TRANSGENDER AUSTRALIA

TRANS
GENDER
AUSTRALIA
A HISTORY
SINCE 1910

NOAH RISEMAN

MELBOURNE
UNIVERSITY
PRESS

MELBOURNE UNIVERSITY PRESS
An imprint of Melbourne University Publishing Limited
Level 1, 715 Swanston Street, Carlton, Victoria 3053, Australia
mup-contact@unimelb.edu.au
www.mup.com.au

First published 2023
Text © Noah Riseman, 2023
Design and typography © Melbourne University Publishing Limited, 2023

Cover design by Design by Committee
Typeset in 11.5pt Baskerville MT Pro by Cannon Typesetting
Printed in Australia by McPherson's Printing Group

 A catalogue record for this book is available from the National Library of Australia

9780522879322 (paperback)
9780522879339 (ebook)

To all the amazing trans and gender diverse people out there. You are absolutely awesome being your fabulous, authentic selves.

Aboriginal and Torres Strait Islander readers are advised that this book contains the names and images of people who are deceased.

FOREWORD

IT IS AN often-stated maxim that to know ourselves we must know our history. That is as true for the trans and gender-diverse community as it is for anyone. Quite a few times over the past thirty years, there have been news stories claiming to be the first time a trans person has done this or that. For example, there have been a number of stories that so-and-so was the first trans person to run for parliament or to get a job in the public service—and those individuals genuinely believed they were the first. The point is that up until now, the history of trans lives in Australia has not been documented in a coherent way, so we have had no idea who was the first, how progress was made, and by whom.

At one level this makes sense, because secrecy was important for trans people. Up until the 1990s it was a common perception that the only trans people who could achieve a safe and liveable life beyond a trans ghetto were those who lived 'high stealth'[1]—who 'passed' so well that no one but their medical carers ever knew they were trans. There are stories of trans individuals who did not even share their personal history with long-term intimate partners. Of course, people living secretly do not routinely document or share their stories. Many of us had secret archives of photos, diaries and newspaper clippings that we destroyed when we felt unsafe.

In the 1970s, the public's knowledge of trans often derived from tabloid stories of trans people who were involuntarily outed, or individuals starting the journey who shared their story and were then ostracised by family, employers and friends. Consequently, trans people measured poorly on human rights and social determinants for health, experiencing social exclusion and being pushed down the social scale.

From the 1990s onwards there was a growing belief among trans people that the only way we could fight for human rights, equity, social justice, better medical treatment and in education was to out ourselves.[2] This era witnessed a growing number of trans people— such as ourselves—living what feminist scholar Judith Butler calls liveable lives.[3] We told personal stories that aimed to demythologise transness, and we critiqued gender norms.

Of course, the other compelling necessity of a trans history is to benefit trans individuals. History helps us find ourselves in the stories of others, both in terms of positive role models and in seeing the journeys we did not want to follow. So many of the publicly shared stories we remember left trans people wary and scared to affirm their gender.

When we first met Noah Riseman as interview participants, we were pleased that he quoted 'Nothing about us without us'—which we consider a great approach to history research, interviews and writing. Such an approach has allowed him to pick the dominant themes while acknowledging the diversity of our communities and empowering our voices. We were very impressed with the thoroughness with which Noah approached the enormous task of documenting changes in societal attitudes to trans and gender-diverse people, as well as the ongoing changes in self-esteem, strategy, assertiveness and political activism of trans people.

This history is based on interviews with over 100 trans and gender-diverse individuals; some are famous, but most are not. It also references trans people's portrayals in newspapers, magazines and other archival sources. Importantly, the book frames trans stories with the joys and huge gains in personal agency and creative lives, as well as the difficulties. We see big-picture activism and the minutiae of disempowered individuals who asserted their authentic selves, making small but cumulative and important changes in their relationships with family, church and helping professions. However, the book is so much more. It describes the miracle that over decades has seen the rich diversity of our trans community—be we Sistergirls, sex workers, lawyers or archivists—make sure and steady progress towards equality and equity, often at horrendous personal cost.

The telling of relevant stories is made more difficult because of the changing language describing gender nonconformity and trans. In this work Noah is highly sensitive to the differing terminology used to describe trans and gender-diverse individuals while acknowledging that certain terminology might be triggering to some individuals, often for very personal reasons. Consequently, he has examined the social changes over a century in the perception of gender non-normativity. For example, we can see trans constructed at different times as deviant personality, connected to same-sex attraction, a psychological disorder, or a deeply held personality trait or belief. But Noah also acknowledges that there is no universally accepted agreement on terminology.

As a self-identifying cis gay man who has lived experience in Australia and the United States, Noah clearly acknowledges his white and middle-class privilege, which he sees as giving him a responsibility to contribute towards equality and affirmation of trans and gender-diverse people. He came to this work seeing a need to broaden trans history following his work with trans and gender-diverse members of the Australian Defence Force. We have been continually impressed with his ability to clearly see the challenges confronting a broad swathe of the LGBTIQ+ communities. But importantly, we have also seen that he has put significant energy into making a positive difference. He has a deep intersectional understanding of Australian Indigenous, military, religious, class and ableness issues that informs his knowledge of LGBTIQ+ health, social justice issues and politics.

More specifically, we are very impressed with Noah's work on trans history, charting changes in Australia that relate to anti-discrimination, gender affirmation, access to affirming health care, and birth certificates. He also examines historical court cases and documents relating to justice issues, such as policing of transgender people and their treatment when incarcerated.

Noah's task was never going to be easy. With changing awareness, language and identities coming to the fore, what to include and what to exclude must have been challenging. Yet in this book he provides important insights into the origins and progress of trans and gender-diverse identities in Australia. It joins other works describing the trans experience, but its breadth of time and description places it apart from most previous ones.

This book will appeal to all trans and gender-diverse people who are trying to find themselves in stories of others, and to those friends and family who wish to support trans and gender-diverse loved ones. Of course, capturing a complete history of such a diverse group of people is beyond any single volume. But we are sure this book will inspire further histories and be referenced as a key text and a solid basis for the retelling of these stories as the language, discourses and social attitudes to gender and gender non-normativity continue to evolve.

Julie Peters, PhD—activist, scholar and author
Jenny Scott, ASAAP (Australian Society of Archivists Accredited Professional)—archivist and activist

CONTENTS

PREFACE

WHEN ORAL HISTORIANS ask questions, we are not trying to stump our interviewees. Sometimes we ask about a particular event, other times we ask about feelings or emotions or relationships, and yet other times we want information about a specific organisation or activity. Then there are the reflective questions, whether they be about the interview participant's own life or a broader historical theme. For this project on transgender history, the last question I asked every interview participant was: How would you like the Australian public to think about the histories and experiences of trans people? I did not anticipate that this question would catch so many interviewees off guard and prove so challenging.

Of course, no answer was the same, but there were two dominant themes that spanned the responses regardless of the interview participant's age, gender, class, ability, race or ethnicity. The first was that trans and gender-diverse people have always been here. Mx Margaret Jones, formerly of trans organisation TransWest and the International Foundation for Androgynous Studies, exemplified this theme in their answer:

I'd like people to realise that trans people have always existed and I'd like them to see through the myths, the incorrect rubbish that is out there. It concerns me, the idea that children are some-how following a fashion—[it's] just so much garbage. I wish that people would understand what the true situation is and not be misinformed … We've always been here, and we've always been around, and if it seems there's more of us, that's just because more people are coming out.[1]

Yes, it is only in the last twenty years or so that trans people have been more visible in the media and public life, but since time immemorial gender-diverse people have occupied this continent.

The second theme that emerged was the importance of uncov-ering, recording and sharing transgender history so that younger generations—be they cisgender, trans or gender-diverse—can learn from it. For instance, Jonathan Paré, the founder of Melbourne-based Transgender Liberation and Care in 1995, said, 'I think it's really important for the community to know its history and to have something documented. I think it's also really important for the individuals [who] will get mentioned, because a lot of us have bled for this, and I think a lot of us feel that we've been abandoned and disregarded.'[2] History teaches about past experiences, reveals how much has changed, dispels myths, and highlights how much more work is needed to progress equality. Eloise Brook from the Gender Centre in Sydney summarised this well:

For all of the way that the trans community is portrayed as being somehow snowflakes who demand or want special or exceptional stakes, I continue to argue that the only thing trans people want is the absolute right to do what everyone else does. That's it. We just want to have the same rights, the same opportunities. I just want to live with my family. I just need the space to be able to live the best life I can.[3]

I commenced this project on Australian transgender history in late 2017 when I conducted my first interview with Erica Roberts in Townsville. I learned a lot from Erica, just like I learned from every interview participant. Erica was born in England in 1941. Even though she was assigned male at birth, from an early age she always felt more comfortable being around girls. From about age fifteen she would secretly dress in her sister's clothes, and later in life she would do the same with her wife's clothes. Erica moved to Australia in 1964 and by 1970 was settled in Townsville and working as a mechanic. Sometimes she would dress in women's clothes and go out to the shops, feeling terrified at the thought of being caught while at the same time experiencing a sense of release. The distress of having to repress her authentic self and live as a man built over time and challenged her mental health. Erica began taking female hormones (oestrogen) around 1988 and then got breast implants. She continued to present as a man during work hours and as a woman at night. Only her wife and adult children knew about her double life. In 1999 she was referred to the Monash Gender Dysphoria Clinic in Melbourne and began to live full time as a woman. She then had further gender affirmation surgery and changed her legal documents to female. Erica went on to found Transbridge—the first social and support group for trans people in and around Townsville.[4]

That interview with Erica was the first piece of the puzzle of recording, documenting and reconstructing Australia's transgender history. Some aspects of her life story and transition journey proved to be common among other trans people, while of course there were parts that were unique to her. Since 2017, I have interviewed 104 trans and gender-diverse people, nineteen health professionals and six longstanding cisgender allies. Some of the trans interview participants have been activists who fought for rights and challenged popular ideas about gender, some were advocates who set up support groups or participated in informal networks of trans people, and some lived their lives quietly away from activism and the trans community. All of them were generous to trust me and share their life stories and often photographs, personal archives, artworks and even musical compositions. They all had the option of being identified or choosing a pseudonym. In this book I use interview participants' first names to reflect our very personable interactions, while for other individuals I use the more formal surnames. Those participants who chose a pseudonym are denoted in quotation marks.

I come to this research as a cisgender, white, upper-middle-class, able-bodied man. Many people wonder why a cisgender man would take up such a project, or indeed if a cisgender man *should* be researching transgender history. The project idea grew out of my previous research on lesbian, gay, bisexual, transgender, intersex and queer (LGBTIQ+) people in the Australian military. I interviewed about a dozen trans and gender-diverse members of the Australian Defence Force (ADF), past and present, and realised something important from their stories: it is not possible to understand the experiences of trans people in an institution such as the ADF without knowing the broader histories—the medical, legal and social. Over dinner, I asked two trans friends what they thought about me doing a bigger project on Australian transgender history; they enthusiastically encouraged me to do it.

Although I am part of the LGBTIQ+ rainbow, as a cis man I am still an outsider to the trans community, which meant I encountered quite a few challenges and learning curves while working on the book. Ethical research as an outsider means constant reflection, centring trans perspectives and voices, and ensuring that the research responds to the needs and desires of the trans community. It means building trusting relationships and working with trans people as research partners, not subjects, and making them part of the research journey. M Paz Galupo's article 'Researching While Cisgender' and Benjamin William Vincent's 'Studying Trans' were particularly helpful at outlining these ethical principles in more detail.[5]

Early in the project, with the assistance of partner investigator Dr Fintan Harte from the Australian Professional Association for Trans Health (AusPATH) and Nick Henderson of the Australian Queer Archives (AQuA), I reached out to transgender representatives from each state and territory to put together a project advisory group. As I explained to the group members, I was not out to create extra work for them but, rather, wanted them as a sounding board for ideas and to hold me to account—to ensure that I was behaving ethically and being responsive to the trans community. Every six months I reported to that advisory group on project progress, and I also regularly updated other trans and gender-diverse people whom I encountered on the research journey. The advisory group was monumental in reaching out to interview participants and organisations, and I cannot thank them enough for their encouragement and support (they are all named in the Acknowledgements).

Two conversations from early in the project were always in my head as reminders of the importance of being self-reflective, conscious of my privileges and ignorance, and open to learning. The first was when I had a meeting scheduled with a trans woman in a local cafe. The night before our meeting, she read a copy of the project information letter and consent form. For some strange reason, the next morning I could not access my email at home. When I arrived in my office and opened my Outlook, I found a series of overnight emails where the person said that I had used a word in my information letter that was associated with TERFs (trans exclusionary radical feminists). Therefore, I must be a TERF and she did not trust my project motives or me. She said she would be at the cafe until a certain time—ten minutes from then—and if I were not there she would leave and cease all communication.

I ran to the cafe and found her waiting. She proceeded to rip my head off (figuratively, of course), accused me of being a TERF, questioned everything about what I was doing and threatened to derail the whole project. When I had the opportunity to speak, I very calmly said I had no idea that the word I had used was a TERF term, and in fact I was grateful she had told me this because now I knew and could both correct my documentation and not use it in the future. I explained why I had used the word: it was historically a term used by trans activists, was in the title of a well-respected scholarly journal, and was a noun. Honestly, I had chosen it for grammatical reasons. I apologised and said I appreciated this learning opportunity. She could see I was genuine and from there the conversation's tone turned positive. I asked if she would read the rest of the information letter and let me know if I had used any other inappropriate terms, and she kindly agreed to do so (aside from the one term, the rest of the letter was fine). Through conversation and dialogue we were able to resolve a misunderstanding, but it was an important lesson for me about the importance of humility and owning mistakes.

The other conversation was with a different person, on the phone. This was someone who had historically been quite active pushing for trans rights, and we were discussing the possibility of an oral history interview. They declined to be interviewed but were supportive of the project, saying that I could draw on anything they had written. They had wanted to chat because they questioned my use of the word 'transgender' for the project. They had transitioned during an era of different language and still self-identified as a transsexual. I explained that I know that language changes over time and that I would never challenge someone's self-identification, but I was trying to use the most up-to-date and inclusive language while still accounting for difference within that language. The person then said something that has stuck with me: 'Noah, I defy you to find terminology that is not going to piss somebody off.'

I share these stories to highlight the importance of language and diversity within the trans community—or, more accurately, communities—particularly because I am an outsider. Words affect people. The wrong words can trigger people. Yet words that trigger one person may be the preferred terminology of another. Some people use inappropriate language with a blatant intention to demean or insult; others do it out of sheer ignorance. That does not change the fact that the language may cause hurt. It can be a learning opportunity, but at the same time it puts an extra burden on trans people who constantly have to educate others. That must be exhausting to have to do on a daily basis. When I write or speak as a trans ally, it is not my existence being discussed, debated or explained to others who have no stake in it. As an outsider, discussions around transgender rights or identity are not personal to me and never can be. That is a form of privilege.

I approached writing this book conscious of that and other privileges, and also aware of how personal and important this history is to the trans people I interviewed and all the other trans and gender-diverse people out there. It tells Australia's trans history since the early twentieth century. Drawing on the oral history interviews along with newspaper and other archival sources, it reconstructs a narrative while acknowledging difference and diversity within that narrative. It is not and never can be a complete history. There are just as many trans histories as there are trans people—or, to quote from the Reverend Josephine Inkpin's oral history interview: 'You know that we have a richer humanity for understanding and owning stories of everybody ... I mean, everyone's got a little bit [of a story]. I don't know whether there's one million, seven billion genders, but we all then can take our own bits of ourselves.'[6] I hope that this book, by illustrating the past, can contribute to the ongoing push for equality and affirmation for trans and gender-diverse Australians.

As a final note, it is not my intention to profit off the histories of transgender people. I do not own these histories but, rather, share them so that everyone—trans, gender-diverse or cisgender—can learn from them. As such, any profits from this book will be donated to a selection of trans charities and support organisations across Australia: A Gender Agenda (ACT), TransFolk of WA, Australian Transgender Support Association of Queensland, Transgender Victoria and the Gender Centre (NSW).

ACRONYMS AND ABBREVIATIONS

AAT	Administrative Appeals Tribunal
ABC	Australian Broadcasting Corporation
ACSA	AIDS Council of South Australia
ADF	Australian Defence Force
AFAB	assigned female at birth
AGA	A Gender Agenda
ALP	Australian Labor Party
AMAB	assigned male at birth
AQuA	Australian Queer Archives
ATSAQ	Australian Transgender Support Association of Queensland
AusPATH	Australian Professional Association for Trans Health
BIPOC	Blak, Indigenous and people of colour
IFAS	International Foundation for Androgynous Studies
IOC	International Olympic Committee
LGBTIQ+	lesbian, gay, bisexual, transgender, intersex and queer
QuAC	Queensland AIDS Council
SWOP	Sex Workers Outreach Project
TAG	Transsexual Action Group
TERF	trans exclusionary radical feminist
TGV	Transgender Victoria
VGLRL	Victorian Gay and Lesbian Rights Lobby
VTC	Victorian Transsexual Coalition
VTRL	Victorian Transgender Rights Lobby

INTRODUCTION
THE CHALLENGES OF TRANSGENDER HISTORY

I N JULY 2013, Lieutenant Colonel Catherine McGregor did an interview on the ABC-TV program *One Plus One*. McGregor had several careers: she was an army officer, a speechwriter and a political adviser for both the Australian Labor Party and the Liberal Party. Her most recent stint was as speechwriter for the Chief of Army, Lieutenant General David Morrison, including drafting his famous video address advising members of the army who could not treat women with respect to 'get out'.

In the *One Plus One* interview, McGregor spoke about her life in the army, her family and upbringing, her past challenges with alcohol and mental health, and her lifetime struggle with gender. Most of the interview was about her gender transition as a serving member of the Australian Army and the reactions from colleagues, both affirming and vitriolic. She talked about the distress of living with gender incongruence and the relief of transitioning:

The grammar for transgendered feelings just doesn't exist. It is incredibly difficult to explain what it feels like to be boiling over with a sense that you're trapped in the wrong body and identity. There's a feeling that you're in a straitjacket, an unfolding nightmare. I was sleepless for months on end. I was experiencing

1

terrible panic attacks. I couldn't see a way forward that offered any level of contentment, and it was a nightmare. At some point, I wonder how much more of it I could have endured, frankly. It seems like a dim memory now, though. It's really interesting that once I actually surrendered to this and decided that I would do what I'm doing, I felt a real calm. And as I've transitioned and been able to express myself as female, I have felt a baseline level of contentment that nothing can rob me of.[1]

The *One Plus One* interview propelled McGregor into the public spotlight. In subsequent months and years she appeared in newspaper features and on the television programs *Australian Story* and *Q&A*, delivered an address at the National Press Club and was 2015 Queenslander of the Year and the state's nominee for 2016 Australian of the Year (an honour she later rescinded).[2] McGregor became a regular newspaper columnist and media pundit, sometimes focusing on transgender matters but also discussing broader political and social issues—not to mention cricket commentating. In 2018, the Sydney Theatre Company performed a biographical play about her life, *Still Point Turning: The Catherine McGregor Story*. She was arguably the most high-profile transgender Australian in the 2010s.

McGregor's public profile coincided with a global moment that *TIME* magazine in 2014 famously dubbed 'The Transgender Tipping Point'. Transgender visibility had increased substantially, and societal attitudes had shifted significantly towards affirming transgender rights.[3] There is certainly evidence to support this claim. All Australian state, territory and Commonwealth governments have amended anti-discrimination laws to protect transgender people. All jurisdictions but one (NSW) now allow trans and gender-diverse people to change their birth certificate without requiring gender affirmation surgery, and all but one (Western Australia) have the option of non-binary gender markers instead of just 'male' or 'female'. At the time of publication, the Western Australian government had flagged impending revisions to birth certificate laws.

Yet legal protections may overplay to what extent Australia and comparable societies have passed a transgender tipping point. Transgender people still consistently face barriers to accessing health care, employment and social services and are subject to daily prejudice and ridicule. Ongoing culture wars and debates around gender binaries and access to affirming health care (especially for children), education programs and sport show that there is a way to go before trans and gender-diverse people are fully accepted. One line from *Still Point Turning* effectively summarises a theme that pervades oral history interviews and other firsthand accounts of transgender Australians: 'The unifying trans experience is rejection and repudiation.'[4]

This book is the first to chart the history of trans and gender-diverse people in Australia in the period since 1910, historicising both the progress and the ongoing battles. The year 1910 is not an arbitrary marker, nor is it intended to deny the existence of gender diversity before that. Indeed, gender-diverse people have been on the continent since time immemorial. This acknowledgement is not, as Aboriginal scholar Madi Day notes is too often the case, meant to exempt contemporary trans settlers from the practices of settler colonialism or to deny the fact that they, too, live on unceded land.[5] As Wiradjuri non-binary scholar Sandy O'Sullivan argues, part of the colonial project was to impose white/British ideas about gender on Aboriginal and Torres Strait Islander communities.[6] This process—like the stealing of land, forced removal of children, forbidding of languages, imposition of Christianity and other practices designed to eliminate Indigenous people and culture—severed many (though not all) expressions of gender that did not align with white/European ideas. As Chapter 5 explores in more detail, white/European trans people, too, have historically disregarded and marginalised Aboriginal and Torres Strait Islander people and knowledges.

The year 1910 is significant, though, because it is when the German sexologist Magnus Hirschfeld published the book *Transvestites: The Erotic Drive to Cross Dress.*[7] Hirschfeld coined the term 'transvestite' and, in doing so, began a discourse around gender diversity where 'trans' became part of the lexicon to describe people whose gender was different from their sex assigned at birth. How that terminology has been applied over time has not always been consistent, and changes in language have never been an even or linear process. Still, every history text needs a starting point, and for this book that is 1910. Before venturing off from 1910, though, I will outline key conceptual and contextual challenges around transgender history.

Terminology and definitions

Language about gender diversity can be challenging for several reasons. First, the dominant vocabulary is derived from European languages and cultures. This can be limiting because language is intricately connected to culture; there are terms for gender diversity in non-European cultures that do not necessarily translate directly, and for which words like 'transgender' do not quite fit. Second, much of this language emerged out of medical and psychiatric discourses. Trans activists of the late twentieth and early twenty-first centuries have fought to depathologise transgender, drawing on social-constructivist ideas of gender rather than embodied biological and binary understandings. Yet it was medicine and sexology that gave language in the West to trans experiences. Third, language around gender diversity has been constantly evolving, and in the twenty-first century especially there have been rapid changes in preferred terminology and a proliferation of new expressions. This links to the final significant challenge: identity is something very personal, and people attach important meanings to the terms they use to describe themselves. Some older trans people, for instance, have been identifying for decades with words that are now generally considered outdated or even offensive (e.g. 'transvestite', 'tranny', 'transsexual'). Understanding transgender history contextualises why people use particular terms and, in that sense, can affirm people's identities while simultaneously acknowledging why the preferred language has evolved.

Michel Foucault famously argued that social discourses constantly (re)create sexual identities. Discourses, be they about sexuality or gender, may define identities and provide ways for people to articulate their sense of self. Indeed, many oral history participants noted that the historical lack of transgender language and visibility left them confused about their gender growing up. Without seeing others like them or hearing words like transgender, transvestite or transsexual, they could not comprehend or articulate their struggles. Yves Rees uses the common adage 'You can't be what you can't see' to explain this sentiment.[8] On the flip side, several interview participants recalled as children or adolescents in the 1960s–80s seeing examples of transgender people in the media.[9] Those interviewees experienced what Peter Ringo refers to as identity events: moments when seeing other trans people facilitated a process of understanding their own gender identities.[10]

While language can give a sense of connectedness and understanding, Foucault also cautioned that discourses are a means of power and social control. That is, in the illusion of empowering people through the proliferation of social discourses, people are in actuality contained and defined to exist within those discourses.[11] To put it another way, labels and definitions contain people within boundaries of fitting particular criteria. Defining who *is* inherently excludes who *is not*. As transgender history shows, when medical professionals defined who *was* transgender (or, to use the more common medical language, transsexual), it was harder for those who *were not* to be affirmed. It is for this reason that scholars such as Surya Monro and Janneke Van Der Ros advocate for what they call gender pluralism—a celebration of diversity that welcomes new gender categories. Gender pluralism need not threaten existing categories (e.g. man, woman): it is about making space for more.[12] Yet, even seeking to broaden gender identities or welcome new categories has been a fraught process. Much of transgender history has been about the tensions between those advocating for a more gender-pluralist approach and those who were wedded to existing terminology and understandings of gender.

Archives scholars KJ Rawson and Cristan Williams trace the first known use of the term 'transgender' to American psychiatrist John Oliven in 1965. Oliven used transgender in contrast to the two dominant psychiatric terms of the time: transvestite and transsexual. Transvestites were heterosexual men who had an urge to dress as women but still identified as men and did not desire any medical or surgical interventions. Transsexuals were those who identified with the opposite sex to that assigned to them at birth, and desired hormones and surgery to live in their affirmed gender. The expression 'opposite sex' is intentional here, because the terms transvestite and transsexual both implied binary understandings of gender. Oliven used the word transgender to refer to a third group who were almost in between: those who wanted to live full time in a different gender from their sex assigned at birth, but who did not desire gender affirmation surgery.[13]

The word transgender was used sparingly in the United States in the 1960s–80s. Over time it evolved into an umbrella term to apply to anyone with a gender identity or expression different from their sex assigned at birth, regardless of medical or surgical interventions. The term slowly spread among trans organisations, with the Aotearoa New Zealand organisation Hedesthia using 'trans-genderism' in 1978 to include transvestites, transsexuals and intersex people.[14] The first known Australian use of the term came from activist Roberta Perkins. In a 1983 monthly spot on Sydney's 2SER community radio program *Gaywaves*, she explained: 'Because a sex refers to the biological state and it is impossible to change this, crossing sex does not take place. As gender is the key to the transsexual condition, transgender is a more appropriate term.'[15] Transgender especially took off in the 1990s after the publication of American activist Leslie Feinberg's *Trans Gender Liberation: A Movement Whose Time Has Come*.[16] By the 2000s transgender was the preferred term and transsexual and transvestite had gone out of fashion, the latter being considered especially derogative. In the 2010s, as non-binary visibility and discourse increased, an even more umbrella expression emerged: trans and gender-diverse. Transgender is still generally considered acceptable, though some non-binary people do not identify as transgender because of the word's historical association with binaries.

Rawson and Williams provide an excellent, concise 2010s–20s definition for transgender: 'An umbrella term (adj.) for people whose gender identity and/or gender expression differs from the sex they were assigned at birth'.[17] Historian Susan Stryker gives a longer explanation for how using transgender as an umbrella term is inclusive of diverse gender experiences and expressions:

> [Transgender] refer[s] to people who cross over (*trans-*) the boundaries constructed by their culture to define and contain that gender. Some people move away from their birth-assigned gender because they feel strongly that they properly belong to another gender through which it would be better for them to live; others want to strike out toward some new location, some space not yet clearly described or concretely occupied; still others simply feel the need to challenge the conventional expectations bound up with the gender that was initially put upon them. In any case, it is the movement across a socially imposed boundary away from an unchosen starting place, rather than any particular destination or mode of transition.[18]

Below is a short list of other significant terms and definitions associated with gender diversity. It is not meant to be comprehensive or complete; rather, these are expressions frequently used in this book. Readers well versed in gender diversity will note that many of the terms have contested meanings and usages. What is presented here is adapted from Stryker's excellent, detailed overview of terminology and ACON's TransHub.[19] These expressions did not exist for much of the 110+ years covered in this book. In some chapters I historicise the terminology, but in other eras—especially the time covered in Chapter 1—there simply was no language around gender diversity. In such cases I can only deploy contemporary terms (e.g. AFAB/AMAB, gender crossing) to describe particular individuals or behaviours, even though such expressions did not exist at the time.

Assigned male at birth (AMAB) and *assigned female at birth (AFAB)*: These expressions refer to a person's presumed gender based on their sex organs when they were born. The terms are preferred to 'biologically male/female' or 'born male/female' because a person's affirmed gender may span their entire life. Some people use the similar expressions 'presumed male/female at birth'.

Brotherboy: Many gender-diverse Aboriginal people with a masculine spirit use the term Brotherboy to describe their gender identity. They may also identify as trans men, but Brotherboy has a distinct cultural context. That said, some Aboriginal people are uncomfortable with the word because the use of 'boy' has connotations of being a child.

Cisgender: This is the term for a person whose gender is the same as their sex assigned at birth. A simple way to think of cisgender is a person who is not transgender or gender-diverse. The expression derives from the Latin 'cis', which means 'same as'. Sometimes the shortened form 'cis' is used (e.g. cis man, cis woman).

Deadname: The name of a person before they transitioned, usually associated with their sex assigned at birth. It is generally considered inappropriate to use a person's deadname and wrong pronouns, even when referring to their life pre-transition. Some trans people are comfortable using their deadname, but that is a personal choice. Deadname is also a verb: to deadname someone is to use their pre-transition name.

Dresser: People who wear clothes generally associated with a gender other than that assigned to them at birth. In the past, dressers often considered themselves distinct from transgender people, but since the 1990s dresser organisations have come to identify under the trans umbrella. Another expression often used is 'cross-dresser', though some dressers find this term offensive.

Gender affirmation: The process or processes a trans person undergoes to live as their defined gender and to be recognised as such by society. Gender affirmation may involve social, medical and/or legal steps, and there is no one way or right way to affirm one's gender. The expression is similar to 'transition', and in popular discourse the two are often used synonymously. The main difference is that 'gender affirmation' moves away from the notion implicit in 'transition' of a before and after, of a change from one gender to another. Instead, affirmation reflects the idea that the person is living and expressing a gender that always existed.

Gender crossing: The experience of assuming a gender different from one's sex assigned at birth. Gender crossing can range from one activity or event through to full-time living in another gender. Gender crossing is a useful expression to describe individuals and situations for which there is no information about their gender identity, because the expression focuses on the action or behaviour rather than assigning or presuming any gender identity.

Gender dysphoria: A medical expression coined in 1973 by American psychiatrist Norman Fisk. Initially it described a spectrum of disorders for people who were experiencing mental distress because their gender identity, expression or presentation was different from their sex assigned at birth. Since 2013, gender dysphoria has been the medical condition listed in *Diagnostic and Statistical Manual of Mental Disorders (DSM) V* to describe trans people. Gender dysphoria can also be used as an expression to describe the distress experienced when people or society do not recognise someone in their affirmed gender.

Gender expression: How people use their body, clothing, language, voice, behaviour and mannerisms to perform their gender. This phrase builds on the work of gender theorist Judith Butler, who argues that people are socialised from a young age to behave or 'perform' gender in particular ways that are culturally and socially constructed.[20]

Gender nonconformists: People whose gender presentation and expression differ from the dominant social and cultural constructs of what constitutes feminine/woman or masculine/man. Gender nonconformists are not necessarily transgender or even gender-diverse. They are simply people whose behaviour, dress, mannerisms or other parts of their life do not follow dominant ideas about gender.

Gender presentation: This phrase is similar to gender expression and refers to how people read or perceive someone's gender. Gender presentation is read based on cultural expectations and norms.

Intersex: This definition is taken directly from Intersex Human Rights Australia:

> Intersex people have innate sex characteristics that do not fit medical norms for female or male bodies. We are a hugely diverse population, with at least 40 different underlying traits known to science. Intersex variations can become apparent at many different life stages, including prenatally through the use of genetic screening technologies, at birth and in early childhood, at puberty, and later in life—for example when trying to conceive a child.[21]

A common myth is that all intersex people are non-binary, but intersex people may be cisgender or transgender just like endosex people (*endosex* refers to individuals whose sex characteristics meet medical norms around male and female bodies).

Non-binary: People whose gender is not exclusively a man or a woman. Some non-binary people may see their gender as closer to male (trans masculine) or female (trans feminine); some may have no gender (agender); some may identify as both man and woman (dual gender); others may experience and express a range of genders (multi-gender). 'Genderqueer' is a synonymous word that was used in the 2000s and early 2010s, but very rapidly 'non-binary' became the more common term.

Sex and *sex characteristics*: These are embodied terms referring to a person's chromosomal biology and based heavily on their reproductive organs. Sex is distinct from gender, which refers to the cultural and social constructs that are attached to a person's presumed sex. Sex characteristics are the physical parts of the body related to development and the reproductive system. Primary sex characteristics are gonads, chromosomes, hormones and genitals, while secondary sex characteristics are those that develop at puberty and may include voice pitch, breast tissue and body hair. People often read an individual's gender in light of their secondary sex characteristics.

Sistergirl: Many gender-diverse Aboriginal people with a female spirit use the term Sistergirl to describe their gender identity. They may also identify as trans women, but Sistergirl has a distinct cultural context. 'Sistagirl' does not refer to gender-diverse Aboriginal people but, rather, is a term of endearment sometimes used more broadly within Aboriginal communities. Similar to Brotherboy, some Aboriginal people are uncomfortable with the term Sistergirl because the use of 'girl' has connotations of being a child.

They/Them: Singular pronouns in the English language have traditionally been gendered (he/him and she/her), while the plural pronouns they/them are gender-neutral. Many non-binary and other gender-diverse people have adopted they/them as a singular pronoun because it is gender neutral. Other gender-neutral neopronouns include ze/hir/hirs, though these have not become as popular.[22] In this book, I use they/them to refer to non-binary individuals and for historical examples when the person's gender was ambiguous or unknown.

Tranny (sometimes spelled *trany* or *trannie*): This word is generally now considered a derogatory slur targeting trans and gender-diverse people. Before the 2000s, it was not necessarily seen as pejorative and was commonly used in transgender organisations. Some older trans people still use it, sparking significant recent debate within transgender communities.[23] Many of the documents and events referenced in this book—especially from the 1990s—use the term, as do a few oral histories, but otherwise it is a word to avoid.

Transition: Similar to gender affirmation, transition refers to a process or movement a person goes through to affirm their gender. Every transition journey is different, though they are commonly spoken about as 'social transition' and 'medical transition'. Social transition refers to the process of living in one's affirmed gender, including adopting a new name, changing pronouns, updating legal documents and coming out to family, friends and workplace. Medical transition may refer to hormonal or surgical interventions some people undertake as part of the process of affirming their gender. A common myth is that all transgender people desire medical transitions. This is not true, and the misunderstanding is in part a legacy of the historical definitions and pathologisation around what it means to be transgender.

Searching for trans before trans

Several historians argue that labelling historical figures as transgender before the word existed is anachronistic.[24] They argue that applying the label transgender to the past risks misrepresenting how historical figures understood their gender identities. These individuals may have had other ways to think about gender that 'transgender' cannot encompass; they may not have sought or desired language to articulate their sense of self, as labels may define but they also restrict.

Yet there is a political imperative to exploring gender diversity in the past. Trans people need to see their roots, to know that they are not alone and have a history. This is the very reason that transgender historians such as Feinberg and Stryker argue that finding historical examples of gender diversity can empower transgender people as experts in their own histories and can contribute to their liberation.[25] Across times, regions and cultures third or multiple genders have been accepted and there have been examples of people who crossed socially constructed bounds of gender normativity. The challenge for historians, then, is to string together historical examples of gender diversity while being cautious not to impose 'transgender' on them. Genny Beemyn advocates:

> The best that we as historians can do is to acknowledge individuals whose actions would seem to indicate that they might be what we would call 'transgender' or 'transsexual' today without necessarily referring to them as such and to distinguish them from individuals who might have presented as a gender different from the one assigned to them at birth for reasons other than a sense of gender difference.[26]

Historians can find themselves going around in circles trying to avoid current language to research, analyse, imagine and write about past cases of gender nonconformity. The concept of trans-historicity breaks out of the potentially paralysing paradox of searching for trans histories before transgender 'existed'. Trans-historicity is itself vaguely defined, though intentionally so. Leah DeVun and Zeb Tortorici express trans-historicity as a methodology

> providing language to describe embodiment across time, and forging a creative space in which evidentiary and imaginative

gestures might meet. Many of these analyses depend on explicit comparisons between trans in the past and trans in the present, and a number of them foreground the emotional needs of living trans people now. They also ask: To what extent must such comparisons assume that we can recognize trans-like phenomena, whether now or before, and that now and before constitute discrete and incommensurate temporal regimes?[27]

Thinking of trans as a lens or method, rather than a set identity, may give new language, explanations and possibilities to historical examples. As Mary Weismantel explains, trans-historicity may make meaning out of a 'past [that] had to wait for transgender scholarship to arrive'.[28] Even taking a trans-historicity approach has its challenges, because historical records are couched in the moral, legal and medical binary-discourses of the era. Scholars need to be careful to read against the grain, searching for trans voices who struggled against those in power who were writing about them.[29] Maria Ochoa describes such histories as complex and messy—and necessarily so, because they reveal how trans people coped with the power structures operating in/over their lives.[30]

The field of trans history

This book adds to growing international interest in transgender histories. The majority of texts on trans history have focused on the United States since the 1850s, most prominently Stryker's canonical monograph *Transgender History*. Stryker examines early examples of gender crossing, then focuses especially on the post–World War II period when trans people forged communities, founded organisations and engaged in activism. Barry Reay's *Trans America* covers similar ground to Stryker (though with minimal engagement with Stryker and other trans scholarship), exploring the emergence of trans as an ever-contested identity in the United States from the 1850s to the 1990s.[31] Feinberg's popular history *Transgender Warriors* is another overview text; it intermixes the author's personal story with global examples of gender diversity across cultures from ancient times until the 1990s.[32] The only overview text from the United Kingdom is Christine Burns' edited collection *Trans Britain: Our Journey from the Shadows*. Burns focuses on the post–World War II era by compiling firsthand accounts, especially from activists, public figures and community leaders.[33]

A dominant theme across twentieth-century trans history is the role that medical professionals, especially psychiatrists and surgeons, played in defining what it meant to be transgender. It has almost been a symbiotic relationship: medical and surgical innovations created new opportunities for transgender people to affirm their gender, yet those opportunities meant that doctors had substantial influence over transgender lives. Joanne Meyerowitz first examined the history of trans Americans since the mid to late twentieth century through the lens of gender affirmation surgery.[34] More recently, Stef Shuster has historicised the very field of trans medicine, focusing more on the doctors' perspectives to highlight changes in training, clinical practice and relationships with trans clients.[35]

Other recent trans history texts—again predominantly from the United States—have focused on particular demographics of trans and gender-diverse people. For instance, Clare Sears' work on laws against cross-dressing from the mid to late 1800s highlights how such legislation created new categories of normative and non-normative gender and gender expression.[36] Emily Skidmore focuses on the late nineteenth and early twentieth centuries to showcase how trans men of various races and classes had 'ordinary' lives in a variety of settings.[37] Jen Manion's *Female Husbands* explores AFAB people in Britain and the United States who lived as men and married women, from the colonial period until World War I.[38] Jules Gill-Peterson uses medicine as a lens to explore the histories of trans and gender-diverse children who have sought gender affirmation since the early twentieth century.[39] C Riley Snorton's highly theoretical book *Black on Both Sides* explores the intersections between Blackness and gender diversity since the era of slavery. Snorton showcases how the policing of Black bodies has consistently erased Black people from histories of gender diversity and in the process reinforced binary understandings of gender.[40] From the United Kingdom, Zoë Playdon uses the little-known but precedent-setting legal case of trans man Ewan Forbes in the 1960s to explore broader historical and contemporary challenges surrounding gender recognition and birth certificates.[41]

In Australia, a handful of historians have explored different aspects of the history of gender diversity. Susanne Davies, Ruth Ford and Mimi Colligan were the first to author book chapters and journal articles examining high-profile case studies of gender crossing in the late nineteenth and early twentieth centuries. The two most famous examples are Gordon Lawrence, arrested in 1888 for being dressed as a woman, and Edward De Lacy Evans, who became a media sensation in 1879 when authorities discovered they had been living as a man for years but were assigned female at birth. The historians are cautious not to label their subjects as transgender or gender-diverse, instead focusing on the ways gender was policed.[42] Lucy Chesser's book *Parting with My Sex: Cross-Dressing, Inversion and Sexuality in Australian Cultural Life* is the most comprehensive exploration of dressing in Australia from the 1870s until the 1920s. Also conscious not to label her subjects as transgender, Chesser focuses on how representations of dressing reflected contemporaneous anxieties about the body, gender and sexuality.[43] The 1920 case of Harry Crawford—discussed in more detail in Chapter 1—has attracted attention from popular and academic historians.[44]

From the post–World War II era, a few historical sources outline aspects of transgender Australians' experiences. These tend to come from the fields of sociology, health or biography. The best historical source is Roberta Perkins' 1983 book *The 'Drag Queen' Scene: Transsexuals in Kings Cross*, based on fieldwork interviews with twelve transgender women in Kings Cross, Sydney in the early 1980s. The book describes the social mores, hierarchies and relationships prevalent in an area of Sydney traditionally associated with alternative, immoral lifestyles.[45] Frank Lewins' 1995 book *Transsexualism in Society: A Sociology of Male-to-Female Transsexuals* compiles information about the experiences of trans people who went through the Monash Gender Clinic—Australia's longest-running transgender clinic and the site of most Australian gender affirmation surgeries.[46]

The majority of published history sources about transgender Australians are biographies and autobiographies. As early as 1907, Marion-Bill-Edwards—who was AFAB but lived for ten years as a man and even married—published a fanciful memoir (though it should be read with a grain of salt).[47] The first published Australian trans autobiography was Peter Stirling's 1989 book *So Different: An Extraordinary Autobiography*.[48] Stirling's life story is particularly intriguing: he was assigned female at birth and later in life learned that he was intersex. He then transitioned and lived as a man. Stirling's autobiography is distinct not only as an early example of a trans man, but also of an intersex Australian. In the 1990s a few more transgender authors published autobiographies, including Katherine Cummings with her award-winning *Katherine's Diary*, and Les Girls star Carlotta Spencer with *He Did It Her Way*.[49] Their books are particularly useful for highlighting how trans people navigated society in eras when there was less visibility and discourse about them.

Since the 2010s there has been an increase in transgender auto-biographies and biographies, both self-published and with trade publishers.[50] Dino Hodge's edited book of LGBTIQ+ Aboriginal and Torres Strait Islander people, *Colouring the Rainbow*, features two Sistergirls' stories. Their narratives reveal the extra challenges of racism that gender-diverse Indigenous Australians experience, as well as the challenges of acceptance for Sistergirls within Aboriginal communities.[51] The 2022 anthology *Nothing to Hide: Voices of Trans and Gender Diverse Australia* has contributions from thirty-eight trans and gender-diverse people, many of whom are Indigenous or people of colour.[52] Finally, an emerging genre in the 2010s has been parents of trans and gender-diverse children writing about their journeys along with their children's.[53] These biographical and autobiographical sources are important starting points that discuss the challenges of transitioning and living transgender in Australia.

Transgender Australia is the culmination of the first research project specifically investigating Australian transgender history in the twentieth century. I began the project in 2017 and it was funded from 2018 to 2022 by an Australian Research Council Discovery grant. I have already produced a series of articles and book chapters addressing specific aspects of Australian trans history, including the debates around the 1996–97 Senate Inquiry into Sexuality Discrimination; AMAB dressers in the interwar period; media representations of trans people in the 1970s; the relationship between personal archives, oral histories and trans histories; and the history of transgender women in Australian sport.[54] I also authored short reports on Victoria's transgender history for Transgender Victoria, New South Wales transgender history for ACON and the Gender Centre, and a report on the history of trans health care in Australia for AusPATH.[55] In a previous project I wrote about the history of transgender people in the Australian Defence Force.[56]

Here, I extend on this scholarship and bring together new oral histories, personal archives, media and other records to produce the first comprehensive history of transgender people in Australia. The rest of this book takes a similar approach to Stryker's *Transgender History*, chronologically and thematically exploring Australian transgender history since 1910. It endeavours to cover similar themes as other texts: medical, legal, media, social and, most importantly, lived and living histories of trans and gender-diverse people.

Chapter 1 picks up where this Introduction leaves off, exploring examples of gender crossing and imagining trans possibilities from 1910 until World War II. It draws heavily on newspaper reports and shows the policing of gender norms, just as European sexology and psychology discourse gradually infiltrated Australia and provided new language and ideas to explain gender crossing.

Chapter 2 focuses on the post–World War II era when advances in medicine presented new opportunities for trans people. At the same time, that meant that doctors and psychiatrists were defining and categorising trans people. The chapter explores how trans people came to understand themselves and navigate the medical system, while new social scenes and opportunities for diverse gender expression were emerging in urban locales, often intertwined with the local camp subcultures.

The 1970s are popularly remembered as a time when the personal became political and when gay and lesbian rights groups emerged across Australia.[57] As Chapter 3 examines, the 1970s were also a period when trans social groups first formed, and by the 1980s activist groups, too, had emerged to fight for trans rights. Activists like Roberta Perkins highlighted the social, economic and health challenges confronting trans people as a direct result of the discrimination they experienced. The small activist groups of the 1980s had minor victories in receiving funding for trans support services and securing changes to gender recognition in particular contexts.

In the 1990s, a new wave of activists swept the country. Some were more radical in their approach—particularly in Sydney—while others were more reformist. Yet what united them were pushes for anti-discrimination protections, more transgender visibility, challenging popular ideas about sex and gender, and access to affirming health care. Chapter 4 examines the rise of various transgender movements and organisations across the country in the 1990s, and the victories they secured in state and territory anti-discrimination and birth certificate laws by the early 2000s.

Most of the trans activism and social groups before the 2010s were dominated by white/European people. Aboriginal and Torres Strait Islander people and other people of colour had distinct social contexts, cultural constructs of gender, and health needs that were on the margins even of the trans community. Chapter 5 highlights the histories of trans and queer Blak, Indigenous and people of colour in Australia, including Sistergirls and Brotherboys. Much of their visibility and activism emerged from the late 1990s, in part in response to their exclusion from other transgender organisations, but also from being marginalised in broader Indigenous, gay and lesbian and sexual health organisations.

Chapter 6 explores the contributions made by trans people to all walks of Australian cultural, political and social life since the 1970s through the theme of firsts—or *perceived* firsts—in sport, the military, religion, culture and politics. It also explores some of the firsts around trans men's activism and visibility in the 1990s as they began to organise and form social and advocacy groups.

The concurrent fights for legal recognition and anti-discrimination reforms brought increased visibility of trans people and rights in the 1990s and 2000s, in both rainbow communities and mainstream Australia. Chapter 7 examines divisions within trans communities and how new advocacy groups and particular pioneers broke down barriers as many facets of Australian society began to adopt new policies and practices to support transgender inclusion.

Finally, Chapter 8 examines the contemporary era since the so-called 'transgender tipping point', when transgender rights have become wrapped up in broader culture wars. At the same time as state and territory governments have passed legislation to make birth certificates and social programs more inclusive, a vocal backlash has weaponised transgender rights as part of a broader conservative agenda. The public battles over Safe Schools (2016), marriage equality (2017), sport, children's health care and birth certificates highlight how opponents of gender diversity continue to deploy the same arguments they have used for over 100 years, but with a significant difference: now, trans and gender-diverse Australians are stronger, more visible and have more vocal allies fighting alongside them for equality and inclusion.

1
IMAGINING TRANS POSSIBILITIES, 1910–39

I N SEPTEMBER 1912, Melbourne's *Age* newspaper published a short article entitled 'Baron Wears Woman's Clothes'. It was about the German Baron von Zobelitz, a poor noble who since childhood had an inclination to wear women's clothes, played with dolls and enjoyed sewing. Zobelitz resisted their parents' demands to dress as a man and consequently suffered at the hands of a violent father. Upon reaching adulthood and living independently, they refused to wear men's clothing, instead making and donning their own women's attire. They even sewed women's clothing for other members of the family. Zobelitz at one stage won a prize at a Berlin competition for the smallest waist; the other competitors did not know that Zobelitz was AMAB because all contestants wore masks. The *Age* article reported that a Berlin court was formally recognising the Countess Geraldine von Zobelitz, thus affirming her identity as a woman.

The article about Zobelitz closed with these two sentences: 'Dr Magnus Herschfeld [sic], an authority on such matters, says transvestitism has been and is common in all ages and all countries. It is an instinctive desire to dress in the clothes of the opposite sex.'[1]

This is the first known Australian reference to transvestism (some-times spelled transvestitism). Over the next two months other regional newspapers reprinted the article, as was common practice in the Australian press.[2] The story did not garner significant attention, nor did the word transvestism enter the Australian lexicon—yet. It would take another twenty years before transvestism and other sexology terms gained traction in the Australian psychology and psychiatry professions and the media.

Examples of AFAB and AMAB people caught dressing in another gender were regular features in the Australian press across the period from 1910 through 1939. Most articles covered a court appearance, be it for charges of vagrancy, offensive behaviour or some other crime. How the press reported and explained these cases shifted over time, with stark differences between the portrayal of AMAB versus AFAB people. There tended to be more understanding, if not acceptance, of AFAB people who presented as men because of an assumption that it was often done for economic or material advan-tage. AMAB people, on the other hand, were generally portrayed as deviant, conflating dressing with other vices such as homosexuality and sex work.

Finding the voice and perspective of dressers themselves is hard, though not impossible. Most articles or court proceedings were brief and only included a few lines maximum from the accused. For AMAB people especially, the defence was often that dressing was part of a joke or a bet of sorts. Reading against the grain, several of these cases talked about dressing on multiple occasions over a period of weeks, months or even years. This suggests that perhaps there was something else driving their dressing. Yet the individuals and the newspaper reports were limited by the language of the time and what contemporaneous biological understandings of sex and gender afforded them. The 1910s started with no language around gender diversity but there were socially accepted tropes, such as the AFAB 'adventure' narrative (see later in this chapter) and the AMAB 'joke' or theatre performance. The policing of gender targeted those people who did not fit these tropes, especially if the gender crossing had a sexual element or there was a hint that the person did not identify as their sex assigned at birth.

By the 1930s, psychologists and psychiatrists were adopting international sexology discourse to explain the desire to gender cross. This gave new language and meanings to gender crossing, but the labels also limited gender nonconformists' agency to craft their own narratives or gender expressions. By the eve of World War II, two important patterns were embedded that would have significant consequences for the rest of the twentieth century: the association of dressing with deviancy, and the association of gender crossing with a mental disorder.

Trans-ing AFAB dressers

Historians of AFAB people who dressed and lived as men in early twentieth-century Australia generally avoid addressing their subjects' gender identity. Ruth Ford argues:

> A totalising approach that depicts all passing wo/men as 'transgender' or 'lesbian' obscures the diverse spectrum of meanings that 'passing' had for different wo/men in particular contexts—and over an individual's lifetime. Women could only conceive of their identities and desires within existing categories—for example, the masquerader or the man-woman. Women who saw themselves as men used the tradition of passing wo/men, but so too did working-class women who loved women—they passed and married.[3]

Ford's point about existing categories is important: dressers and those who wrote about them were limited by the repertoire of concepts available in their time. In 1910s–20s Australia, there was no notion of sex and gender being different. Discourse was about biological sex and this was seen as immutable. There were different traits associated with sex, and in that sense there were ideas of what constituted masculinity and femininity—the former being more physical and the latter more emotional. Dressers and media reports could only draw on these gendered personality traits to explain why they felt more comfortable living or dressing as another sex.

Newspaper coverage was somewhat respectful of AFAB working-class people who assumed men's identities to gain employment and improve their economic situations. The case of Marion-Bill-Edwards was almost genre-setting for coverage of AFAB dressers. Edwards married a woman in 1900, though the couple divorced a few years later. In 1905 Edwards was arrested for burglary in a Collingwood pub. Their ex-wife posted bail, and Edwards moved to Brisbane and assumed a new identity. In 1906, a former acquaintance recognised them and turned them into the authorities. That acquaintance also revealed that Edwards was, in fact, female. Marion-Bill-Edwards, as they became known, attracted significant media attention across the country during the burglary trial. They were acquitted and became part of touring shows. Edwards published a sensational autobiography in 1907 entitled *The Life and Adventures of Marion-Bill-Edwards, the Most Celebrated Man-Woman of Modern Times*. Edwards occasionally appeared in media again, particularly when appearing as a witness in other trials. They continued to live and work as a man in Melbourne until their death in 1956 at age eighty-two.[4]

Lucy Chesser has written extensively about Marion-Bill-Edwards and how the press sensationalised especially around Edwards' sexuality, focusing on their relationship with their ex-wife and other women.[5] Edwards fuelled this interest by highlighting relationships with women in their autobiography. It is not surprising that the press did not question their gender, because the story predated any notions of gender being different from sex. Moreover, nothing in the press coverage or Edwards' autobiography gave any indication that they ever denied being female—though this is not to reject the possibility. To identify publicly as a man may have landed Edwards in a mental asylum like other gender crossers of the late nineteenth and early twentieth centuries. Indeed, even though they never purported to *be* a man, they continued to dress and present as a man for the rest of their life, suggesting a trans possibility.

Edwards' case also crafted a narrative around AFAB people that endured through the 1920s: that gender crossing was a type of adventure in performing masculinity through a combination of dress, physical activity and exhibiting strength. One such example was May McDonald, arrested in Beechworth, Victoria in 1911. McDonald had been living as a man for a year and worked as a horse trainer and rider, earning the nickname 'Jockey Jack'. When questioned why they dressed as a man, 'she answered that she was fond of horses and was as good as any man, and that there were plenty of men who if dressed in female attire would make better women than men'.[6] Nineteen-year-old Tom Ralph, too, was working with horses as a driver and storeman near Ararat. In 1911 they had a riding accident and were brought to the Ararat Hospital unconscious. There, doctors discovered Ralph was AFAB. They had dressed as a man since a young age when both their parents died. The newspaper described Ralph as 'of prepossessing appearance and of exemplary conduct'.[7] Their appearance and conduct suggested a level of respectability, and the point about losing parents from a young age made readers empathise with this person: Ralph was living and working as a man solely because of a difficult upbringing and a lack of role models to teach normative gender behaviour.

In 1929, a more elaborate case appeared in the press of an AFAB gender crosser who had worked as a farmer, railway labourer, horse breaker, drover and hunter. William Smith had moved to Melbourne from the United States when they were seven years old. Their mother died shortly thereafter, and Smith began to dress and present as a man because it was the only way to secure employment. Over the next twenty years they lived as a man and worked on farms and cattle stations in New South Wales, North Queensland and Aotearoa New Zealand. To reinforce the adventure narrative and Smith's masculine nature, one newspaper article relayed the story of

Smith's only ever fight. There was a disagreement, and the other person 'swore, and she [Smith] promptly punched him in the eye. He [illegible] with her, but she has a knowledge of ju-jitsu, and threw him, and secured the little-finger hold. "Don't move, or I'll break your finger," she warned him. He moved, and an instant later his finger was broken.' The article also described Smith's skills hunting kangaroo and wallaby under the subheading 'Adventures Made Her Fearless'.[8] Another article noted that at one point there were no other white people for 25 miles (40 kilometres) from where Smith lived in remote Queensland.[9]

Like so many other examples, Smith only came to the public eye because of a legal case. They were in a wage dispute with a previous employer, who then guessed that Smith was AFAB and brought that fact to police attention. Yet the adventure narrative and physical feats made Smith appear exciting. They had never done anything perceived as sordid, and by participating in a newspaper interview they, like Marion-Bill-Edwards, shaped a sympathetic narrative. Smith never claimed to *be* a man, but was very open about intending to continue *presenting* as a man: 'I could not go back to skirts now … I have done no harm. I have always done a fair day's work. If I can earn a living as a man, why shouldn't I? I save my money, and I don't drink, swear, or gamble, and if I got into dresses I would not be able to earn a living.'[10] Smith was almost bringing together feminine manners with masculine physicality. In so doing, they presented as someone who was not transgressing gender boundaries but, rather, was living *on* the boundary, adopting the best of femininity and masculinity.

A few months later, Smith's wage dispute went to court. Character witnesses testified to their strong abilities as a farmhand, and a doctor indicated 'that Smith was of the female sex. Her muscular development was such that she would be able to perform the work of a man.' The judge ruled in Smith's favour, satisfied that notwithstanding the gender crossing, they had done the work and not been paid.[11] Although doctors insisted that Smith had a fixed female sex, Smith eventually identified as intersex ('hermaphrodite' in the parlance of the era) or 'half and half' to make sense of their gender identity.[12] Such terminology suggests that Smith did not see themself as exclusively a woman; whether they made this assertion because of a genuine intersex variation or to provide a palatable explanation is unclear. Either way, it shows how they deployed the biological understandings of sex available at the time. Smith continued to live as a man and worked on farms from New South Wales to Far North Queensland.[13]

The frequency of AFAB dressers appearing in the press diminished from the 1920s onwards, just as examples of AMAB dressers increased. As the next section explores, this was in part because of the greater association of AMAB dressing with homosexuality and sex work. That said, there were still brief mentions of AFAB dressers, and many of them carried trans possibilities. For instance, in 1921 a person named Bailey sought treatment for rheumatism at Adelaide Hospital and confessed to being assigned female at birth. They had been living as a man for fifteen years, eleven of those residing at a boarding house in Port Adelaide. Bailey had worked as a ship's steward and a farmhand across Australia, and purported to be presenting as a man for the wage opportunity.[14] Like the other AFAB dressers in the media, Bailey's gender crossing was seen as understandable because of the economic motive. Yet the *longue durée* of the gender crossing—over fifteen years—is another hint at a trans possibility.

The adventure narrative proved potent and represented the difference between the celebrated cases of AFAB gender crossing versus socially unacceptable examples. It also reinforced gendered understandings of masculinity as being about physical labour, gruffness, the outdoors and strength. Peers accepted these individuals as men not just because they wore men's clothes, but because they effectively behaved like men. When a person was discovered to be AFAB, the press would highlight the success of their gender performance while reverting to the biological understandings of the time: they were female. Within certain limitations, these individuals could continue to dress and present as men, but not if they denied that they were in fact female.

The Harry Crawford trial

The case of Harry Crawford is the most famous AFAB trans possibility from this era. Crawford, too, came to attention not because of dressing but because of an alleged crime: murder. Unlike the majority of AFAB people arrested in the 1910s–20s, Crawford's case challenged norms around sexuality. Italian emigrant Eugenia Falleni began living as Harry Crawford after arriving in Sydney in 1898, aged twenty-three. In 1913 he married Annie Birkett, a widow with a son. In 1917 Birkett disappeared; a few months later a woman's charred body was recovered not far from where Birkett had last been seen. The body was unidentified and remained so. Three years later Birkett's son approached police to investigate her disappearance. Police brought Crawford, who had remarried, in for questioning. Crawford confessed to being Eugenia Falleni when authorities wanted to conduct a physical exam. He denied having anything to do with Birkett's disappearance, but police still charged Crawford with murder. The trial became a media sensation.[15]

Most of the prosecution's case was circumstantial and speculative. They argued that Birkett had discovered that Crawford was AFAB and Crawford had murdered Birkett to protect the secret. It is an intriguing accusation given, as Jennifer Manion found in the British and American contexts, the majority of women married to 'female husbands' were aware their spouses were AFAB.[16] There was no evidence of abuse or trauma on the remains, nor any evidence that the body was definitely Annie Birkett. Ruth Ford's analysis of the trial notes that the prosecution focused heavily on the notion of Crawford supposedly deceiving Birkett and society by transgressing sexual and gender norms. Indeed, a piece of evidence presented as a climax to the prosecution was a dildo—referred to in the trial and press only as 'the article' and 'something artificial'. Ford argues that this evidence scandalised the court and all but assured Crawford's conviction.[17] Whether Crawford committed the murder remained uncertain, but the conviction certainly policed sexuality—particularly presumed women's sexuality. The sexual dimension is also what set Crawford apart from the other cases of AFAB dressers who encountered the law and the media.

Whereas Ford's analysis of Crawford focuses on sexuality and lesbian possibilities, more recent scholarship by Robin Eames centres on the body and trans (and other) possibilities. Eames considers Crawford as part of Australia's trans-historicity, or what they describe as a 'broader genealogy of queertrans antecedence, recognising him as part of an early trans lineage without erasing his connections to queer and lesbian histories'.[18] Testimony from neighbours and Birkett's relatives made it clear that people knew Crawford was AFAB and wanted to be identified as a man. He requested that people use he/him pronouns and wanted his daughter—born before he assumed the Crawford identity—to call him 'Father'. Eames argues that what generated so many anxieties about Crawford was that he transgressed so many social boundaries around gender, race, class and sexuality and simply did not fit into any preconceived categories.[19] It is also this inability to categorise Crawford that makes him a significant trans possibility.

One other important aspect of Crawford's trial was a precursor to the dominant constructs of transgender in mid-to-late twentieth-century Australia. The defence argued first that there was no definitive evidence that the body was Annie Birkett's; if it were Birkett, there was no evidence of the cause of death; and, if it were a murder, there was no evidence that Crawford was the perpetrator. There was another aspect to the defence that came out in the cross-examination of the government medical officer: the invocation of sexology theories about 'inversion'. The concept of inversion emerged in Continental and then British sexology in the late 1800s, and referred to people of one sex who exhibited traits, behaviour and attractions associated with the opposite sex. To apply it to Crawford, it would mean that they were born with internal male traits but a female body. In the early twentieth century sexologists generally applied inversion to explain homosexuality, which in part explains its invocation in Crawford's trial. As the final section of this chapter will show, it was also part of the genealogy of transgender discourse associated with Hirschfeld and other sexologists of the 1920s–30s.

The government medical officer was sceptical about the possibility that Crawford was a sexual invert. Moreover, the judge was cautionary about the line of questioning and whether the lawyer was trying to argue an insanity defence. Ford identifies the invocation of inversion as a sign that there was an awareness of sexology ideas in the medical profession.[20] The minor, almost haphazard deployment of inversion, as well as the judge's incredulity (and presumably the jury's), highlights its marginality in Australia circa 1920. Yet it was a foreshadowing of things to come. Crawford's fate was unfortunate: the jury convicted him and the judge imposed a death sentence, which was later commuted. Crawford was released from gaol in 1931 and assumed a new woman's identity: Jean Ford. Crawford/Falleni/Ford died in 1938 after being hit by a car.

Trans-ing AMAB cases

How authorities criminalised gender crossing was different for AFAB and AMAB people, and even within these groups there were changing patterns over time. For AMAB people, the main shift was from charges of vagrancy to charges of offensive behaviour. As Adrien McCrory notes, this shift over the 1910s–20s aligned with more intense policing of male homosexuality. McCrory also observes a shift in press coverage of gender crossing: from the 1920s, there were fewer reports about AFAB dressers and more about AMAB people arrested. The policing and discourse shifted away from constructing AMAB dressing as a behaviour towards ideas of its indicating a deviant personality type, generally associated with homosexuality.[21]

AMAB people arrested for dressing were aware that they were committing both social and criminal offences. They gave justifications that could at least mitigate the situation and at best prove socially acceptable. Often the accused would argue in court that their dress was a joke, part of a bet or an isolated case. This is unsurprising given the long history of men impersonating women for theatrical performances, and Chesser notes that theatre and certain social functions were socially acceptable sites of dressing.[22] For instance, in one case from December 1923, Leonard Keith was arrested in Melbourne wearing crepe de Chine—a cloth regularly used for dresses—along with stockings and a necklace. The magistrate dismissed the case when Keith argued that he was dressed as a woman at a carnival where people would win a prize if they guessed he was a man.[23]

Other cases were less clear about a 'legitimate' theatrical or comical purpose for dressing. Cases when someone was dressing for theatre or as a joke were, generally speaking, less likely to lead to arrest and prosecution. In January 1915 Lindsay Campbell claimed to have made a bet with friends to go around Adelaide for two months dressed as a woman and not be caught by police. They claimed to have met numerous men who took them to supper and the theatre.[24] A similar, more elaborate example was from August 1915, when police in Sydney arrested a man dressed in women's clothing and who appeared to be a 'charming young lady'. The accused claimed that a friend had made a bet with them to place advertisements in the newspaper and, dressed as a woman, rent a house, hire a housemaid and employ a gardener. The individual had proven so adept at playing a woman that they often dressed up at night and men would treat them to a life of luxury. *The Sun* reported: 'Theatres, supper, parties, and motor drives frequently came his way. The police say that he told them that he had on one occasion gone through the marriage ceremony.'[25] This is an intriguing example because it shows an individual who secured economic and social gain through performing femininity. What is unclear in the press coverage is whether they genuinely adopted a woman's identity or merely did this to please their suitors.

The majority of press cases resulted in a conviction and fine, indicating that magistrates did not accept the joke defence. Most articles are short and lack any indication about the court proceedings and the magistrates' reasoning, but in some cases readers can infer that dressing was more than just a joke or a bet. For instance, in May 1921 George Augustus Rocake was arrested in Sydney dressed as a woman. The *Sydney Morning Herald* reported: 'The Magistrate asked Rocake why he wanted to get about dressed as he was. Rocake replied that he only did it about once a fortnight, and did it only for a joke; there was no ulterior motive.' It seems odd that Rocake would perform femininity as a joke every fortnight; moreover, the same article reported that Rocake had been seen dressing as a woman by night for the past twelve months.[26] Marjorie Garber argues that 'cross-dressing can be "fun" or "functional" so long as it occupies a liminal space and a temporary time period; after this carnivalization, however ... the cross-dresser is expected to resume life as he or she was'.[27] Cases where dressing was not limited in time and place were seen as transgressive because they crossed the acceptable boundaries of gender binarism. The recurring behaviour suggests that Rocake performed femininity as more than just an occasional joke, bet or theatrical performance.

On 5 December 1925, a short article entitled 'Masqueraded as Woman' appeared in Melbourne's *Argus* newspaper. The fifteen lines described an incident when two police constables spotted a suspicious person in women's clothing at St Kilda Beach. They arrested John Watson, alias William Hopeley, and laid charges of behaving in an offensive manner and being an idle and disorderly person.[28] A longer article in Perth's *Truth* newspaper indicated that Watson's wife was away on holiday, and 'To brighten things up, he dressed himself in some of his wife's clothes. A gingham dress, silk stockings, high-heeled shoes, short coat, a hat and veil comprised his attire for the novel.'[29] In this instance, the magistrate dismissed the charges, accepting the defence claim that there was no law policing men's dress. There is no further information about Watson/ Hopeley's motives or gender identity. Importantly, the practice of secretly dressing in a wife's clothing was common among many contemporary transgender interview participants, further suggesting that this is a trans possibility.

Unspoken in most reports was the undertone of homosexual behaviour. Indeed, Chesser argues that during the interwar period, 'The overt *homosexualisation* of cross-dressing represented a significant and defining addition to the diffuse plurality of meanings that informed cultural understandings of cross-dressing prior to World War One.'[30] A May 1924 report indicated that nineteen-year-old waiter Claud Phillips, dressed as a woman, made the acquaintance of a sea-cook late at night in Sydney. A constable encountered the couple near St Mary's Cathedral, at which time Phillips admitted to being a man.[31] This example raises several uncertainties. It is not clear, for instance, whether the sea-cook was cruising for sex or even realised Phillips was AMAB. The article suggests that the constable approached in response to a complaint from the sea-cook, yet the late-night rendezvous in a known homosexual cruising space raises the possibility that he did know.[32] Phillips' presumed homosexual agenda—and the additional possibility that he lured/ tricked the sea-cook—is what generated public anxieties worthy of the newspaper coverage. This was even reflected in the sensational headline of Phillips' comment to the policeman: 'My God! What will Mother say?'

In another example from July 1922, police discovered an AMAB person dressed 'in the height of female fashion' attending a dance at Sydney's Paddington Town Hall. Like other similar reports— including the story about Phillips—there is a dichotomy between whether the dresser was or was not convincing as a woman. The newspapers reported, 'Many thought that the young man was rather a good-looking girl. He had many partners', but there is also no explanation of how or why police became aware of the person's sex after only an hour. In this case, there was an extra layer of intrigue: the person was quoted as asking the police to let them stay until the end of the dance because they were 'having the time of his life'.[33] Was the person enjoying the attention from male suitors, reflecting possible homosexual inclinations? Or were they enjoying being seen as a woman, reflecting a possible non-normative or diverse gender identity? The newspaper focused especially on the latter possibility, closing with a description of men on a tram who still believed the person to be a woman as the police escorted them away.

When thinking about how these figures conceived their gender identities, there is an important distinction between public and private gender performances. The cases in the press reflect public expressions of gender nonconformity, but they are less revealing about gender practices performed in private.[34] Clare Sears has written about the emergence of laws against cross-dressing in San Francisco in the 1870s as part of a wider push to restrict 'problem' bodies—including Chinese immigrants, diseased people and sex workers—to the private sphere.[35] The Australian states' respective vagrancy laws performed a similar function,[36] restricting public space while imposing a set of acceptable gender boundaries and moral values about who would be permitted to be visible. The majority of Australian dressing cases that made the press thus were those caught in public. Of course, these individuals varied in the boldness of their gender performance, but none of them intended to be apprehended or face the authorities. This suggests that they *wanted* members of the public to see them as women, rather than as men impersonating women.

The distinction between public and private behaviour and its relationship to gender identity is even starker in the few reported cases of individuals exposed for dressing in private. Sears argues that San Francisco laws against dressing in public did not criminal-ise the behaviour entirely but, rather, 'produced a public/private divide through which cross-dressing practices could be managed'.[37] In Australia, newspaper reports of AMAB people caught dressing as women sometimes brought private behaviour into the public domain. For instance, in June 1932 a constable arrested Walter Allison on a street in Brunswick, Melbourne, dressed in some of their wife's clothes. Allison's defence was that they had dressed as a woman to amuse their baby while the wife was out—an ostensibly private activity (though it is unclear why Allison was arrested on the street). The magistrate adjourned the case, but not before saying that such 'foolish freak' was not permissible.[38]

Another case of the private being brought into the public was in February 1932 when police caught farmer Percy Douglas dressed as a woman at a hotel in Melbourne. Douglas had been staying in this semi-private space for three nights. The *Canberra Times* reported: 'The defendant said that while on a lonely farm he amused himself by dressing as a woman, and decided to come to the city to see if he could carry out the impersonation.'[39] Douglas' example suggests possible escalations. They would dress as a woman in private, then reached a point of venturing out to the public. Even in Melbourne it was at the hotel, in a private room, that the police arrested them. It was only Douglas' husky voice upon check-in that alerted the proprietors to contact the police.[40] These cases where the accused mentioned dressing in private raise questions about motives and, particularly, gender identity. It was harder (though not impossible) to argue that they dressed as women as a joke in private.

There are a few cases where the newspaper accounts explicitly suggest that dressing individuals may have seen their gender identity as women, or at least not men. In February 1922 a constable arrested James Scott in central Sydney for being dressed as a woman. The report in the *Evening News* was longer than most, and emphasised that numerous constables believed Scott appeared to be an almost perfect woman; only a tip-off had led to their apprehension. Scott was reported to have been dressing as a woman on nights and weekends 'for as long as he could remember'. Significantly, they did not claim this to be a joke. Instead, the newspaper reported, 'There seemed to be no other motive for the man's strange conduct than a desire to be taken notice of and "admired as a woman".'[41] The accused never explicitly said that they saw themself as a woman, but the notion that they wanted to be admired as a woman suggests a possibility that they did not see their gender as exclusively (or at all) male. That they were so open about this when questioned by police is intriguing given they were not even trying to minimise their gender crossing.

In another relatively candid example, Percy Douglas Baynes of Elwood, Melbourne was arrested in August 1935 for dressing as a woman. It is possible, though not certain, that this was the same person as Percy Douglas arrested in the Melbourne hotel three years earlier. They were the same age and had almost identical names, though that individual was reported as being a farmer from Bannockburn whereas this Percy Douglas Baynes was from Elwood. A police officer had followed them through the city and even to a movie before finally questioning why they were dressed as a woman. The frank response was 'I don't know; I must have a kink.' Baynes did not interact with anyone during this outing, and was reported as saying, 'I just had an urge to do it ... I purchased the women's clothes from several different shops and dressed up after I had finished working in my house, where I live alone.' The magistrate dismissed the charge of offensive behaviour on the grounds that there was nothing illegal about men dressing in women's clothing. The magistrate even asserted that Baynes' appearance as a woman was more modest than how some other women dressed.[42]

Two particular aspects of this case are illuminating, and they link to Baynes' language. The first is the word 'urge': Baynes could not articulate in 1935 language what sensation drove them to dress as a woman, but the word 'urge' suggests that it came from an internal desire to express/perform femininity. The other word, 'kink', links to the language available in 1935. Baynes was drawing on sexology discourse, where gender-non-conforming behaviour was linked to ideas of sexual deviance. This new linkage supposedly explained the urge to gender cross, but it also meant an association with perversion. Gender crossing was no longer being framed as an adventure or a joke, but rather as aberrant and disordered.

Sexology: A new language to articulate trans

Just as the word 'transgender' has antecedents, so too is there a genealogy of the term 'transvestism'. The field of sexology—studying human sexuality and sexual behaviour—emerged in Continental Europe in the late 1800s. Most sexologists of the latter nineteenth and early twentieth centuries tried to explain what were seen as non-normative sexual behaviour and identities, particularly homo-sexuality, and applied their theories to individuals who did not fit dominant gender constructs and behaviours. One example was Karl Heinrich Ulrichs' concept of 'Urnings': people who had a male body but a female soul (and vice versa).[43] Another example was Austrian sexologist Richard von Krafft-Ebing's concept of 'metamorphosis sexualis paranoica', a condition where a person felt like they belonged to the opposite sex. Early twentieth-century sexologists adapted these ideas to the theories of inversion to explain homosexuality.

Magnus Hirschfeld's *Transvestites: The Erotic Drive to Cross Dress* was the first text to distinguish gender crossing from homosexuality. Drawing on firsthand case studies, Hirschfeld described in depth the experiences of people who had an urge to dress in clothing associated with another gender. He gave numerous examples of how and why people dressed, almost presenting a proto-recognition of the differences between gender identity, gender expression, gender presentation and gender nonconformity. Hirschfeld derived the term transvestite from the Latin words *trans* for across and *vestitus* for dressed. He defined transvestites as people 'clearly faced with the strong drive to live in the clothing of that sex that does not belong to the relative build of the body ... the kind of costume is not the chosen expression of an arbitrary mood, but rather is a form of expression of the inner personality as a valid symbol'.[44] He further characterised transvestites thusly:

> in the psyche of these men there is present a feminine admixture— and in the feminine counterpart a masculine one—which presses on to project itself. This alterosexual quota truly must be considerable since, as we discovered, it wants to withstand and does withstand very great resistance and inhibitions, not the least of which is the contrast between body and soul.[45]

Hirschfeld's book did not receive significant attention or dissemination in Australia; nor did the word transvestism gain traction, notwithstanding the 1912 newspaper article about Baron von Zobelitz. Australian doctors and psychologists were aware of British and Continental sexology, but the discipline was on the margins of the medical profession. It would not be until the 1920s that Australian sexologist Norman Haire established a practice in London. Haire was familiar with Hirschfeld's and other sexologists' work and pushed for their field to be respected in Britain and the Empire.[46] The reach to Australia was slow but steady. In one February 1926 case, a doctor testified that the person arrested for dressing in women's clothes was under his care. The doctor never used the term transvestism; he merely stated that the accused 'is not physically or mentally normal, but I believe that the treatment he is now receiving will be more beneficial to him than if he were sent to gaol or a home'.[47] Although the doctor did not have the language to explain the accused's disorder, still his authority marked a shift towards the medicalisation of human sexuality and gender identity.

In the 1930s, there was emerging awareness of the international sexology discourse, at least among the psychology profession, and with some resonance in the Australian press. For instance, in the wake of the 1935 Percy Baynes case, Brisbane's *Telegraph* published an article in which a doctor specialising in psychology said that some people's urge to wear clothing of the opposite sex was a mental condition known as eonism. Havelock Ellis had coined the term eonism in 1928, essentially mirroring Hirschfeld's 1910 theory of transvestism.[48] The *Telegraph* article noted about eonists: 'No vicious tendencies were ever exhibited, and in some cases the condition was one alternating with complete normality.'[49]

Two significant global trans milestones in the 1930s received only minor mentions in the Australian press: Lili Elbe's momentous gender affirmation surgery in 1931 featured briefly in Brisbane's *Telegraph*,[50] and a Czechoslovakian female-to-male surgery in 1935 that appeared in a short piece in at least three Australian newspapers, including Melbourne's *Argus*.[51] Joanne Meyerowitz has written about how Americans who read about European gender affirmation surgeries in the 1930s sometimes investigated the possibility or wrote letters to the journal *Sexology*.[52] Because the stories of gender affirmation surgery did not reach so wide an audience in Australia, there does not appear to have been a similar phenomenon here. As the next chapter explains, in Australia public awareness would come after American Christine Jorgensen's successful surgery in 1952.

Even so, there was some knowledge among Australian psychologists about transvestism/eonism. In August 1932, a doctor responded to a letter from 'L.V.C.' in the 'Talk on Health' section (like a medical 'Dear Abby') of Brisbane's *Sunday Mail*. Though we do not know the contents of L.V.C.'s letter, the doctor's published response talks about transvestism/eonism, suggesting that it was an inherited glandular condition caused when a mother wished for a daughter but birthed a son. The doctor further stated: 'It must not be confused with homo-sexual cases; it might be described as female mind in a male body. But it is impossible to give sufficient detail here. I suggest you read Havelock Ellis's essay on Eonism, contained in the last volume of his Studies in the Psychology of Sex.'[53] The doctor's letter reveals that some professionals with awareness of the sexology and psychology literature could distinguish transvestism from homosexuality. Moreover, just the phrase 'female mind in a male body' alludes to a potential difference between gender (social identity) and sex (body), opening possibilities to imagine the existence of different gender identities.

Transvestism appeared in the newspapers again in the coverage of an August 1937 example from Perth. The case, first published in *Western Australian Clinical Reports*, described a patient who was AMAB but preferred to work as a woman. Over the years since leaving school, the patient had worked as a domestic servant in England and a steward on ships, then for three years as a domestic servant in New South Wales before going to Perth. They never ventured out of the house dressed as a woman; instead, they wore a woman's uniform when working and 'always wears female apparel at night and female underclothing by day'. The doctor diagnosed the patient with the 'rare condition' of transvestism and determined that it had been caused during childhood, when the patient's father was away at war and the patient slept in a cot in the same room as their mother and sister, always wishing to be like the sister. The newspaper reported: 'A young girl a friend of his sister used to assist him to get girls' clothes when his own girls' clothes were taken away from him. When his father returned from the war he made a determined effort to break his son of this practice, but the mother rather sided with the patient.'[54] The doctor's diagnosis aligned with the contemporaneous understandings of transvestism, looking for a familial cause and cure. His report indicated that 'He [the patient] asserts that he has never been addicted to homosexual practices and says that he regards them with even greater loathing than he has for heterosexual indulgence.'[55] The doctor qualified this statement as the patient's assertion, but still his diagnosis reveals early signs of de-linking sexuality from gender identity within the psychology profession.

Interestingly, whereas L.V.C.'s letter and many other cases suggest a sense of shame around their desire to gender cross, this was not the case for the Perth patient. The doctor wrote:

> The patient is not anxious to be cured of the condition. He says that when he continues working as a male he becomes progressively less efficient—usually after a good commencement—and

eventually breaks down in some form of hysterical outburst. At the present time a tolerant attitude is being adopted towards him and he has been placed in congenial employment. His conduct is reported to be good and his work excellent.[56]

This more tolerant approach was almost a precursor to how psychiatrists would approach trans patients in the 1950s. It was, in a sense, easier to be tolerant of gender crossing when it was seen as a disorder rather than deviant behaviour. Yet, as later chapters will show, with diagnoses came rigid criteria and underlying assumptions that restricted trans people's options and excluded those who did not meet doctors' expectations.

The Perth person diagnosed with transvestism contrasts sharply with an example from the east coast two years later: Harcourt Payne. In May 1939 reports appeared in the press about a 64-year-old person who fell ill and was taken by ambulance to an old men's home, and whom doctors discovered was assigned female at birth. Payne had been living as a man since emigrating from England at age thirteen. For the past fifty years they had worked in jobs as a labourer, as a Tramway Department employee and as an assistant town clerk for a municipal council in Sydney's western suburbs. Now Payne was retired and receiving a pension.[57] They were twice married and had been widowed since age thirty; the second wife had passed away four months earlier.

Doctors determined that Payne had a confused mental state and incarcerated them at the Orange Mental Hospital. They searched for a medical explanation for Payne's gender crossing and acknowledged that, like so many other cases of AFAB dressers, Payne probably started presenting as a man for economic opportunities. Yet living as a man for so long had developed into a psychological disorder. An unnamed Sydney psychiatrist explained:

Her appearance and outlook are probably conditioned by a glandular condition known as virilism, which causes masculine development. These physical and economic factors may have been reinforced by a well-known psychological impulse to dress up in the clothes of the opposite sex. Many men have this impulse, and, though they may resist any public exhibition, they often wear women's underclothes.[58]

It is intriguing that the psychiatrist mentioned a 'well-known psychological impulse' to dress, suggesting a growing familiarity with this behaviour within the profession. Virilism—or virilisation—is now understood as an intersex variation related to the production of androgen, which can lead to the development of masculine secondary sex characteristics. The psychiatrist's diagnosis of virilism in 1939 seems to align more with Hirschfeld's concept of transvestism or Ellis' eonism. Later reports indicated that doctors could not figure out why Payne insisted he was a man.[59]

What triggered Payne's commitment to the asylum was their refusal to accept a woman's identity. They were classified as 'certified' and therefore had little prospect for cure or discharge. Ford argues that had Payne convinced the doctors that 'she' now realised she was female, they might have released 'her'. Payne refused to do so and died in the hospital in 1940.[60] Ford is still hesitant to apply the terms lesbian or transgender to Payne, but does acknowledge that 'Payne's adoption of a male identity appeared central to his life and to his sense of himself'.[61]

Payne and the Perth case make for interesting comparisons and contrasts. Whereas doctors declared Payne certifiably insane for refusing to accept a woman's gender, in the Perth case the doctor diagnosed transvestism and adopted a more tolerant response. There are several possibilities behind these contrasting approaches, all of which pose significant questions about gender identity, medicine and madness on the eve of World War II. One possibility is that because Harcourt Payne was AFAB, claiming to be a man was seen as a more serious gender transgression. Moreover, Payne did not approach medical authorities but was caught. The Perth patient, conversely, sought psychological advice even if they did not seek to be cured of transvestism. It is possible the doctors in New South Wales were not aware of transvestism or, even if they were, saw it as a disorder affecting only men—a common misconception.[62] Finally, there is the possibility that the Perth patient may not have seen themself as a woman. This seems unlikely given the description of how they not only preferred to wear female clothing but also adopted a woman's name. Even so, if Payne's insanity were because of a refusal to accept that he was actually a woman, then the Perth patient may have 'accepted' being male, but a male who had a desire to perform a woman's gender role.

A cheeky letter to the *West Australian* commenting on the Perth transvestism case perhaps exemplifies how sexology was reshaping narratives around gender crossing. It was from someone named 'Skipjack' and said, 'We are still waiting to hear the medical name for the condition which makes women want to dress in man's clothing and do man's jobs.'[63] As this chapter has shown, in the 1910s–20s many AFAB people who dressed, presented and worked as men could elicit sympathy because they were seen as adventurous. Now, sexology and psychology discourse was framing dressing and gender crossing as symptoms of a medical disorder. Thus, while there was a new, emerging language to describe gender crossing and gender diversity, so too was that language reshaping—even limiting—how gender crossers could articulate their sense of self.

On the eve of World War II

The era from the 1910s to 1930s presents numerous trans possibilities but also shows how the rise of trans language came with exclusionary power. Of course, we can never fully understand the motivations for those individuals caught dressing or performing a gender other than that assigned to them at birth. These gender nonconformists expose a greater complexity around gender identification in people's lived experience than the language or journalistic coverage of the time permitted. AFAB people caught dressed as men could often elicit public interest and sympathy, particularly if they crafted their life story into a narrative of adventure and seeking opportunities. For AMAB people dressing as women, beyond the realm of the theatre there was no socially acceptable justification for their behaviour. There were only occasionally social or economic advantages to be gained by adopting women's clothing or identities, suggesting that most AMAB gender crossers had other motives. Usually those caught would say they were joking—a plausible defence in some cases, but dubious in others. Where both AFAB and AMAB people ran into trouble was when there was a presumed sexual element to their dressing. Only in rare instances did judges dismiss charges such as offensive behaviour, but those rare exceptions highlight the very nebulousness of the charge.

The few cases where the accused articulated an urge to dress are more enlightening about trans possibilities before World War II. While we cannot definitively label these people as transgender, they reveal what Emily Skidmore describes as a way of 'conveying the open-ended nature of gender being made and remade'.[64] One doctor associated with Harcourt Payne was quoted in *Truth* as saying, 'Unless Annie [Harcourt] Payne reveals the secret of her strange pretence, none of us will ever know the answer to the riddle of her life.'[65] Yet Payne never sought a reason or tried to explain why or how he knew he was a man. He simply was. This is an important reminder: for some people, just being able to present as their authentic self was all that mattered. Did gender nonconformists seek language and explanations for their identities? Or did so-called experts—sexologists, doctors, psychologists—seek labels for people who did not conform to societal explanations? Perhaps it was a bit of both. This symbiotic desire for labels and explanations would become more pronounced after World War II.

2
CONSTRUCTING TRANS
IDENTITIES IN THE POSTWAR ERA

IN DECEMBER 1952, former American GI Christine Jorgensen made global news after undergoing gender affirmation surgery in Copenhagen. Australian newspapers showed great interest, with headlines like 'Man Converted to Woman by Danish Doctors', 'Man Becomes Woman and "She Is Glad"', and '"Converted" Girl Hopes to Marry'.[1] Jorgensen's story even had an Australian angle: she intended to tour the country in late 1954 and appear in a series of fashion parades featuring Australian swimsuits, summer frocks and gowns. She also planned a cabaret-like performance at Sydney's Palladium Theatre and in Melbourne. Local models protested, with one modelling agent saying, 'A fashion parade featuring Miss Jorgensen would reek of the sort of sensationalism that's popular in America, but isn't suitable in Australia. For local girls to parade with him—I mean her—would lower our professional dignity.'[2] The manager of the Palladium cancelled Jorgensen's show and she called off her tour—though she did eventually visit Australia in 1961.[3]

The media presented Jorgensen's gender affirmation as a marvel of modern medicine and the embodiment of white, middle-class femininity.[4] Jorgensen put a face and a name to emerging medical discourse about transsexualism, which American endocrinologist and sexologist Dr Harry Benjamin distinguished from transvestism in 1954: 'It [transsexualism] denotes the intense and often obsessive desire to change the entire sexual status including the anatomical structure. While the male transvestite, *enacts* the role of a woman, the transsexualist wants to *be* one and *function* as one, wishing to assume as many of her characteristics as possible, physical, mental and sexual.'[5] Jorgensen's gender affirmation also presented Australians who were questioning their gender with new possibilities. Her endocrinologist received letters from 465 people around the world inquiring about the possibility of a 'change of sex'. Thirteen such letters came from Australia: nine from AMAB people and four from AFAB people (there were also eight letters from Aotearoa New Zealand).[6]

The changing language and possibilities as embodied in Christine Jorgensen are but one example of evolving understandings and lived experiences of trans people in the postwar period. This chapter addresses multiple strands of trans history from the 1940s through the 1970s, centred especially on three themes: medicalisation, the camp scene and the emergence of trans subcultures. In the early years police continued to arrest dressers, but press reports and court cases—salacious though they were—paid more attention to offenders' motives. The rise of medical discourse about trans-sexualism and surgical options in Melbourne and Sydney offered new explanations and opportunities, particularly for those trans people who adhered to stereotypical ideas of white middle-class respectability. The postwar era also saw the consolidation of camp cultures in the capital cities, bringing together a variety of sexually diverse and gender-diverse people. By the 1970s, the dominant sites of trans visibility were as showgirls and sex workers, shifting the imagery away from the middle-class respectability embodied by Jorgensen.

World War II and its aftermath

Within World War II armed forces there were surprising gender-crossing opportunities and trans possibilities. Drag performances were common as a form of entertainment, and were socially acceptable contexts in which AMAB people—be they gay or trans—could experiment with gender expression.[7] There is also more concrete evidence of trans service members in accounts published after the war. The Chameleon Society of Western Australia published a newsletter that told the tale of a member who served in the Australian Army and was seconded to a British regiment on the Rhine:

> Well one day during a routine inspection, the RSM [regimental sergeant major] was going through the members kits and came across a whole heap of ladies apparel. The RSM grunted and said 'You are Australian aren't you?', 'Yes Sir' said our member. The RSM grunted and moved on leaving our member wondering what in the hell was going to happen. Well what did happen was rather remarkable. A few days later the RSM came across our member and pressed a card into his hand and said 'I can recommend this club.' On it was a[n] address of a crossdressing club in Hamburg.[8]

During and after the war, a few new patterns emerged in media reports that shed light on trends around trans people. Coverage still primarily focused on cases with a salacious element, but one change was that more stories presented perspectives from the dressers themselves. One such example was Patrick John Cowther, arrested in Melbourne in 1944 dressed in women's clothes, a pearl necklace and a gold bangle and wearing lipstick, rouge, powder and eyeliner. Cowther admitted to wearing a pink nightdress to bed and, when their family was not around, dressing as a woman at home. They reportedly said to the police: 'You gentlemen wouldn't understand. It's quite normal. Something inside me makes me want to do it. I've done it all my life. There are hundreds in England like me.'[9]

The tabloid *Truth* included more detailed coverage of this case, even publishing an image of Cowther dressed in women's clothes. Their lawyer argued that there was nothing offensive about how Cowther dressed, and that Cowther dressed in women's clothing as 'an emotional relief ... and to me it is perfectly natural'. The magistrate disagreed: Cowther was convicted and fined £2.[10] It is interesting that their solicitor was making arguments that aligned with contemporaneous understandings of transvestism yet did not use the word. The way Cowther expressed themself and invoked the existence of others was a sign of growing awareness about others 'like them'.

As time went on, medical discourse gradually crept into press reports about dressing—particularly after the publicity surrounding Christine Jorgensen. For instance, police in Adelaide arrested John Martin Vernon Rounsevell while Rounsevell was dressed in women's clothing, a wig and high heels and carrying a handbag. Rounsevell admitted to dressing frequently as a woman and took police to a garage containing several boxes and a wardrobe full of women's clothing. They said to police, 'I cannot help myself. I am not telling lies. I have been to doctors and hope eventually to become a woman.'[11] A psychiatrist testified that Rounsevell had been experiencing transvestism for at least twelve years and this compelled them to dress in women's clothing.[12] The judge accepted that Rounsevell suffered from a neurosis and released them on a £100 bond with the understanding that they would seek medical treatment.[13] Examples of AMAB defendants invoking medical defences, and magistrates accepting them, became more common in the 1960s.

Coverage of AFAB people caught living as men tended to follow the prewar patterns of assuming it was for economic benefits, to seek adventure or to escape from an unhappy marriage. Yet there was the occasional AFAB person who invoked a desire to transition to being a man. In October 1950 *Truth* reported about Bill Armitt, a 22-year-old AFAB person who said that over his lifetime he had gradually developed masculine characteristics. Armitt had been wearing men's clothes and had short hair since age fourteen; in

1949 he had changed his name and lived as a man with his father, working as a bushman. Armitt booked an appointment with a doctor to investigate if he were 'one of those rare cases of a woman who is really a man'—the article implying that the specialist was referring to intersex variations.[14] A few weeks later, *Truth* reported that Armitt had undergone a gynaecological exam and the specialist had conclusively determined that he was a woman. Armitt did not accept this, remarking, 'I don't care what the doctors say. I know in my heart that I am a man and that I will always be a man. I don't know what to do now. What can I do? ... If I can't live as a man, I don't want to live at all.'[15] Armitt was referred to a psychologist but declined the consultation. He returned to Goulburn and his fate is not known.

The other emerging trend during this period was linking gender-crossing cases with the female impersonator scene. Theatre had always been a socially acceptable site for men to dress as women. By World War II, female impersonation represented an extension of this practice, combining dress, acting and singing and with impersonators appealing to audiences because of how convincing they were as women. In the early 1940s Lea Sonia was perhaps Australia's most famous female impersonator, described in one *Truth* article as 'pos[ing] so convincingly as a woman fan dancer as to leave most of the audience still doubtful when the wig is removed at the end of the performances'.[16] Sonia died during a brownout in 1941 when she was hit by a tram while running for a taxi.

One person who cited the spectre of female impersonation was Neville McQuade, alias Colin Carson. McQuade appeared in the press on several occasions in the 1940s when arrested for vagrancy or offensive behaviour. In an interview with *Truth*, they expressed a desire to be famous like Lea Sonia, and regaled readers with descriptions of outfits and hair and desires to be a famous stage performer. McQuade was arrested a second time in 1943 for behaving in an offensive manner, being dressed as a woman and dancing with men.[17] Their third arrest was just after midnight on New Year's Day 1944, for being dressed as a woman and dancing with a man on the streets of Newtown. On that occasion Dr Norman Haire testified for the defence and said McQuade was a 'transvestist type' under his care. The magistrate fined McQuade £3 and released them on a twelve-month good behaviour bond.[18]

McQuade made one more appearance in the Australian media: in 1949 police arrested them, then living as Colin Carson, for having insufficient lawful means of support. Police also accused them of performing sex work with men, but McQuade vehemently denied this. They were quite open about continuing to dress in women's attire and spoke about various social parties and balls that 'were mostly frequented by perverts and their associates'.[19]

McQuade's appearances in the media across the 1940s collectively highlight the continuity and change when it came to gender crossing. Police were still arresting AMAB people dressed as women and laying charges such as offensive behaviour. There were also two emerging patterns that summarised the dominant trans subcultures and discourses until the 1980s: medicalisation and the camp scene. There was overlap between these two sites of trans visibility, but broadly speaking what separated them were the politics of respectability.

Medicalising transgender

In 1951, psychiatrist Dr Herbert Bower saw a patient at Melbourne's Royal Park Mental Hospital who was AMAB but identified as a woman. Bower initially thought the patient was psychotic, but as he came to know them he realised that the individual was well adjusted except for the gender identification.[20] He had no clear diagnosis or treatment for them and subsequently continued to see patients with a different gender identity from their sex assigned at birth.

Bower's early encounters with these individuals were around the same time that international medical discourse was concretising a pathology and language that built on the prewar sexology and new developments in surgery. In 1949 Dr David Caldwell used the word 'transsexual' to describe a person whose gender identification

50

was different from their sex assigned at birth. Dr Harry Benjamin's aforementioned 1954 article 'Transsexualism and Transvestism as Psycho-Somatic and Somato-Psychic Syndromes' explicitly distinguished transvestism from transsexualism. In 1966 Benjamin published *The Transsexual Phenomenon*, which became a global textbook for the medical treatment of transvestites and transsexuals.[21]

Australians were conscious of these overseas developments because of the worldwide press they generated. Still, it was only Bower and a small number of psychiatrists who would treat local trans patients. Much of their work in the 1960s–70s centred on searching for a cause for people's transness, as well as distinguishing between transvestites, transsexuals and effeminate homosexuals. Richard Ball was one such psychiatrist who was associated with what are believed to be Melbourne's first gender affirmation surgeries. The Victorian Health Department ran a 'Transsexualism Consultative Clinic' from 1969. When Ball diagnosed people as transsexuals, he referred them to a surgeon who operated at Royal Melbourne Hospital, usually early on Saturday or Sunday mornings to keep away from conservative 'prying eyes' in the general hospital system.

In 1975 Ball was appointed as professor of psychiatry at St Vincent's Hospital, though the Transsexualism Consultative Clinic continued to run until 1987. Over its eighteen years, according to later media reports, the clinic saw approximately 700 people and referred about 100 of them for gender affirmation surgery. All cases had to go through a review panel before being accepted as a surgical candidate. The clinic's approach represented an early example of a pattern that would echo across the country, as around the world. First, psychiatrists made a distinction between 'transvestites' and 'true transsexuals'. To fit the criteria of a true transsexual, a person had to present as seeing themselves as the opposite gender trapped in the wrong body (this is known as 'wrong body discourse'). What constituted the opposite gender reflected dominant social constructs framed around white, middle-class respectability. The big distinction between transvestites and transsexuals was that the latter had to

51

desire gender affirmation surgery and then to live indistinguishably, quietly, in their affirmed gender. Those individuals who did not meet the criteria would be denied treatment.

Sydney's history of trans health care in the 1960s–70s has points of commonality with Melbourne's, particularly around the role of psychiatrists and the need for a panel of specialists to approve surgery. Unverified newspaper reports and an oral history interview suggest that Sydney was the site of Australia's first gender affirmation surgery, in 1968.[22] There were actually two gender clinics running in Sydney by the early 1970s, both directed by psychiatrists. One was at the Prince Alfred Hospital, but it closed in 1975 when the director accepted a position in Newcastle.

The most prominent personality behind trans psychiatry in 1970s Sydney was Neil McConaghy. McConaghy is a controversial figure in Australia's history of sexuality and medicine because he was a practitioner of gay aversion therapy. When it came to trans people, though, he did not practise aversion therapy; indeed, his research and consultations at the Prince Henry Hospital were more in line with contemporaneous international ideas around transvestism and transsexualism. McConaghy and psychiatrist Ron Barr also regularly deployed a 'penile volume response test'—a mechanism that measured erectile responses to imagery—as part of their assessment process. They believed that true transsexuals were only attracted to men, which of course was a false supposition because sexuality is not the same as gender identity. Justifying this belief, Barr wrote in 1976: 'Patients who show a heterosexual pattern of response may live to regret the loss of the penis following surgery.'[23]

Former patients do not speak fondly of the penile volume response test, which they found not only degrading but also absurd. 'Sascha' recalls:

They would take us and they would connect our bits to a machine and then you'd be watching a film that would be flitting through the zoo and a baboon's arse would flash up, and then you'd go a little bit further and there'd be this large, languid sort of Spanish-looking woman with huge, hairy tits, then she would be sort of lying there going like this and then you'd be flitting through the zoo again and there'd be a man's penis and it was supposedly designed to measure your sexual responses when you came to any of these diversions.[24]

Carlotta similarly writes: 'they wired my penis and brain up and showed me photos of people in Kama Sutra positions, vaginas, penises and animals fucking, to see what my reactions would be. I was so angry and offended that I ripped off all the wires and stormed out.'[25] Although Barr's specific test did not continue after the 1970s, physical examinations including measuring of genitals certainly did—and this was not unique to Sydney.

When Sydney specialists approved trans people for surgery, the operations were performed at Prince of Wales Hospital. Those surgeries stopped in 1978. When questioned in a 1981 interview why, Barr gave the following explanation:

Well, several of us felt that, and the surgeon felt, he wasn't entirely convinced it was helping … I think being a transsexual is primarily an identity problem, not a sexual problem, because transsexuals are willing to take large doses of Oestrogens which greatly reduce/ knock out sex drive and anybody who is primarily interested in sex would not take anything to know [sic] out their sex drive, they are more concerned with identity.[26]

Transgender people have a different recollection about surgeries and why they ceased. Trans people sometimes spoke about surgeons who botched the procedures, with dire consequences.[27] In an article in *Cleo* magazine sometime in the mid-1970s, Trixie Laumonte stated:

I wouldn't have the operation in Sydney. I've seen too many botched up jobs here and it is a real tragedy … Lots of surgeons are in sex change work for the money and I've seen some disgusting jobs. They can make a real mess of you and that's when you get someone who is unhappy afterwards.[28]

A few years earlier, the press reported about a stripper, Tiffany Jones, who died following complications from breast augmentation surgery in a private hospital.[29]

Sascha very bluntly says: 'They [surgeons] mutilated so many people, and so many people just died from stuff that they did. They didn't know what they were doing and it was awful, horrible.' She believes that the Sydney surgeons were not properly trained to perform gender affirmation surgeries and that the trans women they operated on were like guinea pigs. She recollects one friend whom she describes as having been 'butchered' by the surgeons. Eventually, that person died by suicide, which Sascha attributes in part to the surgery complications. Sascha believes the many complications from surgeries led Sydney surgeons to cease operating.[30] Although there are conflicting accounts as to why gender affirmation surgeries terminated in Sydney in 1978, by then viable alternatives had emerged in Melbourne and Adelaide. Those clinics' histories are discussed in the next chapter.

Trans people navigating health care

Before the 1970s there were no trans organisations, no publicly advertised gender clinics and no internet to find doctors with knowledge or referral pathways. Some trans people desperately wrote to the media seeking advice. A letter to a *Truth* advice column published in 1966 read:

> I am a male, and I want very badly to become a female. But I understand this operation is against the law in Australia. I have become very feminine in outlook and even my handwriting has changed. When I walk I roll my hips like a woman. I try not to walk like this, but I can't help it. Can you help me get female hormones? —A.G. (South Australia)

The response was that the person might have a glandular problem and should seek referral to an endocrinologist.[31]

Those trans people who approached psychiatrists had mixed results depending on the psychiatrist's specialist knowledge and the resources available where the person lived. The protocols that psychiatrists developed from the 1960s and 1970s were very rigid: they would assess if a person were a 'true transsexual' and judge whether the person could, if given hormone treatment and gender affirmation surgery, blend indistinguishably with cis women. This was of course quite subjective, but it meant that psychiatrists wielded significant power over trans people's bodies and health care. The psychiatrists expected trans women to wear dresses and apply stereo-typical standards of white femininity (during this era it was almost always trans women, but in later periods psychiatrists would simi-larly expect trans men to dress and present like stereotypical men). Psychiatrists by their own admission would deny treatment to those whom they considered not feminine enough or those who did not live sufficiently respectable lives, such as strippers and sex workers.[32] Those whom psychiatrists diagnosed as 'true transsexuals' would be prescribed hormones by an endocrinologist and must live full time as women for two years—the 'real-life test', as it was called—before the psychiatrists would approve them for gender affirmation surgery. Trans people had to navigate these rigid boundaries and over time came to refer to psychiatrists as gatekeepers.

Trans people who did not meet psychiatrists' approval were, to an extent, able to exercise agency and find other ways to secure hormones. Jazmin Theodora remembers that as far back as the 1960s, 'Someone started taking the hormones to get breasts, and then we all started taking them.' She recalls a Dr Roger Gray who prescribed them without questions—exercising what is now known as the informed consent model.[33] In Melbourne, Dr Harry Imber joined a St Kilda GP clinic in 1972 and by the late 1970s was known in trans circles for his willingness to prescribe hormones with informed consent—he even wrote about it in the *Medical Journal of Australia* in 1976.[34] Other trans people sourced hormones through the black market. In some instances this meant trans women who had legitimate prescriptions shared hormones with their friends. In other circumstances it meant finding a chemist who was willing to sell them off-book, though always for higher than the normal retail price.

When it came to gender affirmation surgeries, trans people had fewer options. Surgeries were limited to a small number of specialists in Melbourne and Sydney—not to mention the rigid gatekeeping expectations just to be eligible. In extreme examples of desperation, people tried to perform gender affirmation surgery on themselves. A case from 1968 made the cover of *Truth*; the person had been taking feminising hormones and said they just could not live as a man. They were rushed to hospital, where they were reported as saying, 'I did it myself with razor blades in the kitchen while my wife was in bed asleep.'[35]

Trans people with some means could travel overseas for gender affirmation surgery. From the 1960s–70s the most common destinations were London (where those with British citizenship could have it done through the public system at Charing Cross Hospital), Hong Kong, Morocco and Egypt. For instance, Jacqueline Durvell Ward reported in the press that:

No Sydney doctors would give me the operation, so I went to London. A Harley Street doctor decided after only six weeks I was ready for a sex operation. I think he realised how determined I was. The Harley Street doctor arranged for me to go to Cairo where a specialist in sex changes carried out the operation.[36]

In 1962, *PIX* magazine ran a three-part firsthand account by a trans woman. In Part 1 she described her lifetime struggle with gender. Part 2 detailed her numerous psychiatric assessments and meetings with surgeons in Melbourne who ultimately declined to perform the operation. She managed to source feminising hormones from a chemist and tried other doctors in Sydney who also declined to refer her for surgery. Eventually, doctors in London approved her for gender affirmation surgery and even waived the costs. The author explained that she was narrating her transition journey because:

> It is the fervent hope that I will instil courage into those who, like me, have been condemned to twilight existence as neuters. Every scorn, every hostility that is heaped upon these poor people is an unnecessary scar. And I would beg of you who have cast the first stone in this direction to stay your hands.[37]

The camp scene

'Camp' is now an old-fashioned word, though it is a useful term that generally captures any expression of sexual and gender diversity. Until the 1970s, it was common lingo and words like 'gay' and, later, 'transgender' were American imports. Another way to think of camp is as an earlier version of 'queer', which historically was a slur but since the 1990s has been reclaimed as a catch-all term for any expression of sexual or gender nonconformity. On the one hand it can be problematic to entwine gender diversity with sexual diversity, but historically, especially during the period to the 1970s, these distinctions were very much blurred in the camp scene.

Australia's camp scene had its origins in the 1920s and especially in the famous 'Artist Balls' and 'Movie Balls'. These were events where attendees would dress in lavish, often homemade costumes and dance the night away. Sydney's first Artist Ball was held in the CBD in 1922, and in Melbourne the first Artist Balls were held in St Kilda around the same period. Sydney's Movie Balls were similar spectacles where guests would dress as famous actors and actresses and movie characters. The balls were not exclusively for the camp crowd, but they attracted many camp people because they were socially acceptable sites for AMAB people to dress as women and AFAB people to dress as men. Karen Chant, who attended her first Artist Ball in 1947, recalls:

The Movie and Artist Ball to us in the thirties/forties is the Mardi Gras today. Everyone wore costumes, glamour, glamour, but as I said we had an hour to get there and had to wear men's underclothing and then after the ball was over you had an hour to go home. If you were caught on the street in drag after that hour you were taken to Central Railway Station, undressed, you were given a towel and they checked out what you were wearing, and if you weren't wearing men's underclothing, they'd charge you with indecent behaviour.[38]

Karen recollects that she and numerous AMAB friends attended the balls hosted at the Sydney Trocadero in the 1940s–50s dressed as movie stars such as Vivien Leigh and Eva Bartok and like mermaids in beautiful handmade costumes. One costume she fondly remembers was a fishtail she diligently sewed for a whole year that was so big the hosts had to open all the doors for her to fit through the entranceway. When that Artist Ball ended, Karen and a friend went to Bondi Beach and threw the dress into the ocean as the sun rose.[39] In 1956 the press reported about an AMAB person arrested at Sydney's Movie Ball, dressed as a woman and wearing a live bantam hen as a headdress. The person was fined for ill-treating the hen.[40]

In 1962, drag queen Dame Sybil Von Thorndyke hosted the first annual Queen's Birthday Ball at a house in Mount Tamborine in south-east Queensland. This was primarily a drag ball but, like so many other camp events of the postwar era, it attracted a variety of attendees. Toye de Wilde was a regular patron of the Queen's Birthday Ball from its earliest years. She recalls:

It started off there were just a few people, and we invited some people, and it got to the stage of where people were just arriving, so we had to move to the local hall, took over that. And then we had to move down off the mountain because everyone was getting so pissed and they were driving off the mountain on the way back down the hill.[41]

The event moved to the Gold Coast, then to suburban Brisbane, and eventually to inner Brisbane by the late 1970s. It continues today and organisers claim it is the world's longest continuously running LGBTIQ+ event.[42]

There were also numerous clubs where every week camp and non-camp people mingled over dinner and a cabaret-esque show, including with female impersonators. The famous trans showgirl and cabaret artist Carlotta recalls that in 1960s Sydney the Latin Quarter in Pitt Street, Chequers in Goulburn Street and André's in Castlereagh Street were the three most popular clubs. She would attend dressed as a woman and remarks, 'I think they liked the glitz we girls brought into the club—we always dressed to the nines and the single guys invariably swamped us. We never had to buy ourselves a drink, that's for sure.'[43] A little later, Belinda Chaplin remembers accidentally encountering Society Five in Melbourne in the early 1970s, which was across several floors of a building near the corner of Swanston and Lonsdale streets. Belinda recalls:

I went, 'Oh my God, I've found it.' It was full of gay people, it was full of drag queens, it was full of trans people, it was like, I think I've just found me, I think I've literally just found myself. It was that instantaneous, it all seemed to makes sense. Then I'd never seen anything, never seen a drag queen or a trans person before, so that was just a real big awakening and I thought, 'I know now what it is.'[44]

Camp people also frequented private parties. Several older trans people recall these parties as their initial exposure to drag—their first time seeing people experimenting with gender expression different from their sex assigned at birth. Jazmin recalls one such party in Sydney in 1955:

We went to this party and this amazing woman, she was buxom and like that ... And I went over and gave her a hug and anyway she raves on about, went back to this friend who took me in. I said, 'God, isn't she the most amazing woman you've ever seen?' And he said, 'It's a drag queen, you idiot' ... So that was the early '50s and she was the first drag queen I saw and she was my mentor, and we became really wonderful friends up until the end.[45]

Private parties could attract the attention of police. Karen recalls a raid on a private party hosted by a dentist in inner-western Sydney. A patron noticed a commotion around the back of the property and people with cameras, and someone shuffled Karen and two other AMAB people dressed as women into a station wagon in the garage. Police sirens went off, as did the bright lights of journalists' cameras. The driver went right through the garage door and Karen was fortunate to get away. The next day, news of the raid was splashed across *Truth* under the headline 'Boys Frocks Shock Cops'. Police arrested and charged the remaining partygoers with indecent behaviour.[46] Toye recalls police raids being common in Brisbane, too:

> The police used to raid all the big parties, and whenever they raided there would be photos taken because they brought photographers. They kept files of photos; they took lots of me and I know that the Queensland police and the Federal police both had a file on me. They knew everything I did and everywhere I went. They also took all the number plates of the cars at a party, or on a Beat or at a gay hotel.[47]

Police regularly accepted payments from nightclub owners as a form of protection, but even that was not necessarily enough to protect employees from harassment or arrest. Jazmin recalls working as a waitress at a coffee shop and restaurant called The Net on Hughes Street in Kings Cross. She was serving drinks to two police officers and one of them shoved his hand up her dress. She slapped the cop and said, 'Don't you ever do something like that to me.' Almost two years later, sometime circa 1958, she encountered that same cop on the street who grabbed her, took £40, and arrested her for vagrancy. The judge sentenced Jazmin to two weeks in Long Bay Gaol. Because trans people were often treated as gay men back then, she was placed in a cell by herself but had to fend off men who wanted sexual relations. She counts herself lucky that a friend was in gaol at the time and helped protect her.[48]

Police across the country regularly harassed camp people on the streets. Karen Chant says, 'I couldn't even walk down from Kings Cross to Town Hall railway station when I was 17–18 [late 1940s] without being pulled up and put in a doorway of a shop by the police',[49] while Belinda Chaplin recalls from early 1970s Melbourne: 'If you're walking down the street at night or whatever they'd stop you, they'd just: "What are you doing? Why are you dressed like that? ... Get home, get out of our sight", all that stuff.'[50] Carmen Rupe was once arrested in early 1960s Sydney and spent two weeks in the remand section of Long Bay Gaol. She writes, 'The effect of all the police harassment was to force me into more or less full-time drag. It was safer in the less suspecting atmosphere of the better-class suburb of Woollahra and I was easily able to carry myself off as female.'[51]

Karen, Carmen and Jazmin all mentioned the famous vice squad detective Frank 'Bumper' Farrell, who had a reputation for being abusive towards camp people around the Kings Cross/Darlinghurst area.[52] Jazmin recalls that early one evening she encountered Bumper on the street and he told her to go home. Later that night she snuck into a club, and when he raided the place he just said, 'I told you to get your arse home.' To Jazmin as well as Carmen, Bumper was one of the nicer cops; Jazmin described so many others as 'homophobic and they belted people all the time and, yeah, I've had kickings from police, and they'd grab your hair and cut a big chunk out of it. And, yes, I don't know how I came through all that because they were very, very heavy'.[53]

Sometime around 1966, thirteen-year-old 'Sascha' was in Kings Cross and the target of police entrapment when an undercover cop tried to solicit her. She ran away and escaped, but later in the evening police arrested her when she was in a taxi and charged her with prostitution. They took her to Darlinghurst Gaol, where she was subjected to horrific violence (content warning for readers):

> They threw me into the cage with everyone. They were all boys. I was in there for quite a while. It wasn't a pretty sight. The following morning, I was put before a magistrate. I was bloody, I was in tears, I'd been smacked around, I'd been slapped around, all of this kind of stuff [by] both [police and the other inmates]. Both. I'd been raped. I'd had the whole lot done ... And then, I went to court. And the judge said to the attorney, 'Couldn't you have had this person hosed down before you had him brought into my court room?'[54]

Police harassment would remain a constant in trans people's lives and is a recurring theme in oral histories. Though it could happen anywhere, it was most pronounced in sites of trans visibility, which by the 1970s were the showgirl, stripper and sex-work scenes.

Showgirls and strippers: The new trans visibility

Showgirl and stripper clubs grew out of the camp and drag scene. Importantly, drag and trans are not the same. Drag refers to people who assume a character role, usually (but not always) of another gender, as part of a performance. That performance is temporary and does not necessarily mean the person identifies with a sex other than that assigned at birth. Yet, as noted earlier in relation to female impersonators, drag was a place where people could experiment with different gender expressions. Many trans people, particularly in eras before medical interventions were accessible, found drag to be an entree—a way they could experiment with diverse gender expressions, even if for a short time and in a confined space.

Drag was common at private parties and sometimes part of the camp scene and other nightclubs. Sydney's first regular drag bar was the Jewel Box, opened in 1961. What separated it from other camp bars was that it explicitly advertised all-male revues. While in the present day that conjures ideas of male strippers, in the 1960s–70s all-male revues referred to female impersonators. The performers were a mix of drag queens and trans women. According to Carlotta, the main distinction between the drag queens and the trans women was that the latter took hormones and grew their own breasts.[55] Toye recalls that at one stage, some showgirls called themselves 'Daughters of the Revolutionary Art Group' rather than 'drag queens'.[56] As numerous former showgirls testify, more often than not the audience could not distinguish the sex of the performers. Sometimes patrons even thought that the venues were false-advertising and the performers were cis women.

The venues in Sydney each played to different clientele. The Jewel Box was, according to Karen Chant, 'very rough';[57] Carlotta says, 'The audience would arrive with flagons of wine or cartons of beer on their shoulders and there would be drunken fights every night. It was hideous, but we didn't mind because we were getting paid $35 a week and we had a chance to strut our stuff as girls.'[58] The Purple Onion opened in 1962 as a venue catering for gay men in the hope of providing a safer place. It quickly grew in popularity; Karen recalls: 'Everybody came to the Onion. My dressing-room wall was autographed by Margot Fonteyn, Rudolf Nureyev—every fabulous person that came to Australia went to the Purple Onion.'[59]

The most famous of the all-male revues, opened in 1963, was Les Girls. Restaurateur Sammy Lee was the main owner and founder, and he was well situated to recruit performers because he already owned the Latin Quarter. Les Girls was not necessarily very different from the other all-male revues; trans women and drag queens bounced around working the different clubs, sometimes to the great ire of the owners. What made Les Girls famous was the publicity it received. Susan Le Gay, one of the first dancers at Les Girls, recalls:

> At first, we just opened, and a few people came, you know, like gay people with their parents, and that sort of thing. And then Mike Willesee, when Carol [Carlotta] came into the show, did a documentary and it was called *The Golden Mile*, about Kings Cross, and Les Girls was in it, and Carol was interviewed.

After that documentary, Les Girls became a household name, packed every weekend, mostly with straight couples who came in from the suburbs for a dinner and a show.[60]

Other cities, too, had burgeoning showgirl scenes of all-male revues. Karen recalls travelling to Melbourne sometime in 1961 or 1962 to help open another Jewel Box. What really kickstarted Melbourne's drag and showgirl venues was when a Les Girls opened at the Ritz Hotel in St Kilda in 1971. A few of the Sydney Les Girls came to Melbourne for short stints, while other performers were homegrown. Belinda Chaplin, for instance, had performed in drag shows at Trisha's Coffee Cup and then in the travelling Hollywood Follies revue before becoming part of Les Girls sometime around 1976.[61]

Parts of regional Australia also had venues with all-male revues. By the early 1970s, Tweed Heads and the Gold Coast in particular had a concentration of shows. A gangster known as the Black Prince opened the Golden Net, which was a converted boathouse located on a pier on the Tweed River.[62] More common in regional areas were touring shows. Belinda toured with three other trans women in the Hollywood Follies show around regional Victoria and they received a positive welcome wherever they went. She states, 'You might only go down there for two nights in a row, but both shows were sold out. You got to get out of the city, have a bit of fun, go horseriding, do whatever, and just do some entertaining.'[63]

In 1978, Belinda joined the travelling Melbourne Les Girls show, which went to country towns all over Australia as well as cities like Adelaide, Perth and Canberra. Vonni joined the touring Les Girls show when it came to Adelaide and had a vacancy. She has similar fond memories of the cast receiving a warm welcome wherever they travelled. She notes one exception: in the NSW town of Bombala, sometime in the early 1980s, the person running the hall where they performed was transphobic. She recalls him saying words to the effect of 'The bathroom's out in the foyer, but you can't go to there. You can't go use those toilets. You can't go to the ladies because you're blokes and you can't go to the blokes because you're deviant.' There was also a small group of picketers in Bombala, so Les Girls left town immediately after their show.[64]

The visibility of travelling shows—not to mention showgirls' appearances on television—could also have positive effects through reaching people who otherwise would have no knowledge or under-standing of trans people. Penny Clifford, for instance, was a guest star at Sydney Les Girls and then a regular performer at Patchs on Oxford Street. From about 1981 to 1987, Penny was part of a touring show called Simone & Moniques Playgirls Revue. The show went all over Australia and even toured to London, Japan, Hong Kong and Aotearoa New Zealand. Simone & Moniques was so popular that it won four Australian Entertainment Mo Awards for the Best Variety Production Show (1977, 1978, 1979, 1981). When the show went to Tasmania in the early 1980s—where it was still illegal for AMAB people to wear women's clothing at night—the showgirls had to carry a letter from Tasmania Police and their doctors saying they were transgender and working at the casino. Describing the effects of such travelling shows on societal attitudes, Penny explains: 'Ten trans women in a show looking beautiful and accepted back in the 1970s, 80s and 90s doesn't get enough credit for starting to get people to see us as more than just freaks.'[65]

Working as a showgirl in the 1960s–80s had its upsides: it was paid employment for trans women in an era when discrimination left few other options. Several former showgirls have remarked on the joy of preparing their own fabulous costumes—though this could at times be challenging on the strict budgets. They also thrived on the crowd and the opportunity to perform, with Toye explaining: 'It gives you a certain amount of satisfaction to think that you're doing something that's creative and appreciated. I love the feeling of giving to somebody else and hoping they'll enjoy it.'[66] Oral history interviews and autobiographies such as Carlotta's are full of the names of local and international celebrities who attended or performed in the shows. Oral histories also note that politicians attended and sometimes flirted with the performers, though the speakers do not divulge any names. Several performers—most notably Carlotta and Susan Le Gay—became celebrities in their own right. When Susan left Les Girls in 1966, she toured for three-and-a-half years with the cabaret singer Tony Monopoly, and even appeared on local television programs.[67] Several Australian trans showgirls and strippers spent time in the 1970s working in Hong Kong or Europe, where they could earn much more money than in Australia.

There was also an underbelly, so to speak, to the showgirl scene. Carlotta's autobiography notes that Sammy Lee could be rough and physically abusive with the showgirls if they were late or upset him in some other way. It was well known that he, along with many of the other venue owners, had gangster connections. Depending on the venue, patrons could be friendly, but they could also be aggressive and were known to sexually harass and grope the performers. Substance abuse was rife among the showgirls. Carlotta explains that booze and drugs were common 'because it was fashionable and it made the pace of our lives more bearable. We worked and played so long and so hard and the drugs seemed to make it easier for us all to cope with the kind of life we led and its disappointments and highs.'[68]

By the 1970s, alongside the burgeoning showgirl scene were the strip clubs. These were not advertised as all-male revues; indeed, venues like La Belle in Adelaide and the Pink Pussycat, Pink Panther and Barrel Theatre in Sydney just advertised women strippers but employed both cis and trans women.[69] One intriguing aspect of these clubs was that often the patrons did not know that several of the strippers were trans women. 'Karolyn' explains that the trans strippers became very adept at using surgical tape to hide their genitals and would wear something like a long coat so that they were not exposed when they turned around.[70]

At times the trans women would be exposed, either intentionally or unintentionally. Audiences sometimes reacted lightheartedly with amusement, but other times this did not end so well. Vonni describes doing what was called a 'tricky dicky': performing a strip number and at the very end flashing her appendage and shocking the audience. Audience reactions were unpredictable. On one occasion, a guy who had been flirting with Vonni before her performance clearly had not realised she was trans. After she flashed the audience, his mates laughed at him and 'When I came out after my show, the guy hit me over the head with a chair and kicked me in the face and broke my nose.'[71]

Both showgirl and stripper venues tended to be located in the rougher parts of a city—Kings Cross in Sydney, St Kilda in Melbourne, Hindley Street in Adelaide. These were areas frequented by gangsters and where police harassment of gay men and trans women was rife. There was generally security within the venues—so long as the girls did not cross the bosses—but outside was different. Dressing as a woman in public was still dangerous, especially in the 1960s. Karen Chant recalls one incident when a Jewel Box performer rushed to a chemist across the street between numbers and was arrested for offensive behaviour. When Karen went to bail her out the next day, police proceeded to harass her: 'As I was walking along I got tripped from behind, and when I got up it was these two policemen [who] said to me: "Tonight's your turn, cunt" … They wanted to get me but they never did.' Karen also recalls police following performers to and from the venues; sometimes she would have her taxi take a circuitous route or drop her off somewhere else so police would not know where she lived.[72]

By the 1970s, as arrests for dressing became less common, Karen and other trans showgirls began living and dressing full time as women. Usually police did not harass them when they were in the venues, in part because the owners often paid regular bribes. Sascha worked as a stripper at several venues in the 1970s before doubling as performer and manager at the Barrel Theatre. During the 1980s she arranged the payments for the cops on behalf of the Barrel's owner, but police corruption was increasingly under public scrutiny. When she heard that the vice squad wanted to check on her, she decided it was time to leave Sydney.[73]

Vonni explains that around 1988 the NSW premier, Nick Greiner, launched a campaign to clean up Kings Cross. She recalls that one night police vans stopped at each end of Darlinghurst Road and went to all the venues: 'They arrested a doorman, ticket seller, a waitress, a barmaid, a stripper from each, even lighting people from each club, and we were all taken and arrested and fingerprinted and put in gaol and charged with aiding and abetting because those places didn't have licences for entertainment or alcohol.' Vonni said that police repeated this over the course of a whole week, but she and others were prepared:

> I could see them [police] on the other side of the road. So I'm up one flight and I'm in my costume, I climbed out of the window onto the rostrum and ran up the rostrum halfway up Darlinghurst Road and then climbed in another window, which was the illegal gambling club where all the ethnics used to do their gambling, and they had topless waitresses. I climbed in the window, so this is one floor up, and the girl said, 'Are you the other waitress?' I said, 'Yes, love, I've just climbed in the window off the rostrum; I'm the other waitress.' And I just stayed there.[74]

Showgirls and strippers also faced the real and dangerous threat of sexual violence. Toye de Wilde spoke candidly about being raped when she was on a Les Girls tour in the town of Julia Creek in

North Queensland. Because the towns were generally welcoming, she thought nothing of it when a patron offered to drive her back to her motel. She explains what happened next (and readers, please be warned this content may cause distress):

> I'd had a lot to drink, and I wanted to go back to the motel, and this guy said, 'I'll drop you off; I'm going past the motel.' He said, 'I'll just get my friend.' And so I stupidly climbed in to the car with them, and they drove me out into the middle of woop woop, where there was nothing but long grass. And they just tore the clothes off me and raped me. And then when they'd finished, they drove me back to the motel.

The rape traumatised Toye, and the reaction of the tour manager only exacerbated her trauma: 'I wanted to call the police, but the manager at the show said it would be very bad publicity for us. All the girls gathered around, and they were great for support. So we just had to go, move on to the next town. And that was terrifying.'[75] Toye was certainly resilient in getting on with life both then and now, but her tale is indicative of not only the violence but also the sense of powerlessness trans women felt when they could not report assaults.

The main reason that most sexual or other assaults went unreported is that police were generally uninterested. As noted across this chapter, police harassment was rampant, and police also could be the perpetrators of the sexual assaults. Ex-stripper Naomi told Roberta Perkins in 1983 about one awful police gang rape:

> One girl was sexually assaulted by nine policemen. The had anal intercourse with her and forced her to perform fellatio. She was picked up walking down the street doing her shopping in the daytime. She had to have stitches in her anus, and she became very depressed after that. If she tried to do anything about it she would have been laughed at and called a 'poofter'. So transsexuals had little choice but to put up with it.[76]

As the next chapter discusses, police harassment and abuse would continue into the 1980s–90s, particularly at the third main site of trans visibility: sex work.

The effects and limits of visibility

As this chapter has shown, trans visibility increased immensely between World War II and the 1970s. In the early period media still primarily centred on salacious stories, but Christine Jorgensen's gender affirmation surgery marked a significant turning point. The emergence of medical discourse and the small number of psychiatrists who worked with trans clients presented new possibilities of medical transition—though on strict terms and targeting those trans people who met white, middle-class standards of respectability. During the same period, the camp scene offered a place for people to experiment with diverse gender expressions. The rise of trans showgirls and strippers in the 1960s–70s then presented new opportunities for trans women.

The showgirl scene was particularly significant because it attracted media attention. Alongside the continuing salacious headlines about trans sex deviants, reports about showgirls showed them to be playful, gentle entertainers. Carlotta used television and other interviews to portray herself as someone who craved a quiet life as a respectable woman.[77] Moreover, many of the all-male revues were targeting straight, cisgender audiences, including families. As the 1970s progressed, television reports and magazines such as *Forum* and *Cleo* often included sympathetic features where trans people were able to share their own perspectives.[78] More often than not the language was couched in the medical discourse of transvestism and transsexualism, but it was still an important shift that could humanise and legitimise trans people.

The visibility of trans showgirls resonated with other trans people who were struggling or questioning their gender identities. John Hewson (who shares his name with a former Liberal Party politician), for instance, began collecting newspaper and magazine clippings relating to drag, trans and other gender nonconformity from 1965 and for almost thirty years pasted this material into a series of scrapbooks. John began dressing in the early 1970s and would continue to do so until 1993.[79] 'Karolyn' recalls:

> My cousin invited me up to Les Girls to see the show. It was my twentieth birthday and my mind just went bang—my world exploded. So yes, that was the moment … when I saw the possibility of what my life could be, that I could actually have a life I could possibly enjoy and feel more myself and not this turmoil. And so I experimented and when the opportunity came, I jumped full on into it.[80]

Karolyn went on to become a stripper herself, but being part of the stripper or showgirl scene was not necessarily a desired outcome for closeted or questioning trans people in the 1970s. Oral histories suggest a bifurcated reaction to media presence of showgirls: on the one hand the speaker had a sense of connection to others like them, but on the other hand many feared that being a showgirl was the only career path, and this drove them deeper into the closet. Yet there were other opportunities emerging for trans people. The next chapter explores the beginnings of trans organisation and support available for both medical and social transitions from the late 1970s through the early 1990s.

3
BEGINNING TO ORGANISE

I N MAY 1971, Rosemary Langton placed a notice in the *Kings Cross Whisper* that read: 'TV enthusiast would like to meet other TV enthusiast for mutual pleasure'. Those in the know realised that TV referred to transvestites. Rosemary received about thirty-five responses (and a few from people who presumed TV meant television). She then convened a meeting at a local Malaysian restaurant, where the attendees founded Seahorse—Australia's first known trans organisation.[1] Within years there were Seahorse chapters or offshoots across the country. Members appeared on television and in magazine and newspaper features and aimed to promote trans dressers as ordinary heterosexual men who just enjoyed adopting female dress part time.

Seahorse catered to a specific demographic of trans people (dressers); by the end of the 1970s other small organisations were popping up across Australia to offer peer support for people who desired or had gender affirmation surgery. This was particularly important when the new Melbourne Gender Dysphoria Clinic and

Flinders Medical Centre Gender Clinic in Adelaide, founded in 1975 and 1978 respectively, meant more opportunities for surgery. In the early 1980s, groups in Victoria and New South Wales shifted from just peer support towards advocacy and activism for trans rights. Roberta Perkins was an especially prominent activist in Sydney who fought for social services and respect for transgender women and sex workers. There were mixed outcomes across the country in each of these spaces as the first generation of trans activists left their mark and laid the groundwork for further reform.

This chapter explores the origins of trans organising and activism in the 1970s–80s alongside the evolving trans subcultures and medical influence. As the medical model continued to distinguish transvestites from transsexuals, so too did different subcultures emerge for these groups. That said, it was not uncommon for someone to identify as a transvestite but then over time to desire hormones and gender affirmation surgery and then identify as transsexual. There were also growing divides between subcultures of trans people who mirrored white middle-class respectability versus those who either did not desire or could not afford gender affirmation surgery. The latter were particularly visible as sex workers in the capital cities, facing brutality and harassment from police and clients alike. As the 1990s rolled in, the distinctions between transvestites, transsexuals and transgender people were stark; it would take a new generation of activists to unite them.

Seahorse and its offshoots

Rosemary Langton was born in Singapore in 1931 and lived in Malaya, the United Kingdom and Hong Kong before she moved to Sydney in 1968. From an early age she dressed in women's clothing, and it was while working in Hong Kong she came across the magazine *Sexology*. She remembers reading an article that mentioned that an American, Dr Virginia Prince, intended to start a new magazine for transvestites. Prince published two editions of *Transvestia: The*

Journal of the American Society for Equality in Dress in 1952, and they are the first known political (as opposed to medical) trans publications from the United States. She relaunched *Transvestia* in 1960 and it would run for another twenty years.[2]

As an avid traveller, Rosemary met Prince in the United States and other trans women in the United Kingdom and Hong Kong. She hosted Prince on a trip to Australia in 1970 and recalls: 'As Virginia left she turned to me and said, "Rosemary, you've got to organise the Australian girls."' It was this exchange that prompted Rosemary to place that advertisement in the *Kings Cross Whisper* in May 1971. When her inner circle met at the Malaysian restaurant, they agreed to organise themselves as a group for dressers with Rosemary as its inaugural president. Rosemary originally proposed that they name themselves after the sea creature called hippocampus, because the male carries the fertilised egg, symbolising a form of gender crossing. The others liked the idea but said they would prefer to go with the animal's more common name: Seahorse.[3]

The Seahorse Club held its first official monthly meeting in August 1971 in Bondi Junction. Over time members met at private residences and, eventually, in locations in Sydney's northern suburbs and on the Central Coast of New South Wales. Generally the members would arrive at the meeting presenting as men, change and put on make-up at the venue, and then return home presenting as men again.[4] An introductory letter sent to new members explained:

> We meet regularly, at least once a month to dress 'en Femme' and enjoy a pleasant social evening. We will assist where possible with make-up, clothing and the buying of feminine items. Meeting attendance is restricted to members or their family and security is a major consideration at these and any other functions, a situation we are sure you will agree with.[5]

Even in its early days, meeting attendance could range from about six people to upwards of twenty.

The club identified as being for heterosexual transvestites, intentionally distinguishing themselves from homosexuals, fetishists and transsexuals. This was part of an effort to portray transvestism as 'normal' and club membership as respectable. For much of its early history, Seahorse had a fraught relationship with sexually diverse people that could even be homophobic. Members consciously distanced themselves from the popularly perceived 'deviance' of the gay and lesbian community, as well as the vice-ridden trans sex workers, strippers and showgirls. Seahorse was a conservative organisation that did not aim to disrupt gender binaries but, rather, to show that some men had a feminine side that they needed to express through feminine dress. Still, by adopting the language of transvestism and, by the 2000s, transgender, Seahorse is considered Australia's first known trans organisation.

Privacy and security were of the utmost importance for Seahorse, so any prospective member needed to go through a screening process, including an interview. Members received a number and used feminine code names, and nobody could ask someone to divulge their real name or other personal information.[6] Members came from all walks of life; a 1974 membership directory listed forty-three members across Australia and one in Aotearoa New Zealand. They had education levels ranging from high school through to trade schools and postgraduate qualifications. Members' hobbies included sports, organ playing, Asian culture, languages, motor racing, knitting and cacti collecting.[7] Oral histories and media from the era indicate that members' employment was also diverse: carpenters, doctors, sports stars, engineers, clerks, lawyers, police-men, teachers and even pastors. By 1977 the NSW group boasted over 600 members.[8] While there was diversity in class, geography and age, the group was very much white and European, and through-out its history Seahorse and its offshoots have remained relatively racially homogenous.

Initially Seahorse was national, though the meetings and leadership were centred in Sydney. To run activities and ensure representation in other states, there were counsellors in Adelaide, Brisbane, Melbourne and Perth. Within a few years of Seahorse's founding, this arrangement proved to be unworkable and other cities formed independent groups. Even before Seahorse, a group of dressers were meeting at a home in Kew, Melbourne, which they dubbed the Kew Castle. By 1975 this group decided it needed a separate structure so that it could effectively plan and run events. Five or six of these dressers convened in a St Kilda East apartment in September 1975, where they founded a separate Seahorse Victoria. A month later they already had a membership list of twelve people,[9] and by 1977 there were 100 members. In 1978, Seahorse Victoria spun off a similar group for dressers known as the Elaine Barrie Project; that group changed its name to Chameleons in 1996 and lasted until about 2011.

Less is known about the origins of Seahorse in other states. John Hewson recalls that sometime around 1973 he placed an advertisement in a magazine to meet other dressers. When people reached out to him, he subsequently founded Seahorse Queensland and ran it until he moved to Sydney a few years later.[10] A 1977 letter to the editor of *The Examiner* indicated the existence of a Tasmanian branch.[11] In 1980 the Tasmanian convenor reported that the group had about ten members, describing them as 'people who are frightened of mixing with others in public and prefer to gather in a home'.[12] By 1975 a distinct South Australian group of Seahorse was organising an annual masquerade ball.[13] Seahorse South Australia's constitution has no date, though it appears to be from the late 1970s.[14] Sometime in the 1980s the SA branch disbanded; in 1985 a new group for dressers, the Carousel Club of South Australia, was founded. In Western Australia, the Chameleon Society was founded in 1974 for dressers and initially had some crossover with Seahorse membership. In 1977, after lengthy negotiations, the two clubs amalgamated and the Chameleon Society became the sole group in the state.[15] There was even a Seahorse group in Aotearoa New Zealand whom Carmen Rupe remembers visited her famous

International Coffee Lounge and Balcony strip club in Wellington.[16] Although all of these groups maintained distinct structures and leadership, they regularly shared items in their newsletters and extended invitations to attend regional or national events.

Among the early national events was the Seahorse NSW–organised Transseminar in May 1976 at a hotel in Sydney's northern beaches. The weekend program included social events and a day of speakers covering topics such as psychiatric perspectives on transvestism, social attitudes towards transvestism, the law, and wives' perspectives. The forum was attended by about 100 Seahorse members, their wives and a small number of invited psychiatrists and other guests, including Dr Bettina Arndt, who at the time was editor of *Forum* magazine.[17] Lady Paula Howard recalls that Transseminar overlapped with a seminar hosted by the Australian Society of Accountants and Auditors, making for interesting interactions at the motel. She writes: 'Astonishingly it worked well and in no time the more liberal of the accountants (and auditors!) were kindly buying rounds of drinks for the more outward-looking and exciting of the transvestites and transsexuals! And to quote Lord Byron "all went merry as a marriage bell".'[18] Seahorse NSW organised a follow-up in 1977 called Transvenue with a similar social and education program but added an extra day 'for professional instruction and guidance in all the arts of femininity. Make-up, wig and fashion advice, fabulous fashion parade by the Seahorse Models, whilst you sit and drink a cool drink alongside the pool.'[19] Most of the Seahorse or equivalent clubs also hosted big annual events such as balls, and smaller functions such as movie or dinner nights.

Early on, the leadership in numerous Seahorse chapters recognised the importance of visibility to changing societal attitudes towards trans people. Seahorse leaders thus were happy to participate in media interviews because they saw them as opportunities to shape a public narrative about the ordinariness of dressers. One of the first opportunities was a radio interview with Melbourne's 3AW in 1974. Shortly after, Sydney's Channel 0-10 extended an invitation for

Seahorse members to appear on *The Mike Walsh Show*.[20] Through the 1970s Seahorse NSW members also appeared on programs such as ABC Radio's *Morning Show* and the Channel 9 program *A Current Affair*.[21]

Another popular medium that Seahorse used to present an image of respectability was 'women's interest' magazines, such as *Forum* and *Cleo*. *Forum* was born out of the sexual revolution, while *Cleo* consciously melded consumerism and fashion with articles that spoke to liberal feminist causes. The author of the first *Forum* article in 1974 attended a Seahorse meeting and interviewed a few members. The article described the transformation of the members from their masculine to feminine appearance and centred trans voices, with members speaking about topics ranging from family relations (especially wives' reactions), their (hetero)sexuality, the difference between trans people and gay people, and why members were hesitant to go out in public. A quote from Trina Taylor closed the article with an effective summary of why Seahorse was important to people's lives: 'It is better with the club. Before the Seahorse Club it was a very lonely life. I always felt I was all dressed up with nowhere to go.'[22] Articles in *Cleo* and *Forum* often included Seahorse contact details, which boosted membership. Trans interview participants who were children or adolescents at the time specifically remember *Cleo* articles about trans people (not just about Seahorse) and feeling a sense of connection that there were others like them.[23]

By the late 1990s and early 2000s, as different ideas around trans and gender diversity were becoming prominent, the dresser groups left behind their identification as 'heterosexual transvestites' and joined the broader transgender umbrella. The organisations mostly withdrew from the media in the 1980s, in part because of privacy concerns, but there was still the occasional feature in broadsheet newspapers. Seahorse NSW, Queensland and Victoria are still around today; Western Australia's Chameleon Society and South Australia's Carousel Club folded in 2015 and early 2023 respectively.

The rise of gender clinics

For those who identified as transsexuals, medical interventions continued to play an important role. In the early 1970s Dr William Walters, an obstetrician/gynaecologist at Melbourne's Queen Victoria Hospital, received a trans patient referral. He did some research and referred the patient to an endocrinologist and then a surgeon. Other GPs then began referring patients to Walters, who along with psychiatrist Herbert Bower prepared a proposal for a multidisciplinary gender clinic. In late 1975 Monash University and the Queen Victoria Hospital board of management agreed to establish the Gender Dysphoria Clinic, with Walters as founding director.[24] It began seeing clients in early 1976 and its first gender affirmation surgery was performed in May of that year.

The Melbourne Gender Dysphoria Clinic was focused almost exclusively on transsexuals and its work centred on screening and preparing people for gender affirmation surgery. Early on, the clinic adopted the procedures outlined in the previous chapter to assess if and when a trans person met eligibility for surgery. Those who fit the criteria of 'true transsexuals' would have hormones prescribed by an endocrinologist and then needed to go through the two-year 'real-life test'.[25] In 1987 Walters moved to Newcastle and psychiatrist Trudy Kennedy became the new clinic director. In October 1988 the Victorian minister for health decided to close the Department of Health's Transsexualism Consultative Clinic and instead devote all public resources to the one gender clinic, renamed the Monash Gender Dysphoria Clinic. The state government would provide $30,000 per annum to support clinical assessment and $75,000 to fund gender affirmation surgeries. This would support six to ten surgeries each year—even though in 1988 there was already a waiting list of more than thirty-five people.[26]

By the 1980s the Monash Gender Dysphoria Clinic was the biggest provider of trans health care in Australia, but it was not alone. The first Australian Conference on Transsexualism was convened in 1979, drawing together specialists from across Australia and Aotearoa New Zealand. It even received a bit of media coverage over a paper presented by Dr Michael Ross of Flinders University that, comparing Australian data with that of Sweden, suggested that Australia had the highest incidence of transsexualism in the world.[27]

Ross was also the driving force behind Adelaide's Gender Clinic at Flinders Medical Centre. There had been sensational press coverage of Adelaide's first gender affirmation surgery performed in 1976.[28] This had the effect of garnering the attention of trans people across South Australia who wanted surgery. In late 1978 Ross and the state deputy director of mental health brought a proposal to Flinders University Medical School to set up a gender clinic similar to the one running in Melbourne. The university agreed, and sometime in late 1978 or early 1979 Ross became director of the new Flinders Medical Centre Gender Clinic.

The Flinders clinic had similar expectations and procedures as Melbourne around the real-life test, prescription of hormones and eventual approval for gender affirmation surgery. By the mid-1980s it was seeing 30–35 new clients per year.[29] In 1988 the Flinders Medical Centre Gender Clinic suspended its operations for up to five years pending a review.[30] Even though the suspension was only meant to be until the review was completed, the clinic did not reopen. In the interim, Ross moved to Sydney and Flinders University declined to continue funding the clinic. Thus, since 1988 the Monash Gender Dysphoria Clinic in Melbourne has been the country's only publicly funded specialist gender service with referrals for gender affirmation surgery.

Self-help and advocacy groups

The possibility of gender affirmation surgery meant more trans people coming out and needing psychosocial support through their transition journeys. A small number of self-help groups emerged in the late 1970s for trans women who desired surgery. One of the first was called Transcare, based in Adelaide. It was founded in 1976 by burgeoning trans activist Marie-Desiree D'Orsay Lawrence and her friend Renée; at the time, they were both training to be pastors in the gay-and-lesbian-friendly Metropolitan Community Church.[31] A 1976 article in *The Mirror* said that the group was supporting twelve people who desired gender affirmation surgery, with a counsellor quoted as saying, 'At Transcare we have contact with the Department of Social Security, an employment service, psychiatrists, beauticians and fashion experts.'[32] Transcare appears sporadically in other records, including a 1979 letter from federal MP Peter Morris advocating for a constituent claiming to be the Newcastle and Hunter Valley representative of Transcare.[33] Brisbane's Metropolitan Community Church attempted to open a branch of Transcare, and a visitor to Adelaide's Transcare formed a spin-off group in Perth called Transfer. Adelaide's Transcare was the most lasting, and by 1982 was focused primarily on social support.[34] It is not known how long these groups lasted, how wide their membership was, or how the organisers facilitated the self-help.

Also in 1976, a small group of trans women in Melbourne organised the Victorian Transsexual Association as a self-help group for those who were seeking or had had gender affirmation surgery. It did not have a membership list per se, but early on anywhere from thirty to fifty people had attended at least one meeting.[35] The association partnered with the mental health and suicide prevention organisation Lifeline, held regular monthly meetings, and offered information about cosmetics, voice modulation appointments offered by the Lincoln Institute Speech Pathology Clinic, electrolysis and strategies for social interactions and becoming more confident as women. By mid-1982 the group's membership and attendance were floundering and by 1983 it essentially existed in name only.[36] In 1988 another group of trans women attempted to form a group hosted in St Kilda called T/S Self Help Group Victoria, though it did not last long either.[37] It would not be until the 1990s that a new generation of activists founded more sustainable peer support groups in Victoria.

Related to the Victorian Transsexual Association was the state's first trans advocacy group: the Victorian Transsexual Coalition (VTC). This group formed in September 1979 after the first Australian Conference on Transsexualism. The initial convenor was Sue Harding, a cisgender counsellor employed by the Commonwealth Rehabilitation Service. Sue had worked with several trans clients in South Australia and believed it was vital to bring together service providers and members of the trans community to offer a support and advocacy service. The initial meeting had a mix of trans and cis representatives from groups including the Victorian Transsexual Association, Transcare, Lifeline, the Metropolitan Community Church and Seahorse Victoria. Once the VTC was established, trans women took on the leadership and shaped the group's direction and objectives. The organisation specifically focused on trans women who had, or intended to have, gender affirmation surgery, and its objectives were to advocate for those women's needs, draw attention to discrimination, and offer resources to assist in social and medical transitions.[38]

Over its nine years of existence, the VTC prepared several documents to offer advice to trans women, including a list of trans-friendly welfare, counselling, legal, accommodation and entertainment services. It also prepared two important guides, one for surgical candidates and the other for families of trans people.[39] The pamphlet for families was titled 'What is Transsexualism?' and provided background on the contemporaneous medical understandings of transsexualism and steps a person must go through to qualify for gender affirmation surgery. The final section of the pamphlet read:

Imagine that you, the parent of a transsexual, awakened one morning, looked into the mirror, and saw an unfamiliar reflection returning your glance: that of the opposite sex. Imagine your shock and dismay! Your feelings were no different from what they had always been; and yet you, with your sense of self, were now trapped in a body that contradicted all that you know yourself to be. Now you have a slight notion of what your child has been experiencing daily, probably since early childhood.[40]

The VTC was also a political advocacy group, with priorities centred on lobbying for legal recognition of trans people in their affirmed genders and anti-discrimination protections. They consistently wrote letters to state and federal politicians, government departments and statutory bodies such as the Commonwealth Rehabilitation Service, Australian Law Reform Commission and Road Traffic Authority (a precursor to VicRoads). The VTC also corresponded with trans organisations in other states and made submissions on proposed legislation for legal recognition in Victoria and South Australia. In 1981 it prepared a petition calling for the Victorian Government to amend birth certificate legislation so that trans people who had had gender affirmation surgery could be recognised in their affirmed gender. The then leader of the opposition, John Cain, tabled the petition with fifty signatures in the Victorian Parliament.[41]

In September 1983, representatives of the VTC met with the Victorian Equal Opportunity Advisory Council to discuss challenges confronting trans women. On the council's advice, the VTC prepared a submission outlining its major areas of concern: revising birth certificates, updating identity documents (e.g. passport, drivers licence, qualifications), identification for credit and government employment, anti-discrimination, and access to rights such as marriage, social security benefits and protections from rape and assault. The submission argued that any person who was undergoing treatment by specialists at a gender clinic should be granted a certificate that would entitle them to legal recognition in their affirmed gender. Once that person had gender affirmation surgery, they should be allowed to amend their birth certificate and that would have the flow-on effect of giving them full access to change all their documents. The VTC further recommended amendments to the Victorian *Equal Opportunity Act* that would redefine the protected attribute of 'the sex' to read 'the sex including reassigned sex'.[42] The advisory council endorsed the addition of 'or reassigned sex' into the *Equal Opportunity Act*,[43] but this did not come to fruition. As the next chapter explores, it would be another seventeen years before Victoria added trans people to its anti-discrimination law.

The VTC also took an interest in health-care provision for trans people, such as advocating for the newly created Medicare (1984) to cover gender affirmation surgeries. It worked closely with the director of the Gender Dysphoria Clinic at Queen Victoria Hospital and also corresponded with the director of the Flinders Medical Centre Gender Clinic. When Monash Health reviewed the operation of the Gender Dysphoria Clinic in 1987, the VTC lobbied for it to retain the essential service. In its letter to the Victorian health minister, the VTC noted that trans clients were at various stages of the real-life test or on waitlists and the cessation of funding for surgeries would have dire effects:

> The psychological stress on all of these patients would be understandably high and they have very few options for alternative assistance. Those patients in a low socioeconomic group by virtue of their history or as a result of lifestyle change are particularly disadvantaged in seeking private surgical intervention.[44]

However, Monash Health ceased funding gender affirmation surgeries and allowed clients to proceed only if they had private insurance. This meant that about half of the people on the clinic's books and ready for surgery could not afford it. Herbert Bower complained to the press, and this contributed to negotiations behind the scenes with the Victorian Department of Health that resulted in the state funding arrangement for the Monash Gender Dysphoria Clinic and the resumption of subsidised surgeries from 1989.[45]

Throughout its existence the VTC never attracted media attention, and this was intentional. The leadership believed that its lobbying work did not require media comment, which would only open the door to the invasion of members' privacy. From 1983, leaders of the organisation sometimes used the name 'Jenny Johnson' as an alias in correspondence and media commentary.[46] The archival trail for the VTC ends in 1988, suggesting that the group folded sometime around then.

Importantly, the VTC was always small and its leaders emphasised politics of respectability, showcasing trans women as ordinary, middle-class women. One subject that the organisation almost entirely avoided was sex work. For instance, in 1985 the Victorian Government conducted an inquiry into prostitution and invited the VTC to prepare a submission. It declined, commenting: 'While we understand that some transsexuals may be involved in prostitution we consider that it concerns people regardless of their gender orientation and therefore the issue is primarily one of criminal law and not of transsexualism.' The VTC noted only that trans sex workers should be recognised in their affirmed gender.[47] Thus, trans sex workers and others who did not fit the norms of white, middle-class respectability would require different champions and activism.

Trans sex workers

By the early 1980s there was a booming trans sex industry in Sydney and smaller trades in the other major cities. Street work was the most visible and stereotypical form of sex work, but it was not the only one. For instance, Sistergirl Elder Vanessa Smith recalls that around age fourteen or fifteen (c. 1966) she began sex work in Perth, trading her body for lodging. She explains: 'That was my trade-off. That's how I survived. That was the exchange ... to give them what they wanted and for me to get what I wanted, and that was a place to stay, a place to live.'[48] Opportunistic sex work was a common way for trans people to enter the industry. Elyse 'Tarks' Coles recalls that in early 1980s Adelaide she was working as an apprentice hairdresser during the day and would find clients at gay establishments such as the Mars Bar at night. Her line when she met men became 'If you're not staying for breakfast, then you're paying.'[49]

More commonly, trans people became sex workers because of discrimination limiting other employment opportunities. Jacqueline Durvell Ward made headlines in the early 1970s when she was arrested for soliciting a man in Brisbane. The tabloids were relatively sympathetic to Ward, describing her troubled upbringing and explaining that she had turned to sex work because she had no other way to earn a living. A follow-up article hinted at possible police abuse, simply mentioning 'a night of bedlam in the watchhouse'.[50] Another example of women turning to sex work for lack of other options comes from Simone Lyndon-Pike, who said in 1984:

> I did not have another profession to go to. I started at 16. Being a transsexual, most jobs do not accept you. Transsexuals are part of a sad story. Most of us have looked for work in other jobs but there are only so many opportunities in places like Les Girls in Sydney. Not everybody can work there. At 16 or 17, you perhaps have an identity crisis as a transsexual. All of a sudden you are a woman; you feel that you are a woman. You want to earn the money to have the operation … Those operations are expensive but that is the only way to earn the money. If you are able to get an ordinary job, you have to ensure that you are not exploited.[51]

Street sex work was common and often centred on a particular road or neighbourhood. Usually this would be the same or adjoining suburb to where cis sex workers operated, but there tended to be defined spaces for gay boys, trans women and cis women. Trans sex worker Bronwyn Walsh, for instance, testified before the New South Wales Select Committee of the Legislative Assembly upon Prostitution in 1984 that approximately twenty sex workers worked the streets of Newcastle and these women tended to cluster around Hamilton Railway Station in Islington and near the Criterion Hotel where gay men hung out.[52] Newcastle sex workers also often worked in Sydney, where they could have more clients in one night.[53]

In Melbourne, St Kilda was the principal site of street sex work. The trans scene was small in the 1980s–90s—maybe only about five trans women per night. Judy, who worked in both Melbourne and Sydney in the early 1980s, noted that Melbourne clients tended to pay more and haggle less. She also explained:

> Working relationships between the girls are quite different. For instance, in Melbourne we used to pack up ten minutes early and go and have coffee together and talk about the night's work … Pimping is a big problem in Melbourne, the pimps just about run prostitution down there. Here [Sydney] none of the transsexuals are under pimps, at least, not yet [1983].[54]

By the late 1980s Greeves Street was where most trans sex workers operated in St Kilda. Latoya Hoeg recalls that when she arrived in Melbourne she met with two 'top dogs' who ran Greeves Street: one from Portugal and the other a blonde trans woman from Aotearoa New Zealand. The New Zealander had a relationship with police so could sometimes warn the girls before raids. Indeed, Latoya recalls the night she met her: 'I got introduced to her and she goes to me, "Oh, don't you worry, look, the cops are going to come around soon." The next minute, cops come around and then they went, "Oh, this is Latoya, la, la, la, la, she's new here, she's going to be working here."' This did not mean that police never hassled Latoya: sometimes they would raid the area and tell the girls to go home, and other times they would arrest them and take them to St Kilda Police Station.[55]

Police in all jurisdictions would often abuse their authority, to demand either bribes or sexual favours from trans women. Paying off the police was common, particularly for top dogs and those with other connections. Simone Lyndon-Pike testified in 1984 that trans sex workers in Sydney used to pay police $150 a week to ensure they were not arrested—though she also noted that this practice stopped in the early 1980s.[56]

The largest, most visible and most documented sex worker scene was in Sydney. Jazmin Theodora recalls soliciting in Paddington in the 1950s, and other trans sex workers say that Boundary Street along the border of Darlinghurst and Paddington near Rushcutters Bay was a regular haunt in the 1960s–70s.[57] From the 1970s, Darley Street in Darlinghurst was a popular site until residents campaigned against the presence of sex workers in their area. In December 1982, a series of police raids nicknamed the Battle of Darlo culminated in the arrest of seventy sex workers, twenty of whom were trans. Subsequently, trans sex workers settled into the laneways around William Street and Premier Lane in Kings Cross/Darlinghurst; by the late 1980s this area was collectively known as 'Tranny Lane'. Submissions from the New South Wales Police and sex worker advocates in 1983 to the Select Committee of the Legislative Assembly upon Prostitution estimated that there were 15–20 trans women working Tranny Lane each night.[58] Trans sex workers recall that this number ballooned to as many as 50–100 on a weekend night by the 1990s.

Surveys that Roberta Perkins conducted with twelve trans sex workers in 1983 found that they worked for anywhere from one month to eighteen years as sex workers, and oral histories reinforce that trans women came in and out of sex work.[59] Tranny Lane had a strict set of unspoken rules, and any new girl who did not learn them could face ostracism or physical abuse. New girls had to start and stay on William Street for a few months as part of their probation before graduating to Premier Lane. Chantell Martin explains, 'There was a hierarchy. There was a top dog there, and the top dog would have maybe four offsiders that would be like foot soldiers or the wardens or whatever. They would monitor Premier Lane and know if you were new and then you'd cop it. You'd get a warning and get told to get downstairs to do your six months.'[60] Sistergirl Kooncha Brown recalls that she cheekily confronted a top dog to keep her time on William Street short. She recalls the exchange:

'Oh, girl, can you work down William Street, you know, just for a week?'
I said, 'Why?'

'Because some of the top dogs here, they don't like the idea that you just walked in.'

I said, 'Walked in where? This is our country, not yours. I'm not going anywhere.'

She said, 'Could you just work down there for one week?'

Well, little did they know I wasn't here for one week, I only come up on the weekend. I said, 'Yeah, okay.'

So the following weekend I just walked back into Premier Lane with my cousin and another friend of ours. But there was lots of fights. Bashings. My cousin got bashed from some of them.[61]

At the top of the social hierarchy—the queen of queens, as Phlan-Michelle Purss described her—was Māori trans woman Carmen Rupe. Carmen had worked as a showgirl, stripper and sex worker in Sydney, Auckland and Wellington and had done street work in Sydney in the early 1960s when police were much more brutal and attacks on trans sex workers were common.[62] When she returned to Sydney in 1982, she had more money and an air of professionalism about her work. Carmen's spot was on the Woolloomooloo side of William Street at the intersection of Forbes Street, but she was not usually working with clients so much as looking out for the girls. Phlan-Michelle recalls that Carmen influenced her to kick a drug habit.[63] Chantell recalls an occasion when a bunch of angry men were chasing her, threatening to beat her up because they had mistaken her for someone else. Carmen saw Chantell running and told her to get behind her, then confronted the men; they finally stopped and saw that Chantell was not the person they were looking for and left her alone.[64] Carmen Rupe passed away in 2011 at age seventy-five.

Those who really broke the rules or crossed the wrong figures were ostracised to part of William Street closer to Kings Cross where only the worst, most dangerous clients were known to tread.[65] Not coincidentally, those trans women with strong drug addictions tended to find themselves on that bottom end of the hierarchy. As Simone summarised in 1984, 'Most of the girls in William Street are junkies. I am not running them down but they have been put into that unfortunate position by the hoons and people that they are working for.'[66]

Demographically, trans sex workers came from all walks of life, though a 1983 police submission to a parliamentary inquiry into prostitution noted that half of the sex workers in Tranny Lane were Māori.[67] Kooncha recalls that on William Street there were different spaces for the Māori, Pasifika, Asian and Aboriginal women, and another space for new girls. Over time those divisions broke down, and the Aboriginal, Māori and Pasifika girls began to look out for one another.[68] The disproportionate number of trans sex workers of colour is a marker of the intersecting racist, sexist and transphobic oppression such women faced. Institutional racism and the legacies of colonialism left people of colour with less access to education and employment opportunities. These preconditions affected trans women of colour across their life spans and transition journeys.

None of the trans sex workers of colour interviewed for this project identified encountering any specific racial discrimination in employment as driving them to sex work. Rather, it was usually something they began opportunistically; lacking other specific skills or job prospects, they just fell into it and the sense of community it provided. Other trans women of colour may have turned to sex work because they could not continue working in their previous profession. For instance, surveys Roberta Perkins conducted in 1983–84 reveal that several Māori, Pasifika and Aboriginal trans women worked in traditionally masculine jobs such as machinist, mechanic or wood turner before they transitioned.[69] As women they did not have the same employment opportunities, nor did they have education or skills that were transferable to traditional women's work. Those trans women of colour who had skills and experience such as clerical work would face not only transphobia but also racial discrimination in hiring practices. In other words, the compounding disadvantages facing people of colour made them more likely to turn to sex work.

Sex workers could see just one client all the way through to more than a dozen per night depending on how much money they were after. They performed the job in a client's car or a doorway, on the streets, or in certain places they knew, to which they would direct their clients. There were relatively set rates, and anyone found to be undercutting would face punishment from the other sex workers. One police submission from 1983 asserted that trans women charged between $20 and $40 for a blow job and could, on a good night, make $700 over four hours.[70] Given the number of trans sex workers who lived in poverty and the questionable mathematics (at a minimum that would equate to eighteen clients or one every twelve minutes), this seems an extreme rather than the norm. A more reasonable estimate came from Simone. When she appeared before the Select Committee of the Legislative Assembly upon Prostitution in 1984, she noted that some nights a girl may make nothing and others she may make a few hundred dollars. On average, though, 'A lot of transsexuals make only $30, $40 or $50, maybe $100, a night and they work four nights a week. That is still a good income.'[71]

Sex work was dangerous, with both clients and police posing threats. Out of twelve surveys Perkins conducted with trans sex workers in 1983, ten workers reported experiencing some form of violence. Four reported having been raped (some multiple times), two knifed, seven bashed (some multiple times) and eight verbally abused.[72] In 1983 Carmen Rupe observed: 'There have been lots of transsexuals threatened with knives, guns, hammers and crowbars. There has been a lot of that happening. It goes with the job and you have to be prepared.'[73] Phlan-Michelle, who performed sex work on Tranny Lane for almost twenty years, was a repeat victim of awful abuse:

I've had knives pulled on me. I've been robbed. I've been bashed. I've been raped. I've had my nose broken. I got stabbed in the right kidney. Stabbed here. Baseball-batted shoulder. I've been kicked with boots, steel-capped boots. I've had bruising here. I've had this ear perforated. If you look carefully on the front, you'll find the knife marks there, across there. There's a few there actually. I've been hot-shotted with drugs.[74]

Often it was not clients who were perpetrating the violence but, rather, carloads of men who came to Kings Cross/Darlinghurst specifically to throw bottles or bash trans and gay sex workers.

At the most extreme end of the violence facing sex workers— and trans people in general—was murder. This is not a distinctly Australian phenomenon: internationally, trans sex workers have been and are still more likely to experience violence, including homicide, than other trans people and the community at large. Many murders went unreported or may have been listed under missing persons (if there was any documentation at all). Gender Centre media officer Eloise Brook's extensive research into the names of trans hate crime victims in Australia has uncovered only three official homicides.[75] Two of those that reached the public eye involved a showgirl and a sex worker. In 1985, a friend found popular showgirl Wendy Wain (sometimes spelled Wayne) dead, naked and face-down in her apartment. The autopsy determined that she had been knocked unconscious with a blunt object, then shot twice at close range in the back and the head. Wendy's murder was never solved.[76] The other high-profile case was Adele Bailey, a sex worker who went missing in Melbourne in 1978 and whose remains were found in country Victoria in 1995. The coroner recorded an open finding over Adele's death in 1999, but there have always been allegations of police involvement in her murder and cover-up.[77]

Starting around 1985, Roberta Perkins and the Australian Prostitutes Collective (founded in 1983) began to compile information about abusive clients in Sydney. They shared this information among sex workers and called it the Ugly Mug List. The early data Roberta collected in 1984–85 included abductions, gang rapes, bashings, stabbings, robberies, beatings and a whole host of awful abuse. A 1987 edition of the Ugly Mug List noted:

> From the violent attacks on workers over the past few years it's obvious there's a lot of sick mugs out there. It's necessary that workers come together and look out for each other. If you must do car jobs get your mates to take down rego numbers. Exercise more caution, really check the client out. If there's the slightest indication that there [sic] a bit odd refuse the job. I know it's not always that easy, as some of these freaked out mugs present as being quite normal. 'Be careful.'[78]

The Australian Prostitutes Collective's successor organisation, Sex Workers Outreach Project (SWOP, founded in 1990), expanded the Ugly Mug List into a pamphlet that was distributed to sex workers every two months. It included as much information as possible, including known names or aliases, location of pick-ups, physical descriptions and an explanation of what happened. Finally, the Ugly Mug List included a list of licence plates to avoid.

Police harassment was also rampant around Tranny Lane and similar sites in other cities. The NSW Parliament partly decriminal-ised sex work in 1979, but many restrictions were reimposed from 1983. For instance, police could still arrest sex workers for violating laws prohibiting soliciting 'near or within view from a dwelling, school, church or hospital' and for committing homosexual acts (which were not decriminalised in New South Wales until 1984).[79] Oral histories talk about police round-ups, which could happen at any time, though the more established sex workers got cluey about when a raid might be imminent.

Police could be violent towards trans people in custody. Phlan-Michelle recalls police taking her and other sex workers to Centennial Park on one occasion and flogging them before taking them to Central Police Station.[80] Kooncha knew of trans women whom police drove to the outer western suburbs, took all their money and shoes, and left them. She remembers one time when an undercover policeman followed a potential client of hers and arrested her just before she could get in his car. He drove her around for almost an hour trying to get her to give him a blow job. Kooncha recalls that the cop pulled out his penis:

> I looked at it and I said, 'Oh, that wouldn't fill a hollow hole in my tooth,' and he looked at me and he said, 'What do you mean?' I said, 'It's not big.' Anyways we kept driving and he said, 'Well come on, so aren't you going to give it to me?' and I said, 'No.' Anyway, he tried to force me, I wouldn't, so I ended up getting locked up in Central Police Station for the long weekend.[81]

More often than not, police would put trans women in men's cells because the law still did not recognise trans people's affirmed gender and it was another way to humiliate and abuse them. Beatings and even rapes by other prisoners were common. Chantell got lucky on one occasion when police put her in the same cell as a big Polynesian man at Surry Hills Police Station. Chantell is Māori and this connection clearly helped her, because the man asked where she was from. She recalls: 'We started talking, and you should have seen the look on those cops' faces. I tell you, they were hoping that he would bash the living daylights out of me, but it turned out he's from Auckland, I'm from Whangārei.'[82]

Sex worker oral histories demarcate 1995 as a turning point in relations with NSW Police, leading to a significant reduction (though by no means an elimination) in harassment and abuse. First, amendments to the *Disorderly Houses Act* effectively legalised brothels and made them commercial businesses. Interestingly, the restrictions on soliciting in view of a church, school, dwelling or hospital remained on the books, but sex workers still generally consider this a moment of further decriminalisation in New South Wales. The other catalyst for change was the 1995–97 Royal Commission into the New South Wales Police Service, more popularly known as the Wood Royal Commission, which exposed entrenched police corruption and led to substantial reform to the NSW Police. Tranny Lane and similar locations in other cities declined beginning in the 2000s due to gentrification and the rise of the internet, which shifted much sex work off the streets and into brothels and parlours and online. The 2000s is also when there was a rise in trans men's sex work, aligning with the rise of trans men's visibility, which is described in more detail in Chapter 6.

An omnipresent challenge facing sex workers was sexually transmitted infections; after 1983, HIV and AIDS were particular risks. Most sex worker testimonies discuss how they used to take precautions and look after each other. Simone testified in 1984:

> I have heard of transsexuals getting disease as a result of after hour activities but not from working. You would not work if you have got something wrong because that would go through the whole street. We have our own rules. If we suspected any person of having anything wrong with them, we would not allow them to work.[83]

When HIV and AIDS entered the scene, the Albion Centre Outreach Bus regularly visited Tranny Lane, and in 1989 it reported an infection rate of 25 per cent of those sex workers known to the program.[84] The Kirketon Road Centre regularly had a van parked near Carmen Rupe's spot, offering condoms and testing to trans sex workers.[85]

The trans sex workers on Tranny Lane had their own informal networks and many were members of the Australian Prostitutes Collective (1983–87) and then SWOP (1990–). Trans sex workers in other states and territories joined the respective sex worker unions that emerged in the 1980s–90s. There was one other figure (besides Carmen Rupe) who featured prominently in 1980s Sydney: Roberta Perkins. It may not have seemed like it for the workers on Tranny Lane, but Roberta's ethnographic research would have significant outcomes for trans organisations and rights in New South Wales.

The Australian Transsexual Association

The group that would have the most enduring legacy for trans rights was the Sydney-based Australian Transsexual Association (ATA). Founded sometime around 1978 by then-61-year-old Noelena Tame, the ATA originally was similar to the Victorian Transsexual Association—a peer support group for trans women who had had or intended to have gender affirmation surgery. Early on, the ATA found a generous ally in the Reverend Bill Crews, who ran the Wayside Chapel in Kings Cross. This became the site of the support group meetings, which were later rebranded as peer counselling sessions facilitated by the ATA secretary, Roberta Perkins.[86] In December 1981 Crews and the ATA facilitated a public forum on transsexualism, bringing together community members, doctors and lawyers to raise awareness of challenges facing trans people.[87]

Noelena in many ways became an accidental activist because of discrimination she faced. As early as 1979, she wrote to federal and state politicians complaining about the fact that she could not change her birth certificate and the ripple effects of that, including access to a passport, the right to marry, and protection under anti-discrimination laws. In a 1980 letter to the Family Law Council, she wrote (original spelling and punctuation retained):

> Please let me know why we [transsexuals] should not marrie as we have had a sex change from mail to femail. For we want to leed a normal moral life as the law has allowed us to have a sex chang legally. Also to have our birth certificate change if not any of these think then the law is making a mokerie and chasing us as idiots in witch we are not. But have feeling like any normal heterosexual femail.[88]

Noelena's activism stepped up a notch in 1982 when her local lawn bowls club discovered that she was trans. The club leadership determined that she was ineligible to join as a woman and ordered her to hand back her membership to the NSW Women's Bowling Association. The story reached the media, and Noelena adeptly portrayed herself as a respectable white middle-class woman who did volunteer work with the blind. She explained in a *Woman's Day* article: 'I'm a normal heterosexual woman and just want to live my life in peace. I have a boyfriend who certainly doesn't think of me as a man. I'm making a big issue of this for the sake of all transsexuals.'[89] Noelena also wrote letters to state and federal politicians pleading her case and calling on them to recognise trans people in their affirmed genders and to protect them from discrimination. Unfortunately, she lost her case because being trans was not a protected category in either New South Wales or federal anti-discrimination law.[90]

The other, more prominent player in the ATA who would lead it down the activist route was Roberta Perkins. Roberta was a sociologist working on a Master of Arts degree at Macquarie University, conducting ethnographic research with trans and cis women sex workers in Kings Cross.[91] She was a remarkable researcher who devoted most of her life from about 1980 until her passing in 2018 conducting surveys and interviews and writing extensively about the challenges facing trans people and sex workers.

The first hint of the ATA shifting from just peer support to an activist stance was in 1981 when Roberta wrote to Michael Kirby, chairman of the Australian Law Reform Commission, about trans women being unable to marry their partners because they were not legally recognised in their affirmed genders. She wrote, 'This lack of recognition causes the medically sex-reassigned person a great deal of pain. It continues to stigmatize them, forces them to see themselves as abnormal, and gives them the status of non-persons.'[92] Kirby's response was similar to what Noelena and Roberta would receive for much of the early 1980s: this was a matter that needed a consistent national approach, and it was under consideration by the Standing Committee of Attorneys-General.

The ATA's flirtation with activism escalated in 1982, when Roberta staged Australia's first known demonstration for trans rights.

The trigger was the conviction of two trans sex workers as men who had committed homosexual prostitution (only heterosexual sex work had been decriminalised). Roberta said in a radio interview that she had received numerous phone calls from devastated trans women, and encouraged trans women to join her for a demonstration on 2 October 1982 at a shopping centre in Manly. The rally did not attract significant publicity, but an article in *The Age* noted that Roberta had taken off her top at it. She was quoted as saying: 'If we are going to be called men, if the law insists that we are men, then we will exercise the privilege of men and remove our tops.'[93] Roberta saw this protest as an important turning point:

I think the time has now come for transsexuals to really start demonstrating to the public through, if necessary, the public demonstrations that were held last Saturday. But show the public that we're not weird, that we're not freaks or anything else. We are people with feminine identities, and these feminine identities are quite firm.[94]

The year 1982 also witnessed an uptake in the ATA lobbying for services. Roberta prepared an ATA submission to the NSW minister for health requesting funding to set up a multidisciplinary gender identity centre. This would be a one-stop shop where trans people could access health, counselling, employment, post-prison reintegration, drug and alcohol rehabilitation, welfare and other social services. The minister declined the proposal, citing a tight budget and referring the ATA to the attorney-general, who countered that this was a responsibility for the minister for health.[95]

In November 1982, the ATA stepped up its campaign for legal recognition of trans people's affirmed genders, sending a submission to all state governments and the federal shadow foreign affairs minister, Senator Gareth Evans. The submission outlined the key areas where trans people needed reform: birth certificates, marriage rights, adoption rights, documents such as passports, anti-discrimination laws, protection from sexual assault, and prisoner rights.[96] Most state governments responded acknowledging the need for reform but, again, deferring to a national approach.

The lack of action and inadequate responses to the ATA's submissions led the group, which was still predominantly centred on Roberta, Noelena and the treasurer, Vivian Sharman, to establish a new activist committee. In an early 1983 statement announcing the committee's formation, the ATA declared:

According to politicians our legal and social issues are not worth discussing. Well, we don't think so. To be the most legally denied group of people in this country is no joke for us. Our government continues to deprive us of basic rights while it preaches democracy and condemns apartheid. 'Apartheid' means 'insensitivity to suffering', and therefore the government by its open refusal to grant us legal recognition is in effect practising apartheid on transsexuals.[97]

The statement announced intentions to meet with the NSW attorney-general, host a series of cabaret fundraisers, and produce a monthly newsletter and a monthly radio program. The latter certainly came to fruition: from March 1983 to December 1986 the ATA had a monthly spot on the 2SER radio program *Gaywaves*, where the hosts discussed topics including trans history, prison experiences, psychiatry, diverse cultures' understandings of (trans) gender, employment, and relations with the gay community.[98] For a brief period in the early 1980s, the ATA had a branch in Melbourne with a couple of members who had a weekly spot on 3CR community radio.[99] In 1985 Roberta stepped down from the leadership of the ATA to pursue other roles (though she never stopped lobbying for trans and sex worker rights). By around 1987 the ATA had lost steam and was no longer active, in part because Roberta's and the organisation's hard work had paid dividends in the form of Tiresias House.

Tiresias House

Although the NSW Department of Health rebuffed the ATA's 1982 proposal for a gender identity centre, Roberta did not give up and tried a new approach. In October 1982 the NSW Government announced the Community Tenancy Scheme, a social housing scheme designed to subsidise community organisations and local governments to allow them to offer affordable housing to groups in need. Roberta wrote to the minister for youth and community services, Frank Walker, outlining a vision where funding for a house under the Community Tenancy Scheme could fulfil the objectives of the gender identity centre proposal. The house would reduce homelessness and double as a site to offer employment, health and welfare services.[100]

One other piece of the puzzle came together in 1983: the publication of Roberta's ethnographic study, *The 'Drag Queen' Scene: Transsexuals in Kings Cross*. The book was groundbreaking, painting a picture of the discrimination and challenges confronting trans women in Sydney. Walker read the book and it moved him. In July 1983 his office reached out to Roberta and they scheduled a meeting. Years later she wrote about what happened:

> [W]hat had impressed—nay, disturbed—him about it most was the semi-nomadic lives young transgenders experienced, forced from their apartments by landlords and unable to get overnight residence in either a men's or a women's refuge—apart from Women's Place in the Cross, which catered for young street women addicts and was always filled to bursting. Walker's words have never left me. 'Roberta, we have got to find them a place where they can lay their heads at night.' Two months later a cheque arrived addressed to me and a house was provided as a refuge strictly for trannies.[101]

Tiresias House opened in Petersham with its first resident on 25 October 1983, and had its formal launch in December that year.[102] The name derived from a Greek god who was said to have transformed from man to woman and back to man again. At the opening, Roberta declared, 'Tiresias House is not the world's first welfare centre run specifically for transsexuals, but it is certainly the world's first run by transsexuals financially aided with government funding.'[103] It was envisioned that Tiresias House would offer accommodation for up to six people for about three months each, and host services relating to employment, health, group and peer counselling, life skills and self-defence.[104] Given the high demand, within months it was already housing sixteen people. Roberta observed that two demographics especially needed housing: young people kicked out of their homes for being trans, and trans people on parole from prison.

In February 1984 Walker's department provided a second house in Haberfield, named Lili Elbe House, which accommodated people on a more long-term basis—for up to a year. Then in August 1984 a third house was acquired, in Ashfield, which focused especially on drug rehabilitation. It was named TRANSITION, an acronym for Transsexual Rehabilitation for Alcoholics and Narcotic Users Service Including Treatment, Initiative and Organising New Direction.[105] At the first-anniversary celebration of Tiresias House, Roberta spoke of the forty-eight people who had applied for accommodation at the houses: 'They have come from everywhere—from the street scene, from the gaols, and from comfortable parental homes. It does reflect the enormous social diversity in the transsexual community.'[106]

The three houses operated differently but had strict rules across the board against violence, abuse and alcohol. House mothers had the role of ensuring that residents obeyed the rules and reported any disturbances to the Tiresias House staff. Roberta prepared a series of signs in texta with supplemental rules such as 'Screw to your heart's content with regular or newfound boy-friends, but don't bring clients home. Remember leave the Cross in the hole it belongs'; 'My shoes and boots fit my feet perfectly. I expect them to keep doing so and not to be put out of shape by "borrowing"';

'You have your own make up, use it not mine. If you feel like a change of shade ask me before "borrowing". The same goes for dresses, undies, jewellery'; and 'Boyfriends are not to use our larder as a cheap means of regularly filling their stomachs. Otherwise, they contribute.'[107]

Workers and residents from Tiresias House in the 1980s presented a mix of stories. In a 1986 radio interview, house parent Anne described her work as 'educational' and elaborated: 'Most of them are younger than me, with a couple of the residents down there very young, and the trauma they've got to go through being accepted as a transsexual, and there are a lot of problems.'[108] Because so many of the residents—the parolees in particular—had substance abuse problems and/or still worked on Tranny Lane, they brought extra baggage. 'Sascha' recalls that when she worked at Tiresias House:

> We'd catch them climbing in the windows and if the staff were there—because they weren't supposed to have locks on the doors, so they'd have the beds stuffed with clothes and things like that— we would ... go in, torch check, and then half an hour later they'd be coming in the windows.[109]

Roberta wrote: '[S]oon, we had guys outside the house yelling they had been robbed, local gangs threatening to break in and rape and bash the lot of us, and police, who had earlier provided protection against local bullies, now banging on the door and carting residents away.'[110]

Notwithstanding these challenges, the founding and operation of Tiresias House were vital interventions that offered the first concrete supports for trans people in New South Wales and Australia. One desperate letter from a trans person seeking a place there said, 'I no longer know what to do with my life. There are only two options left to me: death or prison. Tiresias House and the staff are my only hope.'[111] Despite the problems at the house, as Sascha succinctly summarised, 'There was a lot of joy there. It worked really well for a long time.'[112] From its founding, Tiresias House offered individual and group counselling, doctors' visits, classes and advice on transition options. As time went on, additional funding was directed to youth workers and other case support. Staff played a critical role combating the AIDS epidemic, often travelling to Tranny Lane to hand out condoms and clean syringes.

Although most residents at Tiresias House were trans women, it accommodated trans men as well. At the one-year-anniversary celebration, trans man Ray briefly did an interview on *Gaywaves*. He said, 'I find life has opened up new career opportunities. It's been more fulfilling in as much as I've been able to relax within myself, and relate to other people on a level which is simply more mellow.'[113] The TV program *Midday* did a feature on Tiresias House in 1988 that included a trans man named Tony talking about his life and gender affirmation, and about reuniting with his estranged sixteen-year-old daughter. Tony appeared a few months later in a *Woman's Day* article about trans people; that piece gave more details about his troubled life, including his having been raped and spent time in a women's prison, and noting that he had a second, older child from whom he was estranged. Tony commenced hormones in 1984 and subsequently had both a mastectomy and a hysterectomy.[114]

While the memories of people who worked or resided at Tiresias House in the 1980s to early 1990s focus on the challenges, what stands out from the longer histories is how it became a service delivery hub and a site for trans organising. In 1993, the NSW Department of Health began jointly funding Tiresias House with the Department of Community Services. To reflect the organisation's expanding terms of reference, the house changed its name to the Gender Centre. That same year, it began publishing the magazine *Polare* five times a year. These changes came just as a new generation of trans activists was emerging to push for law reform and new understandings of (trans)gender.

The effects of organising

The 1970s and 1980s witnessed important shifts in the trans community that laid significant foundations. On one front, the medical model of transsexualism became embedded within dominant discourse and provided those who met social norms around respectable femininity with surgical transition options. Those who faced discrimination at home and in the workplace had to find other opportunities, with sex work being a common path. Sex work could provide a sense of community but came with dangers from clients and police. It took brave pioneers like Roberta Perkins, Noelena Tame and other leaders of the Australian Transsexual Association, Victorian Transsexual Coalition and small organisations to begin the call for legal rights and protections. Although these activists were not successful at securing law reform, they did put it on the political agenda and in New South Wales secured funding for the country's first trans refuge and support agency.

Law reform would prove to be a continuing barrier. Whether a trans person worked on Tranny Lane or had gender affirmation surgery and could blend into cis society, the fact that they could not change their birth certificate and could be fired from a job without recourse always posed risks. Indeed, Roberta Perkins concluded her December 1983 speech at the launch of Tiresias House with: 'Now that we have travelled this far and made the important step, we now look forward to the next step, law reform, to enable us to live in our reassigned sex with the same legal rights as everyone else.'[115] That fight would play out in different ways under a new generation of activists in the 1990s.

4
LEGAL RECOGNITION AND ANTI-DISCRIMINATION

I N JULY 1978, at the request of the federal attorney-general, the Family Law Council produced a paper entitled 'Birth Certificate Revision of the Sexually Reassigned'. It outlined different ways to determine a person's sex (e.g. chromosomes, genitals, secondary sex characteristics, psychosocial identity) and areas of law where recognition of a person's gender was important: marriage, inheritance, child custody, sexual offences and sport. The position paper did not make any recommendations around legal reforms, but it did state that 'the first prerequisite for the recognition of the legal rights of transsexuals is revision of birth certificates and this is a matter of State law [so] this is likely to take a long time'.[1] The Family Law Council was not the first to discuss the recognition of trans people's affirmed gender. Yet the report confirmed that any legal recognition came back to birth certificates and that this needed reform in all states and territories.

This chapter traces the push for law reform across Australia in what were the two most significant aspects of legislative change: legal recognition and anti-discrimination laws. These topics were on the political agenda as early as the 1970s, and while there was some law reform in South Australia in 1984 and 1988, most states and territories would not amend their statutes until the late 1990s or early 2000s. The longevity of the reform movement reflects how governments consistently put birth certificate reform in the too-hard basket. Trans people, meanwhile, navigated a patchwork of inconsistent rules across the country, often relying on their trans (in)visibility or judicial common-law rulings.

Because so much of the law reform and activism was state-based, this chapter takes both a chronological and a geographical approach. First, it explores national discussions around law reform from the 1970s–80s. Then, it shifts to the limited reforms around legal recognition and anti-discrimination secured in the courts and the South Australian legislature. Finally, it goes through the other movements and reforms in each state and territory in the 1990s and early 2000s, focusing especially on the different activist organisations and how they approached (trans)gender.

Standing Committee of Attorneys-General

As early as 1959 there were queries within the Department of Immigration asking if a trans Australian could obtain a passport in their affirmed gender. The preliminary advice was yes, if there was medical evidence that they had undergone a change that was 'complete and permanent'.[2] Outside the official archival trail, Jazmin Theodora tells a story about Lorraine Campbell Craig—also known as Bubbles LaRouche—who had gender affirmation surgery in the United Kingdom then applied for a passport with a female gender marker. At first the authorities would not grant this, so she said, 'I'll just have to take off all my clothes here and now, show you and let you feel that I'm a female.' As she started to strip, the officials told her to stop and said they would give her the female passport—which Jazmin says set the precedent for issuing female passports.[3] Whether that story is true or not, it became accepted practice through the

1960s to give those trans people who had gender affirmation surgery legal recognition in their passports.

What changed this was a British legal ruling in 1970 called *Corbett v Corbett*. This was a divorce case involving the trans celebrity April Ashley, whose husband wanted their marriage annulled on the grounds that she was really male. The judge considered four possible criteria to determine a person's sex: chromosomes, gonads, genitals and psychological factors. He acknowledged that a person could change their gender, but when it came to sex he definitively determined that 'the law should adopt, in the first place, the first three of the doctors' criteria, ie the chromosomal, gonadal and genital tests, and, if all three are congruent, determine the sex for the purpose of marriage accordingly, and ignore any operative intervention'.[4]

Corbett v Corbett became accepted law in the United Kingdom until the introduction of the *Gender Recognition Act* in 2004. As it was a common-law ruling, Australian lawyers and judges looked to the case and applied it. Perhaps the first ramification was in regard to passports. In 1972, the Attorney-General's Department advised the Department of Immigration that 'if a person is born biologically a male, his sex for the purposes of the law cannot be changed by subsequent operations'.[5] Trans people who legally changed their names could have their new name on their passport, and during the 1970s there was no requirement to list their sex or a prefix. Two changes in the early 1980s made it harder for trans people to obtain appropriate passports. First, the new 'M' series of passports introduced in 1980 required sex to be included.[6] Then in June 1983 the Department of Foreign Affairs and Trade (DFAT) implemented more rigid evidence requirements for identity documents and required applicants to attend a passport office in person rather than mail in their application.

Numerous trans people and organisations such as the Victorian Transsexual Coalition wrote to DFAT to request that people who had had gender affirmation surgery be granted passports in their affirmed gender. The response was a definitive no, but subsequent lobbying efforts eventually had a positive effect. On 21 November 1984 the attorney-general approved a significant reform: those people who had undergone gender affirmation surgery and had medical evidence attesting to this could obtain passports in their affirmed gender, but with the important caveat that this applied only to their passport and no other identity documents.[7]

The changes to passport rules were part of a growing awareness that legal recognition of people's affirmed gender was a bubbling issue. The first known attempt to get it on the political agenda came out of Victoria in 1976, when a group called the Study Group for Legitimisation of Sex Reassignment prepared a petition calling for the Victorian Government to change the law to allow trans women to change their birth certificate. The petition gathered 315 signatures, and the Australian Labor Party member for Footscray, Robert Fordham, presented it in the Victorian Legislative Assembly. The press briefly picked up on the petition but the parliament never debated birth certificate reform.[8] As noted in the previous chapter, the VTC had prepared a similar petition in 1981, which also met with no further action from the Victorian Parliament.

Around the same time, in October 1976 the NSW attorney-general, Frank Walker, wrote to the federal attorney-general querying whether trans people who had gender affirmation surgery could marry someone opposite to their affirmed gender. The representations came after a number of trans women contacted Walker with concerns about legal recognition of their affirmed gender and the ramifications for issues such as marriage and passports.[9] Walker would consistently prove a champion for trans rights and legal recognition both federally and in New South Wales: he was the minister who first funded Tiresias House in 1983.[10] The federal attorney-general wrote back a few months later saying no, and it was this exchange that led the attorney-general to commission the Family Law Council report. On the back of that report, in May 1979 the topic 'Birth Certificate Revision for the Sexually Reassigned' appeared on the agenda of the monthly Standing Committee of

Attorneys-General, and it would continue to be a standing agenda item through the end of 1985.[11]

In 1984 the Standing Committee of Attorneys-General approved 'the development of legislation to enable a person who has undergone gender reassignment procedures (including surgery) to be regarded for all purposes of the law (subject to limited exceptions) as a member of the sex opposite to that into which they were born'.[12] A subcommittee with representatives from New South Wales, South Australia and Victoria drafted model legislation that would create a mechanism for trans people who had gender affirmation surgery to obtain a certificate of recognition. This document would be as valid as a birth certificate for identification purposes and gender recognition.[13] For reasons unknown, the legislation did not go ahead in Victoria or New South Wales and the standing item was removed from the Standing Committee of Attorneys-General from 1986.

Only the SA Government pushed ahead with what became the *Sexual Reassignment Act*, for a few reasons. First, doctors from the Flinders Medical Centre Gender Clinic lobbied hard for the legislation because, in addition to providing legal recognition for trans people, the bill codified a framework to authorise providers of trans health care in South Australia.[14] The other reason was the high-profile case of an intersex baby born in 1983. The infant was assigned male at birth, but doctors and the mother decided to perform genital surgery and raise the child as a girl. There was a media storm over this case—not because of the forced surgery on an intersex infant, but because state authorities would not change the child's birth certificate. After an eight-month battle, the SA attorney-general intervened to have the child's birth certificate updated as female.[15] Even though the case was about an intersex child, it had trans implications because there was gender affirmation surgery involved. The case loomed large in SA politicians' minds when they were deliberating trans legal recognition.[16]

When the *Sexual Reassignment Act* 1988 passed into law, South Australia became the first jurisdiction with a mechanism to recognise a trans person's affirmed gender. In that sense it was genuine progress, but there were several restrictions in the legislation. It very much followed the medical model of transsexualism, stipulating that— aside from intersex infants' reassignment—a person must undergo counselling and live in their affirmed gender for two years before they could have gender affirmation surgery. The person had to be single and at least twenty-three years old. Once they had gender affirmation surgery, they could apply to the newly established Sexual Reassignment Board, which consisted of medical professionals. The board could then issue a certificate of recognition to the person in their affirmed gender that they could lodge with the Registrar of Births, Deaths and Marriages to obtain a new birth certificate.[17] This became the first template for birth certificate reform, and in the 1990s–2000s other state and territory governments and trans activists would debate the benefits of this approach versus alternative frameworks.

Judicial interpretations

From the 1970s–80s and into the 1990s outside South Australia, the absence of legislation around legal recognition meant that judges were often the ones to decide trans people's gender under the common law. Australian justices applied *Corbett v Corbett* for the first time in the 1979 Family Court case *C and D (falsely called C)*. This case involved an intersex man married to a woman. The judge found that although the husband had male gonads and genitals, because his chromosomes were female he did not satisfy the criteria of being a man and the marriage was invalid.[18]

It was not just marriage and Family Court matters where trans people's gender could prove significant. In various parts of the criminal law (e.g. homosexual acts and sex work), a person's sex determined whether they were perpetrating a crime. This came to public attention in 1982 when NSW Police arrested two trans women, Phillis McGuiness and Vicki Harris, and charged them as men who had procured males for an indecent act. When Harris and McGuiness appeared in court, their defence was that they were women and therefore they had broken no laws. The judge ultimately invoked *Corbett v Corbett* as precedent and ruled: 'It is my view that the law of NSW regards both these people as male persons, despite their belief to the contrary.'[19]

This case devastated trans Australians and, as noted in the previous chapter, prompted Roberta Perkins to lead a public demonstration for trans rights. With the support of the Aboriginal Legal Service (McGuiness was Aboriginal) and Perkins, Harris and McGuiness lodged an appeal.[20] The District Court of Appeals dismissed it in 1984, and Harris and McGuiness lodged another appeal to the Supreme Court of New South Wales. In a momentous 2–1 decision in October 1988, the court overturned Harris' conviction on the grounds that she was indeed a woman because she had undergone gender affirmation surgery. The news was not so positive for McGuiness: recognising her affirmed gender in the absence of surgery proved a bridge too far for the justices. Still, this was significant because it was a direct repudiation of *Corbett v Corbett*. The chief justice, Sir Laurence Whistler Street, wrote in his reasoning: 'The time has come when the beacon of *Corbett* will have to give place to more modern navigational guides to voyages on the seas of problems thrown up by human sexuality.'[21] That same year, a judge in Victoria ruled in *R v Cogley* that a trans woman who had a vagina was therefore a woman—though an appeals court later challenged this determination.[22]

Neither the NSW nor Victorian government enacted legislation, policies or procedures to facilitate change of gender on birth certificates or other documents. Yet there was one reform out of New South Wales in 1987. Estelle Asmodelle (previously Esta) had been a dancer who travelled widely through Australia and Asia. Her passport still had her designated as male, which led to her detention in Singapore at one stage. She lobbied hard for the right to change her gender marker on her passport and her birth certificate and wrote almost daily to the NSW attorney-general until, one day in 1987, she received an invitation to be the first trans person to have a new birth certificate issued in her female name.[23] Under the updated approach, trans people could obtain birth certificate extracts in their new name that did not list their gender. It was not everything trans activists wanted, but as Tiresias House spokesperson Ricca Griffith said, 'It's a step in the right direction; a positive move towards eliminating some of the discrimination.'[24]

In the early 1990s, two cases came before the Administrative Appeals Tribunal (AAT) that again challenged *Corbett*. The first was in 1991 and involved a Cairns trans woman known as HH who had had gender affirmation surgery in 1976. HH had applied for a pension but was rejected on the grounds that she was a man and therefore too young (under the *Social Security Act*, women were entitled to pensions at age sixty and men at sixty-five). The unanimous opinion of the AAT supported HH—for the purposes of the *Social Security Act* only, someone who had had gender affirmation surgery should be considered a woman. That HH had blended into society so indistinguishably with cis women for decades seemed an influential factor in the decision.[25]

Another case went to the AAT in 1992, but with a different outcome. SRA—also known as 'Sally'—was born in 1965 and since age sixteen had known she was trans. She began taking hormones and living full time as a woman when she was eighteen. Doctors approved her for gender affirmation surgery but she could not afford it. She still lived and presented as a woman and entered into a long-term relationship with a cis man known as 'B', and they were receiving independent social security benefits. In 1985 the Department of Social Services sent a case officer to their house, and that person determined that Sally and B were in a domestic relationship and switched Sally to a wife's pension. In 1990, an anonymous phone call to the Department of Social Security advised that B was in a relationship with a man, and further investigation from a case officer led the department to terminate Sally's wife's pension. She appealed the decision in the AAT and won. The tribunal members were satisfied that her psychosocial life as a woman was legitimate, particularly given she had been approved for surgery.[26] The Department of Social Security appealed to the Federal Court of Australia and in December 1993 the court handed down its ruling, which overturned the AAT, asserting that because Sally had not had gender affirmation surgery, she was still legally male.[27]

Sally was devastated by the decision. Her solicitor said in a radio interview, 'It really shows, in a way, how far removed the legal system is from ... people's everyday lives—the people who are relying on the courts to ... make their lives right for them.'[28] Aidy Griffin, leader of the Sydney-based Transgender Liberation Coalition, commented in the media: 'Trannys don't interpret these decisions as a loss of a court case. They're seen as an attack on their identity.'[29] Aidy also said that the case highlighted the urgency of law reform to recognise trans people in their affirmed genders.[30]

The pioneers: South Australia, Australian Capital Territory and Northern Territory

What stands out about South Australia, the Australian Capital Territory and the Northern Territory is that they passed anti-discrimination legislation and introduced birth certificate reform with little organised activism from trans groups. In addition to being the first jurisdiction to allow trans people to change their birth certificates, South Australia was the first state to introduce anti-discrimination protections for some trans people. Although there was no organised trans rights group, individual trans women wrote letters and met with politicians to describe the challenges they faced. One such person was Suzanne James. She presented as a respectable trans woman who worked as a clerk in the public service and lived a quiet life. In a 1982 media interview, Suzanne noted the long process a person had to go through to access affirming health care, and commented: 'I want to be accepted as a female with human respect and dignity, without being treated like a bizarre sexual phenomenon, or some type of sex freak … People don't have to like me, but every human being needs acceptance.'[31]

Suzanne's story struck a chord with one member of the Legislative Council in particular: Australian Labor Party (ALP) member Barbara Wiese. She became the main political champion for trans rights in 1980s South Australia, lobbying both the state and federal governments to enact anti-discrimination and birth certificate reforms.[32] In August 1982 Wiese took the case to the public, writing a long op-ed in the Adelaide *Advertiser* advocating for trans law reform. She outlined the inconsistencies between medical practices that allowed gender affirmation surgery and the law, which would not recognise or respect trans people. Wiese had a good grasp of the legal obstacles confronting trans people and concluded:

Transsexuals are a very small minority of the population. They don't have many votes or a potent lobbying organisation. It would be easy for legislators to continue to ignore the problem. But to do so would cause further quite unnecessary suffering to a small minority whose demands are as modest as they are just.[33]

Wiese's advocacy influenced her party. In October 1983 the SA attorney-general flagged amendments to anti-discrimination law,[34] and in 1984 the SA Government introduced the *Equal Opportunity Bill* into parliament. The legislation added sexuality as a protected category, defined in the law as 'heterosexuality, homosexuality, bisexuality or transexuality [sic]'.[35] On the one hand, making transsexuality a subcategory of sexuality was problematic because it perpetuated the incorrect conflation of gender and sexuality. On the other hand, it made it harder for opponents to strip it from the bill. The bill passed, making South Australia the first jurisdiction to offer anti-discrimination protections to some trans people, meaning those who had gender affirmation surgery. It would not be until 2009 that amendments to the *Equal Opportunity Act* changed the protected category to 'chosen gender', with a definition that explicitly applied to all trans people regardless of medical or surgical interventions.

In the Australian Capital Territory and the Northern Territory the incorporation of trans people in anti-discrimination law received even less fanfare. In 1991 the ACT's Labor government introduced the Human Rights and Equal Opportunity Bill (later dubbed the *Discrimination Act*) as the territory's first anti-discrimination legislation. Included in the bill was the protected category of 'transsexuality', defined as 'those who assume the bodily character-istics of the opposite sex, whether by means of medical intervention or otherwise, or identify themselves as members of the opposite sex, or who live or seek to live as members of the opposite sex'.[36] In the ACT debates over the bill in 1991, there were no controversies or questions at all over the inclusion of transsexuality as a protected category. This marked the Australian Capital Territory as the first Australian jurisdiction to provide anti-discrimination protection for all trans people regardless of medical or surgical interventions. In 1997, the Australian Capital Territory introduced a new *Births, Deaths and Marriages Registration Act* that included provisions to allow trans people who had gender affirmation surgery to change their sex marker. Unlike in larger jurisdictions, debate over this reform was muted.

The NT Legislative Assembly similarly passed its first anti-discrimination legislation in 1992. Like in South Australia, trans people were grouped under the definition of sexuality, which 'means the sexual characteristics or imputed sexual characteristics of hetero-sexuality, homosexuality, bisexuality or transsexuality'.[37] Unlike in South Australia and the Australian Capital Territory, there was no further definition of transsexuality to clarify whether it applied only to people who had gender affirmation surgery. Both A Sharpe and Henry Finlay note that the use of the word 'imputed' means that it could be interpreted as protecting anyone read as, or perceived to be, transsexual, regardless of medical interventions or if the person even is trans.[38] In 1997, again without fanfare, the NT Legislative Assembly passed amendments to the *Births, Deaths and Marriages Registration Act* to introduce birth certificate reforms along similar lines to the SA model. In November 2022 the NT Government finally passed legislation to update the terminology and make 'gender identity' a protected attribute in the *Anti-Discrimination Act*.

New South Wales law reform

After the McGuiness ruling, in 1988 the NSW Law Reform Commission recommended that the state permit trans people who had gender affirmation surgery to have new birth certificates issued in their affirmed gender. The recommendation received media attention in 1990, but the NSW Government did not act on it.[39] It would take pressure from the trans community to facilitate change.

The main activist group in New South Wales, the Transgender Liberation Coalition, was founded in 1991 to pressure the state government to provide more resources for Tiresias House/The Gender Centre. By 1992, new activists under the leadership of Aidy Griffin were in charge of the organisation, and their agenda was more radical: they wanted to challenge the very idea of gender as something that was fixed and binary. They purposely used the word 'transgender' as an umbrella because, as Aidy explained in 1993, 'Transgender is a far broader term that covers everyone. At least the way we use it, it covers everybody who lives outside gender norms. It's not an identity, it's not a condition, it's not a personality type, it's not a category.'[40]

Appearing on ABC-TV's *Lateline* in 1994, Aidy indicated that the two top priorities for transgender people were anti-discrimination protections and legal recognition in their affirmed gender. Aidy acknowledged that anti-discrimination laws would not end all social problems confronting transgender Australians, but that such reforms 'would be sending a signal out to society that this kind of behaviour, the kind of wanton and vicious attacks that occur so often on trannies, is no longer acceptable'.[41] Aidy aimed to build alliances with other trans people and gay and lesbian organisations but found the politics challenging. There was a vocal group called the Lesbian Space Project who refused to recognise trans women as women, and the NSW Gay and Lesbian Rights Lobby was not opposed to trans rights per se but was prioritising its own desired reforms.[42]

Perhaps the most challenging opposition the Transgender Liberation Coalition faced came from trans people who, in line with the medical model, saw gender affirmation surgery as the defining feature of whether someone was a 'true transsexual'.[43] The group who represented this different ideology was the Transsexual Action Group (TAG). Its former secretary Ricki Coughlan recalls that the organisation was made up of only herself and one other person and that they formed as a reaction to the Transgender Liberation Coalition.[44] TAG worked with politicians who considered the Transgender Liberation Coalition's arguments about eliminating gender to be out of touch and 'political poison', and focused their lobbying on birth certificate reforms to apply to trans people who had surgery.[45]

The Gender Centre's magazine *Polare* regularly published letters and opinion pieces in which representatives of both groups attacked each other, sometimes personally. Reading through the letters to the editor and other opinion pieces in *Polare*, it is clear that Sydney's transgender community was split between the Transgender Liberation Coalition's queer ideology and the 'passing politics' of TAG. Jesse (aka Jill) Hooley described the Transgender Liberation Coalition as 'the only group that welcomes and includes all members of the trany community; pre, post and non-op, F to M and M to F— or "queer" or whatever—it is a diverse group of unpaid community activists whose sister/brotherhood has played a leading role in advancing our rights and sense of community'.[46] Others did not see the organisation as being diverse in its advocacy but instead as pushing an ideological agenda that marginalised 'transsexuals' who wished to disappear quietly into society.[47]

Clover Moore, the independent member for Bligh (now Sydney), first introduced an amendment to the NSW *Anti-Discrimination Act* in 1994 to add transgender people as a protected category. In 1995, the ALP won the NSW state election, and attorney-general Jeff Shaw met with representatives of the Transgender Liberation Coalition and drafted an updated version of Moore's bill. The legislation would add transgender as a protected category under NSW anti-discrimination law and update the *Births, Deaths and Marriages Registration Act* to facilitate a process for transgender people to amend their birth certificates. Aidy Griffin, Jesse Hooley and Nadine Stransen lobbied politicians of all stripes, but especially within the Labor Party and crossbench members of the upper house. Aidy was the main strategist, Jesse primed the team with gender theory, and Nadine became an excellent spokesperson for the Transgender Liberation Coalition. Trans man Kelby Evans, too, met with politicians, particularly around the birth certificate part of the legislation. Pindi Hurring did much of the logistical work behind the scenes, chasing politicians' offices to schedule meetings.[48]

The lobbying adopted multiple frameworks and pieces of evidence to appeal to the respective members. They distributed copies of a 1994 research report by Roberta Perkins—the first comprehensive social science study of transgender people in Australia. Her findings on disadvantage among the transgender community were damning about employment discrimination, alarmingly poor health outcomes, hate crimes, family and domestic violence, and high rates of homelessness.[49] Jesse and Nadine also presented data from a study, in progress at the time, that Jesse was conducting about trans people's health needs.[50] Jesse specifically remembers meeting with the upper house member Alan Corbett from the A Better Future for Our Children party. Corbett was a proud Christian, and when he asked Jesse and Nadine what Jesus would think about the anti-discrimination legislation, Jesse pointed out that Jesus regularly spent time with sex workers and the marginalised of society.

Her strong knowledge of the Bible—a consequence of her religious upbringing—proved effective at winning over Corbett.[51]

Where TAG had more influence was on the outcome of the birth certificate reform. It had two main allies in cabinet, and Ricki Coughlan recalls having an impromptu meeting with NSW premier Bob Carr. She told him about the challenges of living as a transgender woman who could not update her documents, and his response was simple: 'This is really easy—it's a matter of equity.'[52] TAG, with some assistance from the Gender Council of Western Australia, used its allies to argue successfully that birth certificate reform should apply only to people who had gender affirmation surgery. The Transgender Liberation Coalition openly expressed disappointment that people could not self-identify their gender marker without surgery, but as Aidy explained in late 1995, 'TLC has not approved the birth certificates legislation. We agreed "not to oppose it".'[53] Importantly, just as ideas around gender and the body have evolved, so, too, does Ricki now accept and espouse social constructivist ideas about gender and support the rights of all trans and gender-diverse people to be able to express themselves, live their truth and be affirmed in law regardless of medical or surgical interventions.

The ALP introduced the bill to state parliament in June 1996, framing the debate around treating transgender people as equals. The Liberal and National parties opposed the legislation, alleging that the Labor Party was catering to special interests, that the definition of transgender was too broad and inappropriate, that this was political correctness gone wrong, and that the law would place burdens on businesses.[54] The legislation passed in 1996 with the support of Moore in the lower house and with the Democrats, the Greens and A Better Future for Our Children in the upper house, making New South Wales the fourth Australian jurisdiction to adopt anti-discrimination protections for transgender people and birth certificate reform.[55]

Western Australia

Western Australia, too, had multiple organisations that advocated for law reform, but these groups operated at different times and did not interact. The Chameleon Society had been a social and support group for dressers since the 1970s, in 1980 a trans person founded Western Australia's first 'transsexual' support association, and in 1984 the wife of a dresser founded a support group for wives of dressers called Mermaids.[56] None of these groups was politically active.

In the 1980s individual trans people such as Norrie made headlines and called for better anti-discrimination protections. Norrie worked in the Department of Social Security in Perth and over time began dressing as a woman even though they were assigned male at birth. In July 1986 they became caught up in fraud charges linked to a boyfriend and were suspended from work. In November 1987 a jury found them guilty of five charges, and the Department of Social Security subsequently dismissed Norrie.[57] Norrie appealed and in June 1988 the Court of Criminal Appeal quashed the convictions.[58] The Department of Social Security reluctantly reinstated Norrie, but they did not receive a warm welcome.[59] Their case did not set any legal precedents, but it highlighted the discrimination trans people faced without recourse. Norrie succinctly explained to the media: 'If someone doesn't like you being Asian, there are anti-discrimination laws to protect you from being dismissed. But there are no laws to protect me. I am a problem and rather than deal with me they have dismissed me.'[60]

In the 1990s a series of trans organisations emerged to challenge the status quo. The first was called the Transexual Movement of Western Australia, originally founded in 1986 to push for the reforms proposed by the Standing Committee of Attorneys-General. The group's lobbying efforts proved effective at getting the WA branch of the Labor Party to pass a resolution in 1989 in support of trans rights.[61] In 1990, the group relaunched after merging with the Transsexual Support Group of WA, founded in 1989. Its principal aim was 'LEGAL REFORM. The T.M.W.A. is seeking to bring about changes to the legal and social status of transexuals in Western Australia.'[62] Little else is known about the group, but it appears that it changed its name to Transperson Support Group of WA and was still operating in 1993. That year, its president wrote to the state and federal governments calling for a sexual reassignment bill in Western Australia and nationally, along with the opening of a gender clinic in the state. The WA justice minister responded that there were no plans to introduce such legislation.[63]

The next active group was the Gender Council of Western Australia, founded in September 1994 and active until around 1996. This group had the same leader and objectives as the Transexual Movement of Western Australia, so can be seen as a successor. It, too, lobbied for legislation along the lines of South Australia's *Sexual Reassignment Act*, and for the establishment of a gender clinic in Western Australia and greater national coordination for trans health care. Its leaders wrote to several state and territory attorneys-general and managed to get the topic back on the agenda of the Standing Committee of Attorneys-General in 1995. In addition to invoking the standard human rights arguments for anti-discrimination, representatives of the Gender Council appealed to economics and how reforms could shift trans people off welfare benefits. Their letters included statements like: 'At present, the cost of discrimination for this generation of transsexuals ... will continue to be born [sic] by the tax payer, YOU' and 'For those of your colleagues who are interested in dollars and cents I wish to remind them that underclasses are expensive.'[64] The Gender Council emphasised that many transgender people were educated and skilled, and it was only the effects of discrimination that were hindering their participation in work.

Members of the Gender Council of WA reached out to activists in South Australia and Queensland to forge the Collective of Australian Gender Councils and the National Gender Dysphoria Advisory Group. Jenny Scott from South Australia recalls that Lea Bontes, president of the Gender Council, did most of the work and used the forums to prepare what looked like a national, representative set of proposals, but that the national collectives really existed in name only.[65]

The Gender Council of WA rejected the term transgender, adopting the medical model of transsexualism. Spokesperson and policy officer Caroline Doust wrote to the federal attorney-general in January 1996:

> I notice that you seem to use the term 'transgender' in your correspondence. The problem with this term is that, as it is commonly applied, it covers an extremely broad range of people, some of whom could not reasonably expect legal recognition of a change in gender. (Some peripheral members of that group would not even wish it.) On the other hand, a gender dysphoric person, who has undergone male to female reassignment surgery is for all legally relevant purposes female.[66]

The Gender Council's distinction between transgender and transsexualism sparked the ire of the Transgender Liberation Coalition, which accused the group of homophobia. A spokesperson for the Gender Council, Laura Seabrook, rejected such accusations, simply pointing out that the group saw transsexualism as a medical condition caused by gender dysphoria, while being transgender was a 'lifestyle'. Seabrook clarified that the Gender Council saw transgender and transsexualism as distinct but still supported anti-discrimination protections for both: 'We support people whether they are pre or post-operative, and that includes non-operatives as well. We recommend that there be no discrimination based on gender [or] assumed gender identification at all.'[67] The Gender Council of WA disappeared from the archival trail in 1996.

The LGBTIQ+ press later reported that the trigger for reform in Western Australia came from a 1994 recommendation by the WA Equal Opportunity Commission that called for laws to be amended to recognise trans people's affirmed gender. The minister for health introduced the Gender Reassignment Bill into the Legislative

Assembly in January 1997, noting that the legislation would establish a Gender Reassignment Board, enable the issue of certificates of recognition and new birth certificates, and 'provide protection from discrimination on the ground of gender history where a person has undergone reassignment procedures'.[68] The bill had the support of the Labor Party but faced opposition from both the gay and lesbian community and members of the Liberal government's own party. Representatives of Gay and Lesbian Equality WA expressed anger that the bill did not extend anti-discrimination protections for sexuality.[69] More influential, though, was the opposition the bill faced from the religious right of the Liberal Party. The party's State Council voted to withdraw the bill, and it was taken off the parliamentary agenda on 30 July 1997. Efforts to resurrect it in late 1998 came to naught, angering members of the state's trans community.[70]

The final organisation based in Western Australia—and that would continue to push for law reform—was the Gender Dysphoria Foundation of Western Australia, later renamed TransWest. The group first met in May 1997; little is known about its early history except that it initially met at the premises of the sex worker outreach group SIERRA and then at the Western Institute of Self Help. As the WA Government stalled and backed away from law reform, representatives of the Gender Dysphoria Foundation spoke to the media. In October 1998 the foundation's spokesperson, Helena Collins, was invited to attend a meeting of the feminist anti-violence organisation Reclaim the Night. Subsequently, organisers of Reclaim the Night rescinded the invitation because Helena was trans, echoing sentiments of Sydney's Lesbian Space Project. Helena lodged complaints with both the Commonwealth Human Rights and Equal Opportunity Commission and the WA Equal Opportunity Commission, but neither body had authority to investigate because being transgender was not a protected category under anti-discrimination laws. Helena commented in the LGBTIQ+ press: 'We can't just walk away after fighting our own battles, such as this, there needs to be a balance and follow up of particular legislation to make decisions such as the one made by RTN [Reclaim the Night] unlawful.'[71]

The Liberal government finally brought the Gender Reassignment Bill back for debate in November 1999. The Labor Party continued to support it, but MLA Diana Warnock expressed disappointment that it did not go further, noting that gay and lesbian people needed anti-discrimination protection and that the category 'gender history' only covered people who had gender affirmation surgery.[72] When the Legislative Council debated the bill in March 2000, the Greens expressed similar sentiments. Still, the Greens, the Democrats and Labor supported the legislation and it passed into law. Thus, in 2000 Western Australia—under a Liberal government—introduced legal recognition and anti-discrimination protections for trans people who had gender affirmation surgery.

Tasmania

The path to trans law reform in Tasmania was less visible, with two factors weighing heavily. First, the campaign for gay law reform took longer there, with male homosexuality only decriminalised in 1997. Second, unique to Tasmania was that it was illegal to dress in clothes associated with another gender. Whereas in other jurisdictions the use of vagrancy laws to criminalise dressing had (mostly) dissipated by the 1970s, in Tasmania the *Police Offences Act* criminalised 'Being a male person, be found in any public place at any time between sunset and sunrise, dressed in female apparel'.[73] Indeed, other versions of this clause had been in Tasmanian laws since at least 1865.[74] It is not known how often authorities prosecuted under it, but it did happen. One instance in 1984 involved a man dressed as a woman trying to enter the Wrest Point Casino after he had been barred by management. A short article in the gay press reported:

As he stalked about that day, stilettos clacking, several people reported 'the strange woman' who was finally tracked down and watched by police. Our unsuspecting drag, however, thought he'd gone unnoticed and proceeded with the second part of his plan. On entry to Wrest Point he was nabbed and defrocked![75]

Notwithstanding Tasmania's smaller population, some efforts were made to form transgender groups in the 1990s. One such group was called Meta-Morphosis: Transsexual Support Association of Tasmania. Founded in 1992, it aimed to offer counselling for trans people and their families and community education about trans issues, and to lobby for law reform.[76] The leaders of Meta-Morphosis worked in solidarity with gay and lesbian groups but wanted distinct trans organisations to represent their own interests. In a 1993 letter to the newly formed Australian Council for Gay and Lesbian Rights, Meta-Morphosis leaders wrote: 'We believe that including trans-sexual/transgenderist rights groups into the Council reinforces some of the heterosexual community's basic prejudices and stereotypes; for example, that "trannies are just confused gay men or drag queens who want to be girls".'[77] The authors expressed sincere appreciation for the solidarity the Tasmanian Gay and Lesbian Rights Group had shown, and it was that solidarity that would influence law reform. That same year, trans advocate Russell Gates appeared on Tasmanian television to talk about trans issues and their own life journey.[78]

After over a decade of campaigning by activists and intervention from the United Nations and the federal government, in May 1997 the Tasmanian Government finally decriminalised male homosexuality. On the heels of this reform, in 1998 the government introduced the state's first anti-discrimination Act. Like in the Northern Territory and South Australia, 'transsexuality' was incorporated within the definition of 'sexual orientation'. The definition included anyone who identified with a gender other than that assigned at birth, regardless of medical or surgical interventions.[79] Amendments in 2013 updated the terminology to transgender, removed it from the definition of sexual orientation, and incorporated the protected attribute of gender identity.

It took further lobbying from trans activists and their allies to put birth certificates and amendments to the criminal code on the parliamentary agenda. Ros Houston (sometimes spelled Roz) and Stephanie Reid were the principal activists in this space. Stephanie worked within the ALP for years to garner support for the amendments,[80] while Ros lobbied from outside political parties. In November 2000, the House of Assembly finally passed amendments to the *Police Offences Act* that repealed the clause that outlawed cross-dressing, and the bill passed the Legislative Council in March 2001. Ros commented: 'A great weight has been lifted from the shoulders of all transgender folk in Tasmania. Discrimination and violence against transgender people remain a problem, but at least now these social ills don't have the sanction of the law.'[81] In May 2001, the government introduced legislation to permit trans people who had gender affirmation surgery to have their birth certificate reissued in their affirmed gender.[82] The bill passed both houses of the Tasmanian Parliament later that year and came into effect from the beginning of 2002.

Victoria

In 1990 the Victorian Law Reform Commission conducted a review of the state's *Equal Opportunity Act*. It exposed several gaps in protections, one of which was around transsexuality; the final report recommended that this be added as a discrete protected attribute in the Act.[83] When the Victorian Government amended the law in 1995 to protect gay and lesbian people under the category of 'lawful sexual behaviour', they did not include transgender. Activist Julie Peters had an important epiphany: 'What we found was they [the politicians] didn't take us very seriously because we weren't a group.'[84]

In 1997, a steering committee formed to found a Victorian Gay and Lesbian Rights Lobby (VGLRL), and two transgender people were represented on the committee. Early on, one of them resigned when she felt that transgender issues were not being given fair consideration.[85] The other transgender member, Julie, remained on the steering committee and pushed hard for the group to become the Victorian Gay, Lesbian and Transgender Rights Lobby. When the VGLRL launched in October 1997, the steering committee decided it would focus on sexuality but advocated to work in solidarity with any separate trans lobby groups.[86]

Julie released a statement expressing her disappointment and announcing her intention to form the Victorian Transgender Rights Lobby (VTRL), which came to fruition a few weeks later.[87] The VTRL initially operated as a subgroup within the support organisation Transgender Liberation and Care but this arrangement proved unfeasible, so in early 1999 the VTRL disbanded. A series of public meetings in April and May 1999 led to the founding of an independent successor organisation, Transgender Victoria (TGV). TGV's leaders identified four key areas as their reform agenda: amendments to the *Equal Opportunity Act*, birth certificates, marriage rights, and better management and medical treatment for transgender prisoners.[88]

Pressure from transgender community representatives put anti-discrimination laws on the Labor Party agenda. At an event during Midsumma Festival in 1998, burgeoning activist Sally Goldner attended an ALP forum that featured the then opposition leader, John Brumby. Goldner asked whether Brumby would commit a Labor government to amend anti-discrimination law to protect transgender people; Brumby answered yes.[89] After winning the 1999 election, the Labor government's main champion for LGBT rights was the new attorney-general, Rob Hulls. Early on, Hulls proposed amendments to the *Equal Opportunity Act* that included the addition of 'gender identity' as a protected category, and in March 2000 his office contacted TGV to advise that he was preparing to introduce the legislation.[90]

The political calculus in Victoria was different from that of other jurisdictions. First, the ALP ran a minority government, meaning they needed the support of either three independents or the

Opposition for legislation to pass the lower house. The government embarked on negotiations with a conservative rural independent who proposed several amendments that the transgender community would not support. Eventually they compromised and accepted one amendment about transgender people needing to be 'bona fide', playing into mythologies that some men may adopt a female persona fraudulently for some alleged gain.[91] Even with the lower house support, the make-up of the Legislative Council was such that the government needed the Opposition either to support the legislation or at least not to oppose it.

This political reality was one reason that TGV worked tirelessly to lobby politicians of all stripes. TGV leaders prepared a political education sheet in November 1999 and sent it to all members of the Victorian Parliament. At the launch of TGV in 2000, co-convenor Kayleen White declared: 'We estimate that 95 per cent of transgender people who transition lose their job when they do so. A recent survey found that 80 per cent of transgender people experience harassment in the workplace.'[92] Numerous politicians from both parties cited the statistical information provided by TGV, including almost every speaker repeating the figure that an estimated 95 per cent of transgender people lost their jobs when they transitioned. The co-convenors of TGV were calm and savvy in their willingness to engage with the Opposition and even conservative media. Sally Goldner recalls: 'The dreaded Steve Price was doing *Drive* on 3AW at the time, and he interviewed me and was reasonable! He just … when I told him that we had stories of cross-dressers being sacked and it's nothing to do with the job, he was like "Oh!" sort of thing.'[93] The anti-discrimination amendments passed unopposed in Victoria in September 2000.

The Victorian transgender community, too, would face divisions over legal recognition of affirmed gender. In 2004, birth certificate reform was finally on the legislative agenda and TGV lobbied for self-definitions of gender regardless of surgical interventions. At one stage Hulls approved a proposal to permit transgender people to change their birth certificate even if they had not undergone surgery, as long as they had been diagnosed with gender dysphoria, were on hormones, and could obtain statutory declarations from two doctors that they had been living in their affirmed gender for at least eighteen months. According to *The Age*, resistance from other transgender community members, as well as gay and lesbian activists, led the attorney-general to abandon this proposal.[94] Finally, in 2004, Hulls introduced amendments to facilitate the change of birth certificates only for those transgender people who underwent 'sex affirmation surgery'.[95] Like the year 2000 amendments to the *Equal Opportunity Act*, the legislation passed with broad support across the parliament.

Queensland

The push for law reform in Queensland was initially tied to the movement to decriminalise homosexuality. Trans activists such as Toye de Wilde worked hard as members of the Queensland Association for Gay Law Reform throughout the 1980s amid the hostile premiership of Sir Joh Bjelke-Petersen. In 1990 the new Labor government of Wayne Goss passed homosexual law reform. From that point on, the solidarity between gay and lesbian and trans activists was tested.

The Australian Transgender Support Association of Queensland (ATSAQ) would become the main advocacy and support group for trans people in the state's south-east. The origins of ATSAQ lie on the Sunshine Coast, where trans woman Kerri Petrie in 1988 founded a group called QCATS: Queensland Collective of Australian Transsexuals. That group did not get much traction; Kerri moved to Brisbane, and on 22 October 1990 she refounded it with Toye. A 1991 article in *Queensland Pride* announcing QCATS' arrival on the scene described the organisation's agenda as 'human rights, legal status, birth registry, proper services to be provided by government departments, police liaison and the establishing of a Sister Tiresias House for the collating of data on case histories and a headquarters for the transsexual movement'.[96] Sometime in 1992, QCATS changed its name to ATSAQ.

Around the time QCATS/ATSAQ was forming, the Queensland Government was preparing to introduce an anti-discrimination bill into parliament. According to longstanding ATSAQ president Gina Mather, the original draft included trans people in the list of protected categories, but by the time it reached the parliament, trans people were no longer included. When parliament updated the Act in 1993, again trans people were not included. Although it is not clear why the final bill excluded trans people, Gina makes one salient observation: gay and lesbian activists did not stand up for trans people to ensure their inclusion.[97]

ATSAQ leaders consistently took whatever opportunities they could to advocate for transgender law reform. Kerri prepared a long submission in 1992 to the Electoral and Administrative Review Commission when it conducted a review into the 'Preservation and Enhancement of Individuals' Rights and Freedoms'. The submission presented information similar to many of the interstate trans organisations and was an early adopter of the language of transgender (or transgenderist) rather than transsexual. Kerri advocated that those people who either could not or chose not to have gender affirmation surgery faced discrimination and psychological challenges and therefore also needed legal protections. She also addressed the challenges as highlighted in other states: birth certificates, other identity documents, prison, rape laws, health care, and workplace and other discrimination. She succinctly noted that 'Inability to gain a birth-certificate is the beginning of a chain of disadvantages to be endured by transgenderists'.[98] The final review document endorsed ATSAQ's submission and recommended legal recognition of transgender people in Queensland.[99] This was a significant endorsement of law reform, but one that the Queensland Government did not implement.

In 1993 Kerri and other founding members of ATSAQ were ready to step down and hand over the leadership. Just in time, Gina Mather attended her first meeting. She remembers that there was a core membership of about twenty people, but they were not experienced at organising or advocacy. Gina came from a union background and, with the blessing of the outgoing leadership, became ATSAQ's new president; Kristine Johnson became secretary. This marked the beginning of a partnership that has extended for thirty years.

Early on, Gina and Kristine targeted their efforts at health-care provision for trans people in Queensland. They worked with doctors in Brisbane and from the Monash Gender Dysphoria Clinic to develop 'Principles and Standards for the Management of Gender Dysphoria in Queensland'. ATSAQ also secured access to the Biala City Community Health Centre on Wednesday afternoons and in December 1994 the Brisbane Gender Clinic opened there, offering primary care and referral pathways to the Monash Gender Dysphoria Clinic. ATSAQ also did outreach with trans sex workers and set up a 24-hour hotline—which in pre-mobile-phone days meant a telephone next to Gina's bed. The hotline would get three or four calls a day from trans people in distress (and calls from cranks and men with a fetish for trans women).[100]

Within months of assuming the presidency, Gina was speaking up and sending letters to the Queensland Anti-Discrimination Commission, the Police Liaison Committee for the Gay, Lesbian and Transgender Communities, and the attorney-general, highlighting the need to add transgender people into the *Anti-Discrimination Act*. Politicians' responses to ATSAQ were consistent: there were no plans to amend the Act, but if there were a review process in the future then its views would be considered. Representatives of the Queensland Anti-Discrimination Commission consistently expressed sympathy but said they did not have the authority to investigate complaints. They did, however, indicate that they were keeping a record of complaints brought to their attention from trans people to report to the attorney-general about the gap in the law.[101]

There was one significant member of parliament with whom Gina had a cordial relationship: Peter Beattie. He was the health minister who had supported ATSAQ to secure space for the Brisbane Gender Clinic. In 1997, when Beattie was opposition leader, Gina wrote to his office noting the challenges facing trans people because they were not protected under the *Anti-Discrimination Act*. When Beattie became premier in 1998, Gina continued to write to him and the new attorney-general pushing them to reform the Act. In May 2000 a letter from the attorney-general's office definitively ruled out changes to the Act and Gina wrote a passionate open letter addressed to 'The People of Queensland'. She invoked the high suicide rates in the trans community and declared: 'After all the years of "setting the record straight", nothing has changed. Our members, your family and friends will continue to die and yes, by their own hand. How can we live in a community that will not afford us the protection that even guide dogs have. (Please, no disrespect meant).'[102] A few months later, she again wrote to Premier Beattie calling for a meeting with him, the attorney-general and representatives of both the Anti-Discrimination Commission and Births, Deaths and Marriages. The premier did not attend, but the attorney-general did.

Gina and Kristine continued to write letters and meet with politicians and other stakeholders. The real turning point came after a meeting with the new attorney-general, Rod Welford, in 2001. It felt like so many they had before: Kristine and Gina presented the challenges confronting the trans community and explained why changes to the *Anti-Discrimination Act* were vital. Welford politely listened, thanked them, and said he would get back to them. Gina was so used to this response and was so cynical that she snapped. She recalls what happened as she was leaving:

I said to him, I must admit I did swear. I said something like: 'You'd be like the fucking rest of them. You fucking won't do anything.'

That's right, I said to him, 'Rod, if your child was fucking born with cystic fibrosis or Down syndrome, you'd do some fucking thing, wouldn't you? You'd give them a quality of life. But if you're born with gender identity, shove it up their arse.'

I did say that, which I shouldn't have, because he was the attorney-general. But that's the way I talk at times.

She [the secretary] said, 'You've offended him.'

I said, 'You cannot offend a parliamentarian. They sit on their shiny fucking leather seat waiting for the day to get their superannuation. [T]he only way you can offend them is to sack them.'

She said, 'No, you have offended him. His daughter's got Down syndrome.'

I said, 'Oh shit. When's the next attorney-general coming on?' …

But within three or four weeks he said, 'Come in again. I want another meeting with you.'[103]

Over the next six months, Gina and Kristine had a series of meetings with both the attorney-general and the premier, who advised them to keep the meetings confidential, especially from the gay and lesbian community. Beattie planned to table a bill in parliament in late 2002 and cautioned Gina and Kristine: 'Be prepared for all hell to break fucking loose.' His prophecy proved accurate: representatives of the gay and lesbian community were furious that amendments to the *Anti-Discrimination Act* had been negotiated behind their backs (as they saw it). It reached the point where Gina and Kristine had to meet with gay and lesbian representatives at the Queensland AIDS Council; Gina reminded them that the gay and lesbian community had not supported trans rights in 1991.[104]

During the negotiations over the *Anti-Discrimination Act* reforms there was tension with one other stakeholder: religious leaders. Some wanted assurances that religious schools would be exempt from any provisions of the Act in relation to the employment of gay, lesbian, bisexual *and* transgender people. Gina recalls one particularly heated meeting she attended with the Catholic archbishop. He was harping on about wanting the right to discriminate, and as she recollects:

> [As] I finished up, he said something that hit a nerve. I was wearing jeans and I stood up. I said, 'Mind you, Archbishop Battersby, while you've been talking, you would notice that I'm wearing jeans and you're the one that's wearing a fucking frock.'
>
> He said, 'I don't have to stand here and be insulted by the likes of you', and Peter Beattie stood up and said, 'Separate! Separate! Archbishop, you're going down to Level 13 or 14. Gina, you stay; [Archbishop,] you're going.'[105]

The archbishop secured the exemptions that he desired.[106]

The bill went to parliament in November 2002. Among a raft of reforms, it added gender identity as a protected category and amended the *Births, Deaths and Marriages Act* so that trans people who had gender affirmation surgery could change their birth certificate. The Liberal and National parties, for their part, supported the addition of trans people as a protected category but opposed the changing of birth certificates. The bill passed the parliament and came into effect in 2003.

The legal situation in the new millennium

As this chapter has shown, the long road to law reform was uneven and chequered across the country. Until the 1970s there was little consideration of whether—let alone how—to recognise trans people in their affirmed gender. This silence could sometimes work in trans people's favour, as they could fall between the cracks and obtain passports or other identity documents in their affirmed gender. From the 1970s, as more government departments applied the British *Corbett* ruling, it became nearly impossible for trans people to change their identity documents.

From the 1980s, state and territory governments began to consider changing their laws to permit trans people to update their birth certificates, as well as to introduce anti-discrimination laws. In places with smaller trans populations, like South Australia, the Australian Capital Territory and the Northern Territory, these changes happened without fanfare or substantial activism. In New South Wales, Western Australia, Victoria and Queensland, trans activists lobbied long and hard until receptive governments were willing to introduce reform. Tasmania, too, required substantial lobbying, often in solidarity with gay and lesbian activists who were also still pushing for law reform.

Visibility was key to lobbying politicians and the media and to generate public support. Indeed, as Transgender Victoria co-convenor Kayleen White effectively explained in 2000:

When we have met with people who do not know transgender people, and they see that we are not the monsters portrayed in folklore (so to speak), we have got them on side. It's a message that was put quite succinctly by one Commonwealth Senator we met: make sure politicians can put a face to transgender issues. In other words, personalise it—which corrects some of the myths and misconceptions.[107]

By 2004, all states and territories had anti-discrimination protections for trans people who had gender affirmation surgery, and most went further to cover all trans people. All jurisdictions also had mechanisms in place for trans people to change their birth certificate, but only if they had gender affirmation surgery. As Chapter 8 explores, the push to extend those rights to all trans people regardless of medical or surgical interventions would fall to yet another generation of activists in the 2010s–20s.

5
QUEER AND TRANS BLAK, INDIGENOUS AND PEOPLE OF COLOUR

WIRADJURI NON-BINARY SCHOLAR Sandy O'Sullivan tweets and writes extensively about what they call the colonial project of gender.[1] It has been well documented how colonialism led to the decimation and mass dispossession of Indigenous people through massacres, disease and displacement. State and territory 'protectors' segregated Aboriginal and Torres Strait Islander people on missions and reserves, and practices such as child removal and banning of traditional languages further attacked Aboriginal cultures. Under protection and assimilation policies, missionaries and government officials attempted to eliminate any beliefs and practices inconsistent with Christianity—including genders beyond the binary and sexualities that were not heterosexual.[2]

As Gomeroi scholar Alison Whittaker observes, it is not surprising that Indigenous people find it difficult to 'prove' the existence of gender diversity before colonisation.[3] Moreover, any 'evidence' Aboriginal people could provide would have to be amenable to, and in the language of, the coloniser. Yet O'Sullivan makes another salient point, questioning the very *need* to 'prove' a precolonial, Indigenous trans-historicity:

> The contemporary desire to trace a history of Indigenous queer representation from time immemorial as evidence that we have not only recently arrived at queerness is analogous to the ways that the colonial project in so-called Australia has insisted on people who were forcibly removed from land now proving persistent occupation to lay claim to that land.[4]

As O'Sullivan also notes, there is not simply one Indigenous perspective on gender (or anything else), and the mere notion of a pan-Indigenous identity or viewpoint is yet another colonial imposition.[5]

There are, of course, plenty of Aboriginal and Torres Strait Islander people who desire to recover and share histories of gender diversity. Those histories are one way of speaking back to the coloniser and to challenge existing trans histories and organisations, which have been dominated by white/European leaders. Exploring Indigenous queer and trans histories can also challenge the myth that Aboriginal and Torres Strait Islander communities are culturally homo/bi/transphobic. Whittaker explains why this misconception is another perpetuation of the colonial project of gender:

> Such disputes on whether Indigenous queerness either exists or emerges from these white liberal centres of enlightenment are arguably part of policing of the periphery of Indigenousness. This entrenches the lateral and colonial unseeing of Indigenous ways of being that see queerness attributed to the 'enlightened' brush of whiteness.[6]

It is not just Indigenous Australians who have had to confront racism and white/European interpretations of how their cultures read gender. Since the late twentieth century, as more non-white/

European immigrants have come to Australia from the Pacific and Asia, other trans people from non-white/European backgrounds have also become more visible here. They, too, have brought different cultural conceptions of (trans)gender that have challenged LGBTIQ+ and trans organisations to be more inclusive of diverse trans people's experiences. They, too, navigated racism and marginalisation, though not necessarily in the same way as Indigenous Australians.

To challenge racism and colonial structures, in recent years 'Blak, Indigenous and people of colour'—sometimes abbreviated as BIPOC—has become a common expression to highlight shared racial oppression and solidarities, while concurrently acknowledging diversity among non-white/European groups. In Australia, Aboriginal artist Destiny Deacon first used 'Blak' in a 1994 exhibition to speak back at racist slurs against Aboriginal people that used 'Black'. The term Blak reclaims the word while at the same time respecting the different experiences of Aboriginal and Torres Strait Islander people versus other non-Indigenous people of colour. Particularly in the wake of the global Black Lives Matter movement, Blak has become more common in Australia as a term of empowerment among Aboriginal and Torres Strait Islander activists.[7] In the context of gender diversity, centring the voices of queer and trans Blak, Indigenous and people of colour thus illuminates a range of cultural experiences and exposes the ways in which trans groups have privileged white/European values and marginalised or discriminated against racial 'others'.

This chapter focuses on the histories and experiences of trans people of colour in Australia, especially Indigenous people. From the 1970s–80s, trans Aboriginal and Torres Strait Islander, Māori and Pasifika people only occasionally appeared in the media. Still, the snippets of information from the media, the life story of high-profile Māori figure Carmen Rupe and oral histories reveal the different experiences of trans people of colour. There has been more visibility since the 1990s, when Sistergirls then Brotherboys and other queer and trans Indigenous people began to organise and advocate for their rights within their own mobs as well as within LGBTIQ+ communities. As the 2000s rolled in, Asian and other trans people of colour, too, founded their own groups and pushed mainstream trans organisations to be more cognisant of the diverse needs, experiences and cultural expressions of gender diversity.

Challenging the colonisers' identity constructions

Aboriginal and Torres Strait Islander cultures are gendered in numerous ways. Particular stories, spaces, dances, knowledges and practices are reserved for women or men, often described in English as 'men's business' or 'women's business'. Yet saying that the cultures are gendered does not mean they are exclusively binary. Brotherboy Elder Dean Gilbert notes that when he went to women Wiradjuri Elders to explain his transition and tell them he wanted to partake in men's business, they responded that this has been happening for hundreds of years.[8] In the Northern Territory, several Aboriginal languages have words for a third gender or someone who does not fit the binary of male and female:

- kwarte kwarte in Arrente
- kungka kungka in Pitjantjatjara and Luritja
- yimpininni in Tiwi
- karnta pia in Warlpiri, which can be interpreted to mean 'like a girl'
- kungka wati in Pintipi and girriji kati in Waramungu, which translate to 'woman/man'.[9]

Many precolonial gender practices have been lost or suppressed, but there is evidence of gender diversity in rock art and oral traditions. For instance, one rock engraving shows a Sistergirl surrounded by animals, fish and a whale.[10] Another part of the country has rock art of a stick figure with breasts and a penis.[11] A Dreaming story from the Nunggubuyu people of the Gulf of Carpentaria in the

Northern Territory tells of a woman who, to protect herself from an approaching spirit, cuts off her hair and wears it as a moustache and beard. Some of the other actions the woman takes—controlling both fire and water and performing traditionally male acts like roasting wallaby in fire ashes—suggest that this is a case of gender crossing.[12]

Translating language, knowledge and culture into English and trying to fit them into Western concepts can be problematic. O'Sullivan writes: 'A key aspect of the colonial project is to insist on compliance and order. The notion of ordering Indigenous people into categories that can be maintained and understood by the coloniser seeps into all aspects of colonial life today.'[13] They write this to challenge the idea that Indigenous people need common terminology to describe their diverse gender experiences and identities. To take O'Sullivan's argument a step further, Indigenous and other cultural understandings of gender do not even necessarily align with Western definitions of what 'trans' is. Aunty Vanessa Smith, a longstanding Sistergirl activist, explains:

We don't have to take hormones. We don't have to have gender reassignment. We don't have to have breast implants. We don't have to dress as women and live as women because our spirit is female, and our spirit is who we are. It's not about the dress; it's not about the physical side of us that you see. Some people might just have a flower over their ear or something like that. Someone might just pluck their eyebrows. Someone might grow their hair, to feel like a female for themselves. But the reality is, it's a spiritual thing with us. It's not about anything else. That's more important than anything—knowing that what's in here is who you are.[14]

Vanessa's description of Sistergirl, Brotherboy and gender-diverse Aboriginal identities focuses on spirit; some cultures focus on character traits and others focus on societal roles. Collectively, all of these gender-diverse Blak, Indigenous and people of colour expose gender for what it is: a construct.

Vanessa also makes an important point that challenges the idea of transness as being just about gender, not sexuality. For some Aboriginal people like Vanessa, the identity as a Sistergirl encompasses both sexual and gender diversity, with the two not necessarily distinct concepts. Aboriginal scholar Madi Day reinforces this point, noting: 'While I recognize that queer and trans are different and separate terms in a Western context, such a divide is not always distinct among Aboriginal and Torres Strait Islander people.'[15] Indeed, Day explicitly deploys the word queer *because* of its broad application to non-normative expressions of gender *and* sexuality.

Queer and trans Indigenous people who do not fit Western constructs of trans have found novel ways to express their identities, especially in recent years. As noted in Chapter 2, drag is not the same as trans, and this is something that Indigenous scholars like O'Sullivan, too, stress.[16] Yet Wodi Wodi scholar Andrew Farrell writes about drag being a means to express their Aboriginality and queerness and to 'gender-fuck'. Farrell's autoethnographic article about their relationship with drag does not present themself as having any specific gender identity except for queer, which Farrell calls 'more of a politics of gender that resists the institution of gender than a gender category ... As a Queer person I aspire to disassociate my identity with the fixed and colonized institution of gender.' Farrell also describes encountering resistance from other LGBTIQ+ people *because* of their refusal to fit within Western-constructed ideas about trans, sexuality and gender:

> I have been constantly interrogated about whether or not I really belong in the transgender community, whether I am a 'woman', whether I will transition, and whether I will adhere to dominant conceptualizations of being transgender or whether I will fix my gender as solely female or male. I have been asked on many occasions whether I am transgender and if not, why not? 'You're already halfway there' people have proclaimed. Macroaggressions relating to my identity have occurred in multiple contexts,

inside and outside of LGBTIQ contexts. It is hurtful when these interrogations sit within what is supposed to be a 'safe space'.[17]

Farrell's deployment of drag thus represents a form of resistance to the colonial project of gender. Moreover, it is the inability of white/ European people—including LGBTIQ+ and trans people—to categorise that they find so distressing.

Looking to other Indigenous cultures reveals words, practices and cultural roles that also do not translate or fit necessarily with Western binaries or conceptualisations of trans. Some cultures have words for people who occupy a third, fourth or other gender; prominent terms and cultures are kathoey from Thailand and hijra from India. Numerous Pasifika languages have words that loosely translate to a third gender or to an AMAB person who is gender or sexually nonconforming:

- faʻafafine in Samoa
- fakaleitī or leitī in Tonga
- vaka sa lewa lewa in Fiji
- fakafifine in Niue
- pinapinaaine in Kiribati and Tuvalu
- akavaʻine in the Cook Islands
- whakawāhine among Māori in Aotearoa New Zealand.

Though less common, there are also terms for AFAB people in Pasifika communities: faʻafatama in Samoa, fakatangata in Tonga, and tanata ira tane among Māori.[18] All of these groups show that gender diversity predates and survived colonial arrivals, and they reflect Madi Day and Wiradjuri scholar Corrinne Sullivan's observation that 'Trans-Indigenous knowledges demonstrate the complexity and heterogeneity of Indigenous experiences illustrating just some of the myriad ways in which queer Indigenous peoples see and experience the world'.[19]

The rest of this chapter explores some of the living experiences and organisational histories of trans and queer Blak, Indigenous and people of colour in Australia. Whether they adopt the Western language of trans, embrace Indigenous terminology such as Sistergirl or Brotherboy, use other cultural expressions or reject any category at all, the examples here highlight the distinct challenges facing racial 'others' within what continues to be a white/European-dominated society. While by no means representing a universal Australian story of trans and queer Blak, Indigenous or people of colour, this chapter illuminates key historical trends, threads, groups and events that speak to the multiple histories of gender diversity surviving and thriving against the colonial project of gender.

Community childhoods

Sistergirl Francene remembers that in her community growing up, there were two Sistergirls who were 'completely accepted'. She explains the role they and other Sistergirls played: 'Mothers will ask you to be their babysitters for the children, caring, because they knew you'd cared for them. You were like a mother. You played that mum, you gave them comfort, you'd feed them, you'd do all those things that a mother would do. And Sistergirls do this today.'[20] Other examples from the mid twentieth century highlight Aboriginal communities that had roles or social positions for people who crossed genders or did not fit into the binary. One of the few anthropological studies to note the presence of gender-diverse people in Aboriginal communities came out of the Tiwi Islands. Arnold Remington Pilling observed that gender-diverse Tiwi people 'had led to no separate social category, although in this case there was labelling of such persons: some were classified by Tiwi as socially female, some as socially male. However, the Tiwi did have a special label for this physiological category, *kita imbalina*, or, in the local English, "little bit female".'[21]

Other oral histories discuss cultural roles for Aboriginal people who crossed genders. Brie Ngala Curtis—an Arrente Sistergirl from the Central Desert who also has Luritja, Warlpiri and Warramunga ancestry—was raised by her grandmother. Her grandmother only had her first contact with white people when she was fourteen years old, so she was well versed in the traditional, precolonial ways. Brie explains:

> The trans women at that time would join the women to do traditional women duties like cooking, collecting bush fruit, growing up the children, and making bush medicine. They'd go through women's ceremony and they'd be respected as women. They'd have relationships with men and be married because they'd be identified as straight women. Back in them days, men could have a lot of wives.[22]

Gender-diverse Indigenous people often describe a tension across their childhoods, with almost contradictory memories of both acceptance and rejection. In a video produced for ACON in 2003, Sistergirl Lillian says, 'The community knew about me long time before I knew about myself. So I said to myself, "Well, I must be this, a Sistergirl."' Yet, later in the video, Lillian also says, 'Being a Sistergirl sometimes—most of the time—I got abused, hit and punched and that, to have sex with.'[23] Kooncha Brown, a Yuin and Gunnai/Kurnai Sistergirl, grew up on the south coast of New South Wales in the 1960s–70s. Her community also had a tradition of Sistergirls, though at the time they did not use that term. Instead, community members used the expression 'funny h' to describe those who were sexually and gender diverse. Kooncha knew multiple Sistergirls growing up, including the community nurse, and recalls family members (her mother's cousins) who were Sistergirls, one of whom married a man in a church. Kooncha says there was some discrimination against Sistergirls but attributes this primarily to outsiders who moved to the community.[24]

Like non-Indigenous people, Sistergirls, Brotherboys and queer and trans Aboriginal and Torres Strait Islander children did not have the vocabulary or understanding to articulate their genders or feelings of difference. Family members reacted in different ways when children exhibited behaviours or dressed in ways not associated with their sex assigned at birth. Kooncha's family, for instance, accepted her then and now: 'I think my family has given me a place within my family, and also created that place within my community. I know of Sistergirls who've been disowned from their family, and they really don't have anywhere else to go.' Lillian had a less favourable experience: 'We were pushed back in the corner and not heard of, not to be seen. I don't want that, and I don't wish that today on the Sistergirls of today.'[25]

An extreme example of family ostracism comes from Vanessa Smith, a Kaneang Sistergirl from Noongar Country. Born in 1951, Vanessa suffered physical, sexual and emotional abuse as a child. She explains: 'I acted out because the man who was abusing me used to call me his girlfriend. So, in a weird sort of way, I believed that I was a girl. So, I acted out as such. As a result of that, my father was embarrassed about it, so he isolated me and excluded me from the closest of the family that I should have enjoyed as a child.' At age sixteen, the Children's Court made Vanessa a ward of the state and sent her to Longmore Remand and Assessment Centre and then Heathcote Mental Hospital. That was a horrific experience, as she recollects:

> They did some pretty horrible things to me as a child insofar as placing me in institutions and treating me with electric shock treatment which they felt was going to cure me of the way, as a child, I was behaving, and that was really mean as well … When they used to strap me down and when I'd wake up, I'd be lying in a padded cell, on the floor, on a mattress. They thought that was meant to cure me … of my acting out effeminately.[26]

The trauma affected Vanessa for her entire life, including bouts of depression and suicide attempts. But she proved a resilient figure and eventually became an influential Sistergirl.

Another high-profile Sistergirl activist is Crystal Love Johnson, who was born in 1970 on the Tiwi Islands to a Tiwi mother and Warlpiri father. Both Crystal and her family faced discrimination when she was growing up in Darwin, as other Warlpiri women used to assault her mother for having a Sistergirl child and men used to abuse her and her brothers. Crystal moved to Sydney in her mid-twenties, and it was there that she learned to accept herself.[27] Crystal proved resilient and returned to the Northern Territory in 2000 at age thirty, where she has since made it her mission to educate remote Aboriginal communities and advocate for Sistergirls. She has also become stronger at standing up for herself. She explained in 2003:

> My family doesn't like it [that I'm a Sistergirl]. They used to use terms like, 'You're not a lubra. You should be a man.' They used to say awful things like, 'You're not a real female. You're a male. You were born as a male; you'll die as a male.' But I always say to my family that 'I was born as a male, but I've got a woman's spirit inside of me'. And I say, 'and no one's going to change that.' And my grandparents knew and they didn't make judgements on me.[28]

Several Sistergirls attributed discriminatory community attitudes to the effects of Christianity and colonialism erasing their cultures. An extra layer of colonial devastation on Sistergirls, Brotherboys and queer and trans Indigenous people was the Stolen Generations. The *Bringing Them Home* report, published in 1997, estimated that between 1909 and 1969, state authorities removed between one in ten and one in three Aboriginal children from their families. Welfare authorities sent some children to institutions, while others went into foster care or were adopted by white families.[29]

It is not surprising that some members of the Stolen Generations were Sistergirls, Brotherboys, queer or gender diverse. Two interview participants are survivors of the Stolen Generations: Kooncha Brown and Ricki Spencer. The welfare authorities removed Kooncha and her brother in the 1960s when she was about three years old and sent her to the Aboriginal reserve at Wallaga Lake before she was fostered out to a kind woman. Kooncha returned to her family four years later, and in that sense she was one of the lucky ones.[30] Ricki was not so lucky. She was born in Melbourne in 1968 and for most of her life thought she was the child of Polish immigrants. When she was in her late forties, after her parents had died, she learned she was Aboriginal. In the past few years Ricki has reconnected with Aboriginal communities in Melbourne, and she is now living as a proud trans Aboriginal woman.[31]

Families of trans people of colour could, like other families, be either accepting or rejecting. Katherine Wolfgramme was born in Fiji in 1972 and moved to Melbourne in 1974, where she was raised by her affirming great-grandparents. She recalls that they did not try to impose gender stereotypes or norms upon her:

I wasn't wearing female clothes, I didn't have a female name, I was just treated as one of the daughters. Now, I know there's a difference. I didn't know as a kid, but I know there's a difference now. Like I said, Nanna taught me to cook, she taught me to clean, and they were my household duties … I never did gardening, I never did lawn mowing, I never helped Grandpa do anything.

Katherine's family was prominent and respected in Fiji, so other members of her Fijian family were not going to challenge her great-grandparents. Still, living in an affirming home did not necessarily shield Katherine from bullying at school and on the streets, or from other societal expectations around gender norms. She really began to explore her gender when she moved out of home at eighteen and found other LGBT people.[32]

Fa'afafine artist, poet and community activist Amao Leota Lu moved from Aotearoa New Zealand to Sydney in the 1980s, when she was twelve, and recalls feeling awkward around teenage boys. She turned to art, music and fashion and found a circle of friends among the unpopular kids. Amao experimented with diverse forms of dress and gender expression but found it hard to be different within her Pasifika community. She explains:

> I wasn't the goody two shoes, church-going Pacific Island Samoan person that Mum and Dad wanted me to be. I was yearning for people to take notice that I was trying to find myself here. I wanted support and not more people saying, 'You can't do this, you can't do that, it's not the church way.' And that I found really challenging, I think. It was traumatic, the church stuff.[33]

Amao, too, would explore her gender when she was an adult.

Most of the other trans people of colour interviewed for this project or whose stories have been published grew up overseas and immigrated to Australia during the 1990s–2000s, so their experiences are told later. They come from Malaysia, Singapore, Samoa and Aotearoa New Zealand, and from Hindu, Muslim and Christian families. They identify as hijra, fa'afafine, whakawāhine or trans, depending on their cultural background. Several report similar tensions between precolonial understandings of gender and the disruptions wrought by colonialism. They also had varying degrees of acceptance from their communities, with one trend standing out: it was after they moved out of home that their families had time to reflect and accept them in their affirmed gender. For those coming from countries where homosexuality or being trans is illegal, it was in Australia that they could be fully open about their authentic selves.

Fragments of queer and trans Blak, Indigenous and people of colour, 1970s–90s

Trans media coverage in the 1970s–80s often did not comment on the racial or ethnic background of a trans person. This reflects the centring of whiteness as the norm, and also rendered trans and queer Blak, Indigenous and people of colour invisible. Usually only in passing might a report mention the person's cultural background.

For instance, Phillis McGuiness' legal battle, described in Chapter 4, garnered media coverage over the period 1982–88. The articles never discussed her Aboriginality except to note that the NSW Aboriginal Legal Service handled her appeals. As another example, a 1979 *Truth* article reported on two trans women abducted on Grey Street in St Kilda—presumably sex workers—one of whom died when she fell from the car. Buried within the article was problematic racial language noting that the deceased was 'born a boy, part-aboriginal, in Alice Springs … However, White had a sex-change operation, which cost $9000, in Cairo several years ago.'[34] In a strikingly similar example, the victim of a physical assault and attempted rape in St Kilda in 1987 was a trans Cook Islander who had migrated to Aotearoa New Zealand in 1974, then Australia in 1979—though it is likely the assailant did not know she was trans when he attacked her. Her perpetrator was one of the few who faced trial and was convicted.[35]

One stand-out article from Brisbane's *Sunday Sun* in September 1979 profiled L Lampton from Palm Island. Notwithstanding the sensational headline 'Sex Change Girl Gets State Ban', the article presented a respectful account of discrimination Lampton faced as an Aboriginal trans woman in Queensland. Lampton emphasised her femininity, as did the journalist, describing her as 'attractive, tall, with light brown skin and an unmistakably feminine figure'. Before transitioning, Lampton had worked in the Queensland Public Service as a project officer at Edward River and the Yarrabah Community Council. She subsequently worked for the Commonwealth Public Service in Adelaide and Sydney, and it was during those job roles that she transitioned. She continued to work in the Commonwealth Public Service, including in the Department of Defence as a receptionist for a senior admiral in the Royal Australian Navy. Lampton said that the Commonwealth Public Service was aware she was transgender and had no problem with it. In 1979 she applied for a project officer job at Yarrabah Community Council and was the successful applicant. She remarked: 'The Community Council knew about my sex change operation and did not have any problem. They were only interested in my job qualifications and that's all anyone should be interested in.'[36]

Unfortunately, higher public figures were interested in the fact that Lampton was trans. Somehow, the Queensland minister for Island and Aboriginal advancement and Premier Joh Bjelke-Petersen got wind of Lampton's appointment and complained to the federal minister for Aboriginal affairs and the prime minister. The minister for Aboriginal affairs, Senator Fred Chaney, subsequently sent a telegram to Yarrabah Community Council advising that Lampton's federally funded appointment was not confirmed. Lampton was upset and, given the lack of anti-discrimination protections at either state or federal level, had no legal recourse. All she could do was tell the media her story and hope that public sympathy could influence a reconsideration.

Some trans women recollect that at Tiresias House in the mid-to-late 1980s, it felt like all of the workers were Pasifika trans women. One such employee, Ricca Griffith, appeared briefly in the media in 1988. Ricca was of Samoan heritage, was raised in Aotearoa New Zealand, and began living full time as a woman at age sixteen before moving to Sydney at age eighteen. Like so many other trans people, she faced discrimination trying to obtain employment so turned to sex work and drugs. As she explained it, 'It's a high price you pay for being a transsexual and you pay it all your life. In bars they'll say: "Out! We don't serve people like you!" At job interviews they say: "You'll give the place a bad name."'[37] Ricca went through rehabilitation and from September 1986 worked at Tiresias House as a drug and alcohol counsellor. She wrote in a job application: 'Since working at Tiresias House I have been able to use my experiences to relate to the problems that many of the young girls come to Tiresias with and help them change their life-styles.'[38]

As noted in Chapter 3, a disproportionate number of trans women who worked on Tranny Lane in the 1970s–90s were Aboriginal, Māori or Pasifika. A small number of these women went on to live at

Tiresias House: among a series of fifty-two questionnaires completed by residents during Tiresias House's first year, 1983–84, two identified as Aboriginal, one as Māori and one as Polynesian.[39] The surveys provide some insights into the life experiences of these women. The Polynesian person was thirty-three and Tahitian, and said that she had known since age three that she was trans. Her parents 'accepted it as normal', but still she faced some bullying at school. She had training as a first-class machinist and in 1976, upon being dismissed from a job, began to live full time as a woman. Her survey had a lot of blank answers and showed a relatively okay experience being trans, particularly when noting her family support and when compared with other surveys. Yet, the fact that she was seeking accommodation at Tiresias House suggests that she likely faced challenges.

The 25-year -old Māori person's survey indicated that her mother was Māori and her father was a French Jew. She identified her racial descent and religion as Jewish. Born in Aotearoa New Zealand, she later lived in Adelaide and then moved to Sydney in 1983. Her answers to questions about her mental health and wellbeing were not as positive as those of the Polynesian respondent; she said she had attempted suicide by overdose because she 'felt like the world was ganging up on me—paranoia'. She had known from age nine that she was trans and had dressed in girls' clothes since age ten, but it was not until she moved to Tiresias House in 1984 that she began to live full time as a woman. Before transitioning she had been a skilled labourer, but like so many other trans women she was now on unemployment benefits. She wrote that her father's reaction to her being trans was 'rejecting' but her mother was 'ambivalent'. One other important insight from her survey was that she said the best moment in her life was 'When I met other transsexuals', and she came to Tiresias House because she 'Read about it and to be with people like myself and seek advice'.

The 24-year-old Aboriginal respondent identified far more challenges. Born in Walgett, she had known since age nine that she was trans and started dressing as a woman when she was fourteen and living full-time as a woman from age twenty. She was not out to her family and even indicated that she had no contact with them in five years. The respondent previously had substance abuse problems, writing that she smoked about ten cigarettes a day and from 1982–83 had taken heroin. She had been performing sex work, but not for the stereotypical or common rationale of lack of other job opportunities. In answer to the question about why she did sex work, she wrote: 'More money—straight jobs don't pay as much in the time as working the street'. She had been subjected to one sexual assault in western Sydney, which she described as 'Forced with axe to have sex in 1982 by strange man'. She had twice been arrested for soliciting and noted verbal harassment by police along with being slapped by a cop. This person had some experience as a clerk and in youth work, so in answer to the question about why she came to Tiresias House she said, 'To help a herion [sic] user kick the habit c/ support from trannys'.

The other Aboriginal person was twenty-two years old and from Barmera, South Australia. This person had even more challenging substance abuse problems, smoking about twenty-five cigarettes a day, having once been hospitalised for a heroin overdose, and having once attempted suicide with pills. She had performed sex work with the reason listed as 'money' and also indicated that she had been raped at age seventeen. She had been arrested for armed robbery and imprisoned for seventeen months at Long Bay Gaol, the main men's prison in New South Wales. She answered the question about what problems she experienced in gaol with 'Denial of female role, harassed, identity crisis'. The 'office use only' section of the survey indicated that this person's parole officer had referred her to Tiresias House.

Aside from the question where they indicated their racial background and that of their parents, there is nothing distinct in these surveys to the respondents' culture. That is in part an indicator of the fact that the questions did not try to account for cultural differences. There is, though, one response that may hint at a distinct experience:

the second Aboriginal respondent answered the question about whether she had been in a children's detention home in the affirmative, with just the word 'Adelaide'. Could this have been related to the Stolen Generations? There is no way of knowing, but it is an important possible intersecting trauma in that person's life.

Organising Sistergirls

Women of colour have consistently asserted that they do not experience oppression in the same way as white women. In 1989 Black feminist Kimberlé Crenshaw coined the term 'intersectionality' to describe how women of colour experience overlapping layers of discrimination: they cannot separate their race, gender or other identities because all of those identities collectively make up the person, and their living experiences of oppression are a reflection of those intersecting identities.[40] It is for this reason that Blak, Indigenous and people of colour have, especially since the 1990s, advocated for their distinct needs within both trans communities and their cultural communities.

Advocacy for Sistergirls and, later, Brotherboys and other queer and trans Aboriginal and Torres Strait Islander people grew out of responses to the AIDS epidemic. In 1994 the Australian Federation of AIDS Organisations (AFAO) hosted Anwernekenhe I, the first national conference for Indigenous gay men and Sistergirls, on Arrente Country in the Northern Territory. AFAO subsequently recognised the need for specific strategies for HIV and AIDS prevention and treatment in Aboriginal and Torres Strait Islander communities. It launched a series of working groups and hosted Anwernekenhe II in 1998.[41] At that meeting, Vanessa Smith was elected chair of the National Indigenous Gay and Sistergirl Steering Committee. For the next four years she travelled across Australia to various Indigenous communities, talking about HIV and AIDS and especially working to break the stigma around HIV. She also talked to and listened to Sistergirls.[42]

In July 1999 Vanessa chaired the First National Indigenous Sistergirl Forum on Magnetic Island, the lands of the Wulgurukaba peoples. The conference brought together thirty-five Sistergirls from across Australia (except for Victoria and Tasmania). There was also an invitation extended to a Brotherboy, but he was unable to attend. Conference topics focused on identity, violence, human rights and substance abuse. The attendees contributed to a final report that made recommendations on the importance of education programs and visibility of Sistergirls within LGBTIQ+ and Indigenous communities and service providers.[43]

Kooncha Brown and Lisa Taylor were two of the attendees at Magnetic Island, and both remember it as a personal and collective turning point for Sistergirls. Kooncha recalls talking about the importance of the Sistergirls not fighting, and working collectively.[44] Lisa similarly praised the power of bringing together Sistergirls from diverse Indigenous communities across the country. She found it personally educative and empowering: 'It was an eye-opener for me to see this umbrella term [Sistergirl] and just go … It was a real wow moment for me … because I always felt a bit different as a trans woman. I always felt I didn't fit the stereotype of what you were meant to be. It was almost like finding myself.'[45]

For the next two decades Vanessa would continue to advocate for Sistergirls and Brotherboys as well as other LGBTIQ+ Indigenous people. She worked with LGBTIQ+ organisations in Perth and in 2015 founded Tekwabi Giz under the National LGBTI Health Alliance (now LGBTIQ+ Health Australia). Tekwabi is a word from the Tiwi Islands and giz is from the Torres Strait; Tekwabi Giz means 'all of us connected'. This working group brought together LGBTIQ+ Aboriginal and Torres Strait Islander people from across the country to advocate for their distinct health needs within broader strategies and organisations.[46] Sadly, Vanessa passed away in January 2022 after a long battle with cancer.

Just as Vanessa was organising nationally, Kooncha Brown was emerging as a fierce advocate for Sistergirls in Sydney. Kooncha attended Tranby Aboriginal College in the early 1990s. She recalls one class when a male student did not realise that she was trans so she gave an impromptu presentation about herself rather than her prepared topic. It was an enlightening experience for the entire class. In 1994, a friend of Kooncha's invited her to attend Anwernekenhe I. Out of that meeting, she became a proxy Sistergirl representative on the Anwernekenhe Working Party. She also did some volunteer work for ACON on its Aboriginal projects, which was her entree into Sistergirl advocacy.

In September 1999 Kooncha was appointed ACON's first Aboriginal and Torres Strait Transgender Sistergirl Project Officer.[47] With the support of her co-workers, Kooncha's role was very much hers to shape. She delivered workshops to service providers, travelled to regional New South Wales as part of the state's Sexual Health Network team, and yarned with local Sistergirls wherever she travelled. She also visited incarcerated Sistergirls. Generally they were housed in men's prisons unless they had had gender affirmation surgery, which led to many challenges. Corrections NSW would contact Kooncha if a Sistergirl inmate was on suicide watch so that she could offer support.[48] She later wrote that her role entailed being a contact point for Sistergirls, client case work, developing health promotion strategies, and training and producing resources to meet the needs of Sistergirls.[49] Kooncha did not limit her advocacy and work just to Sistergirls, though: 'I was working [with] gay men, Sistergirls, lesbians, straight people, because the way we saw it was it was everybody's business when we were talking about HIV and sexual health.'[50]

Kooncha left ACON around 2009 and has continued to support Sistergirls, Brotherboys, and queer, gender-diverse and cis Aboriginal and Torres Strait Islander people. For years she was night manager at an Aboriginal women's refuge, supporting homeless Aboriginal women and children. She was also on the board of the Gender Centre for a few years.[51] In all of these roles, it was her willingness to engage with and empower others that made her successful.

Changing conversations in Indigenous communities

Leaders like Vanessa Smith and Kooncha Brown in the 1990s and 2000s laid important foundations around Sistergirl organising. The conversations began primarily within Aboriginal and Torres Strait Islander LGBTIQ+ communities and the sexual health sector. By the 2010s, a new generation of Sistergirl, Brotherboy, queer and gender-diverse advocates were joining the conversation and targeting the broader LGBTIQ+ and cis-hetero communities.

Lisa Taylor is a Worimi Sistergirl who grew up in Newcastle and in some ways fell into advocacy. In 1998 she was working three casual jobs: doing relief work at the Gender Centre, at SWOP as a receptionist, and in an Indigenous mentor role for Juvenile Justice. Through her work at SWOP, she was invited to attend the 1999 Magnetic Island Sistergirls Forum. She describes the event as 'magical', but it would be another decade before she really came into the fold of Sistergirl activism and advocacy. Around 2009, Vanessa Smith reached out to Lisa and asked her to become the Sistergirl representative on the Anwernekenhe National Aboriginal and Torres Strait Islander HIV/AIDS Alliance. Lisa served in this role for six years, mostly responding to queries and holding meetings to educate service providers. She remembers one specific example when there was a problem in Wilcannia, New South Wales:

> There were some Sistergirls in Wilcannia that were trying to access a domestic violence service and the domestic violence service had a trans policy. They accepted trans women, but ... didn't recognise the Sistergirls as being trans. They thought they didn't look trans enough. So yeah, it was about going in and educating them that not all Sistergirls are going to look the way that ... but they're still trans and they're still under that umbrella.

In 2012 Lisa founded what would prove to be an enduring legacy: a closed Facebook group. It went through a few renditions and name changes but is now known as Sistergirls & Brotherboys + Gender Diverse Mob, and has over 2400 members. During her six years on Anwernekenhe, Lisa pushed hard for greater Brotherboy visibility and representation. At first she met resistance, as some of the other committee members thought that Brotherboys were just butch lesbians rather than men. Lisa persisted, and in 2015 organised a Brotherboy panel at the Anwernekenhe conference. She also worked with Brotherboys to prepare a documentary featuring their stories.[52]

Of course, Brotherboys themselves were also pushing for greater visibility and support. Dean Gilbert is a Wiradjuri trans man who worked in numerous jobs before he transitioned, including running an Aboriginal cultural centre in Wagga Wagga and many years as a prison officer. Employment in the carceral system was challenging because there were so many Aboriginal prisoners, including many who were relatives of his. He witnessed harassment of trans inmates, including Sistergirls. For example:

> I remember one of the Sistergirls came in, they had to be strip searched. And they didn't have the full operation, so they still had their penis and things like that. And just the way the staff would carry on: 'Oh, they've got a big one' and 'Oh, watch it swing' and 'Come in here and let's do …' You know. And then you'd have staff with cameras.

In 2003 Dean moved to Sydney and met Sean Taylor, a trans man who had previously worked at the Gender Centre. Sean told Dean about a popular trans men's group hosted at the Gender Centre: FTM Australia. Dean had no understanding at all about trans men, but went to the meeting to learn. It was an eye-opener: 'When I went and met all these guys, I'm thinking, "Oh fuck!" You know? "This is me. This is me." Like, wow! Ask me today am I still a male trapped in a female's body? No. I don't feel I was born in the wrong body, but I like the idea of being a male. I'm more comfortable.' That was the beginning of his transition journey.

Dean took a role at ACON in its Aboriginal program supporting inmates in Corrections NSW. Almost straightaway he met Kooncha Brown and, as he recalls, 'Kooncha looked at me, and this is the first day I ever heard the saying of Brotherboy. She goes, "Oh hello, you're a Brotherboy." And I went, "What? What's a Brotherboy?" Didn't know.'[53] That was the beginning of Dean's journey of learning and then educating others about Brotherboys. Kooncha was particularly keen for Dean to step up and advocate for Brotherboys, and recalls telling him, 'Dean, I can't talk on behalf of Brotherboys, and neither can gay men or lesbians, so you've got to get out there and talk too. You've got to start educating our mob about Brotherboys and bringing that topic into play.'[54]

Since the mid-2000s, Dean has consistently been a voice of advocacy and support for Brotherboys. He has facilitated workshops, met with service providers, been a contact for younger Brotherboys and done public appearances. In 2014, he and Kai Clancy featured in a short video on YouTube called 'Brotherboys Yarnin' Up'.[55] In 2015, the National Indigenous Television (NITV) program *Living Black* did a special episode that was a short documentary about Brotherboys featuring Dean, Kai and Taz Clay along with relatives and other advocates.[56] Dean worked closely with Lisa Taylor and was one of the people on the Brotherboy panel at the 2015 Anwernekenhe conference. He is also involved in broader advocacy for Aboriginal rights, particularly in the carceral and foster systems.

Dean is fortunate that he has significant support from his family and Wiradjuri mob, but he ran into some difficulties trying to change his name and gender on his Aboriginality papers registered with the NSW Aboriginal Land Council. First he was told he could not do it, then that it would require an affidavit, letters from psychiatrists and other supporting evidence confirming he had had gender affirmation surgery, and that only then would a committee of the NSW Aboriginal Land Council consider it. Dean refused to go through such a tedious, bureaucratic process—not to mention one imposed by the colonial system. Instead, he went to his local Aboriginal land council where, as he explains, 'The people know me there. Met up, spoke to the chairperson, spoke to other people, other women— three of them to be exact. Told them that I want a change and they went yep, fine. Gave me my papers straight away.'[57]

Dean also found great support among Wiradjuri Elders. Given there are so many gendered cultural practices, he wanted to ensure that he followed proper protocols within the community. This long but important quote explains what happened:

So, I approached the Elder women and told them that I feel very much that I've got two spirits. Even though I've come from [deadname], she's still part of my life. All those experiences and whatever, and I'm finding a lot of guys will just try and wipe that side of it. But not me personally. So, I told them about my journey and that I would like to go from women's business into men's business. How do I go about it? Because some people see it as taboo. Some male Elders won't accept it. And it was really hard to navigate. But they were good. The old women, they said, 'Yep, it can be done.' It's been around for hundreds of years, apparently. The only thing is, like, I can't practise any of the women's stuff that was taught to me by my mother—stories, certain paintings, certain designs, things like that. My nephew, who teaches Wiradjuri language in the schools and the university and that, I've actually gone under my nephew's wing around with men's business. It's going out bush and doing some men's stuff. Dancing, doing the men's dance from women's dance.[58]

Dean often shares this experience with other Brotherboys who contact him, many of whom are worried about rites of passage and how to transition from women's business to men's business.

Unfortunately, not all Aboriginal and Torres Strait Islander mobs have been as welcoming. This phenomenon is a bit more pronounced in the stories of Sistergirls from remote communities. At a recent Sistergirls and Brotherboys panel at an AusPATH conference,

Crystal Love Johnson and Brie Ngala Curtis both said that those who had been through initiations in their sex assigned at birth found it harder to be accepted in their affirmed genders. Reflecting on her own experience as a Tiwi and Walpiri person, Crystal recalls: 'My father knew at the time of my initiation that I was a sistergirl. They seen me with long hair, so feminine, still playing with the girls—I came out long before I was initiated. My father thought that putting me through men's business would change me, but it didn't.'[59]

Although some of the cultural challenges have been more pronounced in remote communities, they can affect Aboriginal and Torres Strait Islander trans mob everywhere. Jeremy Anderson, for instance, was raised in the Pilbara and Perth and has also lived in Brisbane and Sydney. He came out as trans at age twenty-six and began living as a man. While he was studying a Bachelor of Contemporary Australian Indigenous Art at Griffith University, he was learning about trans people in Aboriginal culture and was open about this in his study group. He recalls a discussion about the didgeridoo, an instrument traditionally played by men only:

> A girl actually did an interview with an Aboriginal guy, and she was like, 'Do you think that Jeremy should be able to play the didgeridoo?' And he was like, 'Yes, I think he should because he identifies as a man.' But then there was a lot of people in the group that were a bit more old-fashioned, and one woman was like, 'No, you can't play didgeridoo, you have ovaries. That's against our culture.' And that kind of made me feel quite rejected from that group in a way, because I was like, where do I fit in with this whole mob?[60]

In a 2016 short documentary film called *Jemima to Jeremy*, Jeremy expresses anxiety around how Aboriginal communities respond to his gender:

> If I come to these people in this community and say I am transgender, what are they going to say to me? 'Well, you can't

participate in your culture because you're not a man.' I fear they may not see me as a man or a woman. That's the response I've gotten from some people in Aboriginal communities, so it makes me fearful to try and connect with that side of myself, because what if I get rejected.[61]

Jeremy specifically mentions that gathering with other Sistergirls and Brotherboys and trans mob was vital for him to feel comfortable with himself. He was one of about eighty-five Sistergirls and Brotherboys who attended a retreat on Wurundjeri country (Melbourne) in November 2016 called Kungah. In the Ngarigu language from alpine Victoria, kungah means 'gathering'.[62] Dean Gilbert was also at Kungah and summarises how powerful it was: 'There was a lot of yarning, a lot of the Elders coming in, accepting us, and then they'd have little workshops … and it was about us getting together, being able to talk about our journeys and the problems that we're facing. And just seeing, just being in their presence.'[63] About half the attendees were Sistergirls and half Brotherboys, with people from as far away as the Tiwi Islands. Jeremy remembers it as an empowering weekend, with one Brotherboy yarning circle that Dean facilitated having a particular influence on him:

He took us into this Brotherboy circle, and we were like: 'This is our secret men's business and we're going to try and think of a totem for us.' And things like that. It was really cool to have that knowledge and even know what Brotherboy was. When I came back from that conference, I felt so confident in myself and my identity and I went back to uni and was like, 'This is what I know, and I'm here, and I'm proud.'[64]

Sistergirl, Brotherboy, queer and gender-diverse trans mob have worked hard to educate Aboriginal and Torres Strait Islander communities about gender diversity. In the early 2000s, when new men's and women's shelters on the Tiwi Islands would only house people based on their sex assigned at birth, Crystal Love Johnson wrote to the funding body about the need for trans-inclusive shelters. That started a wave of work. First, she held meetings with the Strong Men's Group and Strong Women's Group to educate about gender diversity. Then she lodged a complaint in the NT Anti-Discrimination Commission to force the club on the Tiwi Islands to allow people to use toilets in their affirmed genders. In 2012 she was elected to the Tiwi Islands Regional Council—a significant victory for trans rights and visibility. Crystal still encountered people on the council who would misgender and deadname her, but she consistently spoke out. She recalls saying at a council meeting:

> When I am on this table, my hat is Crystal and I am a female and I represent my people. My people voted me in here, not you mob. You are the same as me. People voted us here to fight for our people's rights and to make our community a better place. When I am out of the room, you can call me Crystal. You have to respect me. These are the laws.[65]

In Central Australia, Brie Ngala Curtis, Rosalina Curtis and the local trans mob worked closely with non-Indigenous ally and youth worker Starlady to set up the organisation Sisters & Brothers NT in 2014. Brie Ngala Curtis says that the trigger for founding the organisation was yet another suicide by a young Sistergirl experiencing discrimination. Sisters & Brothers NT served as a peer support network, with a website that offered resources and referral services. The organisation partnered with the Northern Territory AIDS and Hepatitis Council (NTAHC) to produce a series of posters targeting Sistergirl health. Organisers Brie, Rosalina, Starlady and Crystal also successfully lobbied for the Alice Springs Women's Shelter to welcome trans and queer people. Brie recollects that the organisation's launch at Alice Pride in 2014 was a great success, with senior Elders attending to give a welcome to country. One of the uncles was a cisgender lawman who lamented that so many

LGBTIQ+ members of the Aboriginal community left because they were not accepted.[66] Unfortunately, when Brie and Starlady left Alice Springs a few years later, Sisters & Brothers NT ceased to operate.

The advocacy and visibility of people like Dean Gilbert, Crystal Love Johnson, Brie Ngala Curtis, Rosalina Curtis, Kai Clancy, Taz Clay, Kooncha Brown, Vanessa Smith, Lisa Taylor, Jeremy Anderson and many others have changed conversations around trans(gender) in Aboriginal and Torres Strait Islander communities. Indeed, Dean reflects on the ripple effects of the Brotherboys episode of *Living Black*:

> When we did that documentary and I did speak about my Elders getting behind me and helping me transition from women's business into men's, then other documentaries started coming around about other Elders getting behind there. And I think that's what we've got to keep doing. So, we're bringing the Elders into the [twenty-first] century too and start challenging some of the traditional ways and beliefs.[67]

Trans people of colour: Visibility and advocacy

Just as Aboriginal and Torres Strait Islander trans mob had to educate both Indigenous and non-Indigenous communities, so too have other trans people of colour had to navigate intersectional identities. For some, this meant advocating for inclusion within migrant communities; for others, it meant pushing for rights in their countries of origin. Common across these examples was fighting racism and pushing for greater inclusion within mainstream trans and LGBTIQ+ organisations.

Katherine Wolfgramme is a great example of a prominent trans person whose advocacy has traversed Australia and the world. She did not set out to be an activist: it was out of sheer necessity that she first spoke up for trans rights. In 1997 Katherine wanted to travel overseas with her partner and only had a Fijian passport. She did not want to travel under her deadname, so she contacted the Fijian embassy about changing her name. Staff at the embassy refused to let her assume a woman's name, so she travelled to Canberra to force the issue. She recalls:

> I wore a Chanel suit and pearls, and I had my hair blown out. I looked amazing. And I walked into the embassy, the sliding doors opened, and I was at the front of the reception, and the woman bowed, literally—like, I've always been a bit imperious. And she bowed, and she was like, 'Hello, madam. Welcome. How can I help you?' [laughs] And I said, 'You keep hanging up on me.'

Katherine eventually met with a senior official who said they could not let her change her name to a female one, but after some sweet-talking on Katherine's part, the official agreed to submit the paperwork. A few weeks later a response came: the Fijian solicitor-general would not approve the change, and Katherine would have to meet with him in person.

Katherine went to Fiji on an emergency passport, but the solicitor-general would not meet her. She came from a well-connected family, so she contacted an uncle and told him she was in Fiji and revealed that she was now a woman. The uncle met with her and she explained her dilemma. Katherine feared that if she could not change the name on her passport, she would be strip-searched whenever she travelled. The uncle agreed that was unacceptable and made a few calls to help Katherine secure a lawyer. Eventually she did meet with the solicitor-general, and she remembers it like this:

> He said to me, 'What did you do this for? Why did you do this?' And I said to him, 'Well, because I've always been a girl inside. This is how I feel.' And he said to me, 'Well, you look like a woman to me', and he signed me off. [laughs] And with that,

I became the first transgender woman legally granted a female name by the Fijian Government. And thereafter, all trans women after me have been allowed to change their names.

Katherine describes the entire period as quite traumatic, and says she has only recently begun to speak about it because she recognises the significance of what she achieved for all trans people in Fiji.[68]

In the 2000s there was more visible advocacy for trans rights within Australian multicultural communities. Geeta Nambiar migrated from Malaysia to Sydney in 1998. She lived as a gay man and felt she would only be ready to transition if she had the support of other South Asian people. In 2006 she founded a social support network for South Asian LGBTIQ+ people that she called Salaam Namaste. The group hosted a social event at least once a month where attendees could share challenges they faced with their families and communities. Geeta estimates that the group quickly grew to well over 100 people from a mix of Sri Lankan, Indian, Pakistani and Bangladeshi backgrounds. They entered a float in the Sydney Gay and Lesbian Mardi Gras parade, which was an opportunity for Geeta to be glammed up in a sari. That was an important turning point for her personally: 'I still remember going to the mirror and saying, "This is who I really am. And this is what I must be. Because I'm not a gay person. I'm not a gay man. I'm a woman. And I need to do something about it." Then I started cross-dressing.'

Almost all members of Salaam Namaste were lesbian, gay or bisexual, with gay men especially represented. While Geeta hoped it would be an affirming environment for her as a trans person, it turned out not to be. Many of the group members were Muslim and struggled enough as gay men; affirming or being trans was a bridge too far for them. She explains: 'The people that I interacted with, the people who dressed me up, refused to transition. Because they think that you can only cross-dress; you shouldn't transition because then you're going against God.' Geeta turned to a therapist and found the affirming care she needed. When she eventually came out as trans to the other members of Salaam Namaste, it did not go well:

> Believe it or not, most of them did not accept me. They didn't want me transitioning. They wanted me to be the same gay man who is running this organisation, or the support group. And I said, 'This is me. I can't be in this group anymore. I would like to hand this over to someone else who's comfortable and wants to do that.'

One good outcome of Geeta's experience in Salaam Namaste was that another trans person from Bangladesh transitioned a few months after her. Around the same time that Geeta left Salaam Namaste, a new South Asian LGBTIQ+ group started called Trikone. Geeta's involvement with it was only tangential, but she participated in a forum where she talked about her experience as a trans woman. As with Salaam Namaste, the majority of people involved in Trikone are gay men, but Geeta notes that the leadership is welcoming and accepting of trans people.[69]

Chantell Martin migrated to Sydney from Aoteaora New Zealand in 1984 and was a sex worker for much of the 1980s–2000s. Her entree into trans advocacy came through her employment at SWOP in 2010. Chantell had recently gone through rehab and a friend told her that SWOP was looking for a transgender outreach worker. Chantell applied and was successful, and she held that role until she became co-CEO of SWOP in late 2022. Over the years her job has entailed going to Tranny Lane to hand out clean syringes and condoms, supporting trans sex workers through rehab, meeting with sex workers in prisons, and sitting on numerous advisory committees to advocate for the rights of all sex workers.[70]

Sasja Sÿdek is a proud Indigenous Singaporean trans womxn of colour.[71] Sasja, who migrated to Melbourne in early 2000, is a fierce advocate for trans womxn—especially trans womxn of colour and sex workers. One of her first involvements in advocacy was as a speaker for the 2019 Red Umbrella campaign to stop violence against sex workers. The event proved successful and Sasja was subsequently an invited guest on 3CR radio to discuss her involvement. The hosts invited her back to talk about Trans Day of Remembrance. After several more guest stints, she was offered the opportunity to co-host the weekly program *Behind Closed Doors*, which explores the lives and experiences of sex workers. While of course sex workers come from all walks of life, Sasja makes a conscious effort to include trans and cis womxn of colour, elevating their voices and perspectives to the centre of discussions. She has since left *Behind Closed Doors* and joined *Queering the Air* at 3CR, where her advocacy has expanded beyond sex worker rights. Sasja has also contributed a chapter to *Nothing to Hide: Voices of Trans & Gender Diverse Australia* and is a board member of transfemme.com.au, which works to end violence against trans womxn.[72]

'Aezra' moved to Brisbane from Malaysia in 2012 to commence a PhD on Islam–Asian values. She had been living as a woman for years, but under Malaysian law could not change her name or identity documents to her affirmed gender. It was a challenge to migrate to Australia still under a male name and identity. Aezra connected with ATSAQ in Brisbane and learned that under Queensland law she could change her name by deed poll; she subsequently updated all of her Australian documentation to her affirmed gender. Aezra applied in Malaysia to change her name, but authorities rejected the application because it was contradictory to Sharia law. This was a strategic move on Aezra's part: in 2016 she applied to migrate permanently to Australia as an asylum seeker and used the rejection of her name application as one piece of evidence of the persecution she faced in Malaysia as a trans woman. The Department of Home Affairs approved her application in 2019, and in 2020 she applied for Australian citizenship.

In Brisbane Aezra promoted trans rights and inclusive, intersectional feminism through groups such as Socialist Alternative at the University of Queensland, and campaigned for left-wing political causes at the multi-faith centre attended by many Muslims. She argued that supporting LGBTIQ+ rights was tied to other important causes, such as immigration, the environment and human rights. For a few years she was also involved in ATSAQ, but she left that group because some members expressed problematic views towards Indigenous Australians. Aezra has been a board member of the Forcibly Displaced People Network, ensuring that trans rights were part of the conversations.

Some of Aezra's Muslim friends rejected her when they learned she was trans, including one housemate, who moved out. Aezra also recalls a conversation with someone who wanted to join a women-only gym and was upset to learn that it allowed trans women. Aezra is not afraid to call out homo/bi/transphobia among Muslims, particularly as Muslims are also a marginalised community in Australia. What she says to other Muslims is along the lines of 'You expect people to actually accept Muslim people in Australia ... but you cannot extend this kind of acceptance [to trans people]. How could you be so oblivious?'[73]

Other trans stories highlight how marginalisation within both Muslim and mainstream Australian communities has driven people to homelessness. Carolina was an Iranian refugee who undertook the harrowing journey to Christmas Island in a crowded boat of about 150 people and was then sent to immigration detention. The Australian Government recognised that as a trans woman her safety would be at risk if she were kept with the other single people, so they permitted her to stay with the families. Authorities later relocated her to Adelaide, and while Carolina describes the guards there as kind, she also says it was like a gaol. She was eventually granted refugee status and released into Australia as a permanent resident.

Living at the intersection of two marginalised communities left Carolina to face discrimination on two fronts. She explains: 'Since living in Australia the last five years, it's not easy for me to find somewhere to live. They either don't like that I am transgender or they don't like that I am a Muslim and a refugee, or they don't like the mixture of those things.'[74] In two housing placements, the other Muslim housemates drove Carolina out. On another housing placement a Vietnamese housemate tried to force her to perform sex work.

Carolina eventually found support from the Melbourne-based Australian GLBTIQ Multicultural Council (AGMC). This organisation was founded in 2004 with the aim of researching, advocating and promoting social inclusion of LGBTIQ+ people across diverse faiths and cultures. Over the years it has held educational forums for local governments and service providers, and hosted cultural celebrations of pride. AGMC's leadership lobbied for years to become a member of the Federation of Ethnic Communities Councils of Australia. Committee member Maria Pallotta-Chiarolli describes how AGMC members 'invaded' plenary panels to ask questions about LGBTIQ+ issues, and eventually the AGMC was invited to join the federation.[75]

Trans and queer Blak, Indigenous and people of colour have had mixed experiences with mainstream LGBTIQ+ and trans organisations. Some groups, like the Gender Centre, particularly from the late 1990s onwards, were more inclusive of people of colour. The Gender Centre employed Aboriginal and Torres Strait Islander staff and had representatives on its board. Other groups refused to see difference, which Sistergirl Vanessa Smith explains is a form of racism:

They [Perth LGBTIQ+ groups] just don't support Indigenous people. I can remember when I first started out twenty-odd years ago white gay men. I was confronted by a white gay man who said, 'Why do youse have to be a standalone?' and I said, 'What do you mean?'

'Well, what's so different about you? Aren't our issues all the same?'

I said, 'Well, you're exactly why we need to be standalone.'

He said, 'What do you mean?'

I said, 'Well, your attitude tells me that you're ignorant and you might be racist, therefore we have to overcome that hurdle before we can get to the table to talk about the issues that impact us.'

We have extra load to carry. It's been like that for a while. The 'Well, I can't see ...'—that's controlled by very upper-middle-class white gay men who want to control it for themselves.[76]

Latoya Hoeg, a fa'afafine woman who grew up in Samoa and Aotearoa New Zealand, recalls attending a transgender forum in Victoria sometime in the late 1990s. She found that the other participants, predominantly white/European trans women, were polite but judgemental of her as a sex worker.[77] Such examples show that more often than not, it was not so much blatant hostility towards difference as it was that trans individuals and groups who adhered to white, middle-class values and ideas of respectability tended to exclude those who did not fit those norms—including, often, Blak, Indigenous and people of colour.

Trans people of colour and their allies have used online platforms to promote their culture and acceptance. In early 2011, a group of trans womxn of colour began a YouTube channel called TS Chit Chat. Lily Chang, originally from Malaysia, founded it because vlogs were in vogue at the time. Sasja Sÿdek explains:

TS Chit Chat's first video content was a show about cooking. The filming took place in a hotel where Lily filmed an Indonesian trans womxn who was visiting from Sydney. Gradually we started filming on other topics, from surgeries to fashion to lived experiences. TS Chit Chat started to get responses from the public. They made contact with us, and before you know it we were filming content focusing on trans and gender-diverse advocacy. We were invited to interview local trans advocates and international trans celebrities.[78]

Sasja is one of three founding members of Trans Sisters United, a not-for-profit community group that creates projects that benefit trans and cisgender women. The group began in 2019 when Sasja, Rebeckah Loveday and Miss Katalyna attended a short film on Sistergirls and Brotherboys at the Melbourne Queer Film Festival and went out to dinner afterwards. They decided to form Trans Sisters United to promote trans visibility, particularly for Sistergirls from the Tiwi Islands and trans womxn of colour.[79] Sasja, Rebeckah and Miss Katalyna later founded Trans Pride March Melbourne and hosted a Trans Pride Concert at Federation Square in Narrm (Melbourne) during Midsumma Festival in 2022, showcasing trans performers from Indigenous and multicultural backgrounds.

Performance is a common site of visibility for queer and trans Blak, Indigenous and people of colour. From 2010 to 2019 the Miss Gay and Miss Transsexual Pageant Australia, held in Melbourne, featured a majority of contestants from Asian backgrounds. In 2020 its name changed to the more inclusive Miss Trans Australia. In 2019, Melbourne's LGBTIQ+ bookshop, Hares & Hyenas, a site of trans inclusion since the 1990s, hosted a special 'Trans Voices of Colour Panel' and several artist performances on Trans Day of Visibility. Amao Leota Lu explains why performance is important for her:

I come from a community that's quite supportive of me being Fa'afafine, which is a culturally recognised gender in Samoa. And, as part of my culture, I love to dance and perform. I'm able to bring a different kind of artform to the table by acknowledging my own Indigenous Pasifika culture in what I do. I ride on the shoulders of great people, my own ancestors.[80]

Mama Alto is a jazz singer and cabaret artist of mixed Javanese, Scottish and Irish heritage who has long championed rights and visibility for trans people. Reflecting on the popularity of the arts for LGBTIQ+ people of colour, she says:

Considering these multiple marginalities in the lives of queer POC [people of colour], we can begin to understand the appeal of the arts as a mode of communication, a site of expression, and a medium of community building. In sharing stories: perspectives, questions and explorations, the arts can create empathy, nurture connections, build understanding, foster diversity and confront inequality while giving a platform for empowerment.[81]

From 2021 to 2022, Mama Alto's repertoire expanded when she served as CEO of Transgender Victoria.

Fighting from the margins

If there is one common thread through this chapter, it is how trans and queer Blak, Indigenous and people of colour have faced multiple marginalisations. Even though there are long traditions of gender diversity from time immemorial in Australia and overseas, the impacts of colonialism and imposition of gender binaries have made it challenging for many trans and queer Blak, Indigenous and people of colour to find acceptance in their communities. Within mainstream Australia, including LGBTIQ+ organisations and subcultures, trans and queer Blak, Indigenous and people of colour have confronted everything from overt racism to services and structures that are not cognisant of their distinct needs.

From the 1990s and especially in the new millennium, new activists and organisations emerged to challenge transphobia and racism and to elevate the voices of trans and queer Blak, Indigenous and people of colour. Of course, the outcomes have always been uneven across cities, organisations and time periods. Yet perhaps two recent examples are indicative of how far the LGBTIQ+ community has come. In 2017 a group of thirty Sistergirls from the Tiwi Islands had a prominent float in the Sydney Gay and Lesbian Mardi Gras parade, generating significant media interest,[82] and in 2019, the showcase event at Melbourne's Midsumma Festival was *Gender Euphoria*, a night of performances by ten trans and queer artists from diverse cultural, Indigenous and racial backgrounds. The show was

Harry Crawford's murder trial in 1920 became a media sensation. Crawford was convicted and sentenced to death. The sentence was commuted and Crawford was released in 1931; they died in 1938.

Karen Chant in a fabulous frock at the 1955 Artist Ball in Sydney. Courtesy Karen Chant.

Trans showgirl, singer and performer Susan Le Gay toured with cabaret singer and actor Tony Monopoly around 1969. Susan died in 2019. Courtesy Susan Le Gay.

Left: Trans man Bobbie Nugent (right) and an unidentified woman outside Sammy Lee's Latin Quarter Restaurant, Sydney, 1960s, unidentified photographer. Courtesy AQuA.

Right: Pioneering trans activist and Brisbane businesswoman Toye de Wilde. In 1989 she was the first openly trans person to run for office as an independent. Courtesy Toye de Wilde.

Portrait of Noelena Tame, c. 1982, unidentified photographer. Noelena founded the Australian Transsexual Association around 1978. Courtesy AQuA.

Carmen Rupe, Phyllis and Roberta Perkins at 'The transsexual and society seminar' presented by the Australian Transsexual Association and assisted by the Wayside Chapel, 9 December 1981. Courtesy AQuA.

WHAT DOES THE TRANSVESTITE SEE AS THE MOST IMPORTANT NEEDS?

Only a transvestite realises how strong is the compulsion to express the female part of his personality and the feeling of isolation this creates. Our needs are simple:-
- Understanding by the community to accept us as we are.
- Greater understanding by the medical and related professions. When the "problem" arises advice should be aimed to help. Directions on how to get in touch with organisations which can assist, such as SEAHORSE, rather than being told to forget all about it (the "cold shower" syndrome) as is often the case now.
- The most important need is for family and friends to understand us when they discover we are transvestites; that we have been since birth. We have not changed, only the knowledge of our transvestism has come out into the open.

THE SEAHORSE CLUB OF AUSTRALIA

SEAHORSE is a non profit voluntary organisation dedicated to assisting transvestites and their families throughout Australia. SEAHORSE was formed in 1972 and since then has been active in presenting the role of the heterosexual transvestite in society. The club, through the media, counselling services, government agencies and self help groups seeks to make the community more aware of the "problems" we face. It has initiated a number of research projects and regularly holds public seminars on the subject. SEAHORSE has an active membership of six hundred and regularly publishes and distributes information (which will be forwarded on request), and is established in all State capitals.

For further information contact SEAHORSE through the National headquarters:-

        SEAHORSE
        PO Box 341 Royal Exchange
        SYDNEY NSW 2000

Or the Regional group below:-

THE SEAHORSE CLUB OF AUSTRALIA has prepared this booklet to give some understanding of the subject of transvestism. For a variety of reasons transvestites are one of the most misunderstood groups in Australia today. We have listed the questions we are most frequently asked and hope this brief explanation may be of help as a reference. For any further information please contact us and we will be only too happy to assist.

TRANSVESTISM - A QUESTION AND ANSWER GUIDE

WHAT IS TRANSVESTISM?

In strict clinical or medical terms it is described as a behaviour pattern or personality expression characterised by the compulsion to wear clothing of the opposite sex. However as transvestites we believe it cannot be summed up quite as simply as that. We feel we are best described as "FEMIPHILES", those who love all things feminine.

We MUST at times be able to express our feminine GENDER as this is the only way we can experience part of our character and personality.

WHAT CAUSES TRANSVESTISM?

The cause is still unknown despite extensive research carried out in Australia and overseas. There is no apparent link with transvestism based on hormonal, genetic or hereditary factors. It does appear more related to childhood upbringing and the relationship between child and parents. Almost all transvestites are aware of it well before the age of puberty.

Left: An early brochure from Seahorse NSW, Australia's first known trans organisation founded in 1971 by Rosemary Langton.

Right: SS *Tiresias*, the Tiresias House float at the Sydney Gay Mardi Gras Parade, 1988. Photo by Bob Buckley. Courtesy AQuA.

Roberta Perkins speaking at the Australian Transsexual Association protest, Manly, Sydney, October 1982. Photo by Paul van Reyk. Courtesy AQuA.

Left: Vicky Harris and Phyllis McGuiness outside the Court of Petty Sessions, Sydney, 24 September 1982. Photo by Gerrit Fokkema. Courtesy AQuA.

Right: Gina Mather and Kristine Johnson, leaders of ATSAQ from 1993-2022. Courtesy Kristine Johnson.

Left: Julie Peters and Kayleen White at 2001 Melbourne Pride March. Courtesy Julie Peters.

Right: Shan Short, Aidy Griffin and then-member for Bligh, Clover Moore, at a benefit for the Trany Anti-Violence Project, August 1993. Photo by Tom Luscombe and reproduced with his permission.

TransWest member Mx Margaret Jones at the 2003 Perth Pride Parade. Courtesy Mx Margaret Jones.

Longstanding Sistergirl activist Aunty Vanessa Smith (1951-2022). Photo by Raymond Zada. Courtesy Lisa Taylor.

Sistergirl and Brotherboy advocates Dean Gilbert and Lisa Taylor. Courtesy Lisa Taylor.

Jasper Laybutt, Max Zebra-Thyone and Dale Hewinson at the Boys Will Be Boys Conference, August 1992. Courtesy Jasper Laybutt.

Socialite and fashionista Lady Paula Howard attending Oaks Day in 1978. This dress won Lady Paula a special prize for 'Sheer Elegance'. Courtesy Greer McGearey.

Left: Poster promoting a 2008 show organised by Salaam Namaste. Courtesy Geeta Nambiar.

Right: *Man into woman…the trans-sexual experience* was a documentary with a limited run in Sydney, Canberra and Melbourne. Sabina, 1982. Courtesy AQuA.

Above: Australian Democrats members Natasha Stott Despoja, Julie Peters and Meg Lees, c. 1999. Julie was the first openly trans person to run for the federal parliament in 1996. Courtesy Julie Peters.

Above right: Vote 1 for Crystal Johnson – Wurrumiyanga Ward, Tiwi Islands Regional Council. Printed by Andy Ewing, 7 March 2012. Courtesy AQuA.

Right: Jonathan Paré featuring in a brochure promoting the Victorian AIDS Council Sexuality and Youth Forum, 1995. Courtesy Thorne Harbour Health.

Left: Longstanding trans advocates Jenny Scott and Katherine Cummings (1935–2022) in 1994. Katherine's 1992 memoir *Katherine's Diary* won the Australian Human Rights Award for non-fiction. Courtesy Jenny Scott.

Right: South Australian trans activist Marie-Desiree D'Orsay Lawrence, who died in 2018. Courtesy Jenny Scott.

A Gender Agenda stall at Canberra's 2011 SpringOUT Fair Day. Courtesy Peter Hyndal.

Top: Members of the International Foundation for Androgynous Studies and TransWest march in Perth's 2002 Pride Parade. Courtesy Mx Margaret Jones.

Middle: FTMen–SA (now TransMascSA) at Adelaide's 2017 Feast Pride March. Courtesy Zac Cannell.

Bottom: Author with multiple generations of Gender Centre leadership, March 2023. From left to right: Noah Riseman, Jesse Hooley, Norrie, Elizabeth Riley, Eloise Brook.

so popular that it returned for additional performances later that year at the Melbourne International Arts Festival and in a new form at Sydney WorldPride and again at the Arts Centre Melbourne in 2023. These celebrations of diversity and inclusion are emblematic of the fact that queer and trans Blak, Indigenous and people of colour will no longer be left out of the conversation.

6
TRANS FIRSTS

RACHAEL WALLBANK HAS had a long legal career advocating for the rights of trans people. Social change has been her objective, and the law has been her tool. In 1994 she wrote: 'Every time one of us "stands up" in this way—with considered judgment and dignity—the larger community is advised to positively shift its perception of each one of us.'[1] Rachael's point had significant resonance: even one individual being visible can educate and influence better attitudes towards trans people. It is for this reason that trans pioneers—the 'firsts'—are so significant in the history of trans rights.

It is a brave historian who is willing to call the 'first' of anything. There is always the risk that another person will come forward saying that they accomplished the same thing earlier, or another historian may one day uncover other examples. Yet it is important to recognise the pioneers who challenged the status quo, changed conversations, faced risks, experienced ridicule, and ultimately laid the ground on which future leaders and community organisations built. This chapter explores groundbreaking moments in trans visibility in pop culture, literature, religion, sport, the professions and politics from the 1970s to the 2000s. It also explores the first known organised groups for trans men in the 1990s. Sometimes the pioneers had good experiences that set a positive tone for future trans people in a particular field or industry. Other times the 'first' faced significant scrutiny and even bullying, harassment and prejudice. Whether positive or negative, each first set a precedent—and this too had upsides and downsides. The 'first' at something often became seen as a template that others would follow, meaning later trans people who did not follow the template had to break new ground again. Perhaps most importantly, these firsts show that trans people did not suddenly appear in the new millennium but, rather, have been making contributions to Australian society over a long period of time.

Cultural figures, 1970s–80s

During the 1970s magazines like *Cleo* and *Forum* occasionally ran stories about trans people, and this trend continued in the 1980s–90s in magazines such as *Australasian Post*, *New Idea* and *Woman's Day*. Coverage often had shocking headlines designed to mock, and in *Australasian Post* in particular the stories sometimes included sexualised imagery of trans people. Yet contained within the magazine and newspaper texts were important stories about trans people living their authentic selves in a society that was overwhelmingly hostile. These magazine and newspaper stories also show that trans people came from all walks of life, whether they be a race car driver, a housewife or a retired member of the Australian Defence Force. Sociologist Dave King's analysis of British media coverage of trans people in the 1970s found that 'the press has introduced its readership to (amongst others) the sex change cop, the sex change bride, the sex change sailor, the sex change prisoner, the sex change burglar, the sex change vicar, sex change surgeons, sex change conferences, sex change tennis'.[2] This pattern reverberated in Australia and highlights the first public examples of trans people in different parts of Australian cultural life.

Fashion

Lady Paula Howard was a trans woman who occasionally popped up in the media for her fashion sense. She was born in Wales in 1912, attended Cambridge University, served in the British Army in World War II, where she did female impersonation as part of entertainment for the troops, and then moved to South Africa. She had a global profile in the niche trans scene of the 1960s, appearing on the cover of *Transvestia* magazine in 1964 as well as in mainstream newspaper reports. It was in South Africa that she first took an interest in horseracing and partook in the women's fashion that featured so prominently there.[3]

In the early 1970s Lady Paula left South Africa, first moving to Aotearoa New Zealand and then settling in Melbourne in 1973. She was an early and longstanding member of Seahorse Victoria and presented full time as a woman, including attending numerous social and cultural functions. Her autobiography—which by her own admission includes quite a few embellishments—notes that a friend spotted her on television curtseying to Prince Charles and Princess Diana in the receiving line at the Melbourne Concert Hall in 1983. Lady Paula annually attended the Melbourne Cup Carnival dressed in late Victorian and Edwardian period pieces. In 1978, a dressmaker friend made an extraordinary Edwardian dress for her that, on the famed 'Ladies Day' (Oaks Day), attracted the attention of racegoers and television crews alike. Lady Paula twice won a prize at the Oaks Day fashion contest for sheer elegance.[4] In 1990, an article in *Truth* scandalously described a trans socialite from Toorak who regularly entered the Fashions on the Field and even won one year. The person in that article was identified as 'Lady Sylvia', but the informants were protecting the person's identity and it was likely Lady Paula Howard.[5] Lady Paula died in 2000.

Another trans fashion pioneer was designer Julianne Deen. In 1991 Deen won the Silhouette Award in Australia's Gown of the Year competition, and in 1993 three of her entries were finalists in those awards. Deen designed leather gear for Tina Turner, cloaks for Liberace, outfits for Elton John and the costume for a one-man show by Barry Humphries. Although she transitioned in 1986, she did not publicly reveal that she was transgender until 1993. She also said that before she transitioned she was a pop star with seven hit records and national number ones, though she would not reveal her pre-transition identity.[6] Julianne Deen passed away in 2015.

Television

As detailed in Chapter 2, Les Girls and its headline act, Carlotta, were household names in the 1970s. Carlotta had a short stint on the popular soap opera *Number 96*. This program was known for pushing boundaries around sex and sexuality, including featuring Australia's first openly gay television character. Producers approached Carlotta in late 1972 to appear in a few episodes as a showgirl whom one of the principal characters fell for and then discovered that she was trans. The episodes went to air in February and March 1973, and the producers successfully kept Carlotta's identity a secret, crediting her as Carolle Lea.[7]

Still, substantive trans television storylines would remain few and far between. One 1977 storyline from the program *Pig in a Poke* included a sympathetic subplot with two trans women who faced family hostility, desired gender affirmation surgery, navigated relationships with men and performed as showgirls.[8] In the late 1980s and early 1990s, the ABC program *GP* three times had storylines about trans people, which were all sympathetic. The most prominent was the 1990 episode 'Crossover', about an AMAB pharmacist caught dressed as a woman. The pharmacist approaches the GP clinic desiring gender affirmation surgery while facing ostracism from family and the community. The pharmacist attempts suicide and only survives when the doctor finds him, leading to a reconciliation with the family and commencement of the medical transition process.[9] Actor Peter Whitford played the role and conducted substantial research for it, meeting with trans people including John Hewson and Katherine Cummings.[10]

Film

Trans characters in Australian films were rare in the 1970s–80s and usually entailed a minor cameo such as a showgirl. For instance, Carlotta played a showgirl in the Alvin Purple film *Naked Bunyip* and a choreographer and showgirl in *Dead Easy*.[11] While living in the United Kingdom, Susan Le Gay had a small role in the 1975 Joan Collins film *The Monster* (also known as *I Don't Want to Be Born*); she did a performance involving cracking a whip and appeared in a musical number with other call girls at the end.[12]

In the 1980s there were a few Australian documentaries about trans people that all portrayed them in a sympathetic light. In 1983 the ABC program *Open File* aired 'The Call of the Frock', which explored the challenges facing trans women. Among the featured people was someone going through the final stage of the real-life test before gender affirmation surgery, as well as Roberta Perkins and several trans women attending the Australian Transsexual Association support group. The documentary paid a great deal of attention to the medical model of transsexualism, and the film ended with 'Liz' going into surgery and then waking up in recovery.[13]

Journalist Mike Willesee was the interviewer for *Tommy Doesn't Exist Anymore*, which aired on Channel 9 in 1985. This documentary followed the struggles of three trans women and their families. Two of them had only recently come out as trans, with interviews showing great shock and a sense of failure on their families' part. The third person had been living as a woman for twenty years and was in a relationship with a man. Much of the film (and many critics) focused on the family reactions and their attempts to be supportive even though they could not understand the trans people's lives.[14]

One documentary intended for television could not find a station willing to screen it and subsequently went into limited cinematic release: *Man into Woman*. This 1983 feature covered a breadth of challenges confronting trans people; among the participants in the film were Noelena Tame and Roberta Perkins, and it even included trans man Tony (discussed in Chapter 4).[15] The film did not screen for long—two weeks in Sydney, Canberra and Melbourne—and the main daily newspapers refused to review it. It only received attention from critics in the gay and lesbian press, one of whom noted that it 'deserves support and we need the education'.[16] Unfortunately it faded into obscurity, not to be resurrected until late 2020 for a special screening by the National Film and Sound Archive during Trans Awareness Week.

A few experimental short documentaries appeared in the 1990s—including *F2M* (1992) and *Men Like Me* (1994), both about trans men—but it would not be until the 2000s that there was a revival of feature-length trans documentaries. One of the more prominent was *Becoming Julia* (2003), which followed Julia Doulman early in her transition journey. Julia expressed how surprised she was that people in her hometown of Bathurst were accepting of her as a trans woman going through transition: 'I've told quite a lot of people [I'm trans] and the reactions haven't been as bad as I thought, but I think the test will be when they see me as a female. It is very confronting to a lot of people. And, you know, no one knows more than me how difficult it is to adjust to it.'[17] In 2015 Julia would be a panellist on the ABC program *Q&A*, discussing her experience as a trans woman and the discrimination she encountered.[18]

The most groundbreaking film with a trans storyline was the 1994 hit *The Adventures of Priscilla, Queen of the Desert*. The plot centres on two drag queens and a trans woman who travel from Sydney to Alice Springs in a pink bus named Priscilla. The lead character, played by Hugo Weaving, was based on longstanding Sydney drag queen Cindy Pastel (who is not happy about how much money the film has made for many people but not for her).[19] Along their journey they encounter prejudice, challenge bigots in fights and drinking contests, and perform musical numbers with extravagant costumes in outback pubs and a remote Aboriginal community; and one character finds love. The main actors were cis men, with Terence Stamp playing trans woman Bernadette.

Priscilla is one of the most successful Australian films of all time and became an Australian icon. The closing ceremony of the Sydney 2000 Olympics even included a large Priscilla bus with Cindy Pastel on top and a procession of trans women and drag queens led by Carlotta. Katherine Wolfgramme was one of the participants, and she remarks: 'Words could never express what it was like. I've done some big things in my time, but this is the biggest thing I've ever been a part of.'[20] In 2006, *Priscilla* even spawned a musical. Although the film and all its spin-offs have been widely welcomed for their positive portrayal of gay and trans figures, over time there has also been criticism of the casting of cis straight men in the lead roles. In April 2022, Adelaide trans icon Vonni was cast as Bernadette in the upcoming Gold Coast production of the musical, marking the first major Australian production with a trans person in the role.[21]

Literature

From the 1950s, a small number of trans people began to write and publish autobiographies about their life journeys. Some overseas books that reached Australian audiences were autobiographies by Christine Jorgensen (1967), British travel writer Jan Morris (1974) and British model–actress April Ashley (1982).[22] Importantly, several trans people recollect these books because, just like the media reports and documentaries that featured trans people, they represented a site of visibility and gave a name and language to their internal struggles.[23]

The first books to depict Australian trans people were artistic and ethnographic studies. In 1976, British photographer Barry Kay published *The Other Women*—a series of photographs he had taken on visits to Sydney. The pictures showed trans women from all walks of life, including those who identified as transvestites, transsexuals and drag queens. They highlighted trans women in suburbia, the showgirl scene and the workplace, at the beach, in hair salons and in their ordinary lives.[24] Although not specifically about trans people, the 1977 edited collection *Drag Show* included interviews with two members of Seahorse, who explained the significance of the group and gave their identities as 'transvestites'. It had chapters by psychiatrist Neil Buhrich and legal expert George Zdenkowski that explained medical and legal issues around 'transvestism'.[25] As noted in previous chapters, a few years later Roberta Perkins' *The 'Drag Queen' Scene* (1983) became the first published ethnography of trans women in the Kings Cross/Darlinghurst area.

The first Australian-authored trans autobiography came from an unlikely source. Peter Stirling's life narrative *So Different: An Extraordinary Autobiography* (1989) describes his upbringing as a woman, though he always looked masculine and felt different from others. Stirling joined the Women's Royal Australian Air Force but was kicked out for being in a lesbian relationship. He had a child, but persistent problems and changes to his body took him on a journey through the medical system that culminated in a diagnosis of Klinefelter syndrome (having XXY chromosomes), which is now recognised as an intersex variation. Stirling went on hormone treatment and transitioned, making him both intersex *and* transgender.[26] In one interview, he explained that he wrote the book to help him cope with the anguish of his life, particularly now that his daughter was twenty-one and knew the truth. He hoped that he would not face rejection: 'I tell myself I don't care what people think but in my heart I know how hurt I will be if people turn away from me.'[27]

Garnering much more attention and accolades was Katherine Cummings' memoir, *Katherine's Diary*, published in 1992. Katherine was born in Scotland in 1935 and raised in Kiribati before moving to Australia during World War II. She did two years of national service in the Royal Australian Navy, trained as a librarian in Canada, worked in the United States for a few years and then returned to Australia. While in the United States she came into contact with Virginia Prince's trans groups and forged important friendships with trans people from around the world. In 1986 she decided to transition and live full time as a woman.

During Katherine's two years of the real-life test, a friend suggested that people might be interested in learning about her experiences and encouraged her to reach out to ABC Radio National's *Health Report*. Katherine wrote to the program's host, Dr Norman Swan, and sent a few sample scripts that piqued his interest. For the next two years, she appeared on the show about once a month to talk about her physical and emotional changes. These popular segments were dubbed 'Katherine's Diary'; twice they were nominated for a Human Rights Award. Katherine also received mail, to which she always responded. She explains: 'I have a file of letters written to me after the book and after the broadcast. One very amusing one said, "Why are you writing my life and pretending it's yours?" Because there were so many similarities between us, the way we cope with them.'[28]

The radio segment and its popularity inspired Katherine to write her life story. She wrote a little every day when she came home from work, and at last *Katherine's Diary: The Story of a Transsexual* was published in 1992. It met with great acclaim, winning the Australian Human Rights Award for Literature (Non-fiction). Katherine then became much more involved in the trans community, networking with activists across the country. She went on to work at the Gender Centre as editor of its quarterly magazine, *Polare*, and in support and advocacy roles. She also ran for election to the Australian Parliament for the Australian Democrats in 1998 (discussed in more detail later in this chapter). Sadly, Katherine Cummings passed away in early 2022 at the age of eighty-six.

By the late 1990s and early 2000s more trans Australians were writing their life stories, with several self-publishing. The new millennium and especially the period since 2010 has seen greater public interest in trans issues and the growth of commercially published trans memoirs, but it would not be until 2022 that a mainstream publisher released an anthology featuring all trans writers, many of them Blak, Indigenous and people of colour: it is titled *Nothing to Hide: Voices of Trans and Gender Diverse Australia*.[29] All of these texts owe a great deal to the early pioneers who wrote their life stories in eras when the law did not even recognise their affirmed genders.

Religion

Religion is perhaps a surprising site of trans visibility. In July 1981, Australian newspapers reported about an Anglican priest at St Bartholomew's Church in Burnley, Melbourne who intended to transition. The priest had for years felt like an outsider and only recently embraced her identity as a woman after seeing a television documentary about trans people. She announced her retirement after eight-and-a-half years at that parish on health grounds. With the new name Nerissa Marshall, she was quoted in the press as stating, 'I would have been prepared to serve my parish as a woman and I believe I would have been better at it now because I have faced the reality that I am a woman … But the Church has never been prepared to accept anything, although I don't really want to rubbish the Church.'[30]

Nerissa dressed and presented as a woman for the final few months before her retirement and, according to newspaper reports, parishioners accepted her. After her last sermon, she commented to the media: 'Two-thirds of my people are elderly. They weren't threatened. They said, "We're not going to call you Father any more, we'll call you Vicar."'[31] One letter to *Truth* asserted:

> The real issue is that the church refuses to change its narrow-minded and intolerant attitudes to such important issues as the rights of women, birth control and homosexual law reform. The parishioners of St. Bartholomew's Church were asked if they would accept Nerissa as their minister. The answer was yes. This showed the parishioners have a greater genuine love and tolerance of people than the clergy.[32]

Anecdotally, there were other religious leaders who quietly left their roles in order to transition, but it would not be until the 2010s that another Australian trans cleric was in the public spotlight. Born in Durham, England, Josephine Inkpin was ordained as an Anglican priest in 1987 and completed a PhD in Theology in 1996. She realised that she was trans around 2000 when she read a story about the first openly trans Anglican priest in the United Kingdom, but was not yet ready to live her authentic self. She and her wife, also an ordained Anglican priest, moved to Australia in 2001. In 2017, while teaching at a theological college in Brisbane, Jo came out as trans. Her colleagues were supportive and the archbishop sent a letter to the staff at the college explaining that she was transitioning. A small number of conservatives were unhappy, but the general reaction was positive.

Word spread about Jo's transition. A priest in Adelaide contacted her and told her that she, too, was trans and had transitioned quietly years earlier. Jo remembers the priest saying, 'For years I've thought I'm the only one and now I know I'm not.' She remarks, 'So that was a big thing for me, to realise that there are other people and that there's all this buried history.'[33] The media, too, found out about Jo and was interested. She agreed to appear on ABC-TV's *The Drum* in February 2018, which presented a positive story about 'Australia's first transgender priest'.[34] Although Jo had the support of the Anglican Archbishop of Brisbane, some conservatives within the Anglican Church opposed her continuing ordination and made it difficult for her and her wife to feel secure in their roles or certain of being able to move to other roles in the future. Jo eventually made the decision to move to the Uniting Church, where she believed she could flourish better. In March 2021 she was formally inducted as minister of Sydney's Pitt Street Uniting Church.[35]

In addition to her regular duties as a teacher and parish minister, Josephine Inkpin has been a strong advocate for trans inclusion and affirmation within religious communities. She has a blog called *Blessed Imp* where she writes about queer and trans people of faith, and runs the website *Trans Spirit Flourishing*, which provides scholarly theological resources and writings about gender diversity, spirituality and faith. Jo started the Queensland chapter of Equal Voices, a national alliance of LGBTIQ+ Christians that advocates for equality within civil society and various Christian denominations, and she has been chair of its national board for a number of years.[36] Jo recognises the significance of her role as Australia's first openly trans priest to continue practising, and hopes that her visibility and activism can challenge the loud conservative visions of Christianity that have for so long marginalised LGBTIQ+ people.

Trans professionals

In 1994 Roberta Perkins published the results of Australia's first government-funded study exploring the social, economic and health status of transgender people. Among the sample of 146 transgender people (mostly women) surveyed, 97 per cent had worked in white-collar or professional jobs before their transition. Yet post-transition, only 36 per cent were still employed in those occupations.[37] In 1996, ATSAQ president Gina Mather described a trans man who lost his job as a jumbo jet pilot, and mentioned police and lawyers who also became unemployed after they transitioned. But it was not just professionals affected by discrimination. Gina said: 'We had a situation not so long back where one girl was working for a fast food chain quite successfully for eighteen months, and, unfortunately, two customers who recognised her came in and told the management about her. The next day she had her marching orders. She had no right of recourse because she was a transgender.'[38]

Before anti-discrimination laws, those trans professionals who transitioned and retained their jobs were fortunate to have supportive employers. Julie Peters is one such example. She transitioned in 1990 while working at the ABC in Melbourne and came across a small amount of transphobia, but the majority of her colleagues and some of her supervisors supported her.[39] Others who retained their jobs often worked in specialised fields where clients would still pay for their services. A high-profile example is Professor Abbie Hughes, a distinguished researcher who transitioned in 1987 while director of the National Vision Research Institute within the Victorian College of Optometry.[40]

Three high-profile lawyers transitioned in the 1990s. One was a barrister whose transition inspired a nasty article in Sydney's *Daily Telegraph* in 1996; she subsequently sued for defamation.[41] The second person, Raena (Ray-na) Lea-Shannon, was an associate for a Sydney entertainment lawyer. An article in the *Weekend Australian* noted that she had feared coming out because she could lose her job, but had been fortunate that her employer was incredibly supportive. Moreover, the clients were mostly accepting, perhaps in part because so many were already a bit 'alternative' working in the entertainment industry.[42]

The third lawyer is Rachael Wallbank. She identifies as 'female' rather than as 'trans' or 'transgender', but acknowledges her transsexual background where it is relevant to do so. She transitioned in 1994 and subsequently channelled some of her legal practice into supporting what she refers to as people living with transsexualism—which she understands as a biological phenomenon and an example of human diversity or difference in sexual formation. In the early 1990s Rachael offered free legal advice at the Gender Centre for two hours each week. She also regularly wrote articles for *Polare* discussing topics that affected trans people, such as child custody and legal recognition.

Perhaps Rachael's most lasting mark on the trans community was her work on the 2001–04 legal case *Re: Kevin*. This case involved 'a man of transsexual background'—as he was described in the case—and his wife, who sought a legal declaration of the validity of their marriage in Australia. Kevin had undergone genital reassignment surgery (as it was called at the time, excluding phalloplasty) and had obtained a NSW birth certificate that referred to him as a male. In 1999 he and his partner Jennifer married, but the Commonwealth

Government later contested the validity of the marriage on the grounds that Kevin was AFAB and therefore it was a same-sex marriage.[43] Indeed, as early as 1988 after South Australia passed the *Sexual Reassignment Act*, the federal government maintained that a person's sex assigned at birth was the only valid sex for the purposes of the *Marriage Act*.[44]

Rachael Wallbank represented Kevin and his wife Jennifer as the case went to the Family Court, and on the appeal brought by the Commonwealth Government. In October 2001 the trial judge ruled in Kevin and Jennifer's favour, upholding that Kevin was, for all legal purposes including marriage, a man. In a new precedent that overturned *Corbett*, Justice Richard Chisholm ruled: 'the words "man" and "woman" when used in legislation have their ordinary contemporary meaning according to Australian usage. That meaning includes post-operative transsexuals as men or women in accordance with their sexual reassignment.'[45] He also found that:

in my view the evidence demonstrates (at least on the balance of probabilities), that the characteristics of transsexuals are as much 'biological' as those of people thought of as inter-sex. The difference is essentially that we can readily observe or identify the genitals, chromosomes and gonads, but at present we are unable to detect or precisely identify the equally 'biological' characteristics of the brain that are present in transsexuals.[46]

Rachael subsequently presented numerous university lectures in Australia, Hong Kong, the United States, the United Kingdom and Europe and appeared in several television programs, including an *Australian Story* episode called 'Marriage Matters'. She has published several legal articles and book chapters about the ramifications of *Re: Kevin* and the legal and human rights issues affecting people who experience diversity in sexual formation and gender expression.[47] She also continued to work as a family lawyer, taking part in other cases to support trans people's rights, including the rights of adolescent Australians to have their affirmed sex (as referred to in the relevant cases) recognised for medico/legal purposes. For instance, she appeared for the applicant parents in the Australian Family Court case *Re: Bernadette* where, in June 2005, the first court order was made approving stage one hormones (puberty blockers) for an Australian adolescent who had affirmed her female sex.[48]

Other trans professionals ran into significant opposition in the workplace. Though probably not the first trans teacher, Lee Oliver found herself the subject of a media firestorm in 1996. A front-page *Herald Sun* story reported that Oliver, a teacher at Rosebud Secondary College on the Mornington Peninsula, was going through transition when she was subjected to a disciplinary hearing. The hearing was over her taking drama students to see a play that had male nudity, but there were always undertones that this was cover for discriminating against Oliver for being trans. Parents were angry about the employment of a trans teacher, and even Victorian premier Jeff Kennett said he would not want his children 'subjected to' Oliver during her transition.[49] Although this was before the passage of anti-discrimination protections in Victoria, the Australian Education Union stood by Oliver and threatened to go to the Equal Opportunity Commission if action were taken. Oliver was indeed dismissed, though the Education Department insisted it was not because she was trans but due to a pattern of ongoing behaviour that included sexually inappropriate content, jokes and swearing at students.[50]

In July 2003 another row erupted when the *Herald Sun* ran a cover story headlined 'Sex Swap Cop'. It reported that Victoria Police had received an application from its first openly transgender candidate. This person was not the first trans police officer in Australia, though earlier cops who transitioned had generally had to leave the force.[51] This time there were anti-discrimination laws in place. The headline the following day, 'Revolt on Swap Cop', reported that a survey of readers showed that they opposed transgender people joining the force.[52] Victoria Police, the state government, Premier Steve Bracks and Equal Opportunity Commission Victoria all stood by the anti-discrimination protections (though the opposition leader expressed his disapproval). The following year, the *Herald Sun* continued to refer to the transgender police officer as the 'sex-swap cop' when reporting her graduation from the Police Academy.[53]

As more 'first' trans people came out in the workplace—either by transitioning or applying for jobs—their experiences ranged from full acceptance through to derision, being pushed out of the workforce and being denied employment. Workplace discrimination is still rife, though it is harder to prove. Indeed, as the cases above show, employers may find other grounds to challenge or terminate trans employees, or trans job applicants may be rejected on grounds such as 'cultural fit' or without ever knowing whether it was because they were trans.

Australian Defence Force

There is a surprisingly long, hidden history of trans people enlisting in the armed forces. Veterans of World War II later joined groups like Seahorse and the Chameleon Society of Western Australia, and trans activists like Gina Mather (ATSAQ, Queensland) and Marie-Desiree D'Orsay Lawrence (South Australia) were veterans of the Australian Defence Force (ADF). Yet for most of the ADF's history, trans people had to hide their authentic selves and did not transition until they left the force. In the year 2000, the ADF even brought in an explicit instruction declaring that trans people who wished to transition would need to discharge.

Just before Christmas 2009, Captain Bridget Clinch came out as transgender to her chain of command and then her colleagues. In March 2010 she received a termination notice in line with ADF policy. She challenged the termination in the Australian Human Rights Commission, which entered into a conciliation process with the ADF. Meanwhile, another trans woman in the Royal

Australian Air Force, Amy Hamblin, was also outed as transgender and announced that she intended to challenge the policy.

In September 2010 the pressure applied by the Australian Human Rights Commission paid off: the ADF rescinded the order banning trans people from transitioning while serving. This marked the effective end of the trans ban in the ADF. The next few years were a policy vacuum, and openly trans members consistently had to challenge existing practices. They set precedents on everything from access to hormones, uniforms and toilets to Defence Health payments for gender affirmation surgery. By the mid-2010s, handbooks and online support groups facilitated by trans Defence members were making it easier for new trans recruits and other transitioning members.[54]

Trans people and sport

Although debates about trans people in sport exploded in the late 2010s, there is a long history of trans people participating in sport. The topic first received attention in 1976 when American tennis player Renée Richards was outed as trans and made global headlines. There was even an Australian angle to Richards' story: the Lawn Tennis Association of Australasia declared that it would henceforth require female players to produce a sex certificate, and some Australian players, including Margaret Court, announced that they would not compete against Richards.[55]

Capitalising on the Richards publicity, *Truth* ran a cover story headlined 'Aussie's Bizarre Life in Country Town: Sex Swap Sports Girl Tells All'. It was about Leigh Varis, a transgender woman who played basketball, softball and netball and had 'won complete acceptance as a top player', even being a finalist in the first Pilbara Sportsperson of the Year awards. Leigh noted that early on some teammates and spectators had sniggered, but this had changed, in part because of her feminine appearance.[56]

The first significant public debate about trans women in Australian sport was in April 1991 when media reported that there was a trans woman competing in athletics competitions. That athlete was Ricki Coughlan (then Carne), though her identity remained anonymous at first. As coverage continued, the debate followed what continue to be the main tropes about trans women in sport in the present day: their physical ability or 'unfair advantages' and whether they really were women. NSW Athletics and Athletics Australia consistently supported Ricki's right to compete, though often in a backhanded way by downplaying her skills or saying she did not really look like a 'transsexual'.[57]

In December 1991 the tabloid *Truth* learned Ricki's identity, so to front-foot the story she outed herself to the media. Most of her direct competitors supported her, but some organisations, including the Women in Sport Foundation, vociferously opposed the inclusion of trans people in women's sports. As Ricki explains: 'Their big problem was they could stand there and have a line-up, and they would say, "Pick the transgender athlete", and they wouldn't because I looked the same as all the other athletes because I fit into all of the athletic norms.'[58] Ricki's case was treated as a one-off, and there were no efforts to develop a clear policy within Athletics Australia or other Australian sporting bodies.

The next Australian sport with a transgender competitor attracting media attention was golf. In December 1997, Women's Golf Australia (WGA) announced that five trans women had come into national contention and the organisation was preparing a policy on transgender inclusion. WGA was the peak body for amateur golf, while Australian Ladies Professional Golf governed the professional sport. WGA's proposed policy would permit trans women to compete if they had gender affirmation surgery and were legally recognised as female.[59] WGA did not adopt that policy until early 1999, suggesting it generated significant debate within the association and the golf community.

The big trans figure of Australian golf was Mianne Bagger, who first appeared in the media in June 1999 when the Adelaide *Advertiser* reported that she had won an amateur title. Mianne's gender identity was not news to people who knew her: she had always been open about being a transsexual woman. Amateurs like Mianne could compete in their affirmed gender but under Australian Ladies Professional Golf's policies they would be excluded at the professional level.[60] For the next five years Mianne continued to play around Australia as an amateur, even representing the South Australian state team. She was not allowed to turn professional because international rules since the late 1980s had stipulated that a player must be 'female at birth'. In late 2003 the president of WGA invited Mianne to compete in the 2004 Women's Australian Open. Mianne contacted a friendly journalist at the *Sydney Morning Herald* and shaped the narrative to great effect. She focused on the importance of dialogue to end misunderstandings, acceptance from other players, and the fact that, to her knowledge, she did not have any unfair advantages.[61]

After the Australian Open, Mianne wrote to organisers of professional tours in Europe, Australia and the United States requesting that they amend their rules so she could compete. Meanwhile, the International Olympic Committee changed its rules in 2004, introducing what became known as the 'Stockholm consensus' (because the policy was designed at a meeting of the IOC Medical Commission in Stockholm in 2003): 'sex reassigned' women could now compete if they were legally recognised in their affirmed gender and had gender affirmation surgery, and if at least two years had passed since surgery.[62] Mianne credits this reform as instrumental in convincing the Ladies European Tour to change its eligibility rules. In November 2004 she qualified to play on that tour, and later that month she was granted permission to apply for membership of the Australian Ladies Professional Golf tour.[63] Mianne continued to play professional golf until 2016, though she never won a tournament.

Trans men, too, were likely participating in sport for a long time, but the first public case was a 25-year-old named Will who wanted to play Australian Rules football in 2009. Will met with officials from the Victorian Country Football League to discuss eligibility and to ensure that he would be protected from abuse. The chief executive of the league responded favourably: 'If he's legally and medically certified to be a male, from that point on that's all that matters. We're very impressed by him ... he's just a guy who wants to have a game of footy.'[64] The Victorian Country Football League earned accolades from the state sports minister and both the state and federal human rights commissions for handling Will's case so respectfully.[65]

In the 2000s and 2010s more trans women, trans men and non-binary people joined local sporting clubs across a range of sports. Trans people interviewed for this book have played golf, rugby league, rugby union, athletics, Australian Rules, soccer and field hockey, just to name a few. Their experiences were mixed: most felt acceptance from their own clubs, but how opposition treated them varied from complete acceptance through to hostility and vilification.[66]

Trans people in politics

If visibility could shift attitudes, then one place to garner public attention was through running for political office. The first openly trans candidate in Australia was Toye de Wilde (then Tanya Wilde), who ran as an independent candidate for the Queensland state parliament in the 1989 Merthyr by-election. The inner-Brisbane electorate included the popular gay area Fortitude Valley and other residential areas such as New Farm. Toye's candidacy came out of a public meeting where members of the LGBTIQ+ community expressed that they were tired of being ignored by politicians. Toye already had a significant profile in Brisbane's LGBTIQ+ community: she had been involved in the Queen's Birthday Ball since its founding; had managed several gay bars since the 1960s; was an active member of the Queensland Association for Gay Law Reform, which fought to decriminalise homosexuality; and was a founding board member of the Queensland AIDS Council. The by-election was an opportunity to be heard, so Toye volunteered to run as an independent, knowing it would generate publicity.

Toye's candidacy made headlines across Australia, and she took advantage of the press to talk about the challenges confronting Queensland's LGBTIQ+ community. Several journalists wanted to focus on her trans identity, including asking inappropriate questions such as what her deadname was, but she consistently refused to answer. Instead, she would say, 'I'm not talking about me; we're talking about the situation [in Fortitude Valley].'[67] She commented in a *Woman's Day* article that she had heard all sorts of jokes:

> The one about me not knowing whether I'm Martha or Merthyr, the one about me not being able to decide on my preferences and the one about why they call it queens' land. It's all good fun and I don't care about the jokes. As long as people are starting to sit up and take notice and talk about me, perhaps they will also start listening to what I have to say.[68]

Toye focused especially on social issues, and emphasised that the challenges facing the gay community, such as police harassment, affected other oppressed minorities too. Her approach had an impact, with a *Daily Telegraph* article specifically noting that her policies made her 'more than a sideshow performer'.[69] Toye had meetings with Labor candidates and even the opposition leader, later Queensland premier, Wayne Goss. Toye recalls: 'When I was doing the by-election campaign, Wayne Goss' wife came up to me and said, "Keep doing what you're doing."'[70] In the end she received only 540 first preferences, or 3.14 per cent of the vote. Still, her candidacy kept gay law reform on the agenda—it passed the following year—and set an important template for future trans political candidates. As a pioneering trans advocate in Queensland and Australia, in later years Toye was the recipient of numerous awards and recognition from state premiers and governors, though she considers affirmation from the LGBTIQ+ community to be the most important recognition.

The first openly trans person to run for the federal parliament was Julie Peters, who was an Australian Democrats candidate in the 1996 federal election. In 1995 Julie attended a forum in Fitzroy and spoke to one of the organisers, who said, 'Well, you're very articulate; why don't you sign up to be a candidate?' The Democrats intended to run candidates in all House of Representatives seats, so Julie put her name down for Batman in inner-northern Melbourne. She describes the nomination process as rigorous: she faced an interview panel and was asked about Democrats policies and assessed on her personality. The final question was whether she had any skeletons in her closet that may embarrass the party. She advised them that she was transgender, and recalls the committee chair's response: 'We don't believe that's an issue and we won't discriminate on those grounds. We will assess you in all the other criteria, but thank you for telling us.'[71]

Julie's candidacy hit the headlines in November 1995. During a six-week period she did seven television, twenty-five radio and forty other media interviews. On one day she did fourteen interviews, mostly on radio. Much of the press referred to her as the 'transsexual lesbian' and, as with Toye de Wilde, many questions focused on her identity. Julie was more open than Toye to discussing her life as a trans woman, because it was an opportunity to educate the public. *New Weekly* ran a sensationally headlined article entitled 'Vote for Me: I'm a Transsexual Lesbian'. Yet the contents of the article were quite respectful and it allowed Julie to share her transition journey in her own words. She concluded: 'I guess I see politics as a way of expressing a social conscience. I believe I have dealt with my personal issues and now I want to try to make a difference.'[72] In later interviews, she tried to shift the conversation away from her identity to the Democrats' policies, local issues and the disillusionment that many voters felt in the safe Labor seat. In the end she won just over 6 per cent of first preferences, which marked a 2.5 per cent increase from the previous election.

Also in 1996, Julie made history by being the first openly trans person to run for the Victorian Parliament, for the upper house seat of Monash. That election was only a month after the federal election, so she was busy bouncing from one campaign to the other. Her campaign challenged the privatisations of the Kennett government along with cuts to services and lack of accountability.[73] She garnered 6.5 per cent of first preferences in Monash.

By 1998, Julie was vice-president on the Australian Democrats' Victorian executive. For the 1998 federal election she was nominated to be campaign manager for forty-one candidates for the House of Representatives. She also ran as the candidate in Melbourne Ports, where she garnered almost 8.2 per cent of the primary vote—again an increase from the previous election.[74] Julie again ran in Monash for the upper house in the 1999 Victorian election, increasing the vote to 7.6 per cent. She also ran for a position as councillor in the City of Melbourne. By 2001, Julie felt the Democrats had lost credibility with the electorate. She was disillusioned, having twice not been preselected for a spot on the Senate ticket, which was the Democrats' most realistic chance of electing candidates. She left politics and returned to work at the ABC. In 2016 Julie completed her PhD at Deakin University, published in 2019 as the book *A Feminist Post-Transsexual Autoethnography: Challenging Normative Gender Coercion.*[75]

Julie Peters was actually one of three trans people who ran for the Australian Democrats in the 1998 federal election. One did not identify as trans but, rather, as a woman because she had undergone gender affirmation surgery in 1989. She ran in a safe Liberal seat and had been stealth—private about her trans identity—before being outed during the election campaign.[76] Katherine Cummings was the third trans candidate. She ran in the inner-western Sydney seat of Grayndler—a safe Labor seat held by a young man who was seeking re-election after his first term and years later would become prime minister: Anthony Albanese. Kate recalls him as very nice and positive during the election campaign. At one event in Marrickville, the Labor Party had built a platform from which Albanese was making an address. He spotted Kate in the crowd and, as she recalls, 'He said, "Oh, there's Katherine Cummings. She's standing for the

Democrats" ... He said, "Come on up. Tell them what you think." So I was up there on the platform with him telling him what the Democrats' policies were. He didn't have to do that. Just a nice guy.' When asked about the media reaction to her candidacy, Kate recalls that most of the coverage was respectful and it often did not even mention that she was trans.[77] She won 5.70 per cent of first preferences, which was an increase of .72 per cent from the 1996 election.

By 2001, the political tide had turned for the Democrats. There were already divisions within the party, and its decision to support the introduction of the goods and services tax became its death knell. That said, given the election cycles, it would not be until 2008 that the final members of the party departed the Commonwealth Senate. In the 2004 federal election, Jenny Scott ran as a Democrats candidate for the Senate from South Australia. Party representatives approached her to be fourth on the Senate ticket because of her profile as a campaigner for LGBTIQ+ rights. Jenny's candidacy did not receive as much publicity as Toye's or Julie's, but there was some coverage in the Adelaide *Advertiser*. One article titled 'Transsexual Democrat Gives Voice to Equality' quoted Jenny as saying, 'Somebody has to put their hand up, to combat, what I believe, are lies told about the gay and lesbian and transgender community.'[78]

Jenny's campaign went into a bit of a tailspin when the Democrats did a preference deal with Family First. She was caught off guard and disappointed that the party would do a deal with a right-wing party opposed to LGBTIQ+ rights and other social causes that Jenny had long championed. She faced personal attacks and, as she wrote in a reflection after the campaign,

in the face of personal and direct criticism I had to question myself, consider my position and in the end continue ... With all that going on, possibly the most depressing aspect of the campaign was the perception among some—not all—but some that as soon as you stand for public office your motivation is personal ego.[79]

In the end, the Democrats did not poll well in the 2004 election—though interestingly, despite being fourth on their ticket, Jenny had more below-the-line first-preference votes than candidates two and three combined.[80]

Two years later, Jenny agreed to run for the Democrats in the SA state election for the seat of Mitchell in Adelaide's inner south-western suburbs, making her the first openly trans person to run for the SA Parliament. Responding to an email questioning why she was standing even though her chances of winning were essentially nil, Jenny wrote:

I believe that if only those who had a certain chance of victory ever stood we would not have a democracy at all. Everybody deserves the right to participate in the democratic process. As a woman identified transgender person I belong to an extremely marginalised and maligned group, but that does not exclude me from the democratic process no matter how much some believe it should. I like to think that I bring choice or at least another point of view for people to consider. I may not gain one vote but maybe in five, ten or twenty years time another transgender or similarly marginalised person will stand for election and because of my stand they maybe will not be seen as quite so different.[81]

In the end the result was rather poor, but Jenny has never regretted running in the seat.

In the 2016 federal election, Martine Delaney made national headlines when she ran for the Greens in the seat of Franklin in southern Tasmania. As outlined in the next chapter, Martine already had a profile as a trans rights activist from the early 2000s. One traditionally hostile campaign stop was a candidates forum run by the Australian Christian Lobby. Martine stayed for supper afterwards, and recollects: 'I was sipping on a cup of tea and eating a scone when two little old ladies came up to me and said, "Our husbands wouldn't come tonight because they wanted to watch something on television, but we're going home and we're telling them to vote for you.'" Martine notes that party politics could be nasty; while she has no regrets about running, she would not do it again. In the end, she finished with 13.35 per cent of the vote—the highest personal vote for any Tasmanian Greens candidate in the 2016 election.[82]

There is one site where trans candidates have been successful: local government. Leigh Varis-Beswick—mentioned earlier in this chapter for her sporting prowess—was born and raised in the West Australian mining town of Kalgoorlie. She left when she was fourteen to escape sexual abuse and lived in the Pilbara and, later, Perth before moving back to Kalgoorlie in 1991. She was a sex worker and became owner of the Langtrees 181 brothel, which she ran for twenty years. Leigh's foray into politics came after the local council denied her application for a licence to expand her brothel. In a 2000 documentary, she explained: 'I sort of sat there and I thought well these people aren't doing very well for this town, or this city, so I decided then and there that I was gonna put my hand up and I was gonna try and get into Council and see if I could help.'[83] In 1999, Leigh made history as the first trans person in Australia elected to local government, at the Kalgoorlie-Boulder Council. She had one more claim to fame: in 2001 she began to offer guided tours of one of her brothels—the first tours in the world of an operating brothel.[84] Leigh retired in 2011 and, sadly, passed away in 2020 after a battle with cancer.

Significant though Leigh's victory was, over twenty years later trans representation in all levels of government is sorely lacking. There has still never been a trans member of any state, territory or federal parliament—though two senators (Louise Pratt and Janet Rice) have had trans partners. This is in contrast to other democracies like the United States and Aotearoa New Zealand, where trans people have been elected to multiple levels of government, albeit in small numbers. Māori Labour Party politician Georgina Beyer in 1995 was the world's first openly trans person elected mayor (in Carterton), and in 1999 she became the world's first openly trans member of parliament. Beyer's election made news in Australia, and she even visited Australian LGBTIQ+ communities in 2002. Beyer passed away in March 2023.

In Australian state, territory and federal elections there have been trans candidates, primarily as independents, Greens or other minor party members. As noted in Chapter 5, in 2012 Crystal Love was the first Sistergirl elected to the Tiwi Islands Regional Council. At the time of writing, there are only two openly trans people in any Australian government: one Green in Tasmania's Clarence City Council and one independent in Victoria's Colac Otway Shire Council.[85] In his book *The Children of Harvey Milk*, Andrew Reynolds argues that elected LGBTIQ+ officials are important both as symbols and because they can set pro-inclusion/equality agendas. Just having LGBTIQ+ people at the table makes other lawmakers become more familiar and comfortable with LGBTIQ+ people and issues.[86] On this front, Australia still has a way to go in electing trans people into the halls of council and parliament.

New visibilities: Trans men

As other chapters have shown, there have always been trans men, though until the 1990s they were mostly invisible in medical and public discourse. Some notable exceptions include Bobbie Nugent, who was well known on the butch lesbian scene in Melbourne and Sydney in the 1950s and 1960s; Bobbie travelled through Asia performing as the World's Strongest Woman, and eventually returned to Melbourne in the early 1970s. He was definitely identifying as a man by then and, according to a diary entry, had top surgery in a Melbourne private hospital in the early 1970s.[87] The occasional media report from the 1980s would discuss trans men, such as the features about Tony discussed in Chapter 3 and a 1982 article in Melbourne's *Herald* about 'Michael', a trans man who was happily partnered, had a son, and was running a small business in country Victoria. Michael described his local community as welcoming, commending the hospitable nature of country people.[88]

It was in the 1990s that the first trans men's groups formed in Australia. Jasper Laybutt was well-known in Sydney and across Australia as co-founder of *Wicked Women*, the country's first lesbian magazine with a focus on sadomasochism and erotica. Jasper hosted popular dance parties and competitions catering to lesbians and bisexual women with BDSM interests. He experimented with gender expression, dressing in masculine clothing in daily life and in a more pronounced way when going to clubs and bars. He was unaware that others expressed similar feelings and behaviour and that there was a name for it. Through his networks, Jasper became aware of the American magazine *FTM*, founded in 1986 by Lou Sullivan. Jasper credits *FTM* with changing his life because he learned about the existence of trans men and the possibility of transitioning. He then realised he could physically become the man he felt himself to be.

In 1991 Jasper was going through his transition and was frustrated with gatekeeper health professionals. With his friend Max Zebra-Thyone, he assembled a small group of trans men for a series of meetings. Out of this gathering, Boys Will Be Boys formed—Australia's first known trans men's group. It was a national organisation, but the majority of members and events were in Sydney. Boys Will Be Boys was a mix of a social and support group; it met a few times a year, usually with only four or five people attending, and held a larger annual event that attracted about a dozen people.[89]

Jasper went on a blitz of the LGBTIQ+ press to promote the group. In the first Boys Will Be Boys newsletter published in February 1992, he wrote:

I have been overwhelmed by the response to this support group from women who know they are men. Eight F2M boys have come to my attention within the last two months. Though seemingly a small number, compared to knowing only a handful previously and having met no-one before my gender change, this is quite incredible and only goes to show that there are more of us out there than we may well have imagined.

The monthly newsletter reported on international news and, perhaps more importantly, shared letters and stories. Later issues even had letters from a member in Darwin.[90]

Dale Hewinson (then Crane) became Melbourne's main contact person for a smaller Boys Will Be Boys chapter. Dale had a difficult childhood as a ward of the state and experienced homelessness and incarceration. He was taking testosterone intermittently from his teenage years and lived as a man most of his adult life. He had been out on the gay scene since the late 1980s so was a well-known figure by the time Boys Will Be Boys started. Dale also promoted the visibility of trans men by appearing in a 1994 documentary called *Men Like Me*. One important quote from him in the film summarises the challenges facing trans men:

> As soon as they [people] find out I'm F-to-M [an older expression for trans men], their attitudes change. They're either curious, sometimes dismissive, or really aggressive. It's stressful to always be concerned how people will react when they find out you're different. That's why F-to-Ms disappear into suburbia. It's easier not to be known as who you are.[91]

In Sydney, Jasper was finding it hard to continue his work promoting trans men's visibility. In about 1992 staff at Tiresias House approached him to provide education about trans men. In 1996 the Gender Centre hired him to work as designer on *Polare* and he also provided peer counselling for trans men—though he estimates that he only saw a maximum of two clients each month. Meanwhile, around 1994, Jasper was no longer in a position where he could continue producing the Boys Will Be Boys newsletter and events.[92]

Boys Will Be Boys ended in its original format, but another trans man working at the Gender Centre, Craig Andrews, took over as leader and morphed the organisation into FTM Australia. This, too, existed primarily as a remote organisation, but it grew in membership with the advent of the internet. The basic website set up in

1999 included links to resources for family and friends, details of health professionals, personal ads and a chat page. By the early 2000s, FTM Australia was running a Yahoo discussion group called OzGuys Online and members were receiving a quarterly newsletter called *TORQUE*. In 2003, FTM Australia published a comprehensive resource of over 150 pages for parents, friends and partners of trans men, entitled *Stand by Your Man (and Stay Sane in the Process)*. The organisation also had a series of fact sheets that gave concise information about trans men, identity, terminology and medical transitions.[93] FTM Australia later became a Facebook group and changed its name to Trans Masc Australia, which continues to this day.

In addition to running FTM Australia, from the 1990s Craig worked at the Gender Centre and offered peer support for trans men. Another trans man during that era who features heavily in oral history interviews is Sean Taylor. From 1996 to 2000 he was employed at the Gender Centre and organised social groups and events for trans men, including a bush camp, a winter solstice party and a World AIDS Day commemoration. On Tuesdays Sean hosted a drop-in meal. As a social and support worker he also developed a good relationship with the Department of Housing to assist clients who needed affordable housing, and he helped clients who were having difficulties with Centrelink.[94]

In Melbourne, although there was no discrete trans men's group after Boys Will Be Boys folded, the advocacy and leadership of Jonathan Paré proved monumental. In the early 1990s Jonathan was studying an associate diploma of community development, which he upgraded to a Bachelor degree at Victoria University. For two of his assessments, he conducted participant observation research with trans men and women about their experiences of being transgender. The process of bringing trans people together to discuss matters of concern was, surprisingly, innovative for the time. Most other Australian trans research was either medical/psychological or dealt with trans people one-on-one instead of in focus groups. Out of Jonathan's two reports came a series of recommendations about organising the trans community through a formal group that could provide peer support, education and political advocacy.[95]

Building on his research, Jonathan and a friend, Sharon Saunders, drove to Sydney to meet with peer educators at the Gender Centre. They also met with Trudy Kennedy from the Monash Gender Dysphoria Clinic to obtain support and contacts for other transgender Victorians. In May 1995 Jonathan and Sharon convened the first meeting of Transgender Liberation and Care at the Darebin Community Health Centre in Northcote, attracting about forty-five attendees. The organisation set up a management committee and a subcommittee to focus on community education. Transgender Liberation and Care shared the same initialism as the Sydney-based Transgender Liberation Coalition (TLC), but the two had no connection with each other.

Transgender Liberation and Care was a support group, delivered education to workplaces, facilitated meetings with recently out trans people and their partners and families, provided education for transgender people on a range of topics, and served as an information point for referrals and advocacy. It published its first newsletter in September 1995, which contained information on a long list of topics of importance to members. Among them were body image, safe use of hormones, accommodation difficulties, connecting with trans-inclusive health providers, social gatherings, and community education workshops. The monthly meetings usually had at least twenty participants, and generally a guest speaker.

Although Transgender Liberation and Care aimed to support both trans men and women, the majority of regular participants were trans women. While there were points of common concern, there were also different issues confronting trans men and women, so Jonathan was not surprised that many trans men drifted in and out of the organisation.[96] The archival trail of newsletters from Transgender Liberation and Care ends around 2002. As noted in Chapter 4, its legacy endures through the spin-off group Transgender Victoria.

Breaking ground over and over again

As this chapter has shown, trans people have been making contributions to all walks of Australian life for decades. The people mentioned in this chapter are those who made the public eye, be it intentionally through their advocacy or unintentionally through being outed. For every person identified, there were countless others who either were unable to transition or lived quiet lives out of the spotlight. Being the first at something was rarely easy, but there could never be a second, third or fourth without a first. Those who followed the 'first' may have found a more easily navigable path, but of course this was not universally the case. Trans people whose gender expression or transition journey was different would have to challenge the notion that there was only one trans experience. This was not just a challenge for cisgender people to grasp: as the next chapter shows, trans organisations in the 1990s–2000s, too, faced divisions over understandings of what it means to be transgender.

7
TRANS POLITICS AND ORGANISATIONS, 1990s–2000s

T HE SUCCESS OF trans activism at securing anti-discrimination and birth certificate reforms masked significant divisions that were brewing. As already illustrated in Sydney during the anti-discrimination debates, different ideological perspectives about what constituted trans threatened to derail legislative reform. These divisions—as well as personality clashes—became more pronounced across the country in the late 1990s and early 2000s and led to the formation of splinter trans organisations. This was not necessarily a bad development: offering distinct groups for trans people from different backgrounds meant providing space for trans diversities. Over time, groups who may have started as rivals would come to recognise the strength in diversity.

This chapter explores the dynamics of trans community organisations from the 1990s through the 2000s. Chapter 4 introduced a few of these groups because of their activism around anti-discrimination laws and birth certificates; this chapter brings in other groups who represented particular demographics within the trans community. It also highlights specific individuals who founded these groups and other people outside formal trans organisations—particularly in Tasmania, South Australia and Western Australia—who were instrumental in advancing trans rights and access to services. Sometimes these individuals and groups worked together with complementary interests but shared purpose; other times there were tensions and rivalries that threatened the very movement for trans rights. By the 2010s, though, there was a greater appreciation and acceptance of trans as an umbrella that encompassed various gender expressions and experiences.

Inquiry into Sexuality Discrimination

Although most trans politics and organisations operated at the state/territory level, there was a moment in the 1990s when the federal government examined trans rights. In November 1995, Democrats senator Sid Spindler introduced a Sexuality Discrimination Bill into the parliament. Notwithstanding the title, it was the first proposed federal legislation that included protections for transgender people. In May 1996 the Senate referred the bill to an inquiry by the Senate Legal and Constitutional Affairs References Committee. Nine submissions to the Inquiry into Sexuality Discrimination came from self-identified trans people, and two from trans support organisations in Brisbane (ATSAQ) and Perth (The Gender Council of Australia).

Common themes from the trans submissions were employment discrimination, marriage rights, access to health care and legal recognition. There was a constant tension between positioning transgender people as respectable just like everyone else and arguments about difference and the need to support more diverse understandings of gender identity. While opinions differed on what the definition of transgender should be, trans submissions and witnesses almost universally agreed that all people with diverse gender expressions should be protected under the law.

Opponents of the bill seized on anxieties about gender fluidity and its impact on sport to derail the conversations about transgender discrimination. The Women in Sport Foundation went so far as to describe gender affirmation surgery as 'genital mutilation' and that transgender women were just men who had 'chosen to have healthy reproductive organs removed and cosmetic surgery in order to pass as women'.[1] For transgender witnesses at the hearings, sport was a relatively low priority, and they expressed annoyance at having to address this issue instead of transgender discrimination. Gina Mather of ATSAQ explained:

> There is no advantage to be gained by having gender reassignment just to play sport. Far from it, I think there is a disadvantage to be gained, if anything. Some of the guys get notoriety. You will get public awareness and lose a lot of rights. People will recognise you and, again, you will be victimised, humiliated and vilified.[2]

The final report, tabled in December 1997, was a methodical, respectful document that made a conscious effort to grapple with the issues raised by all parties. It made thirty-three recommendations to improve the Sexuality Discrimination Bill. Among the transgender-related ones were: a precise definition around those who identify with a gender other than that assigned at birth; that refusing to recognise someone's affirmed gender should be considered a form of harassment; to prohibit discrimination on the basis of dress or appearance; and the establishment of a states-Commonwealth working party to discuss document changes for transgender people.[3]

The final report devoted only two pages to sport. It concluded that transgender people should not be excluded from playing sport on the grounds of their gender, but on a case-by-case basis individual organisations could exclude trans people who had physical characteristics that gave them an unfair advantage.[4] Notwithstanding its minor mention, transgender women in sport became the lightning rod for opposition to the entire Sexuality Discrimination Bill. The Liberal and National members of the Senate committee dissented from the majority report, citing trans women in sport in their reasoning. Conservative politicians and columnists denounced the bill in parliament and the media, citing trans women in sport especially (though not exclusively). Although the Australian Democrats and Greens supported the bill, neither the Coalition nor the Labor Party did, leaving it with no chance of passing. It would be over a decade before the federal parliament revisited the rights of LGBTIQ+ people.

New South Wales: The Tranny Wars

Before going into the organisational debates of the era, it is important to remember that many trans people were living their lives quietly away from community groups and politics. There were also trans people who independently organised social gatherings or other events. Penny Clifford, for instance, spent most of the 1990s working as a manager at the DCM nightclub on Oxford Street. She used to host regular trans nights, offering a low-key social event away from the activism and debates playing out elsewhere. She also ran fundraiser nights for Ward 17 South, the AIDS unit at St Vincent's Hospital, raising hundreds of thousands of dollars over the years. In 1991, Penny co-founded the annual Drag Industry Variety Awards (DIVA) to honour and celebrate Sydney's drag queens and the technical supporters behind the scenes.[5] Work by people such as Penny was instrumental in connecting gay, lesbian, bisexual and trans people and building an LGBTIQ+ community.

Away from this social scene, though, trans intra-community politics in New South Wales were the most public and most vicious. As noted in Chapter 4, the Transgender Liberation Coalition led the push for anti-discrimination reform. Coalition members also conducted or participated in research projects to produce evidence about the challenges facing transgender people in New South Wales. One of those projects, which commenced in 1993, was called the Trany Anti-Violence Project. Over a six-month period, twenty-three trans people reported nine incidents of discrimination by employers and service providers, along with thirty-four examples of verbal, physical and sexual assault. Examples included:

- one person living in a country town who was punched by a stranger when she went to purchase a coffee at a local cafe
- a group of men who groped a trans woman's breasts in inner Sydney, then knocked her to the ground and kicked her; the police were rude to the trans woman and refused to enter the house where the assailant lived
- a sex worker's client was angry when he learned that the trans woman had not had gender affirmation surgery; he ripped off her clothing and hit her while shouting homophobic abuse.[6]

Jesse Hooley conducted research for the Central Sydney Area Health Service entitled 'The Transgender Project'. This was one of a few non-psychological/psychiatric, community-driven research projects conducted by and about trans people before the late 2000s. Based on data compiled from ninety respondents, the report reinforced other data about the challenges trans people faced accessing health and welfare services, high levels of physical and sexual assault, the under-utilisation of services offered by the Gender Centre, and dissatisfaction with the outcomes of gender affirmation surgeries and treatment from doctors and psychiatrists. The recommendations focused on services needing to train and employ transgender staff and to co-design models of care.[7] Jesse mostly stepped back from activism after the passage of anti-discrimination reform, but her report would prove a significant piece of evidence that Transgender Liberation Coalition members wielded in their subsequent fights.[8]

After passage of anti-discrimination and birth certificate laws, the Transgender Liberation Coalition turned its attention towards reforming the Gender Centre. This period in late 1996 and the aftermath in 1997 was a divisive moment in the Gender Centre's history and is colloquially known as the Tranny Wars. According to Transgender Liberation Coalition activists like Norrie and Aidy Griffin, the Gender Centre resources, workshops and guidance mostly aligned with the medical model of transsexualism. Some clients complained to the Transgender Liberation Coalition that the majority of counsellors were cisgender and did not adequately understand their needs. Those staying in the refuge had to sign statements promising not to criticise the Gender Centre, and other clients found it difficult to access services such as HIV peer support. The Gender Centre ran events featuring psychiatrists and other doctors as guest speakers. Jesse and three other activists tried to attend one of those sessions to ask a surgeon a question and challenge the prominent view that trans people were pathological or had a mental illness, but the Gender Centre hired a security guard who barred them from entering.[9]

The LGBT press closely followed the Tranny Wars, in part because Norrie and Aidy wrote extensive letters and reports to *Capital Q* and the *Star Observer* as well as to other stakeholders. In a letter to the minister for community services—whose portfolio funded the Gender Centre—Norrie wrote:

> The Gender Centre is still teaching the sickness model outmoded by contemporary medical thought, that is, the model that tranys are 'mentally disordered', 'gender dysphoric', or have 'disorders of gender'. This model is, unsurprisingly, rejected by politically involved tranys, who see it as offensive as the old (once mainstream) notions that all women were 'hysterical' and ill-equipped to vote …
> TLC has called for
> - the immediate removal of all staff responsible for the bans [of trans activists from the Gender Centre],
> - the immediate cessation of teaching that tranys are intrinsically sick, and
> - the employment of tranys in all positions at the Gender Centre, with the exception that where no suitably qualified trany is available, then the position is held part time by a trany who is then upskilled to take over the position full time.[10]

The Tranny Wars came to a head in September 1996 at the Gender Centre annual general meeting. The meeting was a raucous affair, with accusations of what might be called branch stacking by both the Transgender Liberation Coalition and management-aligned candidates. There were fights over procedures and the voting system, not to mention who had a right to speak. One of the more dramatic moments was when Roberta Perkins—who as an elder statesperson had hitherto been silent during the Tranny Wars—rose to speak over the chair's objections. She had held her cards close to her chest, and at last revealed her support for community control and the Transgender Liberation Coalition–aligned candidates. The meeting was so chaotic that the chair adjourned it early, to be reconvened the next week.

In the interim, there was somewhat of a peace deal between the Transgender Liberation Coalition and the Gender Centre management committee. The committee agreed to the coalition's main demands—abandoning the medical model of transsexualism, implementing an affirmative action policy to hire transgender staff, and a review of the centre's management—if Norrie withdrew their candidacy. Norrie agreed to this, believing that coalition candidates could still win the elections and that achieving their aims was more important than Norrie's own candidacy. When the election was finally held the next week, the outgoing management committee's candidates won three positions, Transgender Liberation Coalition–aligned candidates won two, and an independent who had until then supported the coalition won one. The seventh position was a tie; everyone agreed that the winner would be determined by pulling the name out of a hat. The winner was Nadine Stransen, a coalition-aligned candidate. With majority control of the Gender Centre management committee, the Transgender Liberation Coalition had essentially won the Tranny Wars.[11]

Some of the changes that the new management committee ushered in concerned language, shifting away from expressions like 'pre-operative' and 'post-operative' transsexuals to 'non-operative'.

It also shifted away from working with doctors and instead ran workshops and education programs, beginning with a two-day convention in January 1997. The program included sessions covering what transgender is, health services, substance abuse, relationships, families, dressing, and challenges confronting Indigenous trans people and trans people from non-English-speaking backgrounds. The Gender Centre later developed education workshops on anti-discrimination rights and HIV support, and education programs with employers, and embarked on more community outreach.

In oral histories, the Tranny Wars and their aftermath tend to conflate two unrelated but contemporaneous problems. The first was the divisions wrought and the personalities involved. The other was a contested period that followed when many staff left the Gender Centre—some because they no longer felt comfortable in the new environment, but others because of disagreements over management and alleged harassment. Roberta Perkins had to step aside as president of the management committee due to ill health, and the independent member of the management committee took on that role. Although Transgender Liberation Coalition members believed she was aligned with them, she did not agree with them on all issues. For instance, she still subscribed to the difference between transvestites and transgender people and, consequently, wanted to stop Seahorse from holding meetings at the Gender Centre.

There are multiple allegations from various people involved in this period of the Gender Centre's history. Some argue that the chair of the management committee was mismanaging the Gender Centre; others say that staff were permitting men to attend the refuge who were bringing in drugs and alcohol. The new chair of the management committee got a job as a social worker. One version of events says this went against normal practice around conflict of interest and separation between the management committee and staff. The other side of the story is that she had not wanted to be chair and only assumed that role because Roberta had stepped down; really, she always preferred the social worker position.

The chair of the management committee was fired from her role of social worker the same day that she commenced it, officially pushing her out of the Gender Centre, and Roberta returned as chair of the management committee. The person asserted that she then faced a period of harassment from people associated with the Gender Centre, including graffiti at Central Station calling her a man and saying that she was ruining the Gender Centre. This was a painful period of her life and led her to leave trans politics behind. Meanwhile, Elizabeth Riley was appointed manager of the Gender Centre, ushering in a new era of peace and rebuilding the organisation as the Tranny Wars and their aftermath faded into history.

The Gender Centre continued to operate a refuge, HIV support groups, other peer support and counselling programs, workplace education programs and outreach—including to incarcerated or paroled trans people. Indeed, Elizabeth remembers the work with the Department of Corrections system as one of the most significant achievements of her time as general manager. Previously, gaols and prisons had been inconsistent in whether trans people would be housed in facilities for their affirmed gender or for their sex assigned at birth. In men's facilities both trans women and men consistently faced the threat of sexual assault and violence. The negotiations took a long time, and the revisions to the *Anti-Discrimination Act* were instrumental in securing reform.[12] Under revised guidelines released in October 1998, trans inmates would be managed on a case-by-case basis and self-identification would be the cornerstone of determining the inmate's gender. When a prison governor deemed that a person should be housed in a facility for their sex assigned at birth on the grounds of safety, security or good order, the governor would have to submit a report to a case management team for approval. The policy also had checks and balances like a review process, decreed that inmates be referred to by their affirmed name and pronouns (and not as 'it'), and mandated that, even if in a prison for their sex assigned at birth, trans inmates would have access to uniforms and items such as cosmetics for their affirmed gender. Those trans people who were already on hormones would continue to receive them, but those who had not commenced hormones would have to apply for access.[13] In the 2000s, other states and territories adopted similar policies on trans people in custody.

Of course, there are still substantial challenges confronting trans people in the carceral system. Reports from trans inmates show that prison staff have not always applied this policy consistently, and indeed many have not even been aware of it. Trans inmates—particularly trans men—are often placed in facilities or solitary confinement on safety grounds without being given rights to self-determination. Misgendering and harassment from other inmates and prison staff are also common.[14] For this reason, the Gender Centre and other organisations have consistently run outreach programs to support trans prisoners and have lobbied for further reforms.

Recognising that there was not enough support for trans men, Elizabeth aimed to bring in more support programs that specifically targeted them, such as supporting Sean Taylor's peer support groups and other outreach for trans men. The Gender Centre also began to work more actively with Sistergirls and Brotherboys, with an Aboriginal member appointed to the management committee in the late 1990s. From the late 1990s through the 2000s, the Gender Centre organised the annual Tranny Pride Ball. The event began in December 1994 as a fundraiser for a Mardi Gras float being organised by Norrie and Carmen Rupe and, under the Gender Centre's leadership, became an annual celebration of trans life through the early 2000s.

In 2002 the Gender Centre worked with the organisers of the Sydney Gay Games to develop a new policy on transgender inclusion. The Gay Games organisers also met with representatives from Pasifika and Indigenous groups, and adopted a new definition of transgender that shifted away from medical models: 'A transgender person is someone who was born anatomically male or female, but has a strong and persistent, bona fide identification with the gender role other than that assigned at birth. A transgender person may or may not have had medical treatment to transition to their chosen or self-identified gender.'[15] One hundred and fifty-eight transgender athletes from twenty-eight countries registered for the Sydney Gay Games.[16]

The Transgender Liberation Coalition activists mostly left the Gender Centre after the Tranny Wars, and the group disbanded. Aidy Griffin backed away from the transgender scene almost entirely and passed away in October 2021 after a long battle with emphysema. Jesse Hooley—who, incidentally, before she transitioned was a 78er who was at the first Sydney Gay and Lesbian Mardi Gras—became an academic. She was later assaulted in public; she eventually recovered by becoming a visual artist in response to various traumas, as experienced by other trans women, in what was then a more hostile and transphobic society. Over the years Nadine Stransen's mental health deteriorated, and she died under mysterious circumstances in early 2016.[17] Norrie continued to be involved in trans rights activism; they worked as a project officer for SWOP and were a performance artist, and in the 2010s would mount a monumental legal case testing the rights of non-binary people in New South Wales; this is discussed in the next chapter.

Queensland: A site of stability

As outlined in Chapter 4, ATSAQ dominated trans politics in Queensland in the 1990s and 2000s. After the passage of anti-discrimination legislation in 2002, ATSAQ leaders Kristine Johnson and Gina Mather continued to advocate for better access to services, affirming health care and equal rights for trans people. They also ran social functions, including a monthly luncheon, and regularly corresponded with trans people across Queensland offering support, guidance and, in many cases, advocacy. They sat on numerous advisory bodies in relation to the Queensland anti-discrimination law, police and health policy. Gina and Kristine also continued to run the 24-hour hotline at their house and would receive phone calls at all hours from trans people seeking information or who were in distress. Gina has talked about the emotional toll of dealing with so many people in crisis, even having to identify trans people who died by suicide.[18] Although she and Kristine regularly travelled to other parts of Queensland, including Rockhampton, the majority of ATSAQ's work and social membership was based in the south-east.

Filling the void in Far North Queensland was a new organisation that started around 2000 in Townsville. Erica Roberts founded it after a specialist put her in touch with another trans person and she recognised the need for trans people in the region to connect. She advertised on the internet for a new group that she named Transbridge, and it grew from there. Erica also created a brochure that she left at the Townsville Sexual Health Clinic, and spread word through the speech pathology clinic at James Cook University. The membership came from across North Queensland, as far west as Mount Isa and as far south as Gladstone. Erica organised an event one night each month where people would pay $5 and would come to her house for a meal and a social gathering. Similar to Seahorse events, the group would often have a guest speaker attend, be they a health professional or someone selling shoes or make-up. Erica notes that attendance at these events climbed to about thirty before steadily declining until she stopped running them.

Most of Transbridge's membership was older trans women who were transitioning, though a few younger trans men came on occasion. It was a social support group, not a political advocacy group, so most of Erica's work was around providing information and activities such as shopping excursions. Transbridge still has a small internet presence and Erica still gets telephone inquiries from time to time, but for the most part the group has wound down and is not active anymore.[19] The next chapter details the emergence of new trans organisations in Queensland in the 2010s.

Victoria: Fraying unity

Transgender Victoria continued to be the state's main political advocacy organisation in the 2000s, but it too experienced politics and divisions. After lobbying hard for anti-discrimination reforms, Sally Goldner and Kayleen White were exhausted and finished their roles as co-chairs. In 2001–02 there was a split within the organisation. Some members argued that as they had transitioned and had gender affirmation surgery, they were no longer transgender but were just women. This was not a new idea per se: as noted in the previous chapter, one trans candidate in the 1998 election felt the same way. Moreover, in the early 1990s a Victorian activist wrote submissions under the title R.A.W.: Sexually Reassigned Women's Action Group. She argued that 'sexually reassigned women must be included in Human Rights legislation and be legally accepted as females and not just be legally accepted as transsexuals'.[20]

The split in Transgender Victoria led those who rejected the transgender label to form their own online group, called The W-o-m-a-n Network.[21] The W-o-m-a-n Network embraced the medical model of transsexualism and went even further: it argued that transsexualism was an intersex variation. One document outlining its position asserted: 'We who were born with the biological intersexual condition described as transsexualism are as much the subject of "an error made at the time of birth" as any of the 10 per cent of those born with physical hermaphroditism who subsequently claim a mistake was made. And we have to go through hell to get that fact recognised.'[22] The W-o-m-a-n Network was particularly active in lobbying for birth certificate reform to be restricted to people who had gender affirmation surgery, which passed in Victoria in 2004. Its website continued to be updated with trans news, information and comments through 2008.

After the W-o-m-a-n Network splintered off, the leadership of Transgender Victoria was more confident to embrace an umbrella understanding of trans that moved away from the medical model.

Moreover, TGV supported intersex rights but was conscious to distinguish transgender from intersex. At its 2001 annual general meeting, the organisation passed a motion inserting the following clause into its Rules of Incorporation: 'Transgender Victoria recognises intersex as a separate, distinct group from transgender and does not represent nor seek to represent intersex issues or people, although it endorses cooperation with and support of intersex groups where appropriate and of potentially mutual benefit.'[23] In 2007, the group Organisation Intersex Australia—later renamed Intersex Human Rights Australia—was founded; it is now the peak advocacy organisation for intersex people in Australia.

Other Victorian transgender organisations and networks have come and gone over the years, and have changed in their modus operandi. One was the Trans Melbourne Gender Project, which began in 2004 as an online forum and listserv to share announcements and information. In 2006 it produced a 21-page information booklet titled 'GQ Gender Questioning', targeting young people aged sixteen to twenty-five who were questioning their gender identity.

There were sporadic attempts in the 2000s at founding a trans-run health centre. In 2007 a working group ran a public meeting and online survey to discuss the possibility of founding a gender centre in Melbourne. Loosely modelled on Sydney's Gender Centre, the Zoe Belle Gender Centre would be a trans-run organisation that provided health and wellbeing support. The organisation was named after transgender activist Zoe Belle, one of the major proponents of the centre; she passed away in early 2008. Now working under the auspices of community health provider Cohealth, the renamed Zoe Belle Gender Collective offers online resources, diversity-and-inclusion training workshops, and specific programs targeting trans young people.

The broader solidarity with Victorian LGBTIQ+ organisations proved a strength in the 2000s. In 2003, for instance, one conflict between transgender women and a group of radical lesbians went to the Victorian Civil and Administrative Tribunal (VCAT).

The organisers of the 2004 National Lesbian Festival and Conference (Lesfest), to be held in Daylesford, successfully applied to VCAT for an exemption from the *Equal Opportunity Act* to restrict the event to 'lesbians born female only', They argued that this was a matter of security for cisgender lesbians, many of whom had been abused by men.[24]

The transgender community erupted in opposition, affirming trans women's identities as women. There was some coverage in the mainstream media, and the story became front-page news in the LGBTIQ+ press. Most letters published in the LGBTIQ+ press supported trans women, with one arguing: 'When an oppressed group becomes an oppressor group, something is fundamentally wrong in a so-called democratic society.'[25] Within a fortnight, VCAT reversed its decision because the Lesfest organisers had not informed the tribunal of a complaint from a representative of the W-o-m-a-n Network. The complainant was reported as saying, 'The strong support we received for our full acceptance as the women we are was particularly appreciated by people with transsexualism.'[26] The entire saga highlighted the legal protections for trans Victorians and also showcased that the majority of Victoria's LGBTIQ+ community affirmed trans people. The reactionary anti-trans activists would become louder in the 2010s–20s.

South Australia: Individual strides

By virtue of having passed anti-discrimination and gender recognition legislation early, South Australia did not have a trans advocacy group. That is not to say there were no trans activists or advocates in the 1990s–2000s; rather, they tended to work through gay and lesbian organisations in early examples of LGBT unity. One prominent example from the 1990s was Marie-Desiree D'Orsay Lawrence. Originally from Brisbane, Desi, as she was known, began doing drag at age fourteen. She served in the army as a nurse for thirty years before transitioning and settling in Adelaide. Desi always offered her house to support other trans people in need because she had overcome so much trauma—including twice being raped. As noted in Chapter 3, she was co-founder of Transcare in 1976, and by the early 1990s was the convenor of the Carousel Club, which was the only active trans group in South Australia.[27]

When the AIDS epidemic hit, Desi offered support to people living with HIV and AIDS. Her nursing background served her well in this regard, and throughout the 1990s she was a volunteer with the Positive Living Centre. She also performed various volunteer roles with the AIDS Council of South Australia (ACSA) from 1988 onwards, including being dubbed the Mother of the House of ACSA. In 1993 she organised the revival of activist group ACT UP (AIDS Coalition to Unleash Power) in South Australia, with the purpose of targeting businesses and services that discriminated against people living with HIV and AIDS. By the late 1990s she was a volunteer and secretary for People Living with HIV and AIDS (SA) and Feast Festival (South Australia's pride event), and a trustee for the Bobby Goldsmith Foundation, Australia's oldest AIDS charity. In 1995 she ran, unsuccessfully, for president of ACSA. In 1997 she appeared before the Senate Inquiry into Sexuality Discrimination to speak about the challenges of harassment and discrimination confronting transgender people in South Australia. In recognition of her immense voluntary contributions to the LGBTIQ+ community, in 1998 Desi was nominated for the *Adelaide Gay Times* awards in the category of Care & Support.[28]

Desi was very much an advocate of uniting sexually diverse and gender-diverse people, and it was because of people like her that there was early unity in South Australia. As she put it in a speech delivered in 1997 or 1998:

Now after many years of fractions [sic], infighting and squabbles we are at last a united community. Sometimes we forget we come from common stock and it does not matter weather [sic] we are Gay, Lesbian, Transvestite, Transsexual or Bi-Sexual, we have the same battles to fight to become a valued member of the Australian community just as those who claim to be straight.[29]

Though Desi slowed down her activism in the 2000s, she continued to be a strong advocate for the rights of LGBTIQ+ people until she passed away in 2018.

The other prominent figure in SA trans history since the 1990s is Jenny Scott. Jenny transitioned in the early 1990s and then began her foray into South Australia's LGBTIQ+ community. Having recently completed a diploma in Library and Information Management, she began volunteering at the Darling House Library, run by ACSA, in 1993. She subsequently took on other volunteer tasks for ACSA, such as taking photographs at events. ACSA housed numerous organisations, one of which was the Gay and Lesbian Counselling Service, and Jenny quickly got to know the people there and volunteered for them as well. By 1995, she was president of the Gay and Lesbian Counselling Service; she served in that role for two years and in that capacity appeared before the Senate Inquiry into Sexuality Discrimination. From 1996 to 1997 she was the AIDS Council library coordinator and also the elected staff representative on the ACSA board. In 1997 she was employed as an archivist with the State Records of South Australia and cut back her formal roles with ACSA and the Gay and Lesbian Counselling Service, though she continued to volunteer at the Darling House Community Library until 2007.[30]

Jenny's involvement with the LGBTIQ+ community has never waned, and her presence in a variety of committees and organisations has ensured that trans voices are at the table. She has had roles with the SA Police Equal Opportunity Task Group (1997), Dr George Duncan Memorial Committee (2001–02), Gay and Lesbian Health Ministerial Advisory Committee (2004–06), Pride March Adelaide Committee (2003–05), Bfriend Review Reference Group (2012; Bfriend is an organisation supporting LGBTIQ+ people in the Uniting Church), the Feast Board of Management (2002–04; she was chair in 2004), Council on the Aging SA Rainbow

Hub (2017–22), Elder Care LGBTIQ Advisory Group (2019–) and South Australian Rainbow Advocacy Alliance Community Advisory Group (2020–21). She has also served as convener of the Gay and Lesbian Alliance of Museums Australia (2009–13), and is a Parkstone Foundation trustee (2015– ; this organisation funds LGBTIQ+ community projects in South Australia). As noted in Chapter 6, Jenny ran for both federal and state parliament for the Australian Democrats, in 2004 and 2006 respectively. On top of all this, from 2000 until the end of 2019 she was employed as a photographic archivist at the State Library of South Australia. In January 2023, the SA attorney-general appointed her for a three-year term on the State Records Council.

Most of Jenny's work has involved the entire LGBTIQ+ community, but she has also been involved in trans-specific advocacy and support. For instance, beginning in the mid-1990s she regularly gave guest presentations in Gender Studies classes at the University of South Australia to discuss transgender issues. In April 1994, Rob Lyons—the main psychiatrist seeing trans clients in Adelaide— brought together Jenny and a few other trans clients in the hope that social interaction would benefit them. Jenny then set up a formal support group for trans people that became South Australian Transsexual Support. The group met once a month with an attendance of five or six, all trans women. Jenny only stayed with South Australia Transsexual Support for a short period.[31] Although there is not much of an archival trail, correspondence from the Health Insurance Commission indicates that the group lobbied (unsuccessfully) to add trans women to the Pharmaceutical Benefits Scheme listing for anti-androgen medication. The group ended sometime around 1997, and Rob noted that this was in part due to political divisions that were ripple effects of the Tranny Wars in Sydney.[32]

In 2005, in recognition of Jenny's immense contributions to the LGBTIQ+ community, she received the Community Service Award at Adelaide's GLBTI Community Awards (the GALA). In 2017 she was recognised on the South Australian Women's Honour Roll as a 'passionate activist for the LGBTIQ community'. Part of the citation read:

> As a transgender woman she has worked resolutely to provide a voice for members of the community, especially the trans community, and to be a spokesperson raising issues around discrimination and violence. Her intelligence, compassion, knowledge, expertise and experience [have] seen her being involved as a presenter and panel member at a range of community and government forums.[33]

Tasmania: Anti-discrimination wins

Greer McGearey, past and current president of Seahorse Victoria (2005–06; 2009–), lived in Tasmania for a short period in the early 2000s. She recalls that there was a group for dressers called Criss Cross, but otherwise she was not aware of other trans groups in the state.[34] Like Seahorse NSW twenty-four years earlier, Criss Cross began in 1995 when a dresser named 'Tina' placed an advertisement in the newspaper to find others like her. By 1996 it had over a dozen members who met weekly as a social and support group. One announcement in *CentreLines*, the newsletter of Tasmania's Gay and Lesbian Community Centre, explained: 'Some feel they are "trapped in a man's body"; others just need to dress up occasionally, but all of them have a strong need to do so, and to know that they are in safe and understanding company.'[35]

In Tasmania it tended to be individuals who advocated for trans rights. As noted in Chapter 4, one of the state's pioneering trans activists was Ros Houston. In recognition for her work on law reform, in 2001 Ros received a Tasmanian Award for Humanitarian Activities. In her acceptance speech, she declared:

> Transgender and transsexual people experience discrimination and violence far too often and while it is only a tiny minority

who perpetuate this abuse it is made possible by the prejudices, ignorance and apathy of the majority ... Awards like this will help break down this prejudice, ignorance and apathy.[36]

Ros was not involved in major campaigns after that, but she still advocated for trans rights through activities such as training police officers about trans issues.

Ros left one other mark on Tasmanian trans rights through a precedent-setting anti-discrimination case. In February 2000, she went to a neighbouring apartment to complain about excessive noise. The neighbour verbally vilified and threatened her with anti-trans slurs. Ros subsequently called the police, fearing that the neighbour was going to attack her. A day later she lodged a complaint with the Tasmanian Anti-Discrimination Commission, asserting that the nature of the comments and threats constituted discrimination. Over a year later, the case went to the Tasmanian Anti-Discrimination Tribunal. The neighbour alleged that he had been in a fight with his girlfriend that Ros interrupted, but he had not been discriminating against her for being transgender. In June 2003 the tribunal found in favour of Ros, though on narrow grounds that the neighbour had discriminated against her in accommodation (as it was public housing) and sexually harassed her. When it came to broader questions of discrimination, the tribunal determined that while the neighbour had used language that attacked Ros' transness, her being trans was not the motivation for the attack. Still, it awarded her $4000 in damages as compensation for the humiliation and indignity she had suffered.[37] Ros passed away in May 2010 and was honoured as a 'quiet trailblazer'.[38]

Ros Houston and another trans woman, Leslie Williams, were two pioneers whom Tasmanian activist Martine Delaney looked up to. Leslie was a former member of Les Girls living in Hobart whom Martine describes as 'this incredibly proud, out there, happy trans woman who was just out to party themself silly and enjoy being herself. I found her quite inspiring just in the fact that she was this crazy individual who didn't really give a stuff about how society wanted to change her. She was important.'[39]

Jonathan Paré, founder of Transgender Liberation and Care in Victoria, lived in Tasmania from 2001 to 2012 and during that period had several education and training roles in government and non-profit organisations. He took every opportunity he could to add transgender inclusion to anti-homophobia training; among his highlights were facilitating the Pride & Prejudice program in schools and serving as manager of Education Services & Workforce Development with Family Planning Tasmania.[40]

Martine Delaney, mentioned in Chapter 6 for her 2016 Greens election campaign, has been the most prominent trans activist in Tasmania since the mid-2000s. Martine's activism began while she was transitioning in 2002, when she joined the management committee of a suicide prevention organisation called Working It Out. Originally Working It Out was meant to support gay men at risk of suicide, but Martine and others—including Jonathan, who sat on the management committee from 2003–04 and, later, worked for the organisation—ensured that it became inclusive of trans people.[41] In late 2006, Martine convened a group of trans Tasmanians from diverse backgrounds that she referred to as 'TransPlan' whose role was to ensure that Working It Out was meeting the needs of trans Tasmanians. The group strategised about the possibility of peer support groups, social outings and public awareness campaigns to support trans rights.[42]

Martine unintentionally garnered a public profile in 2005 when there was media coverage of her playing women's soccer in a local Hobart football club. Although her teammates were all supportive, an opposition coach complained that she should not be playing for a women's club. As Martine explains, there was no trans policy for soccer, so 'somewhere between FIFA and Football Federation Australia they made a decision to adapt the then IOC rules around trans participation, and since I was two years post-surgery they said, "You can play." I kept on playing. I played for another eleven years.'[43]

Martine's first major foray into activism was a year later, when she challenged religious discrimination against trans and intersex people. During the 2006 Tasmanian state election, the Exclusive Brethren religious group placed advertisements in newspapers claiming that the Greens' support for trans and intersex people was going to destroy Tasmanian families and society. Martine lodged an anti-discrimination complaint against the farmer who had purchased the advertisements. Other trans people—including Julie Peters, who was living in Tasmania at the time—wrote letters of support, noting that the 'claim that helping transsexual people become functional members of society "will ruin our families and society" incites society to discriminate against transsexual people, prevent them receiving the medical care they need and incites hatred and ridicule'.[44]

As the case made its way to the anti-discrimination tribunal, a series of emails emerged that indicated that Liberal Party staff had created the advertisement; Martine subsequently took them to the anti-discrimination tribunal as well. The Liberal Party of Tasmania had to admit its part but would not agree to make a public apology. Martine later met with the then opposition leader, who promised not to make trans people an issue in the looming 2010 election (which his party won). Eventually Martine received a public apology from the Exclusive Brethren as part of a settlement—apparently making her the first person in the world to achieve that feat.[45] As the next chapter shows, she continued to be active in the 2010s, challenging other religious bodies who discriminated against trans people as well as lobbying for marriage equality and the second round of birth certificate reform in Tasmania.

Australian Capital Territory: Pioneering organisations

The two main trans organisations in Canberra emerged in the early and late 2000s respectively. The first is the Canberra Transgender Network, which is not dissimilar to Seahorse, Carousel and the Chameleon Society from the other states. A few Seahorse meetings had been organised in Canberra around 1995–96, but disagreements over the meeting format forced the group to disband. The organiser, Katherine West, then created a group called Transgender Outreach, which was mostly for social gatherings at places such as the Meridian Club. She also organised a popular annual event called the Glitter Ball, but around 2001 or 2002 she stopped planning events. Her successor as organiser of Transgender Outreach was Abbey-Jane, and sometime around 2003 the organisation morphed into the Canberra Transgender Network. This group operates similarly to Seahorse: it caters primarily to dressers, meets monthly and sometimes hosts social nights at a restaurant.[46]

The other Canberra organisation is A Gender Agenda (AGA), whose origins lie with Peter Hyndal. Like so many other trans people, Peter never set out to be an activist or advocate but became one when he confronted discrimination. In the 2000s, he and his partner wanted to go through IVF and came across numerous barriers. He lodged several claims through the NSW Anti-Discrimination Board, and after many years of struggle the cases were settled and Peter successfully went through IVF.[47]

The anti-discrimination cases were one trigger that transformed Peter into an activist for trans rights. The other was his growing education and awareness about human rights principles and their applicability in the Australian Capital Territory. First, he became involved in the gay and lesbian group Good Process as it engaged with the ACT Government in a consultation process on LGBTIQ+ matters. The ACT Government responded favourably to the gay and lesbian causes, but the trans issues—particularly birth certificate reform to remove the surgery requirement—fell by the wayside. Good Process claimed victory and folded, but Peter saw the need for a trans and intersex organisation to continue advocating for those communities' needs. Using the money from his anti-discrimination settlements, in 2005 he founded AGA to do just that.

AGA began slowly and modestly but, most importantly, consultatively. From the beginning it had a human rights framework embedded in its approach. Peter first prepared a community survey to gauge the needs of trans and intersex Canberrans and organised a series of meetings where people could share their experiences. This proved educational for everyone, as different trans people's views about topics such as birth certificates shifted when they heard about others' transition journeys. Peter describes the meetings and learning as organic: 'That theme of finding diversity and commonality at exactly the same moment actually became, I think, a really defining theme in terms of the way that AGA ended up going on to engage with community and encourage community to engage with itself.'

A big turning point for AGA was in 2009, when multiple threads came together. A few young people became involved and injected new energy: they organised social events such as a picnic during Canberra's SpringOUT Festival, a clothes swap, Christmas dinners and movie nights. That same year AGA secured its first funding grant for a social inclusion project around trans people's mental health and wellbeing. The project ran for two years and stimulated growth for the organisation. In 2011 an anonymous donor gave a house to AGA in the suburb of Lyneham. The new premises and funding allowed the organisation to employ a part-time project officer, partner with psychologist Jennie Yates, run a regular calendar of events including a weekly meet-up, and accept drop-ins from trans people seeking support. The success of the project led to AGA receiving recurrent funding from the ACT Government beginning in 2012.[48] One enduring event that still proves popular is community dinners, and Jenni Atkinson was particularly known for bringing lots of food.[49] As the next chapter explores, AGA was instrumental in lobbying for the second round of birth certificate reform in the Australian Capital Territory in 2014.

Western Australia: Resurrection and decline of organised politics

Organised trans groups in Western Australia went through a bit of a boom in the early 2000s. From July 1999 the Gender Dysphoria Foundation, which had lobbied for anti-discrimination and birth certificate reform, became less active. Mx Margaret Jones has heard that there was a split in the organisation over the inclusion of sex workers, who at the time made up about one-third of the membership. For the next few years the International Foundation for Androgynous Studies (IFAS), co-founded in 1997 by an intersex advocate and two academics at the University of Western Australia, did most of the organising around trans and intersex issues in the state. In January 2000 it organised a week-long summer school called Unseen Genders that explored social versus biological constructs of gender, and challenged binaries. IFAS hosted two conferences in 2000 and 2001 entitled InterseXions, and consistently lobbied for both the trans and intersex communities while being cautious not to conflate them. In 2001, intersex IFAS member Alex MacFarlane successfully had a Victorian birth certificate reissued with the sex marker 'indeterminate—also known as intersex', and in 2003 Alex won a court challenge requiring the Australian Government to issue them a passport with the gender marker X.[50]

In early 2001, the Gender Dysphoria Foundation had a revival and in the middle of that year changed its name to 'TransWest: The Transgender Association of WA'. There was overlap in the membership of TransWest and IFAS, and they jointly worked to educate politicians and lobby for further reforms to support trans and intersex people. TransWest held a stall at the Perth Fair Day (part of Western Australia's annual pride festival), participated in the pride parade, and offered referrals and informal counselling for trans and intersex people in need of emotional or health support. Group meetings were held in homes in twenty different suburbs and towns. Mx Margaret Jones even used a spare room in their house for trans or intersex people in need of short-term accommodation. In 2002 TransWest organised Perth's first International Trans Day of Remembrance vigil. The group's convenors also delivered trans awareness training, including presenting to the WA Police Academy from 2002.

In August 2001, after substantial lobbying of the state government by TransWest and IFAS, the WA Equal Opportunity Commission set up a Working Party on Gender Identity. This group, which included trans and intersex representatives from the two organisations, met for the next six months to discuss reforms to the *Equal Opportunity Act* to provide better protections for trans and intersex people.[51] Leading the suite of recommendations was replacing 'gender history' with 'gender identity' as a protected attribute. The final report said that the working party had examined laws from other Australian states and territories and come up with the following definition of gender identity:

the identification on a bona fide basis, through practice, expression, or physical or behavioural attributes, as a person of a sex, whether male or female or indeterminate, other than the sex identified on that person's birth certificate.

The definition of 'gender identity' should include but not be limited to: Transsexual, Transgender, Intersex, Androgyne, Gender Expression, Sistergirls.

The report noted that, if adopted, these reforms would make Western Australia the first jurisdiction in the world to recognise Sistergirls in legislation. It also indicated that Sistergirls themselves should come up with a culturally appropriate definition.[52] The WA Government never released this report, and no future government acted on it.

Just as in New South Wales and Victoria, there were divisions within the WA trans community between advocates of the medical model of transsexualism and social constructionists who rejected binaries and surgery requirements. By February 2003 the divisions came to a head and the advocates for the medical model left TransWest to form a splinter group: TransCommunityWA.[53] That group did not even last a year because its members found the leader to be difficult.[54] In 2003 various trans community representatives came together to form the Perth Gender Centre Umbrella Group, aiming to found an organisation similar to Sydney's Gender Centre. After only six meetings, this group, too, folded.[55] Leaders of TransWest successfully rebuilt its membership to about thirty-four people by August 2004 but then it, too, gradually reduced its activities; it ultimately shifted to being an online Facebook group.

In the absence of trans activist or advocacy groups, it fell to individual trans people to challenge the legal status quo. Leece Johnson, for instance, entered the spotlight in 2004 when she appeared on the cover of the *West Australian* with the headline 'Transsexual Truckie Hails Decision for Girl's Sex Change'.[56] Leece's transition while working as a truck driver—a typically macho, working-class industry—challenged gender norms. Over the next few years she faced difficulties securing jobs and had to challenge transphobia in the workplace and the Transport Workers' Union. Leece has offered support to other trans truck drivers on transitioning, and later in the 2000s began to give presentations about transgender inclusion to various businesses in Perth and regional Western Australia.[57]

One person who delivered significant legal outcomes was Aram Hosie. He already had a public profile as the partner of ALP senator Louise Pratt: in 2007 journalists at the *West Australian* found out he had transitioned and ran a front-page story. Aram did not want the public outing but, since it was going to happen regardless, he participated in an interview in the hopes of shaping the narrative more favourably. This did not stop the *West Australian* from running the sensational front-page headline 'Senator's Sex-swap Partner'.

Although Aram clearly presented and identified as a man, he ran into problems with legal documentation from both the WA and federal governments. The federal government only issued passports in trans people's affirmed genders if they changed their birth certificate. At the time, every state and territory government required people to have gender affirmation surgery to change their birth certificate, which for trans men included both top surgery and a hysterectomy. Aram did not want or need a hysterectomy, a sentiment common among many trans men. He lodged a complaint with the Australian Human Rights Commission and in 2009 was successful in getting his own passport gender marker changed to male. But this was a problem bigger than just Aram, and he wanted to ensure that other trans people, too, could have passports with appropriate gender markers.

Aram's political connections served him well. Around the same time, a group of trans women in then foreign minister Kevin Rudd's electorate met with him to discuss the challenges they faced. Their stories moved Rudd, and he decided he wanted to do something to help trans people. The only relevant policy in his portfolio—which actually was hugely important—was gender on passports. Someone from his office who knew Aram contacted him for advice, and Aram then worked with Rudd's office to set up an advisory group of trans and intersex people to make recommendations about passport reforms.[58] Joining Aram were activists from across the country: Sally Goldner from Victoria, Peter Hyndal from the Australian Capital Territory, Martine Delaney from Tasmania, and Gina Wilson from Sydney, who was president of Organisation Intersex Australia.[59] In 2011, acting on their advice, Rudd changed the rules so that people could self-nominate their gender on passports without the need for medical or surgical interventions, and they also had the option to select the non-binary gender marker 'X'.

Still, the challenge remained that Aram's WA birth certificate was in his sex assigned at birth. He and another trans man whom he knew ('AB') had both applied in 2008 to the Gender Reassignment Board to have their birth certificate changed. Aram knew he would be rejected because he had not had a hysterectomy, but still he lodged the application because he intended to take legal action. What he knew was that the WA *Gender Reassignment Act* specifically said that a person had to have undergone a 'reassignment procedure', defined in the act as 'a medical *or* surgical procedure (or a combination of such procedures) to alter the genitals and other gender characteristics of a person …'[60] When both Aram and AB received rejection letters from the Gender Reassignment Board, they lodged a joint appeal before the State Appeals Tribunal. Aram secured excellent legal representation, and they prepared a case. The tribunal upheld Aram and AB's appeal, saying they should have been granted a certificate of recognition and issued new birth certificates.[61]

The WA Government appealed and the case went before the WA Supreme Court sitting as the Court of Appeal. As Aram recalls, the justices' questions focused less on the hysterectomy and more on the fact that neither he nor AB had a penis. This constituted an even more essentialist interpretation of sex and gender that emphasised genitalia. Aram found the court process incredibly demeaning, with one judge musing out loud about what he and AB would look like in speedos. Photographs of his and AB's chests were tabled as evidence and the judges gave running commentary on how masculine they looked.[62] In a 2–1 ruling in September 2010, the Court of Appeal overruled the State Appeals Tribunal and set an even higher threshold to meet the requirements of the *Gender Reassignment Act*: trans men would need to have a phalloplasty to obtain a certificate of recognition and change their birth certificate.[63]

Even though it was a state law under judicial review, because there was similar legislation in South Australia the ruling could have national ramifications. As such, Aram and AB received special dispensation to appeal their case to the High Court of Australia. This time there were no questions about bodies or genitalia; rather, the justices focused on the legislation. In a unanimous 5–0 decision, the High Court overturned the Court of Appeal ruling and reinstated the decision of the State Appeals Tribunal. The High Court disagreed with the Court of Appeal justices' focus on genitalia while ignoring the broader provisions of the legislation and the physical characteristics of AB and Aram. The justices also noted that significant word 'or', which implied that a person could meet the requirements of gender reassignment through medical interventions without the need for particular gender affirmation surgeries. The justices concluded: 'The options thus provided by the Act do not lend support for a view that a person must take all possible steps, including with respect to their sexual organs, to become as male or female as possible.'[64]

In the aftermath of the High Court case, the then WA attorney-general, Christian Porter, announced that the state government would consider changing the *Gender Reassignment Act*. The premier, however, said that they would leave the matter alone.[65] As such, since 2011 trans people in Western Australia have no longer required gender affirmation surgery to change their birth certificate. They still require medical interventions (e.g. hormones), but just before Christmas 2022 the WA Government announced plans to amend birth certificate legislation—a matter discussed in the next chapter.

When the dust settled

By 2010 Australia's trans communities had gone through rapid changes. Organisations had come and gone, and many of the established groups had weathered internal divisions. Yet, instead of seeing different groups fighting with each other, there was a growing sense of transgender as an umbrella that could encompass all sorts of people with different life experiences. No longer were groups competing over who was more trans; rather, they were coexisting, catering to different demographics under the trans umbrella.

There were other quiet changes during the first decade of the new millennium. Non-medical and psychological research studies were including trans people as a discrete category, providing empirical data about the experiences of trans people in Australia. Doctors were beginning to shift away from acting as gatekeepers and towards an informed-consent model where trans clients had more say over their health care. Doctors began to see trans children and young people seeking affirming care, and the 2000s set important precedents in both law and treatment approaches that would grow exponentially in the next decade. More people challenged binary understandings of gender. As the final chapter shows, the 2010s and 2020s were a time when these ideas came to the fore and trans activists pushed for new legal reforms and rights to reflect more diverse understandings of gender.

8
CONTEMPORARY TRANS AFFAIRS

O N 25 JUNE 2013, the federal parliament passed amendments to the *Sex Discrimination Act* that added sexual orientation, gender identity and intersex status as protected categories. The reform received little media attention because a day later Kevin Rudd replaced Julia Gillard for his second stint as prime minister. Yet this was momentous legislative reform that finally extended federal anti-discrimination protection to LGBTIQ+ people. It came just as trans visibility was reaching its global tipping point. Within weeks the TV show *Orange Is the New Black* would premiere on Netflix, launching trans actor Laverne Cox's public profile. In the next two years, Catherine McGregor and Caitlyn Jenner would be in the Australian and global spotlights respectively.

The 2010s and 2020s represented a time of greater acceptance of trans people and new ideas about non-binary entering popular discourse, challenging both cis and trans people to rethink gender. This period also witnessed a growing conservative movement that fearmongered about gender fluidity, children and sport, hoping that ignorance around these topics would sway the public and politicians to oppose trans and other LGBTIQ+ rights. Put bluntly: now that gay and lesbian people had won mainstream acceptance, conservative forces were targeting trans people.

There has been so much visibility and change in the 2010s–20s that it could fill an entire book. As such, this chapter focuses on the big debates around health care, birth certificates and trans children's rights. These have been global debates, and Australia has proven more progressive than most other developed countries. Still, the vocal anti-trans backlash has taken its toll on the mental health of trans Australians. The past ten years have represented great struggle and vigilance as trans people continue to come out, organise and express themselves in increasingly diverse ways.

From gatekeepers to informed consent

For decades doctors, especially psychiatrists, defined what it meant to be trans. In 1991 American transgender activist Sandy Stone wrote the essay 'The *Empire* Strikes Back', which, according to Eric Plemons and Chris Straayer, spurred trans activists internationally 'to decenter, refract, complicate, or refuse the medical discourses that had for decades defined transsexuals as a group constituted by the desire for sex-altering surgical intervention'.[1] In Australia, as early as 1995 Jesse Hooley and Aidy Griffin attended psychology conferences where they gave papers challenging the medical model of transsexualism and introduced social constructivist ideas about gender. Jesse and Julie Peters also independently gave papers at feminist and queer academic conferences between 1994 and 1999 where they consistently contested the pathologisation of trans people.[2]

In the 2000s the push for doctors to shift away from a gatekeeper model of health care to informed consent gained traction. Informed consent meant trans people deciding what medical interventions they wanted, rather than having to meet psychiatrists' rigid expectations. Initially, doctors at the Monash Gender Dysphoria Clinic continued to adhere to the gatekeeper model; the model even became stricter after detransitioners sued doctors associated with the clinic in 2003 and 2007.[3] The bad publicity triggered reviews of the clinic and forced its temporary closure in 2009. It reopened three months later, and over the next decade the new clinic directors slowly shifted away from the gatekeeper model towards informed consent. Reflecting this new direction, the clinic was renamed the Monash Gender Clinic in 2016 and trans community members became part of a consumer advisory group to co-design its policies and practices.[4]

In the 2010s trans activists also pushed for new peer-controlled primary care clinics. In early 2013, the Queensland Government ended the arrangement in place since 1994 where the Brisbane Gender Clinic operated out of the Department of Health. The national spokesperson for PFLAG (Parents, Families and Friends of Lesbians and Gays), Shelley Argent, donated $20,000 to convert a room at the Queensland AIDS Council (QuAC) into a medical suite to continue running the Brisbane Gender Clinic one day a week.[5] To meet burgeoning demand for services, in 2017 ATSAQ leaders Gina Mather and Kristine Johnson worked with Dr Graham Neilsen to set up another multidisciplinary gender service at the Royal Brisbane and Women's Hospital.[6]

Victoria is the other state that made great strides in primary trans health care. In late 2015 staff associated with the Victorian AIDS Council's free peer-led sexual health clinic, Pronto!, considered the possibility of using the space as a trans health clinic in the daytime. The Victorian AIDS Council supported the idea and brought trans employee Jeremy Wiggins together with clinic's practice manager, Peter Locke, and Dr P Cundill. In July 2016, Equinox opened in Fitzroy as Australia's first peer-led trans health service. In 2019 the Victorian Government funded two more peer-led trans health clinics that opened in Preston and Ballarat.[7]

Other state AIDS councils, too, stepped up their support for trans health and wellbeing in the late 2010s. The most visible example of this is ACON (formerly the AIDS Council of NSW), thanks in large part to the leadership of ACON employee and trans man Teddy Cook. In 2017 three representatives of a group called Rainbow Rights Watch met with ACON's leadership to discuss problems facing the trans community and encouraged ACON to step up its advocacy and support services.[8] ACON facilitated a consultation process and in 2019 produced the document 'A Blueprint to Improve the Health and Wellbeing of the Trans and Gender Diverse Community in NSW'. In March 2020 it launched TransHub, an online resource for trans people, health practitioners and allies that provides information on topics including language, advice on social, legal and medical affirmation, a list of gender-affirming medical practitioners, and education resources. A Yarning Circle advisory group supported the development of TransHub to ensure that the information is accessible for Aboriginal and Torres Strait Islander people.

Across the country, more GPs, psychiatrists and other specialists have been taking up the informed-consent model. AusPATH (originally founded as ANZPATH in 2009) has in many ways mirrored this transition. In its early years the majority of its members were doctors, and trans voices were on the margins, but since 2019 trans community members have made up a majority of board members. On 31 March 2022, AusPATH published its first 'Australian Informed Consent Standards of Care for Gender Affirming Hormone Therapy', centring trans people and seeking to empower clinicians to support trans clients.[9] Finally, AusPATH has become more vocal at advocating for trans rights in a variety of legal and social settings, recognising that securing trans rights is central to trans people's health and wellbeing.

Legal recognition beyond the binary

A study published by the Australian Research Centre in Sex, Health and Society in 2014 found that more than one in three trans and gender-diverse young people identified with genders beyond the binary of man and woman.[10] This explosion of non-binary identifications seems a recent phenomenon, but it is not new. As noted in Chapter 4, in the 1990s a small number of activists, including Aidy Griffin and Norrie, were talking about gender not being fixed or binary. Margaret Jones was using the word 'androgyne' in the late 1990s to describe themself and in 2002 began using the non-binary transgender title Mx.[11] In the 2000s the term 'gender-queer' was popular among young people to describe those who did not identify as exclusively male or female. Since the 2010s, with increased non-binary visibility, more people—especially young people—have had the language to identify as non-binary.[12]

Accompanying the rise in non-binary visibility have been efforts at law reform to recognise genders beyond the binary. In March 2009 the Australian Human Rights Commission published a report entitled *Sex Files: The Legal Recognition of Sex in Documents and Government Records.* Its recommendations all centred on making it easier for people to update their sex and gender markers on legal documents, including removing the requirement for medical or surgical interventions and shifting towards self-identification. The report also recommended that gender categories be updated to allow people to select 'unspecified' rather than be forced into the male/female binary.

A small organisation named Sex and Gender Education (SAGE), founded in 2001, worked hard to support the *Sex Files* report. SAGE founder Tracie O'Keefe thought Norrie could prove an effective test case around the recommendations. Norrie spent several weeks gathering evidence, including two doctors' statutory declarations that confirmed that Norrie's sex was 'not specified'. In November 2009 Norrie lodged the application with the NSW Registry of Births, Deaths and Marriages to change their birth certificate sex marker. In February 2010, they received confirmation that their sex was now registered as 'not specified'.[13]

On Friday 12 March 2010, a *Sydney Morning Herald* cover story reported on Norrie's change-of-sex recognition, and on Monday 15 March, Norrie received word that the NSW attorney-general had overruled the registrar and disallowed their change of sex, asserting that sex could only be male or female. Norrie worked with Tracie to lodge an appeal with the Administrative Decisions Tribunal (the predecessor of the NSW Civil and Administrative Tribunal) and a complaint with the Australian Human Rights Commission. Norrie lost in the Administrative Decisions Tribunal and appealed to the NSW Supreme Court. They won in the Supreme Court, so the NSW attorney-general then appealed to the High Court of Australia. On 2 April 2014 the High Court unanimously ruled that sex need not be binary and ordered that Norrie's sex be legally recognised as 'non specific'.[14] Norrie's High Court victory set the national precedent that state governments could recognise genders beyond the binary for trans people. The ruling had its limitations because the 1996 NSW birth certificate law still applied—namely, to change sex markers on a birth certificate, even to 'non specific', a trans person needed to undergo gender affirmation surgery.[15]

The movements for birth certificate reform focused on two simultaneous changes: removing the requirement for gender affirmation surgery, and introducing gender markers beyond the binary. The first jurisdiction to introduce both reforms was the Australian Capital Territory, though even there it took a bit of time. Following the publication of the *Sex Files* report, Peter Hyndal and A Gender Agenda lobbied heavily for reform, in the process building alliances with other trans groups across Australia and other organisations in the ACT.[16] In January 2011 the ACT attorney-general tasked the Law Reform Advisory Council to conduct an inquiry into the recognition of trans and intersex people. Its report, titled *Beyond the Binary*, was completed in March 2012 but not tabled in the ACT Legislative Assembly until February 2013. It had a suite of recommendations, and one of the most powerful, summative statements read:

The requirement that a person must undergo 'sexual reassignment surgery' to apply to alter the record of their sex can rightly be said to be 'inhumane'; it violates a person's human rights to privacy and to bodily integrity, the right to freedom from torture, and the right to equal legal status unless they submit to invasive medical procedures.[17]

It would be another year before the ACT Legislative Assembly passed birth certificate reform. The final legislation required that anyone changing their gender marker would need a letter from a doctor or psychologist certifying that they had undergone 'appropriate clinical treatment', which was intentionally left open to interpretation. The bill also allowed parents to change their children's birth certificates, and introduced the gender marker 'X' for non-binary people. The bill passed in March 2014 and came into effect in April, making the Australian Capital Territory the first jurisdiction to introduce the option of non-binary gender markers for all people.[18]

The next state to implement birth certificate reform was South Australia. In October 2014, on the heels of the ACT reform and Norrie's High Court win, the Greens member of the Legislative Council, Tammy Franks, introduced the Sexual Reassignment Repeal Bill and it was referred to the Legislative Review Committee for an inquiry. Several LGBTIQ+ and trans organisations, allies, medical professionals and people such as Jenny Scott put in submissions. The final report, tabled in April 2016, recommended repealing the *Sexual Reassignment Act* and introducing amendments to birth certificates akin to those the Australian Capital Territory had already implemented.

The amendments had the support of trans community members, and they lobbied all sides of politics.[19] This was vital because both parties had granted a conscience vote and there was no guarantee the bill would pass. In September 2016 it was defeated in the lower house when there was a tied vote of 19–19; the Speaker of the House cast the tie-breaker vote of no. Several supporters of the bill, including the premier, were absent because nobody had advised that it would be coming to a vote that day. A slightly amended version passed both houses of parliament later that year; the law came into effect in May 2017.[20]

The Northern Territory was the third jurisdiction to pass birth certificate reform, in late November 2018. It followed the same model as the Australian Capital Territory and South Australia: removing the surgery requirement but still necessitating that a doctor or psychologist provide a letter certifying that the person had undergone 'appropriate medical treatment'.[21] In the NT the gender marker options beyond the binary are either 'non-binary' or 'unspecified'.

In other states, the legislation around birth certificate reforms was more progressive but the debates more divisive. Martine Delaney recalls first raising the subject of birth certificates with a Tasmanian attorney-general in 2004, and then discussing the issue with nine attorneys-general over the next fifteen years. Consistently, the answer was that a national approach was needed and birth certificate reform should go through the Standing Committee of Attorneys-General—the same committee that had spent six years deliberating the first round of birth certificate reforms in the 1980s and could not come to an agreement.

In 2017 Martine realised she needed to change tack and conduct a more public campaign. She and the Tasmanian Gay and Lesbian Rights Group founded Transforming Tasmania around the same time as the national marriage equality campaign. This organisation enlisted and skilled up trans people, parents of trans and gender-diverse children, and allies to garner public support and lobby politicians across all parties as well as independents, who are crucial to passing any legislation through Tasmania's upper house. Transforming Tasmania also began drafting birth certificate legislation itself.

The numbers game in the lower house became interesting after the 2018 Tasmanian state election. The Liberals had a majority with 13 seats and Labor and Greens combined had 12. The speaker of the house, Sue Hickey, was a Liberal but known for her independent streak and voting with her conscience. Martine and Transforming Tasmania took a draft bill to the attorney-general but she refused to accept it. They then took the bill to Labor and the Greens, who worked with Transforming Tasmania to refine the legislation. Labor and the Greens tabled the bill in the lower house; in November 2018, the speaker used her tie-breaker vote to pass the legislation. Despite the attorney-general trying to disrupt parliamentary process, the upper house passed the legislation with amendments. When it returned to the lower house, the speaker again used her tie-breaker vote to go against her party, passing Tasmania's birth certificate reform in April 2019.[22]

The Tasmanian reform went further than that of the Australian Capital Territory, South Australia and the Northern Territory. There is no requirement for applicants to provide a doctor or psychologist's certification that they are undergoing medical treatment. People can change their birth certificate at age sixteen without parental consent. In addition to the option to amend their gender to 'non-binary' or 'indeterminate gender', there is an 'other' box, where the applicant can write in their preferred gender term. Finally, gender became optional on birth certificates—a point that became the lightning rod for conservative opposition. Nonetheless, as Martine summarises: 'Despite the best efforts of the government, we got possibly the most progressive birth certificate legislation in the world, and we are the only jurisdiction on the planet that has ever achieved that legislation with a government opposed to it. It's a good feeling so I'm fairly proud of that one'.[23]

It took two attempts for the Victorian Parliament to pass similar progressive legislation. The Andrews Labor government came to power in late 2014 with a strong equality agenda. In its first term it set up the Victorian LGBTI Taskforce, co-chaired from 2015 to 2019 by Transgender Victoria's chair, Brenda Appleton, and appointed Ro Allen as the state's inaugural Gender and Sexuality Commissioner. In 2016 the government introduced a bill similar to the ACT reforms. It passed the lower house but could not get enough cross-bench support in the upper house. Following the 2018 election, the re-elected Labor government again introduced birth certificate reform, only this time it was more like the Tasmanian model. In addition to repealing the surgery requirement, people could identify any gender marker they wished and would not require any letters certifying they had medical treatment. The reforms generated heated debate, but there was more than enough cross-bench support for the bill to pass in August 2019. The law came into effect in May 2020.

Activists in Queensland and Western Australia gained traction after the re-election of Labor governments during the COVID-19 pandemic. In November 2021 the Queensland attorney-general flagged an intention to introduce new birth certificate laws by the end of 2022.[24] After extensive consultations with trans and other stakeholders, the Queensland Government tabled legislation in December 2022 on a similar model to Tasmania and Victoria: there would be no need for medical treatment, and people could elect their own gender descriptors beyond the binary. The Queensland Parliament referred the bill to the Legal Affairs and Safety Committee for detailed consideration and in February 2023 the final report recommended passage of the legislation.[25] The legislation passed the Queensland Parliament in June 2023.

The long road to reform in Western Australia also finally had a breakthrough in late 2022. In 2018 the state's Law Reform Commission recommended the repeal of the *Gender Reassignment Act* and the removal of sex markers altogether from birth certificates. Instead, anyone would be able to apply for a Gender Identity Certificate, which would have the options of male, female and non-binary.[26] As of May 2022, the WA Government still had not considered the recommendations of the report.[27] In September 2022 the president of the Gender Reassignment Board resigned and was not replaced, leading to a backlog of unprocessed applications. The *West Australian* reported on the impasse and how the growing delays were affecting the mental health of trans applicants who were stuck in legal limbo. Then, just before Christmas, the WA Government announced plans to repeal the *Gender Reassignment Act*, abolish the Gender Reassignment Board and replace it with birth certificate reform akin to that in the Australian Capital Territory, South Australia and the Northern Territory.[28]

As of early 2023, it was only in New South Wales that there had been no action or announcement of plans to reform the birth certificate laws. Independent MP Alex Greenwich announced his intention to introduce an omnibus Equality Bill that, among other reforms, would amend birth certificate laws to remove surgery requirements.[29] Neither major party committed to birth certificate reform in the March 2023 election, though the outcome of a Labor minority government gives more prospect for Greenwich's bill to be debated in the new term of parliament.

New and changing trans advocacy

Trans organisations have come and gone over the years, but a few have effectively adapted to changing circumstances. The most obvious examples are Seahorse Victoria and NSW, which continue to host regular social gatherings. Seahorse Victoria celebrated its forty-fifth birthday in 2020 with the publication of a retrospective history, while in 2022 Seahorse NSW hosted a 50th + 1 anniversary ball. ATSAQ is still active in Queensland, continuing to hold monthly luncheons, lobbying for reforms and representing Queensland's trans community at stakeholder engagements. Transgender Victoria continues to be the peak advocacy group in that state. Brenda Appleton was chair from 2002 to 2020 and proved instrumental in improving the organisation's profile and financial viability through developing training programs for aged care providers and other organisations.[30] In New South Wales, a mapping exercise conducted by the Ministry of Health in 2019 found that the Gender Centre still delivers 93 per cent of trans-specific services in the state. The Gender Centre offers peer support groups, counselling and training workshops and has partnered with health services in Sydney and Dubbo to support trans clients through affirming models of care.[31]

In Western Australia, the decline of TransWest left a vacuum in organised trans advocacy. Even the Chameleon Society saw a decrease in members to the point of folding in 2015 when nobody stood for office-bearer roles (the same thing happened to South Australia's Carousel Club in February 2023). Meanwhile, around 2013 Nick Lawrence started the group Trans Men of WA to offer peer support and social opportunities for trans men. Alyce Schotte, who was one of the final organisers of the Chameleon Society, had a conversation with Nick about setting up a group that could sit under the auspices of Trans Men of WA and offer support to other members under the trans umbrella. Nick pondered Alyce's idea and, as she put it, in 2017 'took it to the next level of asking other people and getting other people involved in basically then incorporating the entity which was TransFolk of WA'.[32]

TransFolk of WA rapidly grew into the predominant trans organisation in Western Australia and now operates both online and face-to-face. The original Trans Men of WA group morphed into an online subgroup, and the organisation added other closed Facebook groups for trans women, non-binary people and, later, parents, partners and children and young people. Most of the organisation's work is around advocacy, support and visibility. TransFolk of WA has compiled a list of specialists and trans-friendly health professionals in Western Australia and runs a monthly social event, and representatives attend pride events in Perth, Bunbury, Albany and other parts of the state.[33]

In Brisbane, QuAC founded the group Many Genders One Voice in 2011 as a response to the discrimination and stigma trans people faced in trying to access affirming health care. It was originally known as the Trans Health Action Group and early on focused on peer support and telephone counselling. Trans man Parker Forbes, a finance officer at QuAC, came on board and transformed it to offer tangible support to trans people. He convinced the executive director of QuAC to bankroll the purchase of chest binders to distribute at a subsidised rate or for free. Parker spoke to a manufacturer in the United States and they agreed to offer one free binder for every one purchased for the binder project. Many Genders One Voice also used to run a clothing drive where trans people could purchase a bag of used clothing for a few dollars and have a safe space to try on stuff.

Many Genders One Voice also introduced trans-specific events inspired by existing LGBTIQ+ celebrations in Brisbane. Observing that there were few trans stalls or trans-specific activities at the annual Brisbane Pride Fair Day, in 2016 it began its own Trans Fair Day. That same year, frustrated with the lack of trans representation among winners of the annual Queens Ball Awards, Many Genders One Voice started the Trans Community Awards. The awards honour individual activists, organisations, programs, allies and health professionals for their contributions to Queensland's trans community.[34]

Adrian Barnes' interest in facilitating online spaces led to other new groups. In 1997 Adrian started an online discussion forum called Crossdressing in Australia. In 2001, she moved the site to a different platform and changed the domain name to Trannyradio—a pun on the term tranny, which was still in vogue, and the idea of a transistor radio (as a kid, Adrian always had an interest in transistor radios). By July 2004 Trannyradio had 153 members; this had increased to 500 by March 2007. The membership of active participants—meaning those who posted at least once in a calendar year—peaked at 728 in 2011. That same year, in recognition that 'tranny' was now seen as a derogatory slur, Adrian changed the group's name to TgR.[35]

Other trans people have worked as consultants to elevate trans voices. Examples are too numerous to name them all, but I will mention a few. Starlady has worked for years in Victoria and the Northern Territory to deliver education programs and workshops, with particular attention on supporting Indigenous people, regional communities and young people. Much of the work she does now is through the Zoe Belle Gender Collective—including a ground-breaking project called Transfemme that aims to fight misogyny and support healthy relationships between trans women/trans femme people and cis men.[36] Jenni Atkinson has been a longstanding advocate for trans, intersex and asexual people in Canberra. She used to be part of a collective called TranzAustralia that had a YouTube channel featuring different trans people speaking about their living experiences. She now runs her own consultancy where she delivers trans awareness training to workplaces, schools, charities and religious groups and assists with preparing trans-affirming policies.[37] Rebeckah Loveday spent four years at WorkingOUT, an employment program to support LGBTIQ+ job seekers. From there, she began to deliver trans inclusion training and built a public profile. From December 2017 to January 2021 she co-hosted *The Gender Agenda* on JOY 94.9 radio, elevating trans voices and highlighting their contributions to all walks of life. As noted in Chapter 5, Rebeckah is one of the founders of Trans Sisters United, and she is also a model and actor.[38] Katherine Wolfgramme, too, has long delivered trans inclusion training programs not only within Australia but also to corporations around the world. As recognition for her advocacy, in 2019 she won the Inspirational Role Model of the Year award at the Australian LGBT Awards, and in 2021 she was made a Fellow at the UK-based Royal Society of Arts.[39]

The rise of Facebook and social networking sites generated a plethora of other trans social groups. One such group began in 2015 when a small group of trans people gathered at a cafe in Darlinghurst. Peta Friend wanted to form a new social group that could change the narrative of trans people from one of suffering to one of resilience, vibrancy and celebration. She brought together some longstanding trans community members, including Penny Clifford and Colleen Windsor, and from that first meeting, Trans Pride Sydney was born. The group began with monthly social meetups around days of significance or days when trans people may feel isolated or lonely. When the organisation set up a Facebook page, members joined from across Australia and even overseas. In 2018 the group incorporated and renamed itself Trans Pride Australia.

Organisers subsequently created multiple Facebook groups for allies, for partners, and for parents of trans and gender-diverse people.[40]

Trans Pride Australia member Katherine Wolfgramme in 2016 organised a Trans Day of Remembrance candlelight vigil in Taylor Square—an event she described as Carmen Rupe's dream.[41] Another popular series of events run by Trans Pride Australia was called Trans Stories. It was so successful that Peta pitched it to be part of the Sydney Gay and Lesbian Mardi Gras program in 2018 as *Trans Stories: 40 Years*. The format subsequently became *My Trans Story* and travelled to other parts of Australia, with over sixty speakers having taken part. When the COVID-19 pandemic hit in 2020, Trans Pride Australia began to offer regular online Zoom meet-ups.[42]

Several other new groups offered social environments that fit more specifically to people's interests or specific identity under the trans umbrella. For instance, from about 2003 to 2010, Emma Thorne ran a group called Adelaide Cross-Dress Goddess. She organised an annual show and party titled Stepping Out that brought in big bands and various other performers, attracting upwards of 150 guests.[43] When Emma stopped organising Stepping Out, Adrian Barnes, the organiser of TgR, revamped it from 2010 to 2017 as an annual weekend getaway in Katoomba known as Transformal.[44]

Trans men and trans masculine people have also founded their own peer support and social groups. Although specific population data on trans Australians is hard to come by, community surveys now show trans men represented in similar percentages as trans women (36 per cent and 37 per cent respectively), with the number of non-binary individuals (27 per cent) also on the rise.[45] Andrew Eklund recalls that while he was transitioning, he had a keen desire to meet other trans men. In 2013, he, Dale Hewinson (the former Melbourne convenor of Boys Will Be Boys) and three other trans men founded a new peer support group in Victoria: FTM Shed. They hosted their first formal meeting at the Victorian AIDS Council on 23 June 2013 and fifty people turned up. Originally the organisation identified as for trans men, but as non-binary and trans masculine people became more visible, the committee deliberated about its own identity and how inclusive it should be. Andrew was still on the committee during those debates around 2016 and recalls:

> As gender diversity and non-binary and these identities became more to the fore, there were committee discussions, there were debates about who's this for, bringing that up again. There was a strong voice against it at one point, and I was a strong voice for inclusion, and we went forward and included, and we dropped the FTM out of the name and it became The Shed, and it's changed. The environment has changed.[46]

Trans masculine groups in other states grew from a similar journey of trans men trying to connect with each other. In 2017, Joel Wilson began a Facebook group called Trans Masc Canberra that quickly grew in membership. It hosted monthly meet-ups that could be anything from a cafe gathering to a clothing drive and swap.[47] The South Australian group TransMascSA began in 2016 when Zac Cannell and a friend founded a new social group for trans men called FTMen-SA. The group held fortnightly meetings and quickly attracted over 100 members. Like similar organisations interstate, often there would be a monthly theme such as coming out, how to wear binders, how to access testosterone or top surgery, or where to find packers and other affirming objects. Within a couple of years Zac and the other organisers recognised an increasing number of non-binary and trans masculine members. They held a poll in the group and changed the name to TransMascSA. Although based in Adelaide, the face-to-face meetings attract people who regularly drive in from other places in South Australia, including Victor Harbor and Mount Gambier. Zac said the furthest attendee was someone who drove six hours from Ceduna. He retains demographic data about TransMascSA's membership that is more detailed than that of many other trans organisations. For instance, he is able to cite the percentage of members who are First Nations or culturally and linguistically diverse and knows that they roughly mirror the national average.[48]

Among queer and trans Blak, Indigenous and people of colour, voguing houses and ballroom events have grown in popularity in the 2010s. The voguing and ballroom scene comes from 1970s–80s New York, where Black queer, gay and trans people used to gather for regular stylised dance competitions combined with costume pageantry. The ballroom scene gained international attention in part thanks to Madonna's 1990 hit 'Vogue' but more so through the award-winning documentary *Paris Is Burning* (1990). The American television show *Pose* (2018–21) introduced ballroom to a new generation, catalysing the expansion of a house scene that was already emerging in Australia.

In 2015, Bhenji Ra returned to Sydney after living in New York, where she participated in the ballroom scene. She was disenchanted with the whiteness of so much of Sydney's LGBTIQ+ community so searched for a new place of belonging. Bhenji explained in an interview with *SBS Sexuality*: 'Through one group in Liverpool [western Sydney], a giant group of hip hop dancers, we decided to create a side queer group and work towards occupying spaces and creating something for ourselves. It was really about bridging these gaps between the suburbs and metropolitan city.'[49] This group morphed into western Sydney's House of Slé, a family of queer and trans Pasifika and Asian people.

In 2018, Bhenji organised Australia's first Sissy Ball as part of the Sydney Gay and Lesbian Mardi Gras.[50] It was a huge success and became an annual event, further catalysing the growth of the ballroom and house scene across Australia. Brisbane's own House of Alexander was founded in 2019 and organised its first Alexander Ball in 2020.[51] Other houses in Australia include House of Dévine and House of Klein from Melbourne, House of Reign from Perth, and House of Silky and House of Luna from Sydney. Being part of a house is not just about dancing—it is also about family, affirmation and pride. Xander Khoury, founder of Sydney's House of Silky, explains: 'We've seen from generation to generation just how significant they [chosen families] have been and how much they've helped people through incredibly hard times. When it was illegal to be ourselves. These queer families really supported one another, even in Ballroom's history itself and it still happens today.'[52] The opening concert of Sydney WorldPride 2023 included a ballroom performance featuring the prominent Sydney houses Silky, Luna and Slé, highlighting the significance of ballroom within Australia's contemporary LGBTIQ+ community.

The examples presented here of trans organisations and advocacy in the 2010s–20s are only a sample. Whether aiming to represent all trans people or tailored to a particular demographic, they demonstrate the ongoing need for trans people to be seen and to find places to belong. They also highlight the diverse gender expressions and identities under the trans umbrella and a more visible, younger demographic. This final point has proven especially salient in new debates over trans rights and health care.

Trans children, health care and the law

Many trans people recognise from an early age that there is something different about their experience of gender. Before 2000, GPs, psychiatrists and gender clinics generally only worked with transgender adults or the occasional teenager approaching age eighteen: trans children in Australia were, for all intents and purposes, silenced and invisible. By the early 2000s, as there was more trans visibility in the media and a proliferation of information on the internet, trans children and young people began to come out and seek medical interventions.

Trans children first became a topic of public debate when 'Alex' was referred to the Royal Children's Hospital in Melbourne in 2003. Alex was thirteen years old and wanted to commence puberty-blocking hormones and then testosterone. Endocrinologist

Garry Warne, who had previously worked with intersex children, became Alex's doctor. He did research overseas and determined that what he calls the Dutch approach, which was about affirming care at a young age, was preferable to the British approach, which was about waiting until someone approached adulthood. Garry also consulted with the director of the Monash Gender Dysphoria Clinic, who advised him that all of her clients knew from a young age that they were trans and would have benefited from affirming care.[53]

There was an extra twist in Alex's case: he was under a care order from the Children's Court and therefore doctors had to go to the Family Court to obtain consent for any medical procedure. In 2004 the chief justice of the Family Court approved Alex to commence puberty blockers at age thirteen and testosterone at age sixteen. Still, the case *Re: Alex* set a precedent that would limit trans children's access to medical care: the judge dubbed hormone treatments 'special medical procedures' under the *Family Law Act*. This meant that the Family Court would need to grant permission in *all* cases for children to access hormones.[54] The need to go to the Family Court was costly for families and meant significant delays of sometimes up to ten months before they could access care. The delays had flow-on effects on mental health, not to mention the distress of having to face the court.[55]

In the 2010s an alliance of trans activists, parents and doctors lobbied for legal change, often while at the same time managing their own cases. One of the more prominent examples was Georgie Stone. She and her parents worked closely with Garry and, after his retirement, with Associate Professor Michelle Telfer, the director of the newly formed Royal Children's Hospital Gender Service in Melbourne. Georgie's mother, Rebekah Robertson, has written about the challenges the family navigated to support Georgie, which the Family Court process only exacerbated.[56] In 2011 the Family Court authorised ten-year-old Georgie—known in the case as 'Jamie'—to access stage one hormones: puberty blockers. Still, the family appealed the ruling, arguing that gender-affirming care should not be restricted as a special medical procedure. In 2013 the Family Court ruled in *Re: Jamie* that puberty blockers would no longer be considered a special medical treatment and therefore, so long as both parents consented, trans children would no longer need Family Court authorisation for puberty blockers.[57]

For the next four years, Georgie, Rebekah, Michelle and other families and health professionals advocated for further law reform. In November 2014, the ABC-TV program *Four Corners* aired an episode titled 'Being Me' that brought the challenges facing trans children into the public eye. By 2016, Georgie was free to speak publicly and featured in a moving episode of *Australian Story* titled 'About a Girl' (the same title Rebekah later used for her book). The episode, viewed by more than a million people, introduced in Georgie a new activist advocating for the rights of trans and gender-diverse young people. Georgie, Rebekah, Michelle and other advocates consistently met with state and federal politicians to talk about the importance of law reform and affirming care for trans children.[58]

Ultimately, it was not the politicians but a new series of Family Court rulings that changed the law. In the 2017 case *Re: Kelvin*, the court finally ruled that stage two affirming hormones were not special medical treatment and that parents and trans children could consent to their use. In early 2018, the *Re: Matthew* ruling established that the Family Court would no longer have to authorise gender affirmation surgeries for trans adolescents. The court took a step back in 2020. In *Re: Imogen* one parent was willing to consent to hormone treatment but the other was not. The court ruled that in the absence of unanimous consent among the child, all parents or guardians and the doctors, it would have to approve hormone treatment. That said, it approved the treatment for Imogen.[59]

Trans activists, families and health professionals have continued to lobby for reform because there are still power imbalances. Most important to their arguments is the concept of 'Gillick competence'. This term derives from a 1985 common-law ruling in the

United Kingdom where the court said that children under sixteen could make decisions about their own health care once they were of sufficient intelligence to give informed consent. Gillick competence is recognised in common law in most jurisdictions; only in South Australia is it codified, in the *Consent to Medical Treatment and Palliative Care Act* 1995. Thus, outside South Australia the Family Court rulings essentially overrule Gillick competence when it comes to trans health care. Activists highlight that trans health is the only aspect of children's health care where children who are Gillick-competent still require parental consent.

Advocates for affirming care had a potential breakthrough in a 2022 Supreme Court of Queensland case. A mother and child went to the court in its parens patriae jurisdiction, meaning to allow it to hear the case instead of the Family Court. The Supreme Court not only supported the mother's application to authorise stage two hormones, but also affirmed the applicability of Gillick competence to *all* trans children's health care.[60] The ruling only applies in Queensland, but activists hope that it has set a precedent that other state supreme courts and even the Family Court may apply in the future, leaving health-care decisions in the hands of trans children and their doctors.

Georgie Stone, for her part, has maintained a significant public profile advocating for the rights of trans children and young people. In 2016, Melbourne's Globe LGBTI Awards awarded her the honour of GLBTI Person of the Year, and in 2017 she was named Victorian Young Australian of the Year—the first openly trans person to win that honour. In 2020 she became the youngest person to receive a Medal of the Order of Australia (OAM), along with her mother, Rebekah, for advocacy and support for trans young people. Georgie has made numerous appearances in media and in 2022 was the subject of a short Netflix documentary, *The Dreamlife of Georgie Stone*. In April 2023, 22-year old Georgie became the youngest woman ever to address the National Press Club of Australia. Finally, the young actor became a regular cast member on the long-running TV soap opera *Neighbours* from 2019 until the show's supposed conclusion in 2022—and she will be part of the show's resurrection in the second half of 2023.

The legal challenges and changes have been only one dimension of the rise of public awareness and debate around trans children and their health care. Michelle Telfer recognised the need for specific standards of care for doctors and other professionals working with trans children and young people, and brought together trans children, families, doctors from other gender services and other stakeholders to prepare what would prove a global first. In late 2017 the team at the Royal Children's Hospital Gender Service published the first 'Australian Standards of Care and Treatment Guidelines for Trans and Gender-diverse Children and Adolescents'. The standards of care received the endorsement of AusPATH and in 2018 were published in the *Medical Journal of Australia*. The internationally renowned medical journal *The Lancet* published an editorial endorsing the standards of care, confirming their status as an international trailblazer in providing affirming care to trans children and young people.[61]

Several states and territories have established specialist gender services within their children's hospitals: the Royal Children's Hospital Gender Service in Melbourne (2012), the Children's Hospital Gender Diversity Service in Perth (2015), and the Queensland Children's Hospital Gender Clinic in Brisbane (2016). Other cities' children's hospitals have been seeing trans children and adolescents in the absence of a formal gender service. The Women's and Children's Hospital in Adelaide has been seeing clients since about 2009, Sydney's Westmead Children's Hospital received its first referrals in 2013, Newcastle's John Hunter Children's Hospital also around 2013, and Canberra Hospital in 2014. In 2021 Maple Leaf House opened as a new specialist hub for trans children and young people in Newcastle. Although there are no specialist services in Tasmania or the Northern Territory, there are now doctors there who work with trans children and young people.[62]

Family and peer support

Trans community members have always aimed to create peer support programs to meet differing needs. In 2010, nineteen-year-old Indian-Australian Bachelor of Youth Work student Sim Victor Kennedy was keen to establish projects that met trans young people's needs. After a few years of other community development work that enhanced preplanning, Sim began holding monthly meetings with like-minded peers in a room booked at the ALSO Foundation in Melbourne. Sim then advertised the meetings as a monthly space for trans young people. The group co-created a wish list of wins for trans people in various sections of society. They formed a committee and wrote a constitution, and in January 2011 the group of about twelve—an equal mix of trans men, trans women and non-binary/genderqueer people—voted unanimously to adopt the name YGender. The organisation was originally for anyone under thirty years of age, but that changed to under twenty-five. (Most Australian projects define young people as ages 12–25, including organisations that are recipients of youth suicide prevention funding.)

In January 2011 YGender organised its first event as part of Midsumma Festival and the next month it participated in Melbourne's Pride March. From that time YGender consistently held monthly events that were a mix of peer support and social gatherings. In November 2011 it organised one of Victoria's first commemorations of the Trans Day of Remembrance.[63] With succession planning in place, YGender continued to run after Sim left the group in 2014. Over its life, YGender members—all volunteers—achieved many of the wishes outlined at its inception. Members developed a suite of online resources and videos and focused much of their advocacy on intersectionality and accessibility. In early 2022, after two years of strain wrought by the COVID-19 pandemic, YGender leaders announced on social media that the group was folding.

In the 2010s other existing organisations became more focused on trans advocacy. Minus18, which had been supporting gay, lesbian and bisexual young people in Victoria since 1998, shifted much of its support, advocacy and social events to supporting trans young people. Both Minus18 and YGender contributed to the Safe Schools Coalition's 2016 'Gender Is Not Uniform' campaign, developing a resource guide to support schools to be more inclusive of gender diversity. Minus18 and YGender member Margot Fink coordinated the development of a series of videos and teaching activities for the Safe Schools Coalition (described below) to support the Health and Physical Education area of the Australian curriculum. In recognition of her work with Minus18 to support trans young people, in 2016 Margot was the first openly trans person to be a finalist for Victoria's nomination for Young Australian of the Year—an honour Georgie Stone won two years later.[64]

The NSW equivalent to Minus18 is the organisation Twenty10. Founded in 1982 as a project to support gay young people, by the 2010s it had shifted to support all parts of the LGBTIQ+ rainbow. Among the services it offers are transitional housing for young people at risk of homelessness, counselling and peer support groups. Twenty10 is also the NSW affiliate of the national phone and web counselling service QLife. Most of its services are for people aged sixteen to twenty-five, but counselling is available for children as young as twelve. Some of the peer support groups are trans-specific, and a large proportion of clients across all programs are trans or gender diverse.[65]

The 2010s also witnessed the emergence of new peer support groups founded by and for parents and families of trans and gender-diverse children. Rebekah Robertson wanted to ensure that other parents could have the support and advice her family so craved while supporting Georgie, so in 2012 she founded Transcend, Australia's first parent-led peer support organisation to support families of transgender children and young people. In 2016, Victorian mothers Meagan Macdonald and Karyn Walker founded Parents of Gender-Diverse Children (PGDC) as another peer support and advocacy group.[66] One of the mothers involved in PGDC, Jo Hirst, has authored two children's books affirming and normalising gender diversity, *The Gender Fairy* (2015) and *A House for Everyone* (2018).

Meagan's daughter Evie shot into the public spotlight in 2018 when she sent a video question to Prime Minister Scott Morrison on the television program *The Project*. Morrison had recently criticised the affirmation of trans children in schools, tweeting: 'We do not need "gender whisperers" in our schools. Let kids be kids.'[67] Thirteen-year-old Evie said in her video:

> There are thousands of kids in Australia that are gender diverse. We don't deserve to be disrespected like that through tweets from our prime minister … I know what it's like to be on the receiving end of attitudes like this. I went to a Christian school where I had to pretend to be a boy and spent weeks in conversion therapy. We get one childhood and mine was stolen from me by attitudes like this.[68]

Evie became a public speaker and advocate for trans children's rights. She, too, became an actor, in 2020–22 starring in the ABC ME children's program *First Day*, about a trans teenager starting at a new high school. *First Day* garnered critical praise and won a suite of prizes, most prominently a GLAAD (originally Gay & Lesbian Alliance Against Defamation) Media Award for Outstanding Kids & Family Programming and an International Emmy Kids Award in the category Kids: Live-Action.

In New South Wales, much of the support and activism around trans and gender-diverse children came from parents working in partnership with the Gender Centre. In 2010 Gender Centre employee 'Liz' founded the organisation's first parents support group.[69] At its third meeting, 'Lisa' spoke about the challenges she and her trans child had faced, and quickly the families in attendance were interacting. Lisa continued to attend the monthly meetings and watched as it grew to about sixty families. They came from many ethnic, cultural and socioeconomic backgrounds and their trans children ranged in age from three to their forties. In time, Lisa and other parents became co-facilitators of the group and in 2016 it expanded to hold monthly meetings in Wollongong. More recently there has been a parents support group that meets quarterly in Nowra. There is also an online Facebook group that, as of early 2022, had over 830 members.[70] TransFolk of WA has also run a parents support group since 2016, and Working It Out facilitates a group for parents of LGBTIQ+ children in Tasmania. Since 2013, Transfamily has run out of Melbourne as a peer support group for parents, siblings, extended family and friends of trans and gender-diverse people.

Lisa has also worked with the Gender Centre to offer social activities to support trans children and their families, such as picnics and camp days. She has helped to organise floats in four Sydney Gay and Lesbian Mardi Gras parades, and describes the feeling of marching: 'It is a joyous celebration and I think it's great for our kids who have marched with us to see the beautiful response from the crowd. And it's really good for the crowd to see parents and families who love and support their children out there shining.'[71]

The emergence of parents support groups and other organisations for trans and gender-diverse young people came at an opportune time. There was more trans visibility, the laws around affirming care for children were reforming, and there were more gender services across the country. That said, the demand for services has always outstripped availability, with long waitlists to access services. Many families are under financial and emotional strain because of the delays in accessing affirming health care, the bullying their children experience, and the discrimination they themselves encounter for having a trans child. Numerous research studies have shown the need for education systems and health services to support trans children and young people.[72] The most comprehensive Australian study has been Trans Pathways, a survey of 859 trans young people in Australia and 194 parents or guardians. Some of the damning statistics that Trans Pathways published in 2017 were:

- 79.7 per cent of trans young people have self-harmed
- 74.6 per cent of trans young people have been diagnosed with depression
- 60.1 per cent of participants reported having felt isolated from medical and mental health services
- 48.1 per cent of trans young people have attempted suicide
- 42.1 per cent of participants reached out to service providers who did not understand, respect or have previous experience with gender-diverse people[73]

Bear in mind, of course, that generally speaking it is only the affirming families that seek out support services. Trans children in hostile environments face physical and emotional danger from family, schoolmates, conversion ideology and conversion practices.[74] Exacerbating all of these challenges is the conservative backlash against trans people—particularly weaponising children—that has swept the country since the marriage equality postal survey.

The anti-trans backlash

The year 2017 was an important turning point for LGBTIQ+ rights in Australia. Activists had been lobbying for marriage equality for well over a decade, and opinion polls had long showed majority support for it. Yet politicians on both sides of parliament were intransigent about the issue. In August 2017, the Coalition government announced plans for a postal survey asking all enrolled voters the question: 'Should the law be changed to allow same-sex couples to marry?' The Yes campaign mobilised LGBTIQ+ activists and allies across the country to encourage a yes vote. The final result was 61.6 per cent yes, sparking great jubilation for LGBTIQ+ Australians and their allies. By the end of the year, the federal parliament had passed legislation legalising marriage rights for same-sex couples.[75]

Marriage equality was—or should have been—primarily about gay, lesbian and bisexual people (noting of course that trans people may also be gay, lesbian or bisexual), but the campaign and outcome affected trans people in two ways. First, in almost all jurisdictions a legal requirement for trans people to change their birth certificate was that they first divorce their spouse. One stipulation within the final marriage equality bill was that all states and territories had a year to remove this requirement, and all did so. The other way the marriage equality postal survey affected trans people was by unleashing a wave of transphobia that has never gone away. Much of the no campaign focused not on marriage equality but on superfluous topics involving trans people, hoping that it could tap into transphobia to stoke a no vote. As an example, one of the more prominent 'no' advertisements from the Coalition for Marriage began with a woman saying, 'School told my son he could wear a dress next year if he felt like it.' The entire advertisement played on fears about children and gender diversity, with a tenuous link (at best) to the actual rights of people of the same gender to marry.[76]

The anti-marriage-equality movement built on an ongoing conservative campaign against the Safe Schools Coalition. This was a group of organisations that supported a school program that had two aims: to combat bullying and to affirm young people with diverse sexualities and genders. Safe Schools began in Victoria in 2010, and from 2013 went national with federal funding. In early 2016, conservative politicians and media began to wage a war on the Safe Schools Coalition's school program, arguing that it was so-called cultural Marxism, sexualised young people, was a form of grooming children and was utterly inappropriate. A review commissioned by the federal government found Safe Schools to be above board, but this did not stop the virulent opposition from conservatives and the Murdoch-owned media. Indeed, the press attacks on Safe Schools were so virulent that they led to bomb threats at La Trobe University (where the program was managed), the founder being stalked and several contributors losing their jobs. In other states, too, staff who worked to support Safe Schools recall receiving horrific harassment and threats. One of the most persistent, and blatantly false, accusations levelled against the program was that it included instructions on penis-tucking. Safe Schools became a toxic brand among the political class, resulting in almost every state and territory government saying they would end the program when federal funding finished. Only the Victorian Government stood by the program and even promised to expand it.[77]

The conservative victory over Safe Schools showed the potential effectiveness of mis- and disinformation deployed against trans and other LGBTIQ+ people and emboldened the transphobic discourse both during and after the marriage equality survey. The no campaign had tragic results for the LGBTIQ+ community. Mental health services such as QLife reported a spike in calls, and some trans people died by suicide.[78] Yes campaigners certainly called out the no campaign's misinformation, but the yes campaign made the strategic decision not to engage with the substance of the no campaign's transphobic arguments *because* they were intended to be a distraction. While this decision may have contributed to the strong yes vote, it did not alleviate the awful effects that the campaign disproportionately had on trans people. Many trans people believe that gay, lesbian and bisexual campaigners disregarded trans people during the marriage equality campaign by not doing enough to stand up for their rights and dignity.[79]

The wave of transphobia unleashed by the marriage equality survey has never really gone away. The anti-trans movement broadly draws together two different groups. First is the traditional conservative movement, particularly the religious right, which for decades has campaigned against gay and lesbian rights. Now that gay and lesbian people have won mainstream acceptance, conservatives have turned their attention to trans people. The other anti-trans group consists of radicals who subscribe to binary, embodied differences in sex and refuse to accept gender as a social construct. The origins of this second group lie in one stream of radical feminism, particularly work by American writer Janice Raymond published in 1979, and many members of this group purport to be feminists.[80]

The British cis feminist Viv Smythe is often credited with coining the term TERF—trans exclusionary radical feminist—in 2008 to describe these women.[81] Some of the people described as TERFs consider the term a slur and prefer the expression 'gender critical' to describe themselves. The United Kingdom has proven to be a particular stronghold of TERFs/gender criticals and is sometimes even nicknamed 'TERF Island'. TERFs/gender criticals in the United Kingdom have influenced the derailing of gender-affirming legislation, trans children's health care and the right of trans people to play sports. The free information flow across cyberspace and borders means that British and other TERFs/gender criticals have often targeted Australian trans people online.

One of the most high-profile Australian TERFs/gender criticals is expatriate Germaine Greer, who was writing against trans women's identities as early as the 1980s.[82] Other homegrown TERFs/gender criticals have gained public platforms through the mainstream media and social media, regularly deploying falsehoods and myths about trans people. A common claim is that trans women threaten the safety of cis women, when there is no evidence of trans people systemically assaulting cis women. The media's willingness to give such people a platform has only elevated their voices and catalysed the anti-trans backlash.

Although transphobic campaigners have targeted trans rights in a variety of arenas, they have particularly homed in on two themes that spark emotive reactions: children and sport. Building on the successful campaign against the Safe Schools Coalition, conservative media have weaponised trans children and attacked any moves to provide them with affirming health care.[83] To give an air of legitimacy to their arguments, conservatives have often turned to doctors or academics who do not work in the field of trans health care. Many of these supposed 'experts' have ties to conservative anti-trans organisations. Much of the coverage has also selectively chosen individual examples or research studies as 'evidence' that an affirming model of care is harmful, while ignoring the overwhelming research, evidence and living experience.

Debates around trans women in sport have significantly increased since a turning point in 2017. The Australian Football League excluded trans woman and former handballer Hannah Mouncey from its inaugural women's draft, citing concerns about fairness and safety. This decision prompted public debate and sent sporting bodies to re-evaluate their practices and come up with clear policies and guidelines. Although the public debate has included vocal opponents of trans women in sport, most sporting codes have worked quietly with trans players, trans organisations and human rights commissions to come up with guidelines that land on the side of inclusion. In June 2019 the Australian Human Rights Commission, Sport Australia and the Coalition of Major Professional and Participation Sports published detailed 'Guidelines for the Inclusion of Transgender and Gender-diverse People in Sport'. Cricket Australia announced its trans and gender-diverse inclusion guidelines in August 2019, and in October 2020 eight other peak sporting bodies announced their respective guidelines around trans and gender-diverse inclusion.[84]

Perhaps embodying the present state of trans rights in Australia is the debate over the Religious Discrimination Bill in early 2022. This proposed federal legislation had its origins in the successful passage of marriage equality. As a concession to conservative opponents, the Coalition government initiated a 'Religious Freedom Review', which found that—contrary to the arguments advanced by conservatives—Australia did not have a problem with religious freedom. Still, the review noted that there was no federal anti-discrimination protection on the grounds of religion. This point became the basis for the Coalition's promise of a Religious Discrimination Bill during its successful 2019 election campaign. A draft bill finally went to the federal parliament in early 2022. LGBTIQ+ and allied organisations strongly opposed it, not because they were against the principle of enshrining protection from discrimination on the grounds of religion, but because the bill went further: a clause about so-called 'statements of belief' would have permitted religious individuals and organisations to discriminate against and/or vilify LGBTIQ+ people in a variety of settings, justified on the grounds of their religious beliefs.

Trans children became central to the final debate because of another legislative quirk, little-realised until the Religious Freedom Review. The 2013 amendments to the *Sex Discrimination Act* adding protections for LGBTIQ+ people had an exemption for religious schools. This means that religious schools have the right to discriminate and expel LGBTIQ+ students, at least under federal law (state and territory anti-discrimination laws vary in their exemptions for religious schools). The Labor opposition, the Greens, several independents and a few moderate members of the Liberal Party pushed for the Religious Discrimination Bill concurrently to amend the *Sex Discrimination Act* to remove the exemption for religious schools. Not surprisingly, the conservative religious right opposed this move—because they *wanted* religious schools to be allowed to discriminate against LGBTIQ+ children. Eventually, as a compromise to shore up support from moderate Liberals, the Coalition party room agreed to remove the exemption for gay and lesbian students, but not for trans children.

When the Religious Discrimination Bill went to the House of Representatives in February 2022, the debate went late into the night. A member of the crossbench put forward an amendment that would remove the *Sex Discrimination Act* exemptions that allowed religious schools to expel lesbian, gay, bisexual *and* transgender students. Labor, the Greens and other independents supported the amendment and, in a shocking move, enough moderate Liberals crossed the floor for the amendment to pass. The Religious Discrimination Bill then passed the House of Representatives— still with the controversial statements-of-belief clause, but with this minor victory for LGBT students. The religious right subsequently opposed the bill and the government did not pursue the legislation in the Senate, rendering the bill dead before the 2022 election.

The debate over the Religious Discrimination Bill happened at the same time as the preselection of an outspoken transphobic Liberal candidate for the seat of Warringah in the 2022 federal election. The candidate had a lot of media coverage but lost by a two-party-preferred margin of 61 to 39. These were important victories for trans rights in Australia, but still anti-trans activists would continue their campaign.

In March 2023, as LGBTIQ+ people were feeling (or recovering from) the euphoria of Sydney WorldPride, trans rights were again thrust into the spotlight. Conservative groups sponsored a high-profile anti-trans campaigner from the United Kingdom to go on a public speaking tour of east-coast capital cities. Trans activists and their allies staged protests in every city, but it was what happened in Melbourne that attracted national news. As police held back trans rights protesters, a group of neo-Nazis marched to the event in support of the anti-trans activists. The neo-Nazis stood on the steps of the Parliament House of Victoria and did the Sieg Heil salute. The fallout from this demonstration was manifold, but a few key points are worth noting. The Victorian Government and later the Queensland Government announced plans to outlaw the Nazi salute. The Victorian premier, Daniel Andrews, spoke strongly in favour of trans rights, injected funding to trans organisations for mental health support, and even had the trans flag hoisted at Parliament House. As the anti-trans tour continued in Hobart, Canberra and then Auckland, trans rights supporters consistently outnumbered the anti-trans activists. The pro-trans turnout in Auckland was so strong that the anti-trans campaigner ended her tour early and returned to the United Kingdom. Yet the damage was done. Trans people have described the anti-trans tour as making them feel vulnerable and unsafe. They continue to see their very existence subjected to 'debate', which only reinforces cycles of stigma, discrimination and mental health barriers. Politicians and other commentators may call for a 'respectful' debate, but the anti-trans tour exposed the hollowness of such calls: there is nothing respectful about debating someone's very existence. Even if the voices of trans inclusion were powerful enough to drive away a prominent anti-trans campaigner, as this entire history shows, there will of course be more battles to come.

Conclusion: On the importance of history

Trans rights and visibility have come a long way across the twentieth and twenty-first centuries. The past decade in particular has seen major strides towards self-identification of gender, informed consent, children's access to affirming care, and greater acceptance and inclusion. With each stride have come debate and backlash from the anti-trans movement. These debates cause real hurt to trans people. Indeed, high rates of distress, mental health barriers and suicidal ideation are not the result of anything inherently pathological about being trans. Rather, they are the consequences of ongoing societal stigmatisation and discrimination.

This book began with the adage 'You can't be what you can't see'. It has shown trans possibilities in the early twentieth century and the growing trans visibility and activism in the post–World War II period. Trans people who have lived through the history described in this book have diverse perspectives on the changes they have seen. Older interview participants are pleased to see the strides made towards greater acceptance. They also see strength in people feeling freer to express themselves in different ways. Nevertheless, to flip the saying 'You can't be what you can't see', several interview participants expressed fears about their contributions or identities being erased amid the ever-evolving labels and terminology. Of course, adding more diverse genders into the trans family is not meant to take away from those who are already there, but that is not always how some trans people feel—particularly when those new identities challenge their living experience.

'Susan', for instance, understands the importance of visibility and affirmation for people of diverse gender expressions but identifies strongly with the binary and prefers to live a stealth life:

> The demographic that I was a part of, really, you just want to access the services you need to transition to being female and then you just want to disappear. I don't want to be out and proud. If I can live my life as female—someone else used a great word to describe it: aspirant heteronormative. We don't really identify with the broader trans community. We actually identify with the binary heteronormative community. We just want to disappear.[85]

Andrew Eklund has always identified as a trans man, and he co-founded The Shed with the express purpose of providing a safe space for trans men. Over time, non-binary and trans masculine people have joined the group. While Andrew accepts this, he also expresses a sense of loss of the group being just for trans men:

> We aren't allowed to say on a post, 'Hi guys, hi mates!' I can't call out to other trans men who are male. I have lost some-thing. And does that matter? Well, it's the evolution of the group, and you can't hold that back. I don't believe you should. The population's changed. But it makes me feel old, and it makes me feel isolated again.[86]

Andrew, Susan and several other older interview participants often keep quiet about these feelings because they fear how younger trans activists will respond. They have seen virulent reactions on social media and in person.

Some older trans people may continue to use what is generally considered outdated terminology, be it 'transsexual', 'transvestite' or even 'tranny'. Rosemary Langton, the founder of Seahorse NSW in 1971, still unashamedly uses the word transvestite to describe herself and other dressers because the definition as coined by Magnus Hirschfeld in 1910 still perfectly fits her gender identity.[87] The term tranny is particularly interesting, with activists such as Norrie and Roberta Perkins (before she died) regularly using the word. There is, of course, a distinction between those trans people who claim terms for themselves and outsiders who use the words. In 2017 Katherine Wolfgramme hired solicitors who sent letters to sixteen pubs in New South Wales and the Australian Capital Territory that hosted 'Tranny Bingo' and other events that used 'tranny' in their names, threatening action through the Australian Human Rights Commission if they did not cease using the offensive term. Katherine is quite clear that she has no problem with trans people using the word—but it needs to be theirs to own. She explains: 'So what I did in actual fact was I took a word that was misappropriated. I took it back and I gave it back to the transgender community. Now, what they do with that word is completely up to them.'[88]

Identity is not a zero-sum game and does not have to be a competition. The rise of new labels and categories does not mean that those identities are new; rather, it signifies that people are more comfortable expressing their authentic selves and are finding new ways to explain their gender identity or expression. This is gender pluralism in action—welcoming new categories not as competitors but to sit alongside existing ones. History shows that the evolution of (trans)gender in Australia has not been about erasure but about strength through greater diversity. It is perhaps fitting, then, to let Brenda Appleton have the last word:

I would love that the society as a whole learned to accept difference, and not expect everybody to be the same and to meet society's unreal expectations. I would like that we can be different, be ourselves but be accepted … I think that we are all different. We are different shapes and sizes. We're different ethnicities. We've got different gender and sexualities. We've got different skills and experiences. We live in different places. We have different relationships. We often accept and reject what we are not familiar with, far too easily. I would love that we weren't so judgemental of each other and learned to embrace and celebrate difference, learning about and respecting each other. Vive la différence![89]

ACKNOWLEDGEMENTS

IN SEPTEMBER 2018, Sydney's *Daily Telegraph* ran one of its semi-regular articles attacking Australian Research Council (ARC) funding decisions. The full-page spread had the headline 'Grants for Rants' and featured a huge picture of me taken at Nitmiluk (Katherine) Gorge, lifted from my Facebook page. I was essentially the 2018 poster child for supposedly wasteful research grants. The article criticised funding for my project on the history of 'famous' transgender Australians and described me, pejoratively, as a 'history lecturer, ABC contributor and transgender activist'.[1] While I would relish the opportunity to contribute more to the ABC (producers, take note!), I feel that calling me a transgender activist is an insult to the dozens of trans activists whom I have had the privilege of getting to know and whose stories are told in this book.

Five years since that article, I am proud of everything that the project—which, incidentally, was never just about 'famous' transgender Australians—has produced: three publicly available research reports (two of which were shortlisted for Victorian Community History Awards), media features including an episode of ABC-TV's *Compass*, interviews on podcasts and radio, several scholarly journal articles and book chapters, public lectures, a PhD thesis, submissions to government inquiries and, at last, this book. That *Daily Telegraph* article hangs on my office door with pride along with rainbow and trans flags.

This project would not have been possible without the support of that ARC Discovery grant DP180100322: 'Transgender Australians: The History of an Identity'. Moreover, the grant would not have been successful without the support of so many trans, LGBTIQ+ and academic supporters. First and foremost, thanks to the 105 trans and gender-diverse people who participated in oral history interviews. I learned so much from every interview participant, and it was humbling for so many people to trust me with the most intimate details of their lives. It was not possible to quote from every interview in this book, but rest assured all of them informed the history. Thanks to all of you for inviting me into your homes, workplaces and Zooms and for sharing your life stories. Thanks also to the other interview participants, be they health professionals or cis allies who have long advocated alongside trans people. I conducted all oral history interviews with the approval of the Australian Catholic University (ACU) Human Research Ethics Committee (approval number 2017-35H).

Dr Fintan Harte, former president of AusPATH, was a partner investigator on the ARC grant and was instrumental in early networking with trans community representatives and health professionals. With Fintan's help, I put together a project advisory group with trans representatives from every state and territory as well as the Australian Queer Archives. I extend my sincere gratitude to the advisory group members, who were so generous in suggesting people to interview and were a sounding board throughout the project duration: Belinda Chaplin, Martine Delaney, Sammantha Elmes, Parker Forbes, Aram Hosie, Peter Hyndal, Kristine Johnson, Jenny Scott, and Nick Henderson from AQuA. Early in the piece

Nick Lawrence from TransFolk of WA agreed to join the advisory group, and later Alyce Schotte became the WA representative. Midway through the project I also invited Teddy Cook from ACON to join, and I am grateful for all the support he provided. Finally, longstanding trans advocate Katherine Cummings was a member of the advisory group, but sadly she passed away in January 2022 at age eighty-six (and I extend my condolences to Katherine's biological and chosen families).

In addition to the formal advisory group, many other trans project participants proved to be amazing supporters, be it through suggesting additional interviewees, providing feedback on written material, suggesting where to look for more resources, sharing personal archives or just being a friendly ear. Among those people are Brenda Appleton, Eloise Brook, Ricki Coughlan, Sally Goldner, Leece Johnson, Mx Margaret Jones, Caroline Layt, Greer McGearey, Chantell Martin, Jonathan Paré, Julie Peters, Lisa Taylor, Kayleen White and Jeremy Wiggins. I also want to acknowledge the wonderful Aunty Vanessa Smith (my birthday twin), who, sadly, passed away in January 2022 after a long battle with cancer. I have already mentioned Julie Peters and Jenny Scott, but I want to give them another thanks for generously agreeing to write the Foreword. From the moment I met Jenny (in 2015) and Julie (in 2018), I admired everything about them, and it is an absolute honour to call them friends.

Geraldine Fela proved a wonderful research assistant for this project, and thanks also to Julien Varrenti-Osmond for conducting some of the pilot archival research at AQuA back in 2017. AQuA is an absolutely amazing resource, and LGBTIQ+ Australians are lucky to have such a wonderful collection and great people who manage it. In addition to Nick Henderson, my thanks go to Ange Bailey, Graham Willett, Tim Jones, Claudine Chionh and the army of volunteers at AQuA. In accordance with participants' consent, the majority of oral history interviews have been deposited in AQuA for future use.

Several participants have also donated some of their personal papers to AQuA, with others intending to do so at a later time (::nudge, nudge, Julie::).

Some of the sources that informed this book came from trans people's personal archives, such as Julie Peters' extensive filing cabinets and a series of scrapbooks collected by John Hewson that I accessed at the Queensland AIDS Council (they have since been deposited at AQuA). I also was fortunate to access Roberta Perkins' papers at both the State Library of New South Wales and AQuA. The survival of these papers is thanks not only to Roberta but also to Eurydice Aroney, who also generously connected me with Roberta to conduct an oral history interview before Roberta's unexpected death in 2018.

Scholars both within ACU and externally have been amazing supports throughout this project. The history team regularly provided enthusiastic advice and rigorous peer review. As always, I am indebted to the best team of researchers anyone could work with from the School of Arts and Humanities: Shurlee Swain, Melissa Bellanta, Rachel Busbridge, Nick Carter, Mark Chou, Lorinda Cramer, Hannah Forsyth, Meggie Hutchison (now at UNSW Canberra), Ben Moffitt, Ben Mountford, Nell Musgrove, Maggie Nolan (now at UQ), Jon Piccini, Mike Thompson, Ellen Warne and Naomi Wolfe.

Thanks also to colleagues at other institutions whose support for decades has made this book possible: Pat Grimshaw, Ara Keys and Patty O'Brien. Special thanks to Shirleene Robinson, Yves Rees and Andy Kaladelfos for friendly bits of advice along the way, and also to Andy for alerting me to the existence of the Social Health Press Clippings collection kept at the Melbourne eScholarship Research Centre (coming soon to AQuA, courtesy of a Victorian Local History Grant). Thanks also to the newly minted Dr Adrien McCrory, who completed his PhD on the history of trans people and the criminal legal system in Australia with a scholarship funded by this ARC grant. Adrien's thesis research regularly informed the work in this book, particularly the first chapter.

From Melbourne University Press, thanks to former publisher and CEO Nathan Hollier, editorial coordinator Duncan Fardon, senior editor Louise Stirling, cover designer Josh Durham, copyeditor Katie Purvis, senior publicist Sarah Valle and marketing coordinator Daniel Chelchowski. Thank you also to the two anonymous readers—this book is stronger thanks to your constructive feedback.

As always, final thanks go to the friends and family who supported me on the research and writing journey. This includes the new trans friends I made during the project, many of whom now pop up on my Facebook and Twitter. Thanks to family in both Australia and the United States, where I took time away from holidays and family to draft the final three chapters. Most importantly, thanks to my loving partner, Michael, who somehow tolerates all of my quirks and foibles, not to mention having to listen to all the stories I share about the amazing people I met. For reasons we ourselves still cannot grasp, the COVID-19 pandemic and all the time spent locked up at home brought us closer together.

Some text has previously been published in the following:

A History of Trans Health Care in Australia: A Report for the Australian Professional Association for Trans Health (AusPATH), AusPATH, 2022.
'A History of Transgender Women in Australian Sports, 1976–2017', *Sport in History* 42(2), 2021, pp. 280–307.
New South Wales Trans History, The Gender Centre and ACON, 2022.
'Representing Transgender in the 1970s Australian Media', *Gender and History* 33(1), 2021, pp. 227–48.
'Searching for Trans Possibilities in Australia, 1910–39', *Journal of Australian Studies* 44(1), 2020, pp. 33–47.
'Transgender Inclusion and Australia's Failed Sexuality Discrimination Bill', *Australian Journal of Politics and History* 65(2), 2019, pp. 259–77.
Victoria's Transgender History, Transgender Victoria, 2021.

NOTES

Foreword
1   Brooke Kroeger, *Passing: When People Can't Be Who They Are* (New York: Public Affairs, 2003).
2   Sandy Stone, 'The *Empire* Strikes Back: A Posttranssexual Manifesto', in Julia Epstein and Kristina Straub (eds), *Body Guards: The Cultural Politics of Gender Ambiguity* (New York: Routledge, 1991), pp. 280–304; Julie Peters, *A Feminist Post-Transsexual Autoethnography: Challenging Normative Gender Coercion* (Abingdon, UK & New York: Routledge, 2019).
3   Judith Butler, *Undoing Gender* (New York: Routledge, 2004).

Preface
1   Margaret Jones interview, 28 September 2019, Perth.
2   Jonathan Paré interview, 10 December 2018, Brisbane.
3   Eloise Brook interview, 19 July 2021, via Zoom.
4   Erica Roberts interview, 30 August 2017, Townsville.
5   M Paz Galupo, 'Researching While Cisgender: Identity Considerations for Transgender Research', *International Journal of Transgenderism* 18(3), 2017, pp. 241–2; Benjamin William Vincent, 'Studying Trans: Recommendations for Ethical Recruitment and Collaboration with Transgender Participants in Academic Research', *Psychology & Sexuality* 9(2), 2018, pp. 102–16.
6   Josephine Inkpin interview, 30 November 2018, Brisbane.

Introduction: The Challenges of Transgender History
1   ABC (Australian Broadcasting Corporation), 'One Plus One: Lieutenant Colonel Cate McGregor' [video], *ABC News*, 5 July 2013.
2   Stephen Kerry, 'Australian News Media's Representation of Cate McGregor, the Highest Ranking Australian Transgender Military Officer', *Journal of Gender Studies* 27(6), 2018, pp. 683–93.
3   Katy Steinmetz, 'The Transgender Tipping Point', *TIME*, 29 May 2014.
4   Priscilla Jackman, *Still Point Turning: The Catherine McGregor Story* (Fortitude Valley, Qld: Playlab, 2019).

5   Madi Day, 'Indigenist Origins: Institutionalizing Indigenous Queer and Trans Studies in Australia', *Transgender Studies Quarterly* 7(3), 2020, pp. 370–1.

6   Sandy O'Sullivan, 'The Colonial Trappings of Gender', in Sam Elkin et al. (eds), *Nothing to Hide: Voices of Trans and Gender Diverse Australia* (Sydney: Allen & Unwin, 2022), pp. 136–47; Sandy O'Sullivan, 'The Colonial Project of Gender (and Everything Else)', *Genealogy* 5(3), 2021.

7   Magnus Hirschfeld, *Transvestites: The Erotic Drive to Cross Dress*, trans. Michael A Lombardi-Nash (New York: Prometheus Books, 1991 [1910]).

8   Yves Rees, *All About Yves: Notes from a Transition* (Crows Nest, NSW: Allen & Unwin, 2021), p. 116.

9   Noah Riseman, 'Representing Transgender in the 1970s Australian Media', *Gender and History* 33(1), 2021, pp. 227–48.

10 Peter Ringo, 'Media Roles in Female-to-Male Transsexual and Transgender Identity Development', *International Journal of Transgenderism* 6(2), 2002.

11 Michel Foucault, *The History of Sexuality, Vol. 1: An Introduction*, trans. Robert Hurley (London: Penguin, 1990).

12 Surya Monro, *Gender Politics: Citizenship, Activism and Sexual Diversity* (London & Ann Arbor: Pluto Press, 2005), p. 86; Surya Monro and Janneke Van Der Ros, 'Trans★ and Gender Variant Citizenship and the State in Norway', *Critical Social Policy* 38(1), 2018, p. 72.

13 KJ Rawson and Cristan Williams, 'Transgender★: The Rhetorical Landscape of a Term', *Present Tense* 3(2), 2014, p. 3.

14 Hedesthia, 'Observations on the Phenomenon of Trans-Genderism', June 1978, Australian Queer Archives (hereafter AQuA), Jean Steele papers, box 4.

15 2nd Australian Transsexual Association (ATA) program, *Gaywaves*, 5 May 1983, AQuA.

16 Leslie Feinberg, *Trans Gender Liberation: A Movement Whose Time Has Come* (New York: World View Forum, 1992).

17 Rawson and Williams, 'Transgender★: The Rhetorical Landscape of a Term', p. 1.

18 Susan Stryker, *Transgender History: The Roots of Today's Revolution*, 2nd edn (New York: Seal Press, 2017 [2008]), p. 1.

19 Ibid., pp. 12–40. 'Language', TransHub website, 2021.

20 Judith Butler, *Gender Trouble: Feminism and the Subversion of Identity*, 3rd edn (New York & London: Routledge, 2007 [1990]).

21 'Intersex for Allies', Intersex Human Rights Australia website, 21 November 2012.

22 More information is available at 'Pronouns', TransHub website, 2021.

23 Paul Gregoire, 'Is "Tranny" a Derogatory Term?', *Polare*, August 2014. Other popular articles that discuss the debate over the term include J Bryan Lowder, 'The "Tranny" Debate and Conservatism in the LGBTQ Movement', *Slate*, 30 May 2014; Denton Callander, 'RuPaul's "Tranny" Debate: The Limits and Power of Language', *The Conversation*, 29 May 2014.

24 For example, Ruth Ford, '"And Merrily Rang the Bells": Gender-Crossing and Same-Sex Marriage in Australia, 1900–1940', in David Phillips and Graham Willett (eds), *Australia's Homosexual Histories: Gay and Lesbian Perspectives 5* (Sydney: Australia's Centre for Lesbian and Gay Research, 2000), pp. 42–3.

NOTES

25 Stryker, *Transgender History*; Leslie Feinberg, *Transgender Warriors: Making History from Joan of Arc to Dennis Rodman* (Boston: Beacon Press, 1996); MW Bychowski et al., '"Trans*Historicities": A Roundtable Discussion', *TSQ: Transgender Studies Quarterly* 5(4), 2018, pp. 658–85; Kritika Agarwal, 'What Is Trans History? From Activist and Academic Roots, a Field Takes Shape', *Perspectives on History*, 1 May 2018.

26 Genny Beemyn, 'Presence in the Past: A Transgender Historiography', *Journal of Women's History* 25(4), 2013, p. 113.

27 Leah DeVun and Zeb Tortorici, 'Trans, Time, and History', *TSQ: Transgender Studies Quarterly* 5(4), 2018, pp. 533–4.

28 Mary Weismantel, 'Towards a Transgender Archaeology: A Queer Rampage through Prehistory', in Susan Stryker and Aren Z. Aizura (eds), *The Transgender Studies Reader 2* (New York: Routledge, 2013), p. 321.

29 Agarwal, 'What Is Trans History?'

30 Maria Ochoa, in Bychowski et al., '"Trans*Historicities": A Roundtable Discussion', p. 673.

31 Barry Reay, *Trans America: A Counter-History* (Cambridge: Polity Press, 2020).

32 Feinberg, *Transgender Warriors*.

33 Christine Burns (ed.), *Trans Britain: Our Journey from the Shadows* (London: Unbound Publishing, 2018).

34 Joanne J Meyerowitz, *How Sex Changed: A History of Transsexuality in the United States* (Cambridge, MA: Harvard University Press, 2004).

35 Stef M Shuster, *Trans Medicine: The Emergence and Practice of Treating Gender* (New York: NYU Press, 2021).

36 Clare Sears, *Arresting Dress: Cross-Dressing, Law, and Fascination in Nineteenth-century San Francisco* (Durham, NC: Duke University Press, 2014).

37 Emily Skidmore, *True Sex: The Lives of Trans Men at the Turn of the Twentieth Century* (New York: NYU Press, 2017).

38 Jen Manion, *Female Husbands: A Trans History* (Cambridge: Cambridge University Press, 2020).

39 Jules Gill-Peterson, *Histories of the Transgender Child* (Minneapolis: University of Minnesota Press, 2018).

40 C Riley Snorton, *Black on Both Sides: A Racial History of Trans Identity* (Minneapolis: University of Minnesota Press, 2017).

41 Zoë Playdon, *The Hidden Case of Ewan Forbes: The Transgender Trial That Threatened to Upend the British Establishment* (London: Bloomsbury, 2021).

42 Ruth Ford, '"The Man-Woman Murderer": Sex Fraud, Sexual Inversion and the Unmentionable "Article" in 1920s Australia', *Gender and History* 12(1), 2000, pp. 158–96; Susanne Davies, 'Sexuality, Performance, and Spectatorship in Law: The Case of Gordon Lawrence, Melbourne, 1888', *Journal of the History of Sexuality* 7(3), 1997, pp. 389–408; Ruth Ford, '"Prove First You're a Male": A Farmhand's Claim for Wages in 1929 Australia', *Labour History* 90, 2006, pp. 1–21.

43 Lucy Chesser, *Parting with My Sex: Cross-Dressing, Inversion and Sexuality in Australian Cultural Life* (Sydney: Sydney University Press, 2008).

44 Mark Tedeschi, *Eugenia: A True Story of Adversity, Tragedy, Crime and Courage* (Cammeray, NSW: Simon & Schuster, 2012); Robin Eames, 'Problem Bodies

and Queer Legacies: Rethinking Approaches to Trans History in the Case of Harry Crawford, Sydney, 1920', *Lilith: A Feminist History Journal* 25, 2019, pp. 50–62.

45 Roberta Perkins, *The 'Drag Queen' Scene: Transsexuals in Kings Cross* (Sydney: Allen & Unwin, 1983).

46 Frank Lewins, *Transsexualism in Society: A Sociology of Male-to-Female Transsexuals* (South Melbourne: Macmillan Education, 1995).

47 Marion Edwards, *Life and Adventures of Marion-Bill-Edwards: The Most Celebrated Man-Woman of Modern Times* (Melbourne: WH Williams, Junr, 1907).

48 Peter Stirling, *So Different: An Extraordinary Autobiography* (Sydney: Simon & Schuster, 1989).

49 Katherine Cummings, *Katherine's Diary: The Story of a Transsexual*, rev. edn (Tascott, NSW: Beaujon Press, 2007 [1992]); Carlotta with James Cockington, *He Did It Her Way: Carlotta, Legend of Les Girls* (Sydney: Ironbark by Pan Macmillan, 1994).

50 Some of the more high-profile trade paperbacks are: Jamie Brisick, *Becoming Westerly* (San Francisco: Outpost19, 2015); Sarah Krasnostein, *The Trauma Cleaner: One Woman's Extraordinary Life in Death, Decay & Disaster* (Melbourne: Text Publishing, 2017); Eddie Ayres, *Danger Music: How Teaching the Cello to Children in Afghanistan Led to a Self-discovery Almost Too Hard to Bear* (Crows Nest, NSW: Allen & Unwin, 2017); Rees, *All About Yves*; Nevo Zisin, *Finding Nevo: How I Confused Everyone* (Newtown, NSW: black dog books, 2017); Quinn Eades, *All the Beginnings: A Queer Autobiography of the Body* (North Melbourne: Tantanoola, 2015); Kaya Wilson, *As Beautiful as Any Other: A Memoir of My Body* (Sydney: Picador, 2021).

51 Dino Hodge (ed.), *Colouring the Rainbow: Blak Queer and Trans Perspectives: Life Stories and Essays by First Nations People of Australia* (Mile End, SA: Wakefield Press, 2015).

52 Sam Elkin et al. (eds), *Nothing to Hide: Voices of Trans and Gender Diverse Australia* (Sydney: Allen & Unwin, 2022).

53 Yolanda Bogert, *How I Met My Son: A Story of Love That Transcends Gender* (South Melbourne: Affirm Press, 2016); Rebekah Robertson, *About a Girl: A Mother's Powerful Story of Raising Her Transgender Child* (Milsons Point, NSW: Viking, 2019).

54 Noah Riseman, 'Transgender Inclusion and Australia's Failed Sexuality Discrimination Bill', *Australian Journal of Politics and History* 65(2), 2019, pp. 259–77; 'Searching for Trans Possibilities in Australia, 1910—39', *Journal of Australian Studies* 44(1), 2020, pp. 33–47; 'Representing Transgender in the 1970s Australian Media', pp. 227–48; 'Finding "Evidence of Me" through "Evidence of Us": Transgender Oral Histories and Personal Archives Speak', in Amy Tooth Murphy, Emma Vickers and Clare Summerskill (eds), *New Directions in Queer Oral History: Archives of Disruption* (Abingdon, UK: Routledge, 2022), pp. 59–70; 'A History of Transgender Women in Australian Sports, 1976–2017', *Sport in History* 42(2), 2021, pp. 280–307.

55 *Victoria's Transgender History* (Melbourne: Transgender Victoria, 2021); *New South Wales Trans History* (The Gender Centre and ACON, 2022); *A History of Trans Health Care in Australia: A Report for the Australian Professional Association for Trans Health (AusPATH)* (AusPATH, 2022).

56 'Transgender Policy in the Australian Defence Force: Medicalization and Its Discontents', *International Journal of Transgenderism* 17(3–4), 2016, pp. 141–54; Noah Riseman and Shirleene Robinson, *Pride in Defence: The Australian Military and LGBTI Service since 1945* (Carlton, Vic.: Melbourne University Press, 2020), pp. 169–98, 204–13.
57 Michelle Arrow, *The Seventies: The Personal, the Political, and the Making of Modern Australia* (Sydney: NewSouth Publishing, 2019).

Chapter 1: Imagining Trans Possibilities, 1910–39
1 'Baron Wears Woman's Clothes', *The Age*, 28 September 1912.
2 For example, 'Baron Wears Woman's Clothes', *The Journal* (Adelaide), 8 October 1912; 'Transvestitism an Awkward Malady', *Maitland Daily Mercury* (NSW), 2 November 1912.
3 Ruth Ford, '"And Merrily Rang the Bells"', p. 60.
4 Chesser, *Parting with My Sex*, pp. 238–40; Edwards, *Life and Adventures of Marion-Bill-Edwards*.
5 Chesser, ibid., pp. 238–70.
6 'Masquerading as a Man: Woman's Strange Whim', *Daily Post* (Hobart), 3 January 1911.
7 'Another Masquerade: "Always Dressed as a Boy"', *Sydney Morning Herald*, 12 September 1911.
8 'Woman Works as a Man', *Burrowa News* (Burrowa, NSW), 30 August 1929.
9 'Posed as a Man: Woman's Strange Story', *Daily Advertiser* (Wagga Wagga, NSW), 19 August 1929.
10 Ibid.
11 'Masqueraded as Man: Woman's Claim for Wages', *Sydney Morning Herald*, 14 November 1929.
12 Ford, '"Prove First You're a Male"', p. 7.
13 'Acted as a Man for 20 Years: Woman's Amazing Masquerade', *Daily News* (Perth), 17 December 1932.
14 'Impersonated a Man', *The Sun* (Sydney), 6 September 1921.
15 Ford, '"The Man–Woman Murderer"', pp. 41–66; Robin Eames, 'Problem Bodies and Queer Legacies', pp. 50–62.
16 Manion, *Female Husbands*.
17 Ford, '"The Man–Woman Murderer"', p. 167.
18 Eames, 'Problem Bodies and Queer Legacies', p. 50.
19 Robin Eames, 'Harry Crawford v History: Problem Bodies, Queertrans Cosmogonies, and Historiographical Ethics in Cases of Gender Transgression in Late Nineteenth–Early Twentieth Century Australia', BA (Hons) thesis, University of Sydney, 2018.
20 Ford, '"The Man–Woman Murderer"', p. 169.
21 Adrien McCrory, 'Policing Gender Nonconformity in Victoria, 1900–1940', *Provenance: The Journal of Public Record Office Victoria* 19, 2021, pp. 37–9.
22 Chesser, *Parting with My Sex*, pp. 78–88.
23 'Man Dressed as Woman; Police Charge Fails', *The Argus* (Melbourne), 1 December 1923.
24 'Dressed as a Woman; Adelaide Man Fined', *Weekly Times* (Melbourne), 16 January 1915.

25 'Dressed as a Woman; Man's Impersonation; Motor Drives and Suppers', *The Sun* (Sydney), 22 August 1915.

26 'Man-Woman Case: Rocake Before Court', *Sydney Morning Herald*, 3 May 1921.

27 Marjorie Garber, *Vested Interests: Cross-Dressing & Cultural Anxiety* (New York: Routledge, 2011), p. 70.

28 'Masqueraded as Woman', *The Argus* (Melbourne), 5 December 1925.

29 'Watson Wasn't a Woman, but He Dressed as One', *Truth* (Perth), 2 January 1926.

30 Chesser, *Parting with My Sex*, p. 321. Original emphasis.

31 'Dressed as a Woman: "What Will Mother Say?" Waiter's Escapade', *The Sun* (Sydney), 12 May 1924.

32 Garry Wotherspoon, *Gay Sydney: A History* (Sydney: NewSouth Publishing, 2016), pp. 51–4.

33 'Dressed as Woman: Young Man Arrested', *Bathurst Times*, 21 July 1922.

34 Chesser, *Parting with My Sex*, p. xxi.

35 Sears, *Arresting Dress*, pp. 72–4; 'Electric Brilliancy: Cross-dressing Law and Freak Show Displays in Nineteenth-century San Francisco', in Susan Stryker and Aren Z. Aizura (eds), *The Transgender Studies Reader 2* (New York: Routledge, 2013), pp. 555–6.

36 Davies, 'Sexuality, Performance, and Spectatorship in Law', p. 396.

37 Sears, *Arresting Dress*, p. 73.

38 'Dressed in Wife's Clothes "To Amuse the Baby", He Told a Policeman', *The Sun* (Sydney), 1 June 1932.

39 'Dressed As Woman: Man Discharged With Caution', *Canberra Times*, 4 February 1932.

40 'Man Dressed as Woman: Stayed at City Lodging House for a Joke', *The Age*, 4 February 1932.

41 'Posed as a Woman For Years: Man Arrested in George St; Inquisitive Constable's Surprise', *Evening News* (Sydney), 13 February 1922.

42 'Man Dressed in Woman's Clothes: No Offence, Decides PM', *The Advertiser* (Adelaide), 15 August 1935.

43 Douglas Ogilvy Prestell, *The Correspondence of Karl Heinrich Ulrichs, 1846–1894* (Basingstoke, UK: Palgrave Macmillan, 2020).

44 Hirschfeld, *Transvestites*, p. 124.

45 Ibid., p. 214.

46 Frank Bongiorno, *The Sex Lives of Australians: A History* (Melbourne: Black Inc., 2012), pp. 118–20, 67.

47 'Man in Woman's Dressing Shelter: Masqueraded as Woman: Gets a Month, but Sentence Suspended', *Prahran Telegraph* (Vic.), 12 February 1926.

48 Harry Benjamin, 'Transsexualism and Transvestism as Psycho-Somatic and Somato-Psychic Syndromes', in Susan Stryker and Stephen Whittle (eds), *The Transgender Studies Reader* (New York: Routledge, 2006 [1954]), pp. 43–4.

49 'Wearing Clothes of Other Sex: No Direct Prohibition in Queensland', *The Telegraph* (Brisbane), 15 August 1935.

50 'Man Or Woman: Amazing Case in Denmark', *The Telegraph* (Brisbane), 13 April 1931.

51 'Brief Cable News: Woman Becomes Man', *The Argus*, 30 December 1935; 'Remarkable Operation: Woman Changed into Man', *Daily Mercury* (Mackay), 30 December 1935; 'Woman Now a Man', *Evening News* (Rockhampton), 30 December 1935.

52 Joanne Meyerowitz, 'Sex Change and the Popular Press: Historical Notes on Transsexuality in the United States, 1930–1955', *GLQ: A Journal of Lesbian and Gay Studies* 4(2), 1998, pp. 159–87; Joanne Meyerowitz, *How Sex Changed*, pp. 14–50.

53 'Replies to Queries', *Sunday Mail* (Brisbane), 14 August 1932.

54 'A Double Life: Man Works as Maid', *West Australian*, 14 August 1937; R Gwyn Williams, 'A Case of Transvestitism', *Western Australian Clinical Reports* 1(3), 1937, p. 51.

55 Williams, ibid.

56 Ibid., p. 52. See also 'A Double Life', p. 16.

57 'Lived as a Man for 51 Years: Woman's Masquerade', *The Sun* (Sydney), 13 May 1939.

58 'Lived 51 Years as a Man', *Lockhart Review and Oaklands Advertiser* (NSW), 23 May 1939.

59 'Man-Woman Is Problem for Asylum', *Truth* (Brisbane), 11 June 1939.

60 Ruth Ford, 'Sexuality and "Madness": Regulating Women's Gender "Deviance" through the Asylum, the Orange Asylum in the 1930s', in Catharine Coleborne and Dolly MacKinnon (eds), *'Madness' in Australia: Histories, Heritage and the Asylum* (St Lucia, Qld: University of Queensland Press in association with API Network and Curtin University of Technology, 2003), pp. 112–13.

61 Ford, '"And Merrily Rang the Bells"', p. 59.

62 Garber, *Vested Interests*, pp. 44–5.

63 'One Thing and Another', *West Australian*, 28 August 1937.

64 Skidmore, *True Sex*, p. 10.

65 'Man-Woman Is Problem for Asylum', *Truth* (Brisbane), 11 June 1939.

Chapter 2: Constructing Trans Identities in the Postwar Era

1 'Man Converted to Woman by Danish Doctors', *Canberra Times*, 3 December 1952; 'Man Becomes Woman and "She Is Glad"', *The Sun* (Sydney), 2 December 1952; '"Converted" Girl Hopes to Marry', *Daily Telegraph* (Sydney), 3 December 1952.

2 'Models Boycott Christine's Fashion Show', *The Mirror* (Perth), 20 October 1954, AQuA, G.R. papers.

3 'Visit by Christine Jorgensen "Off"', *The Advertiser* (Adelaide), 24 November 1954; 'Ex-soldier Arrives for Nightclub Act', *Truth* (Adelaide), 29 July 1961, AQuA, G.R. papers; 'Christene [sic] Jorgensen, Sex Change Pioneer, Will Revive Her Nightclub Act in Australia', *People*, date unknown (c. 1977), John Hewson collection, AQuA, notebook 3.

4 Meyerowitz, 'Sex Change and the Popular Press', p. 173; David Harley Serlin, 'Christine Jorgensen and the Cold War Closet', *Radical History Review* 62, 1995, pp. 140–1; Emily Skidmore, 'Constructing the "Good Transsexual": Christine Jorgensen, Whiteness, and Heteronormativity in the Mid-Twentieth-Century Press', *Feminist Studies* 37(2), 2011, pp. 275–7.

5   Harry Benjamin, 'Transsexualism and Transvestism as Psychosomatic and Somatopsychic Syndromes', *American Journal of Psychotherapy* 8(2), 1954, p. 220. Italics in original.

6   Christian Hamburger, 'The Desire for Change of Sex as Shown by Personal Letters from 465 Men and Women', *Acta Endocrinologica* 14, 1953, pp. 363–4.

7   Yorick Smaal, *Sex, Soldiers and the South Pacific, 1939–45: Queer Identities in Australia in the Second World War* (London: Palgrave Macmillan, 2015), p. 84; Brent Coutts, *Crossing the Lines: The Story of Three Homosexual New Zealand Soldiers in World War II* (Dunedin: Otago University Press, 2020).

8   Jenny, 'Did You Hear the One …' *Transceiver* (WA), December 1996, p. 7, State Library of Western Australia (hereafter SLWA).

9   'Dressed as a Woman for Years', *Newcastle Sun*, 8 November 1944.

10   'Man Dressed as Woman for "Emotional Relief"', *Truth* (Sydney), 12 November 1944.

11   'Adelaide Court Claim: Man Seeks Change of Sex', *Truth* (Adelaide), 19 February 1955, AQuA, G.R. papers.

12   'Dressed as a Woman', *The Advertiser* (Adelaide), March 1955, AQuA, G.R. papers.

13   '"Offences" Due to Nerves', *The News* (Adelaide), 31 March 1955, AQuA, G.R. papers.

14   'Amazing "Man-Woman" Goes to Doctor', *Truth* (Brisbane), 15 October 1950; 'Tragic Story of a Girl who Wants to Be a Man', *Truth* (Sydney), 15 October 1950.

15   'Man-Woman Told She's a Lady!', *Truth* (Brisbane), 5 November 1950; '"Man" of the Bush Was a Woman: Tragic Medical Verdict', *Truth* (Sydney), 5 November 1950.

16   'Mystery Fan Dancer "He", Not "She"', *Truth* (Melbourne), 6 January 1940.

17   'Youth Tells Why He Masquerades as a Girl', *Truth* (Sydney), 21 June 1942; 'Dressed as a Woman', *Sydney Morning Herald*, 16 September 1943.

18   'Affectionate Cavorting in Newtown Street Too Much for Cop', *Truth* (Sydney), 9 January 1944.

19   'Police Story about Man-Woman', *Truth* (Sydney), 29 May 1949.

20   Andrew Bock, 'Gender Bender', *The Age*, 9 October 1997: Extra 7.

21   Harry Benjamin, *The Transsexual Phenomenon* (New York: Julian Press, 1966).

22   'Sex Change Shock', *Daily Mirror*, 15 January 1986; 'Nightclub Girl Was Builder's Laborer!', *Truth* (Melbourne), 26 December 1970, AQuA, G.R. papers; 'Interview Seven: Denise', AQuA, Roberta Perkins papers, box 4.

23   Ron Barr and Alex Blaszczynski, 'Autonomic Responses of Transsexual and Homosexual Males to Erotic Film Sequences', *Archives of Sexual Behavior* 5(3), 1976, p. 221.

24   'Sascha' interview, 1 October 2019, Perth.

25   Carlotta and Prue MacSween, *Carlotta: I'm Not That Kind of Girl* (Sydney: Pan Macmillan, 2003), p. 128. See also Carlotta, *He Did It Her Way*, pp. 67–8.

26   'Interview with Dr Ron Barr, Prince Henry Hospital', June 1981, National Archives of Australia (hereafter NAA) C1367, 81/239.

27   Carlotta, *He Did It Her Way*, p. 72.

28   'Sex Change in Australia', *Cleo*, March 1974, p. 57.

29 Cecily Davis, 'Death of a Stripper ... "A Person Known as Tiffany"', publication and date unknown, AQuA, John Hewson collection, notebook 2.

30 'Sascha' interview.

31 'I Want to Change My Sex', *Truth* (Melbourne), 6 August 1966, AQuA, G.R. papers.

32 Tony Maiden, 'Forget About Casablanca: Have Your Sex Change Here, on Medical Benefits', *National Times*, 6–11 May 1974.

33 Jazmin Theodora interview, 12 September 2019, Nimbin, NSW.

34 Harry Imber, 'The Management of Transsexualism', *Medical Journal of Australia* 2(18), 1976, p. 677; Harry Imber interview, 27 January 2019, Melbourne.

35 'Sex Change: Do-It-Yourself Surgery Amazes Doctors!', *Truth* (Melbourne), 28 December 1968, AQuA, G.R. papers.

36 'Sex-change Girl on Streets', newspaper and exact date unknown (1974), AQuA, John Hewson collection, notebook 2.

37 'I Was a Man, Part 3: I Find the Joys of Womanhood', *PIX*, 26 May 1962, AQuA, G.R. papers.

38 Karen Chant interview, 25 April 2018, Central Coast, NSW.

39 Ibid.

40 '"Woman" at Ball Was a Man', *Central Queensland Herald* (Rockhampton), 5 July 1956.

41 Toye de Wilde interview, 11 December 2018, Brisbane.

42 Bill Rutkin, Destiny Rogers and Laurie James Deane, *Queen's Ball: 60th Anniversary* (West End, Qld: Q News, 2021).

43 Carlotta and MacSween, *Carlotta*, pp. 40–1.

44 Belinda Chaplin interview, 30 September 2020, via Zoom.

45 Jazmin Theodora interview.

46 Karen Chant interview; Perkins, *The 'Drag Queen' Scene*, p. 37.

47 Clive Moore, *Sunshine and Rainbows: The Development of Gay and Lesbian Culture in Queensland* (St Lucia, Qld: University of Queensland Press in association with the API Network, 2001), p. 134.

48 Jazmin Theodora interview.

49 Karen Chant interview.

50 Belinda Chaplin interview.

51 Carmen Rupe and Martin Paul, *Carmen: My Life* (Auckland: Benton Ross, 1988), p. 80.

52 Carlotta, *He Did It Her Way*, p. 34.

53 Jazmin Theodora interview. See also Rupe and Paul, *Carmen*, p. 117.

54 'Sascha' interview.

55 Carlotta and MacSween, *Carlotta*, p. 61.

56 Toye de Wilde interview.

57 Perkins, *The 'Drag Queen' Scene*, p. 38.

58 Carlotta and MacSween, *Carlotta*, p. 61.

59 Karen Chant interview.

60 Susan Le Gay interview, 11 December 2018, Brisbane.

61 Belinda Chaplin interview.

62 Karen Chant interview. See also AQuA, John Hewson collection.

63 Belinda Chaplin interview.

64 Vonni interview, 7 December 2021, Adelaide.

65 Penny Clifford telephone interview, 8 March 2023.
66 Perkins, *The 'Drag Queen' Scene*, p. 43.
67 Susan Le Gay interview.
68 Carlotta and MacSween, *Carlotta*, p. 93.
69 Perkins, *The 'Drag Queen' Scene*, p. 62–3; Vonni interview.
70 'Karolyn' interview, 11 September 2019, North Coast, NSW.
71 Vonni interview; Perkins, *The 'Drag Queen' Scene,* p. 63.
72 Karen Chant interview.
73 'Sascha' interview.
74 Vonni interview.
75 Toye de Wilde interview.
76 Perkins, *The 'Drag Queen' Scene*, pp. 75–6.
77 NAA K1129, 1383097; 'Transsexuals: Those Who Have Made the Choice' [television program], *Four Corners*, ABC-TV, 1974; Joanna McIntyre, 'He Did It Her Way on TV: Representing an Australian Transsexual Celebrity Onscreen', *Gay & Lesbian Issues & Psychology Review* 7(1), 2011, pp. 19–32.
78 Noah Riseman, 'Representing Transgender in the 1970s Australian Media', pp. 227–48.
79 John Hewson interview, 31 January 2021, via Zoom.
80 'Karolyn' interview.

Chapter 3: Beginning to Organise
1   Rosemary Langton interview, 13 April 2021, Sydney.
2   Stryker, *Transgender History*, pp. 65, 73.
3   Rosemary Langton interview.
4   Jill Austin interview, 17 December 2021, Sydney.
5   Trina Taylor, letter introducing Seahorse Club, 1974, courtesy Julie Peters.
6   Seahorse Club of Australia, 'An Introduction to the Club and an Outline of It's [sic] Objectives and Membership Rules Pertaining to THE AUSTRALIA TRANSVESTITES GROUP', 1974, courtesy Julie Peters.
7   Seahorse Directory, 1974, courtesy Julie Peters.
8   Trina Taylor, 'The Heterosexual Transvestite in Australia', *Australian Social Work* 30(1), 1977, p. 32.
9   Susan Lardner, 'The First 25 Years: 1975–2000', *Seahorse Times* (July 2000); 'Seahorse Club of Australia, Victorian Division', 6 October 1975, courtesy Julie Peters.
10 John Hewson interview.
11 R.J., 'Calling all TVs', *The Examiner* (Launceston), 4 August 1977.
12 Carlene Ellwood, 'A Bricklayer in Lurex and Lace', *Examiner Express* (Launceston), 9 August 1980.
13 Letter dated December 1975, courtesy Julie Peters.
14 'How a Shocked Wife Coped', *Sunday Mail* (Adelaide), 24 August 1980.
15 'Seahorse Club of Australia: Amalgamation and Election Notices', 1977, courtesy Julie Peters; Barbara Burrows, 'Barbara B. Reports', *New Femme: The Official Newsletter of the Chameleon Society of WA* 6, March–April 1977, pp. 1–2.
16 Rupe and Paul, *Carmen*, pp. 173, 212.
17 'Trans-seminar '76', courtesy Julie Peters; 'That's No Lady; That's My Husband', *Cleo*, August 1976, pp. 28–9.

18 Lady Paula Howard, *Frocks, Frills and Furbelows: The Story of Lady Paula Howard—An Embellished Biography of Transvestism Spanning Forty Years and Four Continents* (Norwood, SA: Peacock Publications, 1999), p. 57.
19 'Transvenue 77', courtesy Julie Peters.
20 Trina Taylor, 'TV is Both Transvestism and Television', *Feminique* 5, 1974, p. 26.
21 Trina Taylor, 'Seahorse and the Media', *Feminique* 9, 1975, p. 16.
22 'A Night Out with the Boys', *Forum* 2(8), 1974, p. 21.
23 Riseman, 'Representing Transgender in the 1970s Australian Media', pp. 227–48.
24 William Walters interview, 23 April 2019, Sydney.
25 Riki Lane, '"We Are Here to Help": Who Opens the Gate for Surgeries?', *TSQ: Transgender Studies Quarterly* 5(2), 2018, pp. 207–27; Simon Ceber interview, 6 November 2020, via Zoom.
26 'Public to Pay for Sex Changes', *Truth* (Melbourne), 27 May 1989; Calvin Miller, 'Sex Change Program on Again', *The Herald* (Melbourne), 29 June 1989.
27 Several newspapers reported this, including Jeff Wells, 'Changes in Sex: We Lead West in "Trapped People"', *The Age*, 2 June 1979; 'We Are Tops in World of Trans-sex', *Courier-Mail* (Brisbane), 2 June 1979; and Carolyn Armstrong, 'The Big Desire for Changing Their Sex', *The Australian*, 2 June 1979. Ross' paper was published two years later as Michael Ross et al., 'Cross-cultural Approaches to Transsexualism: A Comparison between Sweden and Australia', *Acta Psychiatrica Scandinavica* 63, 1981, pp. 75–82.
28 'More in Line for Sex Change', *The Mirror* (Sydney), 15 November 1976; Julie Clarke, 'Sex-Change Surgery', *Cleo*, August 1977, p. 55.
29 Michael Ross interview, 24 September 2020, via Zoom.
30 Kevin Murphy, 'Cut-off Point for Sex-swaps?' *The Bulletin*, 3 May 1988.
31 Desiree, 'Transexuality: A Life History', *Catch 22* (Adelaide) 2(8), September 1984, pp. 16–17.
32 'More in Line for Sex Change'.
33 Peter Morris MP, to MJR McKellar MP, Minister for Immigration and Ethnic Affairs, 3 October 1979, NAA A1838, 1622/1/44 PART 1.
34 Michelle Jayne Goodman, secretary, Transcare, to Victorian Transsexual Coalition, 13 November 1982, AQuA, Jean Steele papers, box 1; 'Help for Transsexuals', *The Scene* (Brisbane), April 1982, p. 5.
35 Victorian Transsexual Coalition meeting minutes, 1 November 1979, AQuA, Jean Steele papers, box 1.
36 Victorian Transsexual Association Self-Help Group, undated letter, 1982, courtesy Julie Peters; Victorian Transsexual Association brochure; Jeane Steele, secretary, Victorian Transsexual Coalition, to Michelle J Goodman, secretary, Transcare, 26 February 1983; Victorian Transsexual Coalition meeting minutes, AQuA, Jean Steele papers, box 1.
37 T/S Self Help Group Victoria, 'Re: Formation T/S Self Help Group Victoria', 10 February 1988, AQuA, Jean Steele papers, box 1.
38 'Minutes of a meeting held at the Metropolitan Community Church, Toorak, 13/9/79', AQuA, Jean Steele papers, box 1; Victorian Transsexual Coalition, 'General Information Circular', NAA A1838, 1622/1/44 PART 2.

39 Victorian Transsexual Coalition, 'After Sex Change Surgery', n.d. (1980s), courtesy Simon Ceber.
40 Victorian Transsexual Coalition, 'What is Transsexualism?', n.d. (1980s), courtesy Simon Ceber.
41 John Cain, MLA, Victorian Legislative Assembly, Official Hansard, 1 December 1981, 3884–3885; AQuA, Jean Steele papers, boxes 1 and 2.
42 Victorian Transsexual Coalition, 'Submission: Equal Opportunity Bill 1983', November 1983.
43 Ian Sharp, Chair of Victorian Equal Opportunity Advisory Council, to Premier John Cain, 21 September 1983, Julian Phillips papers, University of Melbourne Archives, 92/165, folder 8.
44 J Johnson, secretary, Victorian Transsexual Coalition, to the Honourable David White, Minister for Health, 25 February 1988, AQuA, Jean Steele papers, box 1.
45 'Public to Pay for Sex Changes', *Truth* (Melbourne), 27 May 1989; Calvin Miller, 'Sex Change Program on Again', *The Herald* (Melbourne), 29 June 1989.
46 Jean Steele, secretary, to William Walters, 13 September 1984, AQuA, Jean Steele papers, box 2; Jean Steele to Miss Jo Anne Frend, 10 April 1987; Victorian Transsexual Coalition meeting minutes, AQuA, Jean Steele papers, box 1.
47 J Johnson to the Commissioner, Inquiry into Prostitution, 4 February 1985, AQuA, Jean Steele papers, box 1.
48 Vanessa Smith interview, 27 September 2019, Perth.
49 Elyse 'Tarks' Coles interview, 1 July 2019, Tweed Heads, NSW.
50 'Jackie Was a Tough Boy!', unknown newspaper, Brisbane, c. 1971/2, AQuA, John Hewson collection, notebook 2.
51 Simone Lyndon-Pike, 'Minutes of Evidence Taken in Camera Before the Select Committee of the Legislative Assembly upon Prostitution', 11 July 1984, p. 18, State Library of NSW (hereafter SLNSW), Roberta Perkins papers, box 9B.
52 Bronwyn Walsh, 'Minutes of Evidence Taken in Camera Before the Select Committee of the Legislative Assembly upon Prostitution', 11 July 1984, p. 3, SLNSW, Roberta Perkins papers, box 9B.
53 'Lisa' interview, 12 July 2021, via Zoom.
54 Roberta Perkins, *The 'Drag Queen' Scene*, p. 119.
55 Latoya Hoeg interview, 9 August 2019, Melbourne.
56 Simone Lyndon-Pike, 'Minutes of Evidence Taken in Camera Before the Select Committee of the Legislative Assembly upon Prostitution', 11 July 1984, p. 18, SLNSW, Roberta Perkins papers, box 9B.
57 Jazmin Theodora interview; 'Minutes of Evidence Taken in Camera Before the Select Committee of the Legislative Assembly upon Prostitution', 11 July 1984, p. 7, SLNSW, Roberta Perkins papers, box 9B.
58 Roberta Perkins, 'Transexuals and Police Persecution', *Alternative Criminology*, June 1983, pp. 6–7; SLNSW, Roberta Perkins papers, box 9A.
59 Ibid.
60 Chantell Martin interview, 12 September 2021, via Zoom.
61 Kooncha Brown interview, 10 May 2022, Sydney.
62 Rupe and Paul, *Carmen*.

63 Phlan-Michelle Purss interview, 11 May 2021, Sydney.

64 Chantell Martin interview, 19 September 2021, via Zoom.

65 Phlan-Michelle Purss, walking tour with Noah Riseman, 15 April 2021, Sydney.

66 Simone Lyndon-Pike, 'Minutes of Evidence Taken in Camera Before the Select Committee of the Legislative Assembly upon Prostitution', 11 July 1984, p. 4, SLNSW, Roberta Perkins papers, box 9B.

67 'Statement by the NSW Police Force to the Select Committee of the Legislative Assembly upon Prostitution', 16 May 1983, SLNSW, Roberta Perkins papers, box 9A.

68 Kooncha Brown interview, 10 May 2022.

69 AQuA, Roberta Perkins papers, box 1.

70 'Statement by the NSW Police Force to the Select Committee of the Legislative Assembly upon Prostitution', 16 May 1983, SLNSW, Roberta Perkins papers, box 9A.

71 Simone Lyndon-Pike, 'Minutes of Evidence Taken in Camera Before the Select Committee of the Legislative Assembly upon Prostitution', 11 July 1984, p. 4, SLNSW, Roberta Perkins papers, box 9B.

72 Surveys conducted for submission to NSW Select Committee of the Legislative Assembly upon Prostitution, SLNSW, Roberta Perkins papers, box 9A.

73 Perkins, The 'Drag Queen' Scene, p. 124.

74 Phlan-Michelle Purss interview, 11 May 2021.

75 Eloise Brook (host), 'Do I Believe in Ghosts?' [podcast], Counting the Dead, 30 October 2019, The Gender Centre Inc.; Eloise Brook interview.

76 AQuA, John Hewson collection, notebooks 9, 10 and 13.

77 Robin Bowles, No Justice (Sydney: Pan Macmillan, 2000).

78 'Ugly Mug List no. 17', c. December 1987, SLNSW, Roberta Perkins papers, box 5A.

79 New South Wales, Prostitution (Amendment) Act 1983, sec 8A. This clause is still in the Summary Offences Act 1988, sec 19(1).

80 Phlan-Michelle Purss interview, 11 May 2021.

81 Kooncha Brown interview, 10 May 2022.

82 Chantell Martin interview, 19 September 2021.

83 Simone Lyndon-Pike, 'Minutes of Evidence Taken in Camera Before the Select Committee of the Legislative Assembly upon Prostitution', 11 July 1984, p. 9, SLNSW, Roberta Perkins papers, box 9B.

84 Paul van Reyk, 'Future Directions for the AIDS Council of NSW: A Strategic Planning Document', March 1989, p. 82.

85 Phlan-Michelle Purss interview, 11 May 2021.

86 John Ruane (director), Man into Woman: The Transsexual Experience [documentary film], Sabina Productions, 1983; 'Call of the Frock' [television program], Open File (season 1, episode 4), ABC-TV, 1983, NAA C2831, 1056252; NAA C475, 1056252.

87 'Sex Change Seminar: Doctor Does Castrations', Canberra Times, 10 December 1981; '"Rip Off" in Sex Changes', Daily News (Perth), 9 December 1981.

88 Noelena Tame to Family Law Council, 8 August 1980, NAA A463, 1987/G1019.

89 "'They Won't Bowl Me Out"; Barred Bowler to Challenge Sex Ruling'; Liz Hickson, 'Sex Change Grandma: "I Was Born into a Male Body"', *Woman's Day*, 17 January 1983, AQuA, John Hewson collection, notebook 5.

90 Riseman, 'A History of Transgender Women in Australian Sports, 1976–2017', pp. 284–5.

91 Roberta Perkins, interview with Noah Riseman, 28 February 2018, Sydney.

92 Roberta Perkins to Michael Kirby, 1981, AQuA, Roberta Perkins papers, box 2.

93 Deirdre Macken, 'Law Turns a Blind Eye to Transexuals', *The Age*, 11 October 1982.

94 Roberta Perkins, interview on *Gaywaves*, 7 October 1982, AQuA.

95 Australian Transsexual Association, 'A Submission for the Establishment of a Gender Identity Centre', 1982; LJ Brereton to Roberta Perkins, 7 July 1982, AQuA, Roberta Perkins papers, box 2.

96 Australian Transsexual Association, 'Submission on Behalf of Transsexuals in Australia for Legal Identification in Accordance with Their Psychosexual and Gender Identities', 5 November 1982, AQuA, Roberta Perkins papers, box 2.

97 c. 1983, AQuA, Roberta Perkins papers, box 1; 'Transsexuals Make a Showing', *Campaign*, March 1983.

98 *Gaywaves*, 'Australian Transsexual Association (ATA) program', recordings all available in AQuA.

99 Australian Transsexual Association (Vic.), n.d., AQuA, Jean Steele papers, box 1.

100 Roberta Perkins to Frank Walker, 25 March 1983, AQuA, Roberta Perkins papers, box 2.

101 Roberta Perkins, 'Tales of Tiresias', *Polare* 54, October–November 2003, p. 18.

102 *Gaywaves*, 1 November 1984, AQuA.

103 Roberta Perkins, 'Speech by R Perkins for Opening Ceremony of Tiresias House', AQuA, 13 December 1983, Roberta Perkins papers, box 3.

104 Paola Totaro, 'House Aims to Help "Oppressed, Misunderstood" Transsexuals', *Sydney Morning Herald*, 14 December 1983.

105 Roberta Perkins, 'Tales of Tiresias'; *Gaywaves*, 12 July 1984, 1 November 1984.

106 *Gaywaves,* 1 November 1984.

107 AQuA, Roberta Perkins papers, box 1.

108 *Gaywaves,* 7 August 1986.

109 'Sascha' interview.

110 Roberta Perkins, 'Tales of Tiresias'.

111 'Arthur or Martha' [television program], *Midday*, Nine Network, 10 February 1988.

112 'Sascha' interview.

113 *Gaywaves*, 1 November 1984, AQuA.

114 'Arthur or Martha', *The Midday Show*, 15 February 1988; Megan Gressor, 'The Trauma of Being a Transsexual', *Woman's Day*, 26 April 1988. Tony also featured in a 1990 *Cleo* sealed section article about trans people, but going by a different name. Paula Goodyer, 'Changing Sex', *Cleo*, May 1990, p. 145.

115 Perkins, 'Speech by R Perkins for Opening Ceremony of Tiresias House'.

Chapter 4: Legal Recognition and Anti-Discrimination

1 Family Law Council, Working Paper No 1, 'Birth Certificate Revision of the Sexually Reassigned', July 1978, p. 13, NAA A432, 1983/005019/01; NAA A432, E1976/6463 PART 1.
2 NAA A1838, 1622/1/44 PART 1.
3 Jazmin Theodora interview.
4 *Corbett v Corbett* [1970] 2 All ER 33.
5 NAA A1838, 1622/1/44 PART 2.
6 NAA A1838, 1622/1/44 PART 1; NAA A432, E1976/6463 PART 2.
7 Director, Passports Policy Section, 'Issue of Passports to Trans-Sexuals', 8 January 1985, NAA A432, 1985/12478; NAA A432, CF1984/14098.
8 Robert Fordham, MLA, Victorian Legislative Assembly, Official Hansard, 16 November 1976, 4164; 'Sex Change Rights Denied: Petition', *The Sun* (Melbourne), 17 November 1976; 'MPs to Debate Petition on Sex Change', *The Age*, 17 November 1976; 'A Queer Deal!', *Sunday Observer* (Melbourne), 28 November 1976.
9 Correspondence between NSW Attorney-General Frank Walker and others, 1976–81, AQuA, Jean Steele papers, box 2.
10 Angela Bell, 'In Sexual Limbo', *Sydney Morning Herald*, 23 January 1989.
11 NAA A432, 1983/005019/01; NAA A432, 1983/012942-01; NAA A432, E1976/6463 PART 2; NAA A432, E1976/6463 PART 1.
12 SCAG 6/12/85 Item No. 9, NAA A432, 1985/10784.
13 NAA A432, 1985/10784; NAA A432, CF1984/14098; Public Records Office Victoria (hereafter PROV), VPRS 17369, P0001, unit 228, 902/L02/01523; PROV. VPRS 18024, P0002, unit 33, 93/65/36/2.
14 This part of the Act would set back health-care provision in South Australia after the closure of the Flinders Medical Centre Gender Clinic. See Riseman, 'A History of Trans Health Care in Australia' (AusPATH, 2022), pp. 31–2.
15 NAA A1838, 1622/1/44 PART 2; 'Baby Kylie ... the Girl in a Boy's Body', *The Sun* (Melbourne), 9 August 1983; 'S. Australian Officials Insist that Boys Won't Be Girls', *Canberra Times*, 9 August 1983; 'Kylie's a Girl!', *The Sun* (Melbourne), 30 March 1984; 'Sex Change Approved', *West Australian*, 30 March 1984; 'Baby "Girl" Compo Claim', *The Herald* (Melbourne), January 1985.
16 South Australia Attorney-General and Minister of Corporate Affairs, 'Media Release: Sexual Reassignment Bill', 2 December 1987, NAA A432, 1985/12478.
17 South Australia, *Sexual Reassignment Act* 1988.
18 *C and D (falsely called C)*, Family Law Cases 90–636, 1979.
19 'Transsexuals Still Men, CSM Rules', *Sydney Morning Herald*, 25 September 1982.
20 Paola Totaro, 'Courts Must Decide on Transsexuals: SM', *Sydney Morning Herald*, 14 February 1984.
21 Street CJ, *R v Harris and McGuiness*, 17 NSWLR 158, pp. 161–2.
22 *R v Cogley*, [1989] VR 799; Henry Finlay, 'Transsexuals, Sex Change Operations and the Chromosome Test: *Corbett v Corbett* Not Followed', *Western Australian Law Review* 19, 1989, pp. 155–6.

23 Kassia Byrnes, '"They Arrested Me": Australia's First Legally Recognised Trans Woman on a Life in the Spotlight', *news.com.au*, 8 March 2022.

24 'Sex Change: Now You Can Be on Record', *Sydney Morning Herald*, c. October 1987, NAA A432, CF1984/15506 PART 1.

25 President O'Connor J and D W Muller, *Re Secretary, Department of Social Security v 'HH'*, 23 ALD [1991], 64. See also NAA A432, 1990/011585-01; Greg Roberts, 'Sex Change Now Passport to an Early Pension', *Sydney Morning Herald*, 24 April 1991.

26 Jennie Curtin, 'Man Is Female, Tribunal Says', *Sydney Morning Herald*, 5 September 1992; Rod Campbell, 'Surgery Not Necessary for Transsexual to Be a Woman: Tribunal', *Canberra Times*, 12 October 1992.

27 Justice John Lockhart, *Secretary, Department of Social Security v SRA*, 31 ALD 1 [1993]: pp. 25–6.

28 Jane Mussett on *Life Matters* [radio program], ABC Radio National, 13 December 1993, NAA C100, 1582651.

29 Daphne Sider, 'Pension Lost in Gender Dispute', *Sydney Morning Herald*, 2 December 1993.

30 Janet Fife-Yeomans, 'Transsexual Loses Landmark Appeal', *The Australian*, 2 December 1993; NAA A432, 1993/504751 PART 1.

31 'MLC Joins Suzanne's Sex Battle', *The Herald* (Melbourne), 8 October 1982.

32 Barbara Wiese MLC, 22 January 1982, NAA A432, E1976/6463 PART 2; 13 December 1983, NAA A432, 1983/012942-01.

33 Barbara Wiese, MLC, 'The Case for Change', *The Advertiser* (Adelaide), 12 August 1983.

34 'Transexuals [sic] Protected', *The Australian*, 17 October 1983.

35 South Australia, *Equal Opportunity Act* 1984, sec 5.

36 Henry Finlay, 'Appendix A', *Transsexualism in a Modern State: Options for Reform* (Hobart: HA Finlay, 1995), pp. 8–9.

37 Northern Territory, *Anti-Discrimination Act* 1992, sec 4.

38 Finlay, 'Appendix A', *Transsexualism in a Modern State*, p. 17; A. Sharpe, 'Transgender Performance and the Discriminating Gaze: A Critique of Anti-Discrimination Regulatory Regimes', *Social & Legal Studies* 8(1), 1999, p. 11.

39 New South Wales Law Reform Commission, 'Names: Registration and Certification of Births and Deaths', (Sydney, 1988), pp. 50–3, courtesy Kim Dorin; 'New Sex—"New Birth Certificate"', *Sydney Morning Herald*, 9 May 1990; 'Report Backs Sex-change Marriages', *Newcastle Herald*, 11 May 1990.

40 Teresa Rizzo (director), *On Becoming* [video], AFI Distribution, 1993.

41 'Changing Gender' [television program], *Lateline*, ABC-TV, 12 April 1994, NAA C475, 1719712.

42 Aidy Griffin interview, 26 November 2019, Sydney.

43 See Dr Herbert Bower in 'Changing Gender'.

44 Ricki Coughlan interview, 26 April 2019, Sydney.

45 Ricki Carne, 'Transsexual Action Group T.A.G.', *Polare* 10, December 1995, pp. 10–11.

46 J Hooley, 'A Response to T.A.G.'s Perspective', *Polare* 12, May 1996, p. 8.

47 Caroline Layt, 'A Response' and J Deering and J Scott, coordinators, South Australian Transsexual Support Group, 'Removal of the Medical Model', *Polare* 16, 1997, pp. 4–5; Rahnee, 'Offended', *Polare* 18, 1997, pp. 4–5.

48 Aidy Griffin interview; Jesse Hooley interview, 9 May 2022, Sydney; Pindi Hurring interview, 10 May 2022, Sydney.

49 Roberta Perkins, *Transgender Lifestyles and HIV/AIDS Risk: National Transgender HIV/AIDS Needs Assessment Project*, School of Sociology, University of New South Wales, 1994; Aidy Griffin interview.

50 This report was eventually published as *The Transgender Project: A Needs Assessment for People with Transgender Practices* (Central Sydney Area Health Service, 1996).

51 Jesse Hooley interview.

52 Ricki Coughlan interview.

53 Aidy Griffin, 'Tranys Win Law Reforms: What will they mean?', *Polare* 10, 1995, p. 8.

54 New South Wales, Legislative Assembly, Official Hansard, 22 May 1996, 1344–1361.

55 For an overview of the movement and effects of anti-discrimination reform in NSW, see Jesse Hooley, 'Normalising Transgender and Policing Transgression: Anti-Discrimination Law Reform Ten Years On', *Australian Feminist Law Journal* 25, 2006, pp. 79–98.

56 Lea R-M Bontes-Bright to the Chairperson, Electoral and Administrative Review Commission, 14 January 1993, in Kerri Joy Petrie, *A Report on a Submission to the Electoral and Administrative Review Commission, Response from the Commission, and from the President of the Australian Transgenderists Support Association of Queensland, Incorporated on a Queensland 'Bill of Rights'*; 'Transvestites in Open: Self-help Group Set Up', *Truth* (Melbourne), 24 November 1984.

57 Norrie interview, 28 August 2019, Sydney; Norrie, *Ultrasex: An Autobiography by Norrie May-Welby* (Sydney: Norrie, 2019), pp. 47–8, 55–6.

58 *Norrie v R* [1988] WASC 181 (29 June 1988).

59 Norrie, *Ultrasex*, p. 63.

60 'Dismissal Biased, Says Transsexual', unknown newspaper, likely *West Australian*, c. June 1988, courtesy Norrie scrapbook.

61 Transexual Movement of Western Australia to Victorian Transsexual Coalition, 3 July 1986 and 17 April 1990, AQuA, Jean Steele papers, box 1.

62 Transexual Movement of WA (1990), brochure, SLWA, PR14249. Document also in AQuA, Jean Steele papers, box 3; 'Work Shop for Transexuals in June', *Westside Observer*, June 1990.

63 NAA A432, 1993/481534 PART 1.

64 Lea Rose-Marie Bontes CD, Gender Council of Western Australia, to Senior Crown Solicitor, 'Re: Standing Committees of Attorney's General Agenda', 28 November 1994, NAA A432, 1995/68617 PART 1; Caroline Doust to Honourable Cheryl Edwardes, Attorney General (WA), 1 July 1995, NAA A432, 1996/19460 PART 1.

65 Jenny Scott interview, 8 December 2021, Adelaide.

66 Caroline Doust to Attorney-General Michael Lavarch, 9 January 1996, NAA A432, 1996/19460 PART 1.

67 Gavin McGuren, 'Gender Council Denies Homophobia', *Westside Observer*, 5 August 1995.

68　The Honourable Kevin Prince, Western Australia, Legislative Assembly, Hansard, 9 April 1997, 1361.

69　'Trany Recognition Goes West', *Capital Q*, 27 March 1997.

70　Samantha Dowling, 'WA Stalls on Transgender Reform', *Brother-Sister* (Melbourne), 24 December 1998.

71　Samantha Dowling, 'Trannie Debate Strikes Reclaim the Night', *Westside Observer*, 9 October 1998.

72　The Honourable Diana Warnock, Western Australia, Legislative Assembly, Hansard, 24 November 1999, 3763.

73　Tasmania, *Police Offences Act* 1935, sec 8(1)(d).

74　Tasmania, *Police Act* 1865, sec 14.

75　'Tasmania Is Not Such a Drag After All', unknown newspaper, 1984, in John Hewson collection, notebook 7, AQuA.

76　'Metamorphosis: Transgender Counselling and Support Association', *Pink Thylacines* (Tasmania), December 1992, p. 13.

77　Gyan Wilson and Russell Hunter to Australian Council for Gay and Lesbian Rights, 19 May 1993.

78　Jordan Hirst, 'Transgender Day of Visibility: Hobart Council Flies Trans Pride Flag for First Time', *QNews*, 30 March 2021.

79　Tasmania, *Anti-Discrimination Act* 1998, sec 3.

80　Equality Tasmania, 'Stephanie Reid Talks About Changing Tasmanian Law' [video], YouTube, 31 March 2021.

81　'Upper House Says "Yes" to Transgender Law Reform (13th Mar)', *GLC Newsletter* (Hobart), April 2001, p. 9.

82　'New Birth Certificates for Tassie Trannies', *Queensland Pride*, 30 May 2001, p. 4.

83　Law Reform Commission of Victoria, *Review of the Equal Opportunity Act*, Report No. 36, October 1990, p. 26.

84　Julie Peters interview, 23 February 2018, Melbourne. See also Anna Langley interview, 17 March 2019, Cambridge, UK.

85　Letter to members of the Gay, Lesbian and Transgender Rights Lobby Steering Committee, 10 July 1997, courtesy Julie Peters.

86　*The Gay and Lesbian Rights Lobby of Victoria: Steering Committee Report*, October 1997, courtesy Julie Peters; Julie Peters interview.

87　Jodie Joyce, 'MPs Target of Gender Lobby Group', *Brother-Sister*, 13 November 1997.

88　Riseman, 'Victoria's Transgender History', pp. 26–7; Kayleen White interview, 28 January 2019, Melbourne; Sally Goldner interview, 27 August 2018, Melbourne.

89　Sally Goldner interview.

90　Kayleen White interview.

91　Sally Goldner interview; Kayleen White interview.

92　Kayleen White, speech at Transgender Victoria Launch, Transgender Victoria launch kit, 26 April 2000, courtesy Julie Peters.

93　Sally Goldner interview.

94　Richard Baker, 'State to Move on Transsexual Status', *The Age*, 4 March 2004. See also Sally Goldner interview.

95　Victoria, *Births, Deaths and Marriages Registration (Amendment) Act* 2004.

96 Christina Dodd, 'Transsexual Movement Firing Up Again', *Queensland Pride*, 2, March–April 1991, p. 15. See also 'Support, Guidance & Justice: Transgender Support Association (Queensland)', *Queensland Pride*, 30 January 2004, p. 20; Toye de Wilde interview; Gina Mather interview, 4 July 2019, Brisbane.
97 Gina Mather interview.
98 Kerri Petrie, 'A Submission to the Electoral and Administrative Review Commission Concerning Transsexual and Transgenderist Issues, August 1992, by the Australian Transgenderists Support Association of Queensland', 14 August 1992.
99 Queensland Electoral and Administrative Review Commission, *Report on the Review of the Preservation and Enhancement of Individuals' Rights and Freedoms* (Brisbane, August 1993), p. 378.
100 Kristine Johnson interview, 3 July 2019, Brisbane.
101 Danielle Dillon, Queensland Anti-Discrimination Commission, to Gina Mather, 8 February 1994, State Library of Queensland (hereafter SLQ) 27358, box 16013.
102 Gina Mather to the People of Queensland, 6 June 2000, SLQ 27358, box 16013.
103 Gina Mather interview.
104 Ibid. See also Kristine Johnson interview.
105 Gina Mather interview.
106 Rob Whiddon, Chief of Staff to Premier, to Gina Mather, 29 November 2002, SLQ 27358, box 16013.
107 Kayleen White, *Transgender Victoria Newsletter* (February 2000), courtesy Julie Peters.

Chapter 5: Queer and Trans Blak, Indigenous and People of Colour

1 O'Sullivan, 'The Colonial Project of Gender (and Everything Else)'.
2 O'Sullivan, 'The Colonial Trappings of Gender', p. 139.
3 Alison Whittaker, 'The Border Made of Mirrors: Indigenous Queerness, Deep Colonisation and (De)fining Indigenousness in Settler Law', in *Colouring the Rainbow*, p. 226.
4 Sandy O'Sullivan, 'Challenging the Colonialities of Symbolic Annihilation', *Southerly* 79(3), 2022, p. 19.
5 O'Sullivan, 'The Colonial Trappings of Gender', p. 141.
6 Whittaker, 'The Border Made of Mirrors', p. 226.
7 Jack Latimore, 'Blak, Black, Blackfulla: Language Is Important, But It Can Be Tricky', *Sydney Morning Herald*, 30 August 2021; Kate Munro, 'Why "Blak" not Black? Artist Destiny Deacon and the Origins of This Word', *NITV*, 29 June 2020.
8 Dean Gilbert interview, 15 August 2021, via Zoom.
9 Damien W Riggs and Kate Toone, 'Indigenous Sistergirls' Experiences of Family and Community', *Australian Social Work* 70(2), 2017, p. 230.
10 Kooncha Brown interview, 10 May 2022.
11 Vanessa Smith interview.
12 AC van der Leeden, 'Thundering Gecko and Emu: Mythological Structuring of Nunggubuyu Patrimoieties', in LR Hiatt (ed.), *Australian Aboriginal Mythology: Essays in Honour of WEH Stanner* (Canberra: Australian Institute of Aboriginal Studies, 1975), pp. 88–90.

13 O'Sullivan, 'The Colonial Trappings of Gender', p. 141.

14 Vanessa Smith interview.

15 Day, 'Indigenist Origins', p. 368.

16 Sandy O'Sullivan, 'The conflation of trans with drag is a problem ...' [Tweet], 6 January 2023.

17 Andrew Farrell, 'Lipstick Clapsticks: A Yarn and a Kiki with an Aboriginal Drag Queen', *AlterNative: An International Journal of Indigenous Peoples* 12(5), 2016, p. 581.

18 Alan Weedon, 'Fa'afafine, Fakaleitī, Fakafifine: Understanding the Pacific's Alternative Gender Expressions', *ABC News*, 31 August 2019.

19 Corrinne Tayce Sullivan and Madi Day, 'Indigenous Transmasculine Australians & Sex Work', *Emotion, Space and Society* 32, 2019, p. 100591.

20 *Sistergirls: Stories from Indigenous Australian Transgender People*, produced by ACON, 2003.

21 Arnold Remington Pilling, 'Homosexuality among the Tiwi of North Australia', in Stephen O Murray (ed.), *Oceanic Homosexualities* (New York & London: Garland Publishing, 1992), p. 27.

22 Brie Ngala Curtis, 'Kungakunga: Staying Close to Family and Country', in *Colouring the Rainbow*, p. 37.

23 *Sistergirls*.

24 Kooncha Brown interview, 10 May 2022.

25 *Sistergirls*.

26 Vanessa Smith interview.

27 Crystal Love, 'Napanangka: The True Power of Being Proud', in *Colouring the Rainbow*, pp. 21–8; Crystal Love Johnson, as told to Sam Elkin, 'Yimpininni', in *Nothing to Hide*, pp. 10–15.

28 *Sistergirls*.

29 Human Rights and Equal Opportunity Commission Australia, National Inquiry into the Separation of Aboriginal and Torres Strait Islander Children from Their Families, *Bringing Them Home: Report of the National Inquiry into the Separation of Aboriginal and Torres Strait Islander Children from Their Families* (Sydney: Human Rights and Equal Opportunity Commission, 1997).

30 Kooncha Brown interview, 10 May 2022.

31 Ricki Spencer interview, 21 January 2022, via Zoom.

32 Katherine Wolfgramme interview, 2 June 2022, via Zoom.

33 Amao Leota Lu, as told to Bobuq Sayed, 'Dancing with My Ancestors', in *Nothing to Hide*, p. 185.

34 Jack Ayling, 'Bizarre Case of the Sex-change Corpse', *Truth* (Melbourne), 21 April 1979.

35 *R v Cogley*, [1989] VR 799; *The Queen v Shane Alexander Cogley*, Supreme Court of Victoria, 20 February 1989, AQuA, Jean Steele papers, box 2; *The Queen v Shane Alexander Cogley* sentence, 31 October 1988, NAA A432, CF1984/15506 PART 1.

36 Ken Blanch, 'Sex Change Girl Gets State Ban', *Sunday Sun* (Brisbane), 9 September 1979.

37 Megan Gressor, 'The Trauma of Being a Transsexual', *Woman's Day*, 26 April 1988.

38 Ricca Griffiths, application for full-time employment, 19 May 1987, AQuA, Roberta Perkins papers, box 1.
39 AQuA, Roberta Perkins papers, box 1. A fifth person noted that her parents' nationality was originally 'Indonesian', but she listed her racial background as Dutch and her religion as Catholic, suggesting that her parents may have been born in Indonesia but were Dutch settlers.
40 Kimberlé Crenshaw, 'Demarginalizing the Intersection of Race and Sex: A Black Feminist Critique of Antidiscrimination Doctrine, Feminist Theory and Antiracist Politics', *University of Chicago Legal Forum* 1, 1989, pp. 139–67.
41 Michael Costello and Rusty Nannup, *Report of the First National Indigenous Sistergirl Forum: A Forum for All Indigenous People Who Identify as a Sistergirl or Who Have Transgender Qualities* (Darlinghurst, NSW: AFAO, 1999), p. 3.
42 Vanessa Smith interview.
43 Costello and Nannup, 'Report of the First National Indigenous Sistergirl Forum', pp. 9–10.
44 Kooncha Brown interview, 10 May 2022.
45 Lisa Taylor interview.
46 Vanessa Smith interview.
47 Kooncha Brown interview, 22 March 2022, via Zoom; Kooncha Brown interview, 10 May 2022.
48 Kooncha Brown interview, 22 March 2022.
49 Kooncha Brown, '"Sistergirls": Stories from Indigenous Australian Transgender People', *Aboriginal and Islander Health Worker Journal* 28(6), 2004, p. 26.
50 Kooncha Brown interview, 22 March 2022.
51 Kooncha Brown interview, 10 May 2022.
52 Lisa Taylor interview.
53 Dean Gilbert interview.
54 Kooncha Brown interview, 22 March 2022.
55 Trans Health Australia, 'Brotherboys Yarnin' Up: Kai and Dean' [video], YouTube, 23 August 2014.
56 'Brother Boys' [television program], *Living Black* (season 22, episode 10), NITV/SBS, 8 June 2015.
57 Dean Gilbert interview.
58 Ibid.
59 Love, 'Napanangka', p. 23.
60 Jeremy Anderson interview, 28 August 2021, via Zoom.
61 'Jemima to Jeremy' [television program], *Our Stories* (season 1, episode 36), NITV, 17 August 2016.
62 Margaret Burin, 'Sistergirls and Brotherboys Unite to Strengthen Spirits', *ABC News*, 21 November 2016; Matthew Wade, 'New Retreat for Trans and Gender Diverse Aboriginal People', *Star Observer*, 17 May 2016.
63 Dean Gilbert interview.
64 Jeremy Anderson interview.
65 Love, 'Napanangka', p. 32. See also Love Johnson, 'Yimpininni', pp. 17–19.
66 Curtis, 'Kungakunga', p. 46.
67 Dean Gilbert interview.
68 Katherine Wolfgramme interview.
69 Geeta Nambiar interview, 11 April 2021, Sydney.

70 Chantell Martin interviews, 12 and 19 September 2021.
71 Womxn is an alternative spelling for 'woman', popular especially in intersectional feminism, which challenges the centring of 'man' as part of the spelling.
72 Sasja Sÿdek interview, 4 August 2019, Melbourne; Sasja Sÿdek, 'The Magic Art of Not Giving a Fuck', in *Nothing to Hide*, pp. 44–50.
73 'Aezra' interview, 1 February 2021, via Zoom.
74 Maria Pallotta-Chiarolli (ed.), *Living and Loving in Diversity: An Anthology of Australian Multicultural Queer Adventures* (Adelaide: Wakefield Press, 2018), pp. 67–8.
75 Maria Pallota-Chiarolli interview, 28 October 2020, via Zoom.
76 Vanessa Smith interview.
77 Latoya Hoeg interview.
78 Sasja Sÿdek interview.
79 Rebeckah Loveday interview, 16 August 2019, Melbourne; Sasja Sÿdek interview.
80 Amao Leota Lu, 'Dancing with My Ancestors', p. 186.
81 Mama Alto, 'Multiple Margins: Queer People of Colour in the Arts', in *Living and Loving in Diversity*, p. 19.
82 Avani Dias, 'Tiwi Islands Sistagirls Prepare to Wow Sydney Mardi Gras, Want to Show Indigenous LGBTIQ Culture', *ABC News*, 2 March 2017; Helen Davidson, 'Their First Mardi Gras: A Journey for Tiwi Island Sistagirls Decades in the Making', *The Guardian*, 3 March 2017.

Chapter 6: Trans Firsts
1   Rachael Wallbank, 'Legal Counselling Service: An Introduction', *Polare* 4, August 1994, p. 4.
2   Dave King, *The Transvestite and the Transsexual: Public Categories and Private Identities* (Aldershot, UK: Avebury, 1993), p. 101.
3   Howard, *Frocks, Frills and Furbelows*, p. 38; scrapbook of Lady Paula Howard, courtesy Seahorse Victoria.
4   Howard, ibid., pp. 60–3; scrapbook of Lady Paula Howard, courtesy Seahorse Victoria.
5   Ric Turner, 'Socialites Field a Queer Question', *Truth* (Melbourne), 17 April 1990, AQuA, John Hewson collection, notebook 24.
6   Nadine Williams, 'Julianne Beats Gender Barrier', unknown newspaper, 1993, courtesy Julie Peters.
7   Carlotta and MacSween, *Carlotta*, p. 125.
8   'Lisa's Story' [television program], *Pig in a Poke* (season 1, episode 6), ABC-TV, 1977.
9   NAA C612, GP EPISODE 74 30330445.
10 John Hewson interview. See also Garry Shelly, 'When James Becomes Jane...', *TV Week*, 13 October 1990, AQuA, John Hewson collection, notebook 24.
11 Carlotta and MacSween, *Carlotta*, p. 126.
12 Susan Le Gay interview.
13 NAA C2831, 1056252; NAA C475, 1056252.
14 Ian Munro (director), *Tommy Doesn't Exist Anymore* [documentary film], Transmedia for the National Nine Network, 1985. See also AQuA, John Hewson collection, notebook 9.

15 John Ruane (director), *Man into Woman*; *Man into Woman* draft script, AQuA, Jean Steele papers, box 2.

16 Graeme Stephen, '*Man into Woman*', *Outrage*, August 1983.

17 Ruth Cullen (director), *Becoming Julia* [documentary film], Australian Film Commission in association with the New South Wales Film and Television Office, 2003.

18 Julia Doulman interview, 26 April 2018, Central Coast, NSW.

19 Vanessa Wagner, 'The Colourful Life of Dame Cindy Pastel', *OUTinPerth*, 7 November 2008.

20 Katherine Wolfgramme interview. See also Carlotta and MacSween, *Carlotta*, pp. 226–7.

21 Nicole Dyer, Tom Forbes and Kirsten Webster, 'Transgender Actor Vonni Lands "Role of a Lifetime" in Gold Coast Priscilla Production', *ABC News*, 26 April 2022.

22 Christine Jorgensen, *Christine Jorgensen: A Personal Autobiography* (New York: Bantam Books, 1967); Jan Morris, *Conundrum* (London: Faber and Faber, 1974); Duncan Fallowell and April Ashley, *April Ashley's Odyssey* (London: J Cape, 1982).

23 'Sascha' interview; Peta Friend interview, 9 May 2022, Sydney.

24 Barry Kay, *The Other Women* (London: Mathews Miller Dunbar, 1976).

25 Kevin Chan and Ken Israel (eds), *Drag Show* (Sydney: Currency Press, 1977).

26 Stirling, *So Different*.

27 Jayne Newling, 'Tragedy of the Mum who Became a Man', *New Idea*, 22 April 1989.

28 Katherine Cummings interview, 4 March 2018, Central Coast, NSW.

29 Elkin et al. (eds), *Nothing to Hide*.

30 Russell Robinson, 'Vicar to Live as a Woman', *The Sun* (Melbourne), 1 July 1981; 'Priest Quits to Live as a Woman', *West Australian*, 1 July 1981.

31 'Last Sermon for Priest who Became a Woman', *Sydney Morning Herald*, 28 July 1981.

32 M & R Holland, North Hobart, Vic., 'Church Is Narrow-minded', *Truth* (Melbourne), 25 July 1981.

33 Josephine Inkpin interview.

34 Julia Baird, 'Meet Australia's First Transgender Priest', *ABC News*, 23 February 2018.

35 Stephanie Boltje, 'The Sydney Uniting Church Appoints History-making Transgender Minister', *ABC News*, 31 March 2021.

36 Josephine Inkpin interview.

37 Perkins, *Transgender Lifestyles and HIV/AIDS Risk*, p. 27.

38 Gina Mather, Australia, Senate, Legal and Constitutional References Committee, 'Reference: Sexuality Discrimination Inquiry', Brisbane, 1 October 1996, p. 790.

39 Julie Peters interview.

40 Philip McIntosh, 'From Man to Woman', *The Age Saturday Extra*, 22 August 1987.

41 'Cassandra Carr' interview, 19 October 2017, Melbourne.

42 Ruth Ostrow, 'Legal Eagle's Change of Sex Wins Respect', *Weekend Australian*, 22 May 1993.

43   The Honourable Daryl Williams, Attorney-General, to Prime Minister John Howard, 15 February 1942, NAA M4326, 1521.

44   The Honourable Lionel Bowen, Commonwealth Attorney-General, to the Honourable CJ Sumner, South Australian Attorney-General, NAA A432, CF1984/15506 PART 1.

45   *Re: Kevin*, [2001] FamCA 1074.

46   Ibid., paragraph 272.

47   Rachael Wallbank, 'Re Kevin in Perspective', *Deakin Law Review* 9(2), 2004, pp. 461–502; 'The Legal Status of People who Experience Difference in Sexual Formation and Gender Expression in Australia', in Jens M Scherpe (ed.), *The Legal Status of Transsexual and Transgender Persons* (Cambridge: Intersentia, 2015), pp. 457–525.

48   *Re: Bernadette* [2010] FamCA 94. For further information on Rachael Wallbank, see her page on the *Australian Women Lawyers as Active Citizens* website.

49   Simon Pristel, 'Sex Change Uproar', *Herald Sun*, 18 October 1996. See also Simon Pristel and Tanya Giles, 'Sex Switch Teacher Row', *Herald Sun*, 16 October 1996.

50   Maree Curtis, 'Sex-change Teacher Swore at Students', *Sunday Age*, 9 March 1997.

51   Brian Blackwell, 'Male Cop Becomes a Woman', *Australasian Post*, 27 August 1988; Penny Rataj, 'Sex-Change Policeman: "I'm Myself at Last"', *Woman's Day*, 1 May 1990.

52   Geoff Wilkinson and Michael Warner, 'Sex Swap Cop', *Herald Sun*, 9 July 2003; Paul Anderson, Michael Warner and Geoff Wilkinson, 'Revolt on Swap Cop', *Herald Sun*, 10 July 2003.

53   Sarah Wotherspoon, 'Sex-swap Cop Earns Stripes', *Herald Sun*, 30 October 2004.

54   Riseman and Robinson, *Pride in Defence*, pp. 145–69; Riseman, 'Transgender Policy in the Australian Defence Force', pp. 141–54.

55   'Sex Tests: LTAA Decides', *The Age* (Melbourne), 7 October 1976; 'Ban on Renee', *Sunday Sun* (Brisbane), 28 November 1976; 'I Just Want to Prove I'm Human' and 'Margaret Too Busy for Challenge from Renee', unknown dates and newspapers, c. 1976, AQuA, John Hewson collection, notebook 2.

56   'Sex-change Leigh's the Talk of the Town', *Truth* (Melbourne), unknown date, c. 1976, AQuA, John Hewson collection, notebook 3.

57   Michael Cockerill, 'Sex Row Athlete Allowed to Run', *Sydney Morning Herald*, 30 August 1991.

58   Ricki Coughlan interview.

59   Tom Salom, 'Gender Bender: Golf Transsexuals to Vie for Female Contests', *Herald Sun*, 4 December 1997.

60   Mianne Bagger interview, 21 May 2019, Melbourne; Charles Happell, 'Golf Gets Bagger, Better', *The Age*, 30 June 1999.

61   Mianne Bagger interview; Brendan Maloney, 'Born a Man, But Now in the Women's Open', *Sun Herald*, 15 February 2004. See also Patricia Davies, 'Bagger Experiences Another Life Change', *The Australian*, 5 November 2004.

62   Sheila L Cavanagh and Heather Sykes, 'Transsexual Bodies at the Olympics: The International Olympic Committee's Policy on Transsexual Athletes at the 2004 Athens Summer Games', *Body & Society* 12(3), 2006, pp. 75–102.

63 Bruce Mathews, 'Just One of Girls', *Herald Sun*, 5 November 2004; 'Bagger Delighted to Qualify for Tour', *The Advertiser* (Adelaide), 6 November 2004; AAP, 'Bagger's Acceptance Is Now in the Bag', *The Australian*, 27 November 2004.

64 Jill Stark, 'I'm Just an Ordinary Guy who Wants to Play Footy', *Sunday Age*, 7 June 2009.

65 Rob Mitchell, 'Australian Sports Commission Gets Red-carded on Equality', *The Age*, 9 June 2009.

66 Riseman, 'A History of Transgender Women in Australian Sports, 1976–2017', pp. 292–300.

67 Toye de Wilde interview.

68 Suzy Anderson, 'Transsexual Politician: "I've Heard All the Jokes"', *Woman's Day*, 18 April 1989.

69 'Odd Quip Helps Make a Case for Merthyr's Quaint Campaigners', *Daily Telegraph*, 18 April 1989.

70 Toye de Wilde interview.

71 Julie Peters interview.

72 Marianne Docherty, 'Vote for Me: I'm a Transsexual Lesbian', *New Weekly*, 15 January 1996.

73 Julie Peters, 'Australian Democrats Candidate for Monash Policy Statement', 1996, courtesy Julie Peters.

74 Julie Peters interview.

75 See also 'The Accidental Archivist' [television program], *Compass* (season 36, episode 18), ABC-TV, 10 July 2022.

76 'Trannie Stands', *Westside Observer*, 28 August 1998; 'The Honourable Dismember', *Queensland Pride*, September 1998.

77 Katherine Cummings interview.

78 Vivienne Oakley and Greg Kelton, 'Transsexual Democrat Gives Voice to Equality', *The Advertiser* (Adelaide), 4 September 2004.

79 Jenny Scott, 'Election Memories', 26 October 2004, State Library of South Australia, Jenny Scott papers.

80 Jenny Scott interview, 8 December 2021, Adelaide.

81 Jenny Scott, email, 30 January 2006, State Library of South Australia, Jenny Scott papers. See also Jenny Scott interview, 8 December 2021.

82 Martine Delaney interview, 11 September 2021, via Zoom.

83 Sanchia Robinson (director), *More Than a Woman* [documentary film], Third Eye Productions, 2000. See also Phoebe Pin, 'Former Kalgoorlie Brothel Madam Loses Battle with Cancer', *Kalgoorlie Miner*, 24 March 2020.

84 David Weber (presenter), 'Kalgoorlie Brothel Tour Traces the History of Goldfields' [radio program], *The World Today*, ABC Radio, 12 April 2001.

85 Shibu Thomas, 'Councillor Jade Darko Makes History as First Trans Woman Elected to Public Office in Tasmania', *Star Observer*, 18 November 2022.

86 Andrew Reynolds, *The Children of Harvey Milk: How LGBTQ Politicians Changed the World* (New York: Oxford University Press, 2019).

87 Anna Brownfield (director), *A Big Life* [documentary film], Nanna Moles Studios and Poison Apple Productions, 2021.

88 Carol Veitch, 'Helen Stopped Conforming, and Became Michael', *The Herald* (Melbourne), 27 October 1982.

89 Jasper Laybutt interview, 21 August 2019, Newcastle; Max Zebra-Thyone interview, 26 August 2019, Newcastle.
90 *Boys Will Be Boys* newsletters, Digital Transgender Archive.
91 Susan Long (director), *Men Like Me* [documentary film], 1994.
92 Jasper Laybutt interview.
93 Craig Andrews (ed.), *Stand by Your Man (and Stay Sane in the Process)*, 3rd edn (Glebe, NSW: FTM Australia, 2007); 'Fact Sheet: TG and TS Table', FTMA Network, 16 May 2005, courtesy Jonathan Paré.
94 Lesley Findlay, 'Good-bye Sean … 1996–2000', *Polare* 36, August–September 2000, p. 8.
95 Jonathan Paré, 'The Experiences of Being Transgender: Personal, Community & Social Consequences', November 1994, courtesy Jonathan Paré.
96 Jonathan Paré interview.

Chapter 7: Trans Politics and Organisations, 1990s–2000s
1 Australia, Senate Legal and Constitutional References Committee, Sexuality Discrimination Inquiry, Submission 69, Women in Sport Foundation, 15 July 1996.
2 Gina Mather and Kristine Johnson, Australia, Senate, Legal and Constitutional References Committee, 'Reference: Sexuality Discrimination Inquiry', Brisbane, 1 October 1996, pp. 795–96.
3 Australia, Senate Legal and Constitutional References Committee, *Inquiry into Sexuality Discrimination* (Canberra, December 1997), pp. ix–xvii.
4 Ibid., p. 117.
5 Penny Clifford telephone interview.
6 *Trany Anti-Violence Pilot Project Draft Report*, 1994, courtesy Shan Short. See also Shan Short interview, 30 April 2021, via Zoom.
7 *The Transgender Project: A Needs Assessment for People with Transgender Practices*, Central Sydney Area Health Service, 1996, AQuA, Roberta Perkins papers, box 4 and courtesy Jesse Hooley.
8 Jesse Hooley interview.
9 Norrie interview, 10 September 2019, Sydney; Aidy Griffin interview; Jesse Hooley interview.
10 Norrie May-Welby to the Minister for Community Services, 29 July 1996, courtesy Norrie.
11 Norrie interview, 10 September 2019; Aidy Griffin interview.
12 Elizabeth Riley interview, 6 July 2021, via Zoom.
13 NSW Department of Correctional Services, 'Management of Transgender Inmates', 1998.
14 Adrien McCrory, 'Policing (Trans)gender: Trans and Gender Diverse Interactions with the Australian Criminal Legal System Since the Twentieth Century', PhD thesis, Australian Catholic University, 2023.
15 Claire F Sullivan, 'Gender Verification and Gender Policies in Elite Sport: Eligibility and "Fair Play"', *Journal of Sport and Social Issues* 35(4), 2011, p. 411.
16 Caroline Symons, *The Gay Games: A History* (London & New York: Routledge, 2010), pp. 211–15.
17 Cathy Brooker, 'Fighting for Nadine', *Saturday Paper*, 25 November 2017.
18 SLQ 27358, box 16013; Gina Mather interview; Kristine Johnson interview.

19   Erica Roberts interview.
20   PROV 10977/P1/unit 16. Original emphasis.
21   Julie Peters interview.
22   'The Intersexual Nature of Transsexualism', The W-o-m-a-n Network, 6 July 2003, courtesy Julie Peters.
23   Transgender Victoria, Annual General Meeting minutes, 28 November 2001, courtesy Julie Peters.
24   Adam Carr, 'Lesfest Bans Trannies', *Melbourne Star*, 18 September 2003; Andrew Milne, 'Queer Spaces?' *MCV*, 19 September 2003.
25   'Letters to the Editor', *MCV*, 3 October 2003.
26   Sherele Moody, 'Lesfest Ban Quashed', *Melbourne Star*, 2 October 2003 and 'Lesfest Bans Overturned', *MCV*, 3 October 2003.
27   Marie-Desiree D'Orsay-Lawrence, 'Reference: Sexuality Discrimination Inquiry', Adelaide, 16 August 1996, p. 511; Desiree D'Orsay-Lawrence, 'Queering Agendas', c. 1997–98, courtesy Julie Peters; Desiree, 'Transexuality: A Life History', pp. 16–17.
28   'Actor Wanted', *Adelaide Gay Times*, 13 August 1993; 'ACTUP Returns to Adelaide', *Adelaide Gay Times*, February 1993; 'Nominees for the Presidency', *Accent*, August 1995; 'Fruit: A Fabulous Entree at Adelaide GT's Community Awards Dinner', *Adelaide Gay Times*, 18 September 1998; 'Individual: Marie-Desiree d'Orsay Lawrence', *Adelaide Gay Times*, 24 December 1999; Desiree d'Orsay Lawrence, 'Farewell to a President', *Adelaide Gay Times*, 23 July 1999.
29   Desiree D'Orsay-Lawrence, 'Queering Agendas'.
30   Jenny Scott interview, 8 August 2018, Adelaide.
31   Jenny Scott interviews, 8 August 2018 and 8 December 2021, Adelaide; State Library of South Australia, Jenny Scott papers.
32   Health Insurance Commission to South Australian Transsexual Support Group, 17 November 1997; Rob Lyons, letter to Chief Medical Officer, 8 April 1997, courtesy Rob Lyons.
33   Government of South Australia, Office for Women, *2017 South Australian Women's Honour Roll*, November 2017, p. 11.
34   Greer McGearey interview, 1 September 2018, Melbourne.
35   'Into the Odd Frock—Seriously', *CentreLines* (Hobart), May 1996.
36   'Tas Transgender Activist Receives Human Rights Award (5th Dec)', *GLC Newsletter* (Hobart) 9(1), January 2001.
37   *Houston v Burton* [2003] TASADT 3.
38   Andie Noonan, 'Goodbye to "Quiet Trailblazer"', *Star Observer*, 12 May 2010.
39   Martine Delaney interview.
40   Jonathan Paré interview.
41   Martine Delaney interview; Jonathan Paré interview.
42   TransPlan emails and minutes, 6 December 2006 and 31 January 2007, courtesy Julie Peters.
43   Martine Delaney interview. See also Riseman, 'A History of Transgender Women in Australian Sports, 1976–2017', p. 294.
44   Julie Peters, 26 March 2007, courtesy Julie Peters.
45   Martine Delaney interview.

46 Julia Adams interview, 23 October 2019, Canberra.
47 Peter Hyndal interview, 15 February 2019, Canberra; Riseman, 'A History of Trans Health Care in Australia', p. 47.
48 Peter Hyndal interview, 21 October 2019, Canberra.
49 Jenni Atkinson interview, 25 May 2019, Canberra.
50 Margaret Jones interview; Mx Margaret Jones, 'A Brief History of Transgender, Transsexual, Intersex and Cross-Dresser Events and Organisations in Western Australia', *Mx Margaret Dylan Jones* website, 2019.
51 Margaret Jones interview.
52 Moira Rayner, Assistant Commissioner for Equal Opportunity, to Attorney General, 10 December 2002, courtesy Margaret Jones.
53 Margaret Jones interview
54 Leece Johnson interview, 30 September 2019, Perth.
55 Mx Margaret Jones, 'A Brief History of the Time We've Spent on Working Towards a Gender Centre' (2003), *Mx Margaret Dylan Jones* website.
56 Peta Rasdlen, 'Transsexual Truckie Trapped in Man's Body', *West Australian*, 15 April 2004.
57 Leece Johnson interview.
58 Aram Hosie interview, 12 April 2019, Melbourne.
59 Martine Delaney interview.
60 Western Australia, *Gender Reassignment Act* 2000, sec 3. Emphasis added.
61 Aram Hosie interview; *AB & AH v Gender Reassignment Board (WA)* (2009) 65 SR(WA) 1.
62 Aram Hosie interview.
63 *Western Australia v AH* [2010] WASCA 172.
64 *AB v Western Australia* and *AH v Western Australia* [2011] HCA 42.
65 Aram Hosie interview.

Chapter 8: Contemporary Trans Affairs

1   Eric Plemons and Chris Straayer, 'Introduction: Reframing the Surgical', *TSQ: Transgender Studies Quarterly* 5(2), 2018, p. 164. See also Stone, 'The *Empire* Strikes Back'.
2   Jesse Hooley interview; Aidy Griffin interview; Julie Peters interview.
3   Riseman, 'A History of Trans Health Care in Australia', pp. 48–50.
4   Jaco Erasmus, 'Monash Gender Clinic: An Overview of the Current Model of Care', *Australasian Psychiatry* 28(5), 2020, pp. 533–5; Riseman, 'A History of Trans Health Care in Australia', pp. 61–2; Riki Lane, 'We Are Here to Help', pp. 207–27.
5   Riseman, 'A History of Trans Health Care in Australia', p. 58. Gale Bearman interview, 11 January 2021, via Zoom; Gina Mather interview.
6   Gina Mather interview; Graham Neilsen, email correspondence, 30 May 2022.
7   Jeremy Wiggins interview, 24 June 2021, via Zoom; Riseman, 'A History of Trans Health Care in Australia', pp. 72–3.
8   Teddy Cook interview, 3 February 2022, via Zoom; Nic Parkhill interview, 23 February 2022, via Zoom.
9   AusPATH, 'Australian Informed Consent Standards of Care for Gender Affirming Hormone Therapy', 31 March 2022. For AusPATH history see Riseman, 'A History of Trans Health Care in Australia', pp. 4–6.

10   Elizabeth Smith et al., 'From Blues to Rainbows: The Mental Health and Well-being of Gender Diverse and Transgender Young People in Australia' (Melbourne: Australian Research Centre in Sex, Health and Society, 2014), p. 11.

11   Margaret Jones interview.

12   Stephanie D Clare, *Nonbinary: A Feminist Autotheory* (Cambridge: Cambridge University Press, 2023), pp. 30–42.

13   Norrie interview, 10 September 2019.

14   Norrie, *Ultrasex*, pp. 182–6. *NSW Registrar of Births, Deaths and Marriages v Norrie* [2014] HCA 11 (2 April 2014).

15   NSW, *Birth, Deaths and Marriages Registrations Act* 1995, sec 32A.

16   Peter Hyndal interview, 21 October 2019.

17   ACT Law Reform Advisory Council, *Beyond the Binary: Legal Recognition of Sex and Gender Diversity in the ACT*, ACT Law Reform Advisory Council Report 2, March 2012, p. 38.

18   Kirsten Lawson, 'Transgender People Will Be Able to Alter Birth Certificates', *Canberra Times*, 17 March 2014.

19   Zac Cannell interview, 24 July 2021, via Zoom.

20   Lauren Novak, 'Gender Switch "Trojan Horse"', *The Advertiser* (Adelaide), 23 September 2016; Lauren Novak, 'Jay's Top Priority Is Social Agenda', *The Advertiser* (Adelaide), 3 November 2016.

21   Elias Clure, 'Birth Certificate Changes to Broaden Rights for Trans, Gender-neutral, Intersex People in NT', *ABC News*, 29 November 2018.

22   Martine Delaney interview; Alexandra Humphries and Ellen Coulter, 'Tasmania Makes Gender Optional on Birth Certificates after Liberal Crosses Floor', *ABC News*, 10 April 2019.

23   Martine Delaney interview.

24   Jordan Hirst, 'Queensland Attorney-General Gives Update on Delayed Trans Reforms', *QNews*, 3 August 2022.

25   In the interests of transparency, I sent a submission to the inquiry drawing on history and expressing my support for the Births, Deaths and Marriages Registration Bill 2022.

26   Law Reform Commission of Western Australia, *Project 108 Final Report: Review of Western Australian Legislation in Relation to the Registration or Change of a Person's Sex and/or Gender and Status Relating to Sex Characteristics*, 6 December 2018.

27   Leigh Andrew Hill, 'No Action on Trans and Intersex Rights from WA Government', *OUTinPerth*, 18 May 2022.

28   Caitlyn Rintoul, 'WA Government Abolishes Gender Reassignment Board to Streamline Recognition Process', *West Australian*, 21 December 2022.

29   Lucy Cormack, '"World Is Watching": MP Seeks Equality Bill Ahead of WorldPride and State Election', *Sydney Morning Herald*, 17 March 2022.

30   Brenda Appleton interview, 21 February 2018, Melbourne.

31   Eloise Brook interview; Noah Riseman, 'New South Wales Trans History', pp. 70–2.

32   Alyce Schotte interview, 20 January 2021, via Zoom.

33   Ibid.

34   Parker Forbes interview, 16 September 2019, Brisbane.

35 Adrian Barnes interview, 16 December 2021, Sydney; Adrian Barnes, *My Knight's Quest* (Morrisville, NC: Lulu, 2022), pp. 66–71.
36 Linc Jenkin, 'Starlady: Shining Bright', *Star Observer*, 15 April 2022; Sam Elkin and Gemma Cafarella (hosts), 'Starlady' [podcast], *Transgender Warriors*, 19 March 2020, JOY 94.9; https://www.transfemme.com.au/.
37 Jenni Atkinson interview.
38 Rebeckah Loveday interview; 'My Career', *Rebeckah Loveday Official* website, 2018.
39 Katherine Wolfgramme interview.
40 Peta Friend interview, 7 March 2022, via Zoom; AJ Brown interview, 24 February 2022, via Zoom.
41 Katherine Wolfgramme interview.
42 Peta Friend interview, 7 March 2022.
43 Emma Thorne interview, 18 September 2021, via Zoom.
44 Adrian Barnes interview, 21 December 2021; Barnes, *My Knight's Quest*, pp. 91–9.
45 Ingrid Bretherton et al., 'The Health and Well-being of Transgender Australians: A National Community Survey', *LGBT Health* 8(1), 2021, p. 42.
46 Andrew Eklund interview, 7 February 2022, via Zoom.
47 Joel Wilson, interview with Noah Riseman for LGBTIQ+ military history project, 15 May 2018, Canberra.
48 Zac Cannell interview.
49 Samuel Leighton-Dore, 'Sissy Ball Founder Bhenji Ra on How Voguing Became a Lifeline', *SBS Sexuality*, 26 February 2020.
50 'Sissy Ball Set to Transfix Sydney at Mardi Gras', *Australian Pride Network*, 19 December 2017.
51 Tristan Niemi, 'Meanjin Is Burning', *Nothing Ever Happens in Brisbane*, 3 November 2021.
52 Merryana Salem, 'House of Silky Is Determined to Breathe Life Back into Australia's Ballroom Scene', *Junkee*, 3 March 2022.
53 Garry Warne interview, 20 July 2021, via Zoom.
54 Kim Atkins, 'Re Alex: Narrative Identity and the Case of Gender Dysphoria', *Griffith Law Review* 14(1), 2005, pp. 1–16; Eithne Mills, 'Re Alex: Adolescent Gender Identity Disorder and the Family Court of Australia', *Deakin Law Review* 9(2), 2004, pp. 365–73.
55 Michelle Telfer et al., 'Transgender Adolescents and Legal Reform: How Improved Access to Healthcare Was Achieved through Medical, Legal and Community Collaboration', *Journal of Paediatrics and Child Health* 54(10), 2018, p. 1097.
56 Robertson, *About a Girl*.
57 Michael Williams, John Chesterman and Phil Grano, 'Re Jamie (No 2): A Positive Development for Transgender Young People', *Journal of Law and Medicine* 22(1), 2014, pp. 90–104.
58 Robertson, *About a Girl*; Telfer et al., 'Transgender Adolescents and Legal Reform', pp. 1096–9.
59 Riseman, 'A History of Trans Health Care in Australia', p. 63.
60 *Re A* [2022] QSC 159.

61 Michelle Telfer interview, 12 July 2021, Melbourne; Michelle M Telfer et al., 'Australian Standards of Care and Treatment Guidelines for Transgender and Gender-diverse Children and Adolescents', *Medical Journal of Australia* 209(3), 2018, pp. 132–6; 'Gender-affirming Care Needed for Transgender Children', *The Lancet* 391, 2018, p. 2576.

62 Riseman, 'A History of Trans Health Care in Australia', pp. 66–7.

63 Sim Victor Kennedy interview, 6 January 2021, Melbourne.

64 Riseman, 'Victoria's Transgender History', p. 39.

65 'Ash' interview, 2 March 2022, Sydney.

66 Robertson, *About a Girl*, pp. 166–89; Kimberley Caines, '"I'd Rather Go to Heaven than Live Here as a Boy": Inside the Lives of Australian Trans Children, Part One', *9News*, 29 January 2019.

67 Tyron Butson, '"Gender whisperers": Scott Morrison criticised for "hateful" tweet about trans students', *SBS News*, 5 September 2018.

68 Ella Braidwood, '13-year-old Trans Kid Confronts Australia's Prime Minister over His Views on Trans Children', *PinkNews*, 6 September 2018.

69 'Liz' interview, 8 July 2021, via Zoom.

70 'Lisa' interview, 28 April 2022, via Zoom.

71 Ibid.

72 Tiffany Jones, 'Evidence Affirming School Supports for Australian Transgender and Gender Diverse Students', *Sex Health* 14(5), 2017, pp. 412–16.

73 Penelope Strauss et al., *Trans Pathways: The Mental Health Experiences and Care Pathways of Trans Young People. Summary of Results* (Perth Telethon Kids Institute, 2017).

74 Tiffany Jones et al., 'Religious Conversion Practices and LGBTQA+ Youth', *Sexuality Research and Social Policy* 19(3), 2022, pp. 1155–64.

75 Alex Greenwich and Shirleene Robinson, *Yes Yes Yes: Australia's Journey to Marriage Equality* (Sydney: NewSouth Publishing, 2018).

76 Megan Palin, 'Anti Same-sex Marriage Campaign Airs: "School Told My Son He Could Wear a Dress"', *news.com.au*, 30 August 2017.

77 Benjamin Law, *Moral Panic 101: Equality, Acceptance and the Safe Schools Scandal*, Quarterly Essay 67 (Carlton, Vic.: Schwartz Publishing, 2017).

78 Brenda Appleton interview.

79 Amy Thomas, Hannah McCann and Geraldine Fela, '"In This House We Believe in Fairness and Kindness": Post-Liberation Politics in Australia's Same-sex Marriage Postal Survey', *Sexualities* 23(4), 2019, pp. 475–96; Jessica Gerrard, 'Boys in Dresses: Same-sex Marriage, Children and the Politics of Equivalence', *Australian Feminist Studies* 35(103), 2020, pp. 70–80; Martine Delaney interview.

80 Janice Raymond, *The Transsexual Empire: The Making of the She-Male*, 2nd edn (New York: Teachers College Press, 1994 [1979]).

81 Viv Smythe, 'I'm Credited with Having Coined the Word "TERF": Here's How It Happened', *The Guardian*, 28 November 2018.

82 Germaine Greer, 'Once a Man, Always a Man', *The Age*, 13 September 1989; Calla Wahlquist, 'Germaine Greer Tells Q&A Her Trans Views Were Wrong, but Then Restates Them', *The Guardian*, 11 April 2016.

83 Law, *Moral Panic 101*.

84 Victorian Equal Opportunity and Human Rights Commission, *Guideline: Trans and Gender Diverse Inclusion in Sport* (Carlton, Vic.: VEOHRC, 2017); Australian Human Rights Commission, *Guidelines for the Inclusion of Transgender and Gender Diverse People in Sport* (Sydney: AHRC, 2019); 'Transgender and Gender Diverse Governance in Sport', *Pride in Sport* website, 2020.
85 'Susan' interview, 19 January 2022, Victoria.
86 Andrew Eklund interview.
87 Rosemary Langton interview.
88 Katherine Wolfgramme interview.
89 Brenda Appleton interview.

Acknowledgements
1 Jack Houghton, 'Grants for Rants', *Daily Telegraph* (Sydney), 28 September 2018.

BIBLIOGRAPHY

Oral history interviews

Adams, Julia. 23 October 2019. Canberra.
'Aezra'. 1 February 2021. Zoom.
Anderson, Jeremy. 28 August 2021. Zoom.
Appleton, Brenda. 21 February 2018. Melbourne.
'Ash'. 2 March 2022. Sydney.
Atkinson, Jenni. 25 May 2019. Canberra.
Austin, Jill. 17 December 2021. Sydney.
Bagger, Mianne. 21 May 2019. Melbourne.
Barnes, Adrian. 16 December 2021. Sydney.
Bearman, Gale. 11 January 2021. Zoom.
Brook, Eloise. 19 July 2021. Zoom.
Brown, AJ. 24 February 2022. Zoom.
Brown, Kooncha. 22 March 2022. Zoom.
——10 May 2022. Sydney.
Cannell, Zac. 24 July 2021. Zoom.
'Carr, Cassandra'. 19 October 2017. Melbourne.
Ceber, Simon. 6 November 2020. Zoom.
Chant, Karen. 25 April 2018. Central Coast, NSW.
Chaplin, Belinda. 30 September 2020. Zoom.
Clifford, Penny. 8 March 2023. Telephone.
Coles, Elyse 'Tarks'. 1 July 2019. Tweed Heads.
Cook, Teddy. 3 February 2022. Zoom.
Coughlan, Ricki. 26 April 2019. Sydney.
Cummings, Katherine. 4 March 2018. Central Coast, NSW.
de Wilde, Toye. 11 December 2018. Brisbane.
Delaney, Martine. 11 September 2021. Zoom.
Doulman, Julia. 26 April 2018. Central Coast, NSW.
Eklund, Andrew. 7 February 2022. Zoom.
Forbes, Parker. 16 September 2019. Brisbane.

Friend, Peta. 7 March 2022. Zoom.
——9 May 2022. Sydney.
Gilbert, Dean. 15 August 2021. Zoom.
Goldner, Sally. 27 August 2018. Melbourne.
Griffin, Aidy. 26 November 2019. Sydney.
Hewson, John. 31 January 2021. Zoom.
Hoeg, Latoya. 9 August 2019. Melbourne.
Hooley, Jesse. 9 May 2022. Sydney
Hosie, Aram. 12 April 2019. Melbourne.
Hurring, Pindi. 10 May 2022. Sydney.
Hyndal, Peter. 15 February 2019. Canberra.
——21 October 2019. Canberra.
Imber, Harry. 27 January 2019. Melbourne.
Inkpin, Josephine. 30 November 2018. Brisbane.
Johnson, Kristine. 3 July 2019. Brisbane.
Johnson, Leece. 30 September 2019. Perth.
Jones, Margaret. 28 September 2019. Perth.
'Karolyn'. 11 September 2019. North Coast, NSW.
Kennedy, Sim Victor. 6 January 2021. Melbourne.
Langley, Anna. 17 March 2019. Cambridge.
Langton, Rosemary. 13 April 2021. Sydney.
Laybutt, Jasper. 21 August 2019. Newcastle.
Le Gay, Susan. 11 December 2018. Brisbane.
'Lisa'. 28 April 2022. Zoom.
'Liz'. 8 July 2021. Zoom.
Loveday, Rebeckah. 16 August 2019, Melbourne.
Martin, Chantell. 12 September 2021. Zoom.
——19 September 2021. Zoom.
Mather, Gina. 4 July 2019. Brisbane.
McGearey, Greer. 1 September 2018. Melbourne.
Nambiar, Geeta. 11 April 2021. Sydney.
Norrie. 28 August 2019. Sydney.
——10 September 2019, Sydney.
Pallota-Chiarolli, Maria. 28 October 2020. Zoom.
Paré, Jonathan. 10 December 2018. Brisbane.
Parkhill, Nic. 23 February 2022. Zoom.
Perkins, Roberta. 28 February 2018. Sydney.
Peters, Julie. 23 February 2018. Melbourne.
Purss, Phlan-Michelle. 11 May 2021. Sydney
——Walking tour with Noah Riseman. 15 April 2021. Sydney.
Riley, Elizabeth. 6 July 2021. Zoom.
Roberts, Erica. 30 August 2017. Townsville.
Ross, Michael. 24 September 2020. Zoom.
'Sascha'. 1 October 2019. Perth.
Schotte, Alyce. 20 January 2021. Zoom.
Scott, Jenny. 8 August 2018, Adelaide.
——8 December 2021. Adelaide.
Short, Shan. 30 April 2021. Zoom.

Smith, Vanessa. 27 September 2019. Perth.
Spencer, Ricki. 21 January 2022. Zoom.
'Susan'. 19 January 2022. Victoria.
Sÿdek, Sasja. 4 August 2019. Melbourne.
Taylor, Lisa. 12 July 2021. Zoom.
Telfer, Michelle. 12 July 2021. Melbourne.
Theodora, Jazmin. 12 September 2019. Nimbin.
Thorne, Emma. 18 September 2021. Zoom.
Vonni. 7 December 2021. Adelaide.
Walters, William. 23 April 2019. Sydney.
Warne, Garry. 20 July 2021. Zoom.
White, Kayleen. 28 January 2019. Melbourne.
Wiggins, Jeremy. 24 June 2021. Zoom.
Wilson, Joel. Interview for LGBTIQ+ military history project. 15 May 2018. Canberra.
Wolfgramme, Katherine. 2 June 2022. Zoom.
Zebra-Thyone, Max. 26 August 2019. Newcastle.

Personal archives shared courtesy:
Simon Ceber
Kim Dorin
Mx Margaret Jones
Sim Victor Kennedy
Rob Lyons
Norrie
Jonathan Paré
Julie Peters
Shan Short
Kayleen White

Australian Queer Archives (AQuA)
Australian Transsexual Association (ATA) radio program, *Gaywaves*
G.R. papers
John Hewson collection
Roberta Perkins papers
Jean Steele papers

National Archives of Australia
NAA A432, 1983/005019/01
NAA A432, 1983/012942-01
NAA A432, 1985/10784
NAA A432, 1985/12478
NAA A432, 1990/011585-01
NAA A432, 1993/481534 PART 1
NAA A432, 1993/504751 PART 1
NAA A432, 1995/68617 PART 1
NAA A432, 1996/19460 PART 1
NAA A432, CF1984/14098

NAA A432, CF1984/15506 PART 1
NAA A432, E1976/6463 PART 1
NAA A432, E1976/6463 PART 2
NAA A463, 1987/G1019
NAA A1838, 1622/1/44 PART 1
NAA A1838, 1622/1/44 PART 2
NAA C100, 1582651
NAA C475, 1056252
NAA C475, 1719712
NAA C612, GP EPISODE 74 30330445
NAA C1367, 81/239
NAA C2831, 1056252
NAA K1129, 1383097
NAA M4326, 1521

Other archives
Public Record Office Victoria. PROV 10977/P1/unit 16 and 10977/P1/unit 17.
——VPRS 17369, P0001, unit 228, 902/L02/01523.
——VPRS 18024, P0002, unit 33, 93/65/36/2.
State Library of New South Wales (SLNSW). Roberta Perkins papers.
State Library of Queensland (SLQ). ATSAQ papers. SLQ 27358, boxes 16012–16013.
State Library of South Australia. Jenny Scott papers.
State Library of Western Australia (SLWA). PR14249.
University of Melbourne Archives. Julian Phillips papers. 92/165, folder 8.

Judicial rulings
AB & AH v Gender Reassignment Board (WA) (2009) 65 SR(WA) 1.
AB v Western Australia and *AH v Western Australia* [2011] HCA 42.
C and D (falsely called C), Family Law Cases 90–636, 1979.
Corbett v Corbett [1970] 2 All ER 33.
Houston v Burton [2003] TASADT 3.
Norrie v R [1988] WASC 181 (29 June 1988).
NSW Registrar of Births, Deaths and Marriages v Norrie [2014] HCA 11 (2 April 2014).
R v Cogley [1989] VR 799.
R v Harris and McGuiness (1988) 17 NSWLR 158.
Re A [2022] QSC 159.
Re: Bernadette [2010] FamCA 94.
Re: Kevin [2001] FamCA 1074.
Re Secretary, Department of Social Security v 'HH' 23 ALD [1991].
Secretary, Department of Social Security v SRA 31 ALD 1 [1993].
Western Australia v AH [2010] WASCA 172.

Legislation
New South Wales. *Birth, Deaths and Marriages Registrations Act* 1995.
——*Prostitution (Amendment) Act* 1983.
——*Summary Offences Act* 1988.
Northern Territory. *Anti-Discrimination Act* 1992.
South Australia. *Equal Opportunity Act* 1984.

——*Sexual Reassignment Act* 1988.
Tasmania. *Anti-Discrimination Act* 1998.
——*Police Act* 1865.
——*Police Offences Act* 1935.
Victoria. *Births, Deaths and Marriages Registration (Amendment) Act* 2004.
Western Australia. *Gender Reassignment Act* 2000.

Newspapers and magazines
AAP
Adelaide Gay Times
The Advertiser (Adelaide)
The Age (Melbourne)
The Argus (Melbourne)
Australasian Post
The Australian
Bathurst Times
Brother-Sister (Melbourne)
The Bulletin
Burrowa News (Burrowa, NSW)
Campaign
Canberra Times
Capital Q (Sydney)
Catch 22 (Adelaide)
Central Queensland Herald (Rockhampton)
CentreLines (Hobart)
Cleo
Courier-Mail (Brisbane)
Daily Advertiser (Wagga Wagga, NSW)
Daily Mercury (Mackay)
Daily Mirror
Daily News (Perth)
Daily Post (Hobart)
Daily Telegraph (Sydney)
Evening News (Rockhampton)
Evening News (Sydney)
The Examiner (Launceston)
Examiner Express (Launceston)
Forum
The Guardian
The Herald (Melbourne)
Herald Sun (Melbourne)
The Journal (Adelaide)
Kalgoorlie Miner
Lockhart Review and Oaklands Advertiser (NSW)
Maitland Daily Mercury (NSW)
MCV (Melbourne)
Melbourne Star (Melbourne)
The Mirror (Perth)

The Mirror (Sydney)
National Times
New Idea
New Weekly
Newcastle Sun
The News (Adelaide)
OUTinPerth
Outrage
People
Pink Thylacines (Tasmania)
PIX
Prahran Telegraph (VIC)
QNews (Brisbane)
Queensland Pride (Brisbane)
Saturday Paper
The Scene (Brisbane)
Star Observer
The Sun (Melbourne)
The Sun (Sydney)
Sun Herald (Sydney)
Sunday Age (Melbourne)
Sunday Mail (Adelaide)
Sunday Mail (Brisbane)
Sunday Sun (Brisbane)
Sunday Observer (Melbourne)
Sydney Morning Herald
The Telegraph (Brisbane)
Truth (Adelaide)
Truth (Brisbane)
Truth (Melbourne)
Truth (Perth)
Truth (Sydney)
TV Week
Weekend Australian
Weekly Times (Melbourne)
West Australian
Westside Observer (Perth)
Woman's Day

Newsletters
Accent (AIDS Council of South Australia)
Boys Will Be Boys (Digital Transgender Archive)
Feminique (Seahorse NSW)
GLC Newsletter (Hobart)
New Femme: The Official Newsletter of the Chameleon Society of WA
Polare (The Gender Centre, NSW)
Seahorse Times (Seahorse Victoria)
Transceiver (Chameleon Society of WA)

Audiovisual

A Big Life [documentary film]. Anna Brownfield (director). Nanna Moles Studios and Poison Apple Productions. 2021.

'The Accidental Archivist' [television program]. *Compass* (season 36, episode 18). Tracey Spring (producer). ABC-TV. 10 July 2022.

'Arthur or Martha' [television program]. *Midday*. Nine Network. 10 February 1988.

Becoming Julia [documentary film]. Ruth Cullen (director). Australian Film Commission in association with the New South Wales Film and Television Office. 2003.

'Brother Boys' [television program]. *Living Black* (season 22, episode 10). NITV/SBS. 8 June 2015.

'Brotherboys Yarnin' Up: Kai and Dean' [video]. Trans Health Australia. YouTube. 23 August 2014.

'Do I Believe in Ghosts?' [podcast]. *Counting the Dead*. Eloise Brook (host). 30 October 2019. The Gender Centre Inc.

'Jemima to Jeremy' [television program]. *Our Stories* (season 1, episode 36). NITV. 17 August 2016.

'Kalgoorlie Brothel Tour Traces the History of Goldfields' [radio program]. *The World Today*. David Weber (presenter). ABC Radio. 12 April 2001.

'Lieutenant Colonel Cate McGregor' [television program]. *One Plus One*. ABC-TV. 5 July 2013.

'Lisa's Story' [television program]. *Pig in a Poke* (season 1, episode 6). ABC-TV. 1977.

Man into Woman: The Transsexual Experience [documentary film]. John Ruane (director). Sabina Productions. 1983.

Men Like Me [documentary film]. Susan Long (director). 1994.

On Becoming [video]. Teresa Rizzo (director). AFI Distribution. 1993.

Sistergirls: Stories from Indigenous Australian Transgender People. Produced by ACON. 2003.

'Starlady' [podcast]. *Transgender Warriors*. Sam Elkin and Gemma Cafarella (hosts). 19 March 2020. JOY 94.9.

'Stephanie Reid Talks About Changing Tasmanian Law' [video]. Equality Tasmania. YouTube. 31 March 2021.

Tommy Doesn't Exist Anymore [documentary film]. Ian Munro (director). Transmedia for the National Nine Network. 1985.

'Transsexuals: Those Who Have Made the Choice' [television program]. *Four Corners*. ABC-TV. 1974.

TranzAustralia. YouTube channel.

Online sources

AusPATH. 'Australian Informed Consent Standards of Care for Gender Affirming Hormone Therapy'. 31 March 2022.

Australian Human Rights Commission. *Guidelines for the Inclusion of Transgender and Gender Diverse People in Sport*. Sydney: AHRC, 2019.

Australian Women Lawyers as Active Citizens website. Rachael Wallbank page.

Baird, Julia. 'Meet Australia's First Transgender Priest'. *ABC News*. 23 February 2018.

Boltje, Stephanie. 'The Sydney Uniting Church Appoints History-making Transgender Minister'. *ABC News*. 31 March 2021.

Braidwood, Ella. '13-year-old Trans Kid Confronts Australia's Prime Minister over His Views on Trans Children'. *PinkNews*. 6 September 2018.

Burin, Margaret. 'Sistergirls and Brotherboys Unite to Strengthen Spirits'. *ABC News*. 21 November 2016.

Butson, Tyson. '"Gender whisperers": Scott Morrison criticised for "hateful" tweet about trans students'. *SBS News*. 5 September 2018.

Byrnes, Kassia. '"They Arrested Me": Australia's First Legally Recognised Trans Woman on a Life in the Spotlight'. *news.com.au*. 8 March 2022.

Caines, Kimberley. '"I'd Rather Go to Heaven than Live Here as a Boy": Inside the Lives of Australian Trans Children, Part One'. *9News*. 29 January 2019.

Callander, Denton. 'RuPaul's "Tranny" Debate: The Limits and Power of Language'. *The Conversation*. 29 May 2014.

Clure, Elias. 'Birth Certificate Changes to Broaden Rights for Trans, Gender-neutral, Intersex People in NT'. *ABC News*. 29 November 2018.

Dias, Avani. 'Tiwi Islands Sistagirls Prepare to Wow Sydney Mardi Gras, Want to Show Indigenous LGBTIQ Culture'. *ABC News*. 2 March 2017.

Dyer, Nicole, Tom Forbes and Kirsten Webster. 'Transgender Actor Vonni Lands "Role of a Lifetime" in Gold Coast Priscilla Production'. *ABC News*. 26 April 2022.

Government of South Australia, Office for Women. *2017 South Australian Women's Honour Roll*. November 2017.

Humphries, Alexandra and Ellen Coulter. 'Tasmania Makes Gender Optional on Birth Certificates after Liberal Crosses Floor'. *ABC News*. 10 April 2019.

'Intersex for Allies'. Intersex Human Rights Australia website. 21 November 2012.

Jones, Mx Margaret. 'A Brief History of Transgender, Transsexual, Intersex and Cross-Dresser Events and Organisations in Western Australia'. *Mx Margaret Dylan Jones* website. 2019.

Leighton-Dore, Samuel. 'Sissy Ball Founder Bhenji Ra on How Voguing Became a Lifeline'. *SBS Sexuality*. 26 February 2020.

Loveday, Rebeckah. 'My Career'. *Rebeckah Loveday Official* website. 2018.

Lowder, J. Bryan. 'The "Tranny" Debate and Conservatism in the LGBTQ Movement'. *Slate*. 30 May 2014.

Munro, Kate. 'Why "Blak" not Black? Artist Destiny Deacon and the Origins of This Word'. *NITV*. 29 June 2020.

Niemi, Tristan. 'Meanjin Is Burning'. *Nothing Ever Happens in Brisbane*. 3 November 2021.

O'Sullivan, Sandy. 'The conflation of trans with drag is a problem …' [Tweet]. 6 January 2023.

Palin, Megan. 'Anti Same-sex Marriage Campaign Airs: "School Told My Son He Could Wear a Dress"'. *news.com.au*. 30 August 2017.

Salem, Merryana. 'House of Silky Is Determined to Breathe Life Back into Australia's Ballroom Scene'. *Junkee*. 3 March 2022.

'Sissy Ball Set to Transfix Sydney at Mardi Gras'. *Australian Pride Network*. 19 December 2017.

'Transgender and Gender Diverse Governance in Sport'. *Pride in Sport* website. 2020.

TransHub. 'Language'. *TransHub* website. 2021.

Victorian Equal Opportunity and Human Rights Commission. *Guideline: Trans and Gender Diverse Inclusion in Sport.* Carlton, Vic.: VEOHRC, 2017.

Weedon, Alan. 'Fa'afafine, Fakaleitī, Fakafifine: Understanding the Pacific's Alternative Gender Expressions'. *ABC News.* 31 August 2019.

Websites

Equal Voices. https://equalvoices.org.au/

Inkpin, Jo. *Blessed Imp.* https://www.blessedimp.org/

——*Trans Spirit Flourishing.* https://www.transspirit.org/

Transfemme. https://www.transfemme.com.au/

Twenty10. https://www.twenty10.org.au/

Published sources and unpublished theses

ACON. 'A Blueprint for Improving the Health and Wellbeing of the Trans and Gender Diverse Community in NSW'. Sydney: ACON, 2019.

ACT Law Reform Advisory Council. *Beyond the Binary: Legal Recognition of Sex and Gender Diversity in the ACT.* ACT Law Reform Advisory Council Report 2, March 2012.

Agarwal, Kritika. 'What Is Trans History? From Activist and Academic Roots, a Field Takes Shape'. *Perspectives on History.* Published electronically 1 May 2018.

Amao Leota Lu, as told to Bobuq Sayed. 'Dancing with My Ancestors'. In Sam Elkin, Alex Gallagher, Yves Rees and Bobuq Sayed (eds), *Nothing to Hide: Voices of Trans and Gender Diverse Australia.* Sydney: Allen & Unwin, 2022, pp. 182–8.

Andrews, Craig (ed.). *Stand by Your Man (and Stay Sane in the Process).* 3rd edn. Glebe, NSW: FTM Australia, 2007.

Arrow, Michelle. *The Seventies: The Personal, the Political, and the Making of Modern Australia.* Sydney: NewSouth Publishing, 2019.

Atkins, Kim. 'Re Alex: Narrative Identity and the Case of Gender Dysphoria'. *Griffith Law Review* 14(1), 2005, pp. 1–16.

Australia. Human Rights and Equal Opportunity Commission. National Inquiry into the Separation of Aboriginal and Torres Strait Islander Children from Their Families. *Bringing Them Home: Report of the National Inquiry into the Separation of Aboriginal and Torres Strait Islander Children from Their Families.* Sydney: Human Rights and Equal Opportunity Commission, 1997.

Australia. Senate Legal and Constitutional References Committee. *Inquiry into Sexuality Discrimination.* Canberra, December 1997.

——'Reference: Sexuality Discrimination Inquiry', Adelaide, 16 August 1996.

——'Reference: Sexuality Discrimination Inquiry', Brisbane, 1 October 1996.

Australian Human Rights Commission. *Sex Files: The Legal Recognition of Sex in Documents and Government Records.* Canberra: Australian Human Rights Commission, 2009.

Ayres, Eddie. *Danger Music: How Teaching the Cello to Children in Afghanistan Led to a Self-discovery Almost Too Hard to Bear.* Crows Nest, NSW: Allen & Unwin, 2017.

Barnes, Adrian. *My Knight's Quest.* Morrisville, NC: Lulu, 2022.

Barr, Ron and Alex Blaszczynski. 'Autonomic Responses of Transsexual and Homosexual Males to Erotic Film Sequences'. *Archives of Sexual Behavior* 5(3), 1976, pp. 211–22.

Beemyn, Genny. 'Presence in the Past: A Transgender Historiography'. *Journal of Women's History* 25(4), 2013, pp. 113–21.

Benjamin, Harry. *The Transsexual Phenomenon*. New York: Julian Press, 1966.

——'Transsexualism and Transvestism as Psycho-Somatic and Somato-Psychic Syndromes'. In Susan Stryker and Stephen Whittle (eds), *The Transgender Studies Reader*. New York: Routledge, 2006 [1954], pp. 45–52.

——'Transsexualism and Transvestism as Psychosomatic and Somatopsychic Syndromes'. *American Journal of Psychotherapy* 8(2), 1 April 1954, pp. 219–30.

Bogert, Yolanda. *How I Met My Son: A Story of Love That Transcends Gender*. South Melbourne: Affirm Press, 2016.

Bongiorno, Frank. *The Sex Lives of Australians: A History*. Melbourne: Black Inc., 2012.

Bowles, Robin. *No Justice*. Sydney: Pan Macmillan, 2000.

Bretherton, Ingrid, Emily Thrower, Sav Zwickl, Alex Wong, Daria Chetcuti, Mathis Grossmann, Jeffrey D. Zajac and Ada S Cheung. 'The Health and Well-Being of Transgender Australians: A National Community Survey'. *LGBT Health* 8(1), 2021, pp. 42–9.

Brisick, Jamie. *Becoming Westerly*. San Francisco: Outpost19, 2015.

Brown, Kooncha. '"Sistergirls": Stories from Indigenous Australian Transgender People'. *Aboriginal and Islander Health Worker Journal* 28(6), 2004, pp. 25–6.

Burns, Christine (ed.). *Trans Britain: Our Journey from the Shadows*. London: Unbound, 2018.

Butler, Judith. *Gender Trouble: Feminism and the Subversion of Identity*. 3rd edn. New York & London: Routledge, 2007 [1990].

——*Undoing Gender*. New York: Routledge, 2004.

Bychowski, MW, Howard Chiang, Jack Halberstam, Jacob Lau, Kathleen P. Long, Marcia Ochoa, C Riley Snorton, Leah DeVun and Zeb Tortorici. '"Trans★Historicities": A Roundtable Discussion'. *TSQ: Transgender Studies Quarterly* 5(4), 2018, pp. 658–85.

Carlotta and Prue MacSween. *Carlotta: I'm Not That Kind of Girl*. Sydney: Pan Macmillan, 2003.

Carlotta with James Cockington. *He Did It Her Way: Carlotta, Legend of Les Girls*. Sydney: Ironbark by Pan Macmillan, 1994.

Cavanagh, Sheila L and Heather Sykes. 'Transsexual Bodies at the Olympics: The International Olympic Committee's Policy on Transsexual Athletes at the 2004 Athens Summer Games'. *Body & Society* 12(3), 2006, pp. 75–102.

Chan, Kevin and Ken Israel (eds). *Drag Show*. Sydney: Currency Press, 1977.

Chesser, Lucy. *Parting with My Sex: Cross-dressing, Inversion and Sexuality in Australian Cultural Life*. Sydney: Sydney University Press, 2008.

Clare, Stephanie D. *Nonbinary: A Feminist Autotheory*. Cambridge: Cambridge University Press, 2023.

Colligan, Mimi. 'The Mysterious Edward/Ellen De Lacy Evans: The Picaresque in Real Life'. *La Trobe Journal* 69, 2002, pp. 59–68.

Costello, Michael and Rusty Nannup. *Report of the First National Indigenous Sistergirl Forum: A Forum for All Indigenous Poeple Who Identify as Sistergirl or Who Have Transgender Qualities*. Darlinghurst, NSW: AFAO, 1999.

Coutts, Brent. *Crossing the Lines: The Story of Three Homosexual New Zealand Soldiers in World War II*. Dunedin: Otago University Press, 2020.

Crenshaw, Kimberlé. 'Demarginalizing the Intersection of Race and Sex: A Black Feminist Critique of Antidiscrimination Doctrine, Feminist Theory and Antiracist Politics'. *University of Chicago Legal Forum* 1, 1989, pp. 139–67.

Cummings, Katherine. *Katherine's Diary: The Story of a Transsexual*. Rev. edn. Tascott, NSW: Beaujon Press, 2007.

Curtis, Brie Ngala. 'Kungakunga: Staying Close to Family and Country'. In Dino Hodge (ed.), *Colouring the Rainbow: Blak Queer and Trans Perspectives*. Adelaide: Wakefield Press, 2015, pp. 35–47.

Davies, Susanne. 'Sexuality, Performance, and Spectatorship in Law: The Case of Gordon Lawrence, Melbourne, 1888'. *Journal of the History of Sexuality* 7(3), 1997, pp. 389–408.

Day, Madi. 'Indigenist Origins: Institutionalizing Indigenous Queer and Trans Studies in Australia'. *TSQ: Transgender Studies Quarterly* 7(3), 2020, pp. 367–73.

DeVun, Leah and Zeb Tortorici. 'Trans, Time, and History'. *TSQ: Transgender Studies Quarterly* 5(4), 2018, pp. 518–39.

Eades, Quinn. *All the Beginnings: A Queer Autobiography of the Body*. North Melbourne: Tantanoola, a literary imprint of Australian Scholarly Publishing, 2015.

Eames, Robin. 'Harry Crawford v History: Problem Bodies, Queertrans Cosmogonies, and Historiographical Ethics in Cases of Gender Transgression in Late Nineteenth–Early Twentieth Century Australia'. BA (Honours) thesis. University of Sydney, 2018.

——'Problem Bodies and Queer Legacies: Rethinking Approaches to Trans History in the Case of Harry Crawford, Sydney, 1920'. *Lilith: A Feminist History Journal* 25, 2019, pp. 50–62.

Edwards, Marion. *Life and Adventures of Marion-Bill-Edwards: The Most Celebrated Man-Woman of Modern Times*. Melbourne: WH Williams, Junr, 1907.

Elkin, Sam, Alex Gallagher, Yves Rees and Bobuq Sayed (eds). *Nothing to Hide: Voices of Trans and Gender Diverse Australia*. Sydney: Allen & Unwin, 2022.

Erasmus, Jaco. 'Monash Gender Clinic: An Overview of the Current Model of Care'. *Australasian Psychiatry* 28(5), 2020, pp. 533–5.

Fallowell, Duncan and April Ashley. *April Ashley's Odyssey*. London: J Cape, 1982.

Farrell, Andrew. 'Lipstick Clapsticks: A Yarn and a Kiki with an Aboriginal Drag Queen'. *AlterNative: An International Journal of Indigenous Peoples* 12(5), 2016, pp. 574–85.

Feinberg, Leslie. *Trans Gender Liberation: A Movement Whose Time Has Come*. New York: World View Forum, 1992.

——*Transgender Warriors: Making History from Joan of Arc to Dennis Rodman*. Boston: Beacon Press, 1996.

Finlay, Henry. 'Transsexuals, Sex Change Operations and the Chromosome Test: *Corbett v Corbett* Not Followed'. *Western Australian Law Review* 19, 1989, pp. 152–7.

——*Transsexualism in a Modern State: Options for Reform*. Hobart: HA Finlay, 1995.

Ford, Ruth. '"And Merrily Rang the Bells": Gender-crossing and Same-sex Marriage in Australia, 1900–1940'. In David Phillips and Graham Willett (eds), *Australia's Homosexual Histories: Gay and Lesbian Perspectives 5*. Sydney: Australia's Centre for Lesbian and Gay Research, 2000, pp. 41–66.

——'"The Man-Woman Murderer": Sex Fraud, Sexual Inversion and the Unmentionable "Article" in 1920s Australia'. *Gender and History* 12(1), 2000, pp. 158–96.

——'"Prove First You're a Male": A Farmhand's Claim for Wages in 1929 Australia'. *Labour History*, 90, 2006, pp. 1–21.

——'Sexuality and "Madness": Regulating Women's Gender "Deviance" through the Asylum: The Orange Asylum in the 1930s'. In Catharine Coleborne and Dolly MacKinnon (eds), *'Madness' in Australia: Histories, Heritage and the Asylum*. St Lucia, Qld: University of Queensland Press in association with the API Network and Curtin University of Technology, 2003, pp. 109–19.

Foucault, Michel. *The History of Sexuality, Vol. 1: An Introduction*. Translated by Robert Hurley. London: Penguin, 1990.

Galupo, M Paz. 'Researching While Cisgender: Identity Considerations for Transgender Research'. *International Journal of Transgenderism* 18(3), 2017, pp. 241–2.

Garber, Marjorie. *Vested Interests: Cross-Dressing & Cultural Anxiety*. New York: Routledge, 2011.

'Gender-Affirming Care Needed for Transgender Children', *The Lancet* 391, 30 June 2018, p. 2576.

Gerrard, Jessica. 'Boys in Dresses: Same-sex Marriage, Children and the Politics of Equivalence'. *Australian Feminist Studies* 35(103), 2020, pp. 70–80.

Gill-Peterson, Jules. *Histories of the Transgender Child*. Minneapolis: University of Minnesota Press, 2018.

Greenwich, Alex and Shirleene Robinson. *Yes Yes Yes: Australia's Journey to Marriage Equality*. Sydney: NewSouth Publishing, 2018.

Hamburger, Christian. 'The Desire for Change of Sex as Shown by Personal Letters from 465 Men and Women'. *Acta Endocrinologica* 14, 1953, pp. 361–75.

Hirschfeld, Magnus. *Transvestites: The Erotic Drive to Cross Dress*. Translated by Michael A Lombardi-Nash. New York: Prometheus Books, 1991 [1910].

Hodge, Dino (ed.). *Colouring the Rainbow: Blak Queer and Trans Perspectives: Life Stories and Essays by First Nations People of Australia*. Mile End, SA: Wakefield Press, 2015.

Hooley, Jesse. 'Normalising Transgender and Policing Transgression: Anti-Discrimination Law Reform Ten Years On'. *Australian Feminist Law Journal* 25, 2006, pp. 79–98.

Howard, Lady Paula. *Frocks, Frills and Furbelows: The Story of Lady Paula Howard: An Embellished Biography of Transvestism Spanning Forty Years and Four Continents*. Norwood, SA: Peacock Publications, 1999.

Imber, Harry. 'The Management of Transsexualism'. *Medical Journal of Australia* 2(18), 30 October 1976, pp. 676–8.

Jackman, Priscilla. *Still Point Turning: The Catherine McGregor Story*. Fortitude Valley, Qld: Playlab, 2019.

Jones, Tiffany. 'Evidence Affirming School Supports for Australian Transgender and Gender Diverse Students'. *Sex Health* 14(5), 2017, pp. 412–16.

Jones, Tiffany, Jennifer Power, Adam O Hill, Nathan Despott, Marina Carman, Timothy W Jones, Joel Anderson and Adam Bourne. 'Religious Conversion Practices and LGBTQA+ Youth', *Sexuality Research and Social Policy* 19(3), 2022, pp. 1155–64.

Jorgensen, Christine. *Christine Jorgensen: A Personal Autobiography*. New York: Bantam Books, 1967.

Kay, Barry. *The Other Women*. London: Mathews Miller Dunbar, 1976.

Kerry, Stephen. 'Australian News Media's Representation of Cate McGregor, the Highest Ranking Australian Transgender Military Officer'. *Journal of Gender Studies* 27(6), 2018, pp. 683–93.

——*Trans Dilemmas: Living in Australia's Remote Areas and in Aboriginal Communities*. Abingdon, UK: Routledge, 2018.

King, Dave. *The Transvestite and the Transsexual: Public Categories and Private Identities*. Aldershot, UK: Avebury, 1993.

Krasnostein, Sarah. *The Trauma Cleaner: One Woman's Extraordinary Life in Death, Decay & Disaster*. Melbourne: Text Publishing, 2017.

Kroeger, Brooke. *Passing: When People Can't Be Who They Are*. New York: Public Affairs, 2003.

Lane, Riki. '"We Are Here to Help": Who Opens the Gate for Surgeries?' *TSQ: Transgender Studies Quarterly* 5(2), 2018, pp. 207–27.

Law, Benjamin. *Moral Panic 101: Equality, Acceptance and the Safe Schools Scandal*. Quarterly Essay 67. Carlton, Vic.: Schwartz Publishing, 2017.

Law Reform Commission of Victoria. *Review of the Equal Opportunity Act*. Report No. 36, October 1990.

Law Reform Commission of Western Australia. *Project 108 Final Report: Review of Western Australian Legislation in Relation to the Registration or Change of a Person's Sex and/or Gender and Status Relating to Sex Characteristics*. 6 December 2018.

Lewins, Frank. *Transsexualism in Society: A Sociology of Male-to-Female Transsexuals*. South Melbourne: Macmillan Education Australia, 1995.

Love, Crystal. 'Napanangka: The True Power of Being Proud'. In Dino Hodge (ed.), *Colouring the Rainbow: Blak Queer and Trans Perspectives*. Adelaide: Wakefield Press, 2015, pp. 21–34.

Love Johnson, Crystal, as told to Sam Elkin. 'Yimpininni'. In Sam Elkin, Alex Gallagher, Yves Rees and Bobuq Sayed (eds), *Nothing to Hide: Voices of Trans and Gender Diverse Australia*. Sydney: Allen & Unwin, 2022, pp. 10–19.

Mama Alto. 'Multiple Margins: Queer People of Colour in the Arts'. In Maria Pallotta-Chiarolli (ed.), *Living and Loving in Diversity: An Anthology of Australian Multicultural Queer Adventures*. Adelaide: Wakefield Press, 2018, pp. 18–23.

Manion, Jen. *Female Husbands: A Trans History*. Cambridge: Cambridge University Press, 2020.

McCrory, Adrien. 'Policing Gender Nonconformity in Victoria, 1900–1940'. *Provenance: The Journal of Public Record Office Victoria* 19, 2021, pp. 33–42.

——'Policing (Trans)gender: Trans and Gender Diverse Interactions with the Australian Criminal Legal System Since the Twentieth Century'. PhD thesis. Australian Catholic University, 2023.

McIntyre, Joanna. 'He Did It Her Way on TV: Representing an Australian Transsexual Celebrity Onscreen'. *Gay & Lesbian Issues & Psychology Review* 7(1), 2011, pp. 19–32.

Meyerowitz, Joanne. *How Sex Changed: A History of Transsexuality in the United States*. Cambridge, MA: Harvard University Press, 2004.

——'Sex Change and the Popular Press: Historical Notes on Transsexuality in the United States, 1930–1955'. *GLQ: A Journal of Lesbian and Gay Studies* 4(2), 1998, pp. 159–87.

Mills, Eithne. 'Re Alex: Adolescent Gender Identity Disorder and the Family Court of Australia'. *Deakin Law Review* 9(2), 2004, pp. 365–73.

Monro, Surya. *Gender Politics: Citizenship, Activism and Sexual Diversity*. London & Ann Arbor: Pluto Press, 2005.

Monro, Surya and Janneke Van Der Ros. 'Trans★ and Gender Variant Citizenship and the State in Norway'. *Critical Social Policy* 38(1), 2018, pp. 57–78.

Moore, Clive. *Sunshine and Rainbows: The Development of Gay and Lesbian Culture in Queensland*. St Lucia, Qld: University of Queensland Press in association with the API Network, 2001.

Morris, Jan. *Conundrum*. London: Faber and Faber, 1974.

New South Wales. Legislative Assembly. Official Hansard.

New South Wales Law Reform Commission. 'Names: Registration and Certification of Births and Deaths'. Sydney, 1988.

Norrie. *Ultrasex: An Autobiography by Norrie May-Welby*. Sydney: Norrie, 2019.

O'Sullivan, Sandy. 'Challenging the Colonialities of Symbolic Annihilation'. *Southerly* 79(3), 2022, pp. 16–22.

——'The Colonial Project of Gender (and Everything Else)'. *Genealogy* 5(3), 16 July 2021.

——'The Colonial Trappings of Gender'. In Sam Elkin, Alex Gallagher, Yves Rees and Bobuq Sayed (eds), *Nothing to Hide: Voices of Trans and Gender Diverse Australia*. Sydney: Allen & Unwin, 2022, pp. 136–47.

Pallotta-Chiarolli, Maria (ed.). *Living and Loving in Diversity: An Anthology of Australian Multicultural Queer Adventures*. Adelaide: Wakefield Press, 2018.

Perkins, Roberta. *The 'Drag Queen' Scene: Transsexuals in Kings Cross*. Sydney: Allen & Unwin, 1983.

——'Transexuals and Police Persecution'. *Alternative Criminology*, June 1983, pp. 6–7.

——'Transgender Lifestyles and HIV/AIDS Risk: National Transgender HIV/AIDS Needs Assessment Project', School of Sociology, University of New South Wales, 1994.

Peters, Julie. *A Feminist Post-Transsexual Autoethnography: Challenging Normative Gender Coercion*. Abingdon, UK & New York: Routledge, 2019.

Pilling, Arnold Remington. 'Homosexuality among the Tiwi of North Australia'. In Stephen O Murray (ed.), *Oceanic Homosexualities*. New York & London: Garland Publishing, 1992, pp. 25–31.

Playdon, Zoë. *The Hidden Case of Ewan Forbes: The Transgender Trial that Threatened to Upend the British Establishment*. London: Bloomsbury, 2021.

Plemons, Eric and Chris Straayer. 'Introduction: Reframing the Surgical'. *TSQ: Transgender Studies Quarterly* 5(2), 2018, pp. 164–73.

Prestell, Douglas Ogilvy. *The Correspondence of Karl Heinrich Ulrichs, 1846–1894*. Basingstoke, UK: Palgrave Macmillan, 2020.

Queensland Electoral and Administrative Review Commission. *Report on the Review of the Preservation and Enhancement of Individuals' Rights and Freedoms*. Brisbane, August 1993.

Rawson, KJ and Cristan Williams. 'Transgender*: The Rhetorical Landscape of a Term'. *Present Tense* 3(2), 2014, pp. 1–9.

Raymond, Janice. *The Transsexual Empire: The Making of the She-Male*. 2nd edn. New York: Teachers College Press, 1994 [1979].

Reay, Barry. *Trans America: A Counter-History*. Cambridge: Polity Press, 2020.

Rees, Yves. *All About Yves: Notes from a Transition*. Crows Nest, NSW: Allen & Unwin, 2021.

Reynolds, Andrew. *The Children of Harvey Milk: How LGBTQ Politicians Changed the World*. New York: Oxford University Press, 2019.

Riggs, Damien W and Kate Toone. 'Indigenous Sistergirls' Experiences of Family and Community'. *Australian Social Work* 70(2), 2017, pp. 229–40.

Ringo, Peter. 'Media Roles in Female-to-Male Transsexual and Transgender Identity Development'. *International Journal of Transgenderism* 6(2), 2002.

Riseman, Noah. 'Finding "Evidence of Me" through "Evidence of Us": Transgender Oral Histories and Personal Archives Speak'. In Amy Tooth Murphy, Emma Vickers and Clare Summerskill (eds), *New Directions in Queer Oral History: Archives of Disruption*. Abingdon, UK: Routledge, 2022, pp. 59–70.

——*A History of Trans Health Care in Australia: A Report for the Australian Professional Association for Trans Health (AusPATH)*. AusPATH, 2022.

——'A History of Transgender Women in Australian Sports, 1976–2017'. *Sport in History* 42(2), 2021, pp. 280–307.

——*New South Wales Trans History*. The Gender Centre and ACON, 2022.

——'Representing Transgender in the 1970s Australian Media'. *Gender and History* 33(1), 2021, pp. 227–48.

——'Searching for Trans Possibilities in Australia, 1910–39', *Journal of Australian Studies* 44(1), 2020, pp. 33–47.

——'Transgender Inclusion and Australia's Failed Sexuality Discrimination Bill'. *Australian Journal of Politics and History* 65(2), 2019, pp. 259–77.

——'Transgender Policy in the Australian Defence Force: Medicalization and Its Discontents'. *International Journal of Transgenderism* 17(3–4), 2016, pp. 141–54.

——*Victoria's Transgender History*. Melbourne: Transgender Victoria, 2021.

Riseman, Noah and Shirleene Robinson. *Pride in Defence: The Australian Military and LGBTI Service since 1945*. Carlton, Vic.: Melbourne University Press, 2020.

Robertson, Rebekah. *About a Girl: A Mother's Powerful Story of Raising Her Transgender Child*. Milsons Point, NSW: Viking, 2019.

Ross, Michael, J Walinder, B Lundström and I Thuwe. 'Cross-cultural Approaches to Transsexualism: A Comparison between Sweden and Australia'. *Acta Psychiatrica Scandinavica* 63, 1981, pp. 75–82.

Rupe, Carmen and Martin Paul. *Carmen: My Life*. Auckland: Benton Ross, 1988.

Rutkin, Bill, Destiny Rogers and Laurie James Deane. *Queen's Ball: 60th Anniversary*. West End, Qld: Q News, 2021.

Sears, Clare. *Arresting Dress: Cross-dressing, Law, and Fascination in Nineteenth-century San Francisco*. Durham, NC: Duke University Press, 2014.

——'Electric Brilliancy: Cross-dressing Law and Freak Show Displays in Nineteenth-century San Francisco'. In Susan Stryker and Aren Z Aizura (eds), *The Transgender Studies Reader 2*. New York: Routledge, 2013, pp. 554–64.

Serlin, David Harley. 'Christine Jorgensen and the Cold War Closet'. *Radical History Review* 62,1995, pp. 136–65.

Sharpe, A. 'Transgender Performance and the Discriminating Gaze: A Critique of Anti-Discrimination Regulatory Regimes'. *Social & Legal Studies* 8(1), 1999, pp. 5–24.

Shuster, Stef M. *Trans Medicine: The Emergence and Practice of Treating Gender.* New York: New York University Press, 2021.

Skidmore, Emily. 'Constructing the "Good Transsexual": Christine Jorgensen, Whiteness, and Heteronormativity in the Mid-Twentieth-Century Press'. *Feminist Studies* 37(2), 2011, pp. 270–300.

——*True Sex: The Lives of Trans Men at the Turn of the Twentieth Century.* New York: New York University Press, 2017.

Smaal, Yorick. *Sex, Soldiers and the South Pacific, 1939–45: Queer Identities in Australia in the Second World War.* London: Palgrave Macmillan, 2015.

Smith, Elizabeth, Tiffany Jones, Roz Ward, Jennifer Dixon, Anne Mitchell and Lynne Hillier. 'From Blues to Rainbows: The Mental Health and Well-being of Gender Diverse and Transgender Young People in Australia'. Melbourne: Australian Research Centre in Sex, Health and Society (ARCHS), 2014.

Snorton, C Riley. *Black on Both Sides: A Racial History of Trans Identity.* Minneapolis: University of Minnesota Press, 2017.

Steinmetz, Katy. 'The Transgender Tipping Point'. *TIME*, 29 May 2014.

Stirling, Peter. *So Different: An Extraordinary Autobiography.* Sydney: Simon & Schuster, 1989.

Stone, Sandy. 'The *Empire* Strikes Back: A Posttranssexual Manifesto'. In Julia Epstein and Kristina Straub (eds), *Body Guards: The Cultural Politics of Gender Ambiguity.* New York: Routledge, 1991, pp. 280–304.

Strauss, Penelope, Ashleigh Lin, Sam Winter, Angus Cook, Vanessa Watson and Dani Wright Toussaint. 'Trans Pathways: The Mental Health Experiences and Care Pathways of Trans Young People: Summary of Results'. Perth Telethon Kids Institute, 2017.

Stryker, Susan. *Transgender History: The Roots of Today's Revolution.* 2nd edn. New York: Seal Press, 2017 [2008].

Sullivan, Claire F. 'Gender Verification and Gender Policies in Elite Sport: Eligibility and "Fair Play"'. *Journal of Sport and Social Issues* 35(4), 2011, pp. 400–19.

Sullivan, Corrinne Tayce and Madi Day. 'Indigenous Transmasculine Australians & Sex Work'. *Emotion, Space and Society* 32, 2019, p. 100591.

Sÿdek, Sasja. 'The Magic Art of Not Giving a Fuck'. In Sam Elkin, Alex Gallagher, Yves Rees and Bobuq Sayed (eds), *Nothing to Hide: Voices of Trans and Gender Diverse Australia.* Sydney: Allen & Unwin, 2022, pp. 44–50.

Symons, Caroline. *The Gay Games: A History.* London & New York: Routledge, 2010.

Taylor, Trina. 'The Heterosexual Transvestite in Australia', *Australian Social Work* 30(1), 1977, pp. 29–33.

Tedeschi, Mark. *Eugenia: A True Story of Adversity, Tragedy, Crime and Courage.* Cammeray, NSW: Simon & Schuster, 2012.

Telfer, Michelle, Fiona Kelly, Debi Feldman, Georgie Stone, Rebekah Robertson and Zeffie Poulakis. 'Transgender Adolescents and Legal Reform: How Improved Access to Healthcare Was Achieved through Medical, Legal and

Community Collaboration'. *Journal of Paediatrics and Child Health* 54(10), 2018, pp. 1096–9.

Telfer, Michelle M, Michelle A Tollit, Carmen C Pace and Ken C Pang. 'Australian Standards of Care and Treatment Guidelines for Transgender and Gender-diverse Children and Adolescents'. *Medical Journal of Australia* 209(3), 6 August 2018, pp. 132–6.

Telfer, Michelle, Michelle Tollit, Carmen Pace and Ken Pang. 'Australian Standards of Care and Treatment Guidelines for Trans and Gender-diverse Children and Adolescents: Version 1.1'. Melbourne: Royal Children's Hospital, 2018.

Thomas, Amy, Hannah McCann and Geraldine Fela. '"In This House We Believe in Fairness and Kindness": Post-Liberation Politics in Australia's Same-sex Marriage Postal Survey'. *Sexualities* 23(4), 2019, pp. 475–96.

The Transgender Project: A Needs Assessment for People with Transgender Practices. Central Sydney Area Health Service, 1996.

van der Leeden, AC. 'Thundering Gecko and Emu: Mythological Structuring of Nunggubuyu Patrimoieties'. In LR Hiatt (ed.), *Australian Aboriginal Mythology: Essays in Honour of WEH Stanner.* Canberra: Australian Institute of Aboriginal Studies, 1975, pp. 46–101.

van Reyk, Paul. 'Future Directions for the AIDS Council of NSW: A Strategic Planning Document'. March 1989.

Victorian Legislative Assembly. Official Hansard.

Vincent, Benjamin William. 'Studying Trans: Recommendations for Ethical Recruitment and Collaboration with Transgender Participants in Academic Research'. *Psychology & Sexuality* 9(2), 2018, pp. 102–16.

Wallbank, Rachael. 'The Legal Status of People who Experience Difference in Sexual Formation and Gender Expression in Australia'. In Jens M Scherpe (ed.), *The Legal Status of Transsexual and Transgender Persons.* Cambridge: Intersentia, 2015, pp. 457–525.

——'Re Kevin in Perspective', *Deakin Law Review* 9(2), 2004, pp. 461–502.

Weismantel, Mary. 'Towards a Transgender Archaeology: A Queer Rampage through Prehistory'. In Susan Stryker and Aren Z Aizura (eds), *The Transgender Studies Reader 2.* New York: Routledge, 2013, pp. 319–34.

Western Australia. Legislative Assembly. Hansard.

Whittaker, Alison. 'The Border Made of Mirrors: Indigenous Queerness, Deep Colonisation and (De)fining Indigenousness in Settler Law'. In Dino Hodge (ed.), *Colouring the Rainbow: Blak Queer and Trans Perspectives, Life Stories and Essays by First Nations People of Australia.* Adelaide: Wakefield Press, 2015, pp. 223–37.

Williams, Michael, John Chesterman and Phil Grano. 'Re Jamie (No 2): A Positive Development for Transgender Young People'. *Journal of Law and Medicine* 22(1), 2014, pp. 90–104.

Williams, R Gwyn. 'A Case of Transvestitism'. *Western Australian Clinical Reports* 1(3), July 1937, pp. 51–2.

Wilson, Kaya. *As Beautiful as Any Other: A Memoir of My Body.* Sydney: Picador, 2021.

Wotherspoon, Garry. *Gay Sydney: A History.* Sydney: NewSouth Publishing, 2016.

Zisin, Nevo. *Finding Nevo: How I Confused Everyone.* Newtown, NSW: black dog books, 2017.

INDEX

endosex people, defined 11
eonism 39, 42; *see also* transvestism
Equal Opportunity Act (South Australia)
    114–15
Equal Opportunity Act (Victoria) 83–4,
    126–9, 220
Equal Opportunity Act (Western
    Australia) 231
equal opportunity acts; *see also* anti-
    discrimination laws
Equal Opportunity Commission
    (Western Australia), Working Party
    on Gender Identity 230–1
Equal Voices 185
Equinox (peer-led trans health service)
    238
ethnographic studies *see* research
Evans, Edward De Lacy 16
Evans, Kelby 118
Exclusive Brethren religious group 227

F2M documentary 179
Facebook groups 156–7, 203, 232, 247,
    249–50, 251, 261
Falleni, Eugenia 28; *see also* Crawford,
    Harry
family and peer support for trans
    children and young people 258–62
Family Court 110, 187, 188, 254–6
Family First (political party) 197
Family Law Act (Commonwealth)
    254–5
Family Law Council 96, 105, 108
family law reform concerning trans
    children's health care 253–7
Farrell, Andrew 141
Farrell, Frank 'Bumper' 61
fashion pioneers (public examples of
    trans people in Australian life)
    176–7
fearmongering *see* transphobia
Feast Festival 221
federal government
    Australian Labor Party 233, 236
    Coalition 208–9, 262, 266–8
federal parliamentary candidates 182,
    195–9
Federation of Ethnic Communities
    Councils of Australia 169
Feinberg, Leslie 6, 13, 14–15
Female Husbands (Manion) 15, 28
female impersonators 49, 59, 63–6

feminism, radical 264–5
Fiji
    trans women 147, 163–5
    see also Pasifika people
films 178–80; *see also* television
    programs
Fink, Margot 259
Finlay, Henry 115
First Day (television program) 260
First National Indigenous Sistergirl
    Forum 154, 156
firsts (public examples of trans people in
    Australian life) 20, 174–5, 205
    armed forces xvi, 1–2, 47, 181,
        189–90
    fashion 176–7
    film 178–80
    literature 180–3
    politics 193–200
    professional occupations 185–9
    religion 183–5
    sport 190–3
    television 177–8
Fisk, Norman 9
Flinders Medical Centre Gender Clinic,
    Adelaide 73, 80, 109
Forbes, Ewan 16
Forbes, Parker 247–8
Forcibly Displaced People Network 168
Ford, Jean 30; *see also* Crawford, Harry
Ford, Ruth 16, 23, 28–30, 42
Fordham, Robert 108
Forum magazine 77, 78, 175
Foucault, Michel 5
Franks, Tammy 242
Friend, Peta 249
FTM Australia 157, 202–3
FTM magazine 201
FTM Shed 250–1
FTMen-SA 251
F-to-M *see* trans men

Galupo, M Paz xvi
gangsters 64, 66, 67
Garber, Marjorie 32
Gates, Russell 125
gay (term) 57
gay and lesbian community
    attitudes to Aboriginal trans people
        169–70, 172–3
    attitudes to trans people 117, 141–2,
        165–6